BROOKLANDS
BOOKS

CW00545870

Morgan Plus 4 & Four 4

Gold Portfolio

1936-1967

Compiled by
R.M. Clarke

ISBN 1 85520 1895

Booklands Books Ltd.
PO Box 146, Cobham, KT11 1LG
Surrey, England

Printed in Hong Kong

BROOKLANDS BOOKS

CONTENTS

BROOKLANDS BOOKS

CONTENTS - *Continued*

BROOKLANDS BOOKS

ACKNOWLEDGEMENTS

This is very far from being our first book on Morgans. In fact, books on Morgans featured among our very first motoring titles, more years ago than we care to remember! Enthusiasm for the marque continues to flourish undiminished, and we are pleased now to be able to give the extended, 180-page Gold Portfolio treatment to the four-cylinder cars to complement our Gold Portfolio on the eight-cylinder models.

As regular readers of our publications will know, our aim at Brooklands Books is to make available once again previously published material which is now hard to come by. Without the kind co-operation extended to us by the original publishers of that material, we could not of course fulfil this aim. Our grateful thanks on this occasion therefore go to the publishers of *Autocar, Autosport, Car and Driver, Cars and Car Conversions, Light Car, Motor, Motor Rally, Motor Sport, Road & Track, Small Car, Sports Cars Illustrated, Sports Car World,* and *Thoroughbred and Classic Cars.*

Lastly, we must thank motoring writer James Taylor for his introductory words to this book, and Morgan owner David Brownell whose 1961 Plus 4 is the subject of our cover picture.

R.M. Clarke

Who would have guessed in 1936 that Morgan's new four-wheeler sports car would still be in production without fundamental change 30 years later? But then, who can predict what will become traditional and what will simply be ephemeral? The four-cylinder, four-wheeled Morgan, has become a tradition, and it would be hard to imagine motoring life without it.

Of course, the 1967 4/4 and Plus 4 models were not *quite* the same as the original 1936 model. They were faster, and they were more practical, thanks to the Morgan policy of keeping their mechanical specification abreast of the times while retaining their Thirties sporting character. In fact, Morgan had little choice but to do that: unable to manufacture their own engines, they bought in whatever was available that seemed to fit the bill, and so were able to update the cars almost without thinking about it. The customers loved it, but as soon as Morgan dared to alter the traditional body styling, the customers reacted adversely: just 26 of the GRP-bodied fixed-head Plus Four Plus of the mid-1960s found buyers. The only real styling change which the company did get away with was to change the original flat radiator for a curved grille in the early 1950s!

A list of the engines Morgan used in its 4/4 and Plus 4 models between 1936 and 1967 makes fascinating reading. Before the War, the original 4/4 had an IOE Coventry Climax engine; immediately after the War it had a specially-built OHV Standard type; and then there was a Standard engine again in the longer-wheelbase Plus 4 introduced in 1951. In 1954 came the first of the related Triumph TR engines which saw the Plus 4 range right through to the end of the 1960s. The 4/4, meanwhile, was revived in 1956 after a five-year lapse, and worked its way steadily through a succession of Ford engines, initially side-valve and later OHV types.

Few people have the opportunity to become acquainted with the whole range of Morgans in the metal, but this book offers the chance to meet them all through the medium of road testers' opinions. As a record of the reactions to each "new" Morgan over the years, it is unique.

James Taylor

New Morgan Car

Interesting Design of a Four-wheel High-performance Open Two-seater by Makers of a Famous Three-wheeler

INDEPENDENT front wheel springing and a very attractive appearance are features of a new car which is being placed upon the market by The Morgan Motor Company, of Malvern, well known for many years as the makers of the redoubtable Morgan three-wheeler. The new car bears little resemblance to the latter, however, for it is a four-cylinder four-speed four-wheeler. Named the Morgan "4-4" and priced complete at £180, the vehicle is a two-seater of the sports type, and, being fitted with an engine of 1,122 c.c. developing 34 brake horse-power, it should possess a lively road performance, for the total weight is 13 cwt.

There are several interesting features in the design, but without doubt the first point to take the eye is the appearance. The Morgan is unusually low in build, and, having a wheelbase of 7ft. 8in., looks long and graceful. As will be seen from the illustrations, it is of

The 9.8 h.p. Morgan two-seater.

a distinctive design, with a long bonnet, plentifully louvred, running back to the scuttle, which is surmounted by a metal-framed screen arranged to fold flat forwards when required. Aft of the seat is a compartment, in the top of which the folded hood is concealed, for the housing of luggage. Behind is a nine-gallon fuel tank. The tail slopes streamline fashion to match the contour of the rear wings, and countersunk vertically into the tail are two spare wheels.

From a mechanical point of view the layout of the chassis has many interesting features. The first point is the independent front wheel suspension. This follows along the well-tried practice of the Morgan three-wheeler. Braced to the front of the frame by a steel pressing are two horizontal tubes, placed laterally and mounted one considerably above the other. The top tube has diagonal tie-bars

on each side to add to the stiffness. On each side the ends of the tubes are joined by a vertical pillar, and on this a stub axle assembly is free to slide up and down, and to rotate for steering purposes.

Above the stub axle bracket a strong coil spring is enclosed in short telescopic tubes; this provides the suspension. Below the stub axle bracket a lighter coil spring accommodates rebound motion. The vertical movement of the stub axle is further checked by a Newton telescopic shock absorber of the hydraulic type. Steering arms project forward from the stub axle bracket and are coupled by a ball-jointed track rod, whilst the drag link is disposed transversely. The steering gear is mounted well forward and allows a considerably raked steering column, which is surmounted by a spring-spoked steering wheel. To increase fore-and-aft rigidity of the suspension system radius rods run back from the outer ends of the lower tube to the frame sides. The frame of the car is underslung, and consists of Z-section side members cross braced by inverted U-section members.

The bottom edges of the side members are joined by a wood floor from just behind the engine to just in front of the rear axle. Underslung half-elliptic rear springs checked by Hartford shock absorbers are employed, and in place of shackles the rear end of each master leaf passes through a slot in a trunnion piece which is neatly housed

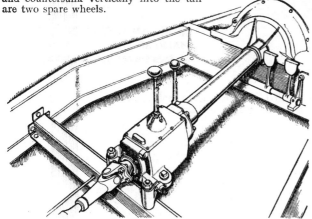

The four-speed gear box is rigidly attached to the clutch housing by a 3in. tube.

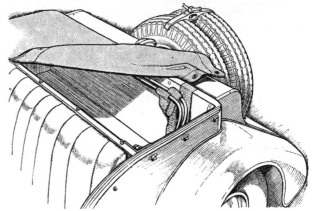

Luggage compartment, nine-gallon tank, and spare wheels follow current sporting fashion.

New Morgan Car

within the end of a tubular rear cross-member on each side.

The engine is a Coventry Climax. Since some 90,000 Coventry Climax engines have been built up to date, and have given excellent service in the hands of the public in cars of many different makes, the soundness and reliability may be taken for granted. The engine used in the Morgan is a 9.8 h.p. model, four cylinders, 63×90 mm. (1,122 c.c.), with push-rod and rocker-operated overhead inlet valves and side exhausts. Before delivery by the makers each one of these engines is well tested and has to pass a standard of developing 34 brake horse-power at 4,500 r.p.m.

The design of the transmission is unusual. Drive through the Borg and Beck single-plate cushioned clutch is taken through an enclosed shaft back to the gear box, which is mounted well back in the car and avoids thereby the need

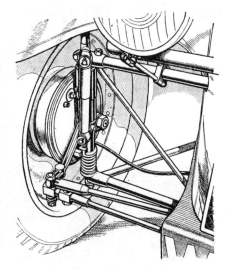

for remote control. This box provides four speeds, with synchromesh for easy changing on third and top. The overall gear ratios are: first 17.5, second 12, third 7, and top 5 to 1, the tyre size being 16×5in. Actually, the gear box casing is directly connected to the engine, for a stout 3in. tube, which embraces the clutch shaft, is bolted to the clutch housing at one end and to the gear box at the other.

The equipment includes Girling brakes, Stevenson four-wheel jacking system, and a 12-volt Lucas set, with coupled 57 ampere-hour batteries mounted away from the heat of the engine.

The main dimensions of the Morgan "4-4" are: wheelbase 7ft. 8in., track 3ft. 9in., overall length 11ft. 8in., height 3ft. 8in., or with hood up 4ft. 1in., width 4ft. 6in.

The independent front wheel suspension.

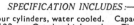

TO THE READER.—By mentioning " THE LIGHT CAR " when replying to advertisers, the progress of the small car movement will be assisted.

The Morgan 4-4 in Improved Form

Detail Modifications Add to the Attractions of an Unusual Small Car

As an open car, the Morgan is very attractive and capable of a snappy performance. It costs £194 5s.

INTRODUCED as a fast touring two-seater, the Morgan 4-4 was first described in *The Motor* on January 7, 1936. Since that time development has proceeded and the 1937 model, which will be exhibited at Olympia, is in several respects an even better car than the type which is already on the road in the hands of many private owners.

It may be recalled that an outstanding feature of the Morgan is its independent suspension system. At the front of the chassis frame is a girder built up of tubes and tie rods. This forms a rigid part of the frame and at each end there was a vertical spindle. On this there was a sliding lug which carried the wheel spindle and which was controlled by coil springs, together with a Newton hydraulic shock absorber.

While retaining this general principle on the new model, the detail work has been altered and would appear to be very greatly improved. The fixed "vertical" spindle is now inclined backwards and the sliding member is a steel forging with a phosphor-bronze bush at top and bottom. Combined with this forging is the steering arm and a face to which the brake plate is bolted at four points.

Numerous advantages accrue from the alteration. A better càstor action is obtained by tilting the pin on which the wheel mounting slides. Moreover, the provision of separate bushes makes it a simple matter to look after any wear which may take place in consequence of the sliding motion. This, however, is not likely to be great because the spindle diameter has been increased from ¾ in. to 1 in. and the space inside the forging between the two bushes forms a reservoir for lubricant which can be forced into it through a conventional greasegun nipple.

In addition, the new method of mounting the brake plate on a large

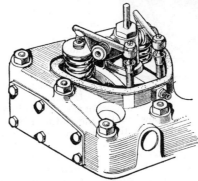

The modified o.h. inlet valve gear: the cup is now fitted at the top of the push rod and will hold lubricant.

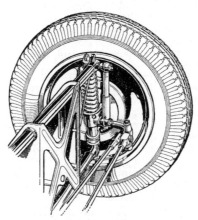

The fixed spindle for the front springing is now inclined backward slightly giving better castor action.

and rigid face stiffens the plate itself and so enables the Girling brakes to operate even more smoothly and certainly than in the past. Finally, so far as these modifications are concerned, it seems that the inclination of the sliding axis gives rather a better suspension—perhaps because any blow or

shock received by the road wheel is not purely vertical but must have some horizontal component so that if the wheel can slide slightly backwards as well as forwards it travels more in the path which it would naturally choose.

There is another improvement in the steering mechanism which has been made since the Morgan was first described. Instead of the original arrangement in which a reduction gear was housed half-way down the steering column, as on the three-wheelers of this make, a Burman-Douglas steering box is now used with a conventional continuous column from the Ashby spring steering wheel. The drag link runs across the front of the chassis from the drop arm to a ball joint on the track rod close to its connection with the near-side steering arm.

In the power unit also changes are to be observed. The four-cylinder Coventry Climax engine still has its inlet valves placed overhead and operated by push rods and rockers, but the arrangement of the cup and ball joint between push rod and rocker has now been inverted. That is to say the cup is in the top of the push rod, where it will retain lubricant, and the ball is attached to the rocker.

At the same time, the method of adjusting tappet clearance has been made more convenient. Instead of incorporating this in the push rod, it forms part of the attachment of the ball to the rocker, where it can be reached more easily.

To improve the flow of cooling water through the block, the connection from the bottom of the radiator is now larger and is taken to the off side of the cylinder jacket at its lowest point. Further to improve the cooling a thicker radiator block is employed. This is of the tubular type, so that altogether the engine runs appreciably cooler than in

CONTINUED ON PAGE 12

No. 1072.—10 H.P. MORGAN 4-4 TWO-SEATER

Newcomer Among Small Sports Cars Which Makes a Most Favourable Impression By Its Steady Cornering and General Handling

Restarting on the slippery chalk surface of Maiden's Grove Hill, near Henley (1 in 5 gradient).

ALTHOUGH the Morgan four-wheeler car is new, and really was seen for the first time publicly in the wide sense at the last Olympia Show, the name is, of course, familiar to many through the three-wheeler which for years past has had an enthusiastic following. This has always made its chief appeal to a driver who appreciates performance, and in the same way the new car, the Morgan 4-4, as it is called, is designed to attract the owner who wants a small, reasonably priced and economical sports car. It is provided with a well-tried design of four-cylinder engine of slightly more than 1,100 c.c., having overhead inlet valves and side exhaust valves, mounted in a particularly low-built and rigid frame fitted with an improved form of the special Morgan independent front-wheel suspension.

With its neat open sports two-seater body, the complete car has a smart and attractive appearance. Also, a new and acceptable shape of radiator has been evolved, no easy thing to-day, and in tail view the car is particularly pleasing, the effect being finished off in a practical way by the mounting behind the petrol tank of two spare wheels rigidly clamped in position.

Entirely fresh as this car is to one at the outset, observation of its behaviour on the road is apt to be unusually keen. At once several particularly good things can be said from the point of view of the owner to whom it is intended to appeal. This Morgan is outstandingly steady, and corners exceptionally well, has light, accurate steering, extremely effective braking, and a lively, willing performance. There is no doubt of the appeal made in these directions by this new car to the type of driver concerned.

Straightaway one is struck, of course, by the exceedingly low build, it being possible to touch the road surface from the driving or passenger seat. This construction no doubt has a good deal to do with the remarkable feeling of safety

that is speedily induced in the driver, though it does result in seating positions which, from the point of view of entry and exit, are best suited to the younger and more agile members of the fraternity. Once seated, however, driver and passenger find themselves to be comfortable, and vision is very satisfactory, the bonnet line not being unduly high even in relation to the low seating position.

As to the performance, the four-cylinder engine is a unit that pulls particularly well at low speeds on top gear or will keep the car swinging along happily at 50 to 60 m.p.h., besides lending itself to use of the gears, third being valuable for extra acceleration and fast hill-climbing. There is a noticeable exhaust note, though this is not of a nature to annoy either those in the car or others outside it, while the engine is quiet mechanically at ordinary speeds and smooth as well. The gears are inclined to make more sound than is usual to-day, especially second and first.

Undeniably, the car has distinct possibilities by reason of the good points already outlined. Certainly an outstanding feature is the sure and accurate way in which it can be put round either a fast open road bend or, for instance, a sharp turn of the modern arterial road roundabout type, with no tendency whatsoever to heel or sway, and only a mild "scream" from the low-pressure tyres under such extreme use to show that anything out of the ordinary is being done. This ability is contributed to not only by the special type of front springing, the underslung rear springs, and the low build, but also by a steering gear which is finger-light, though quick and high-geared, at the same time free from road shocks and possessing enough caster action. It needs only 1¾ turns from lock to lock. At speed or slowly, it can be one-hand steering, so well does the car control, besides which it feels "solid."

DATA FOR THE DRIVER

10 h.p. MORGAN 4-4 TWO-SEATER.

PRICE, with open two-seater body, £194 5s. Tax, £7 10s.
RATING : 9.8 h.p., four cylinders, i. over e. ; 63 ×90 mm., 1,122 c.c.
WEIGHT, without passengers, 14 cwt. 0 qr. 14 lb.
LB. (WEIGHT) per C.C. : 1.41.
TYRE SIZE : 16 ×5.00 in. on bolt-on steel disc wheels.
LIGHTING SET : 12-volt ; 10 amps at 30 m.p.h. ; two-rate charging.
TANK CAPACITY : 9 gallons ; fuel consumption, 35 m.o.g. (approx.).
TURNING CIRCLE (L. and R.) : 37ft. GROUND CLEARANCE : 6in.

ACCELERATION

Overall gear ratios	From steady m.p.h. of		
	10 to 30	20 to 40	30 to 50
5.00 to 1	10.9 sec.	11.6 sec.	12.0 sec.
6.50 to 1	8.2 sec.	8.7 sec.	10.9 sec.
12.00 to 1	5.5 sec.	—	—
17.60 to 1	—	—	—

From rest to 30 m.p.h. through gears, 6.1 sec.
From rest to 50 m.p.h. through gears, 15.9 sec.
From rest to 60 m.p.h. through gears, 28.4 sec.
25 yards of 1 in 5 gradient from rest, 5.3 sec.

SPEED.

				m.p.h.
Mean maximum timed speed over ¼ mile	...	...		—
Best timed speed over ¼ mile	...			77.59

Speeds attainable on indirect gears :—

1st	...	...	...	16-21
2nd	...	...	...	29-35
3rd	...	...	...	51-60

Speed from rest up 1 in 5 Test Hill (on 1st and 2nd gears) 19.69

Performance figures for acceleration and maximum speed are the means of several runs in opposite directions.

(Described in "The Autocar" of October 2nd, 1936.)

Again, complete confidence is produced by the Girling brakes, which are light to apply, smooth and progressive even in an emergency stop, and exceedingly good as regards ordinary slowing down. The driving position has a big influence upon one's general opinion of a car, of course, and the fact that the steering column of the Morgan is well raked, that vision is good, and that both wings are in sight of the driver have much to do with the feeling experienced right from the commencement of being able to do anything one chooses with it. It is a most handy size of machine in town streets or on a busy main road, and, steering as it does to the proverbial inch, can get through safely where many another car would be held back. It feels very safe on wet roads, also. As to the controls, the steering wheel is spring-spoked, and thin and comfortably shaped in the rim. The gear lever, too, is admirably placed. The box, it will be remembered, is some two feet aft of the engine. This arrangement has the advantage of bringing the gear lever into a convenient position immediately above the box itself, with no need for remote control mechanism, and of shortening the open propeller-shaft, which passes in the ordinary way to the rear axle final drive.

The gear change handles very well indeed; first is reasonably low and really need not be used for starting on the level. The clutch gives a quite smooth start and is light to operate. The change from first to second is a deliberate one in the ordinary way, or, alternatively, for a quick get-away a very rapid pull-through change can be made from first to second, with a single clutch depression. From second to third a quick movement is possible, synchromesh on the latter gear assisting, as also between third and top on either the upward or the downward change. In a convenient position to the left of the gear lever is the hand-brake lever, this being of fly-off type, engaging its ratchet only when the knob is pressed down; it will hold with absolute certainty on a 1 in 4 gradient, on which, too, a very easy restart can be made.

This car's suspension is admirable on ordinary surfaces, on the firm side over certain types of less good surfaces at low speed, and inclined to be hard over a really severe potholed section. During the course of a test of some 300 miles the Morgan was taken up several well-known gradients of the kind used until quite recently in trials. There is plenty of power for this sort of thing, the engine revving freely.

Though fixed by screws, and in one section, the seat back rest can, of course, be set at the commencement

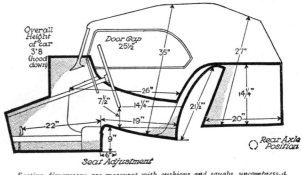

Seating dimensions are measured with cushions and squabs uncompressed.

POSITIONS OF THE VARIOUS CONTROLS

29 feet
(Damp Concrete Surface)
from **30 M.P.H.**

to suit any individual driver's ideas. Actually, with the seat as arranged on this particular car both an average-height man and a tall one were comfortable. Some people prefer more support in the lower part of the back than this seat gives. The body sides are fairly high; if protection were not thereby sacrificed it would probably be an advantage as regards the driver's right arm if his door could be cut away partially. The windscreen can be folded flat on the scuttle, and it was with this down that the best timed speed recorded in the table was taken, the speedometer then showing a reading of 82. With the windscreen up normally, the best timed speed was 74.38 m.p.h., the speedometer then not going above 78. The full circuit of Brooklands could not be used for gaining speed, and, in the circumstances, to have recorded a mean timed speed would have been unfair. At 30 the speedometer was but 0.8 m.p.h. fast, and at 50 was 2.1 m.p.h. fast.

Behind the seats is a good space for luggage, protected by a tonneau cover. The hood framework is easily raised, and the detachable fabric clips on to the body sides and to the top of the windscreen with quick-action fasteners. There is a side screen to fill in the space above each door. The driving mirror, mounted on the wing, is quite effective when adjusted for an individual driver. As was specially noticeable from driving the car along muddy by-ways, the mudguarding is very effective.

The engine is generally accessible, including plugs and ignition distributor, dynamo, and oil filler—admirably so—while both radiator and fuel tank have well-placed quick-action filler caps. It is noticeable that the engine runs to, and stays at, a high temperature, about 95 deg. C., but no more. Starting is ready.

In tail view the Morgan 4-4 is particularly satisfactory; two spare wheels are provided.

IN BRIEF

ENGINE: Four cylinders; overhead inlet and side exhaust valves; 63 mm. by 90 mm.=1,122 c.c.; power output, 37-40 b.h.p. at 4,500 r.p.m. Tax, £7 10s.

TRANSMISSION: Single dry-plate clutch; four-speed gearbox with synchromesh for third and top. Ratios, 5, 7, 12 and 17.5 to 1; reverse, 22.6 to 1. Final drive by open propeller shaft and spiral bevel.

GENERAL: Girling brakes; helical springs front and semi-elliptic rear; 9-gallon rear tank.

DIMENSIONS, Etc.: Wheelbase, 7 ft. 8 ins.; track, 3 ft. 9 ins.; overall length, 11 ft. 8 ins.; overall width, 4 ft. 6 ins.; weight, 13 cwt. 3 qrs. 7 lb.; turning circle, 37 ft.; width across seats, 36½ ins.; legroom (squab to pedals) 40-46 ins.; luggage space 35 ins. long, 14 ins. deep, 14-20 ins. wide.

PERFORMANCE: See text. Petrol consumption, 35 m.p.g.

PRICE: £194 5s.

MORGAN MOTOR CO., LTD.,
MALVERN LINK,
WORCS.

The MORGAN 4-4

A Car of Really Sporting Appearance and Performance which Does Not Belie Its Good Looks

ALTHOUGH the first detailed announcement of the Morgan 4-4 appeared almost exactly a year ago, it was not until the Motor Show in October that many motorists were able to examine the car at close quarters for the first time. Since then, the works at Malvern have been working at high pressure supplying the demand that close inspection created. The task of coping with this demand has kept the makers fully occupied, and it was not until recently that we were able to subject the car to an extended road test.

Shorter runs in early models had already convinced us that in matters of performance, road holding and cornering, the Morgan 4-4 was a vehicle that would instantly appeal to those who want more in a car than mere reliability and comfort. Further acquaintance with the 4-4 in its final production form, served to confirm in full measure all the previous favourable impressions, and show, in addition, that one or two items originally open to slight criticism are now above reproach.

Modified Steering Layout.

The steering is a case in point. As described on October 2, the layout has been modified since the model was first introduced. With this new design the front suspension is more comfortable than before and the steering also is appreciably improved. Only 1½ turns of the steering wheel are required to move the road wheels from lock to lock, but, in spite of this rather high ratio, the car is light to handle.

Further, it keeps its course well. Travelling either fast or slow, we noticed no tendency to wander. Even with the speedometer (which we found to be more accurate than most) showing 75 m.p.h., the car followed a straight line if left to itself, and obeyed the wheel precisely when required. As might be expected from the look of the Morgan, fast cornering causes no anxiety; the worst that happens is a gentle slide which is easily controlled under normal conditions.

So far as performance is concerned, repairs to Brooklands Track unfortunately prevented our obtaining the usual stop-watch figures. The makers speak of 80 m.p.h., and we can add that, according to our past experience, the Morgan concern does not usually make exaggerated claims. Moreover, from the general performance of the

The lay out of facia board ensures that instruments are easily read, whilst all controls are conveniently placed. At the top of the page is a three-quarter rear view which shows the sporting lines and the neat mounting of the two spare wheels.

car on the road, there is every reason to suppose that stop-watch figures for a timed quarter-mile would indicate a speed not very different from that claimed.

As for acceleration and hill-climbing, one has only to drive the 4-4 for a short distance to realize that here is a car in which hills assume much less importance, and modern problems of overtaking cease to be of much moment—a car, in fact, which revels in high averages.

The clutch is smooth in operation and gear changing calls for no special skill. Top and third gears have synchromesh, but the others also are easy to engage. As to the brakes, which are Girlings, it will be unnecessary to say more than that they are amongst the smoothest and most effective we have yet tried. The hand brake by the way, has a ratchet of the press-on or racing variety, and is placed conveniently on the near side of the gearbox.

A stubby gear lever is mounted directly on the

separate gearbox, which is placed amidships. To engage bottom gear, the lever is moved towards the steering column and then forwards. For second it is pulled straight back towards the driver's seat. Third is forward away from the column, and top is back towards the passenger. Reverse, alongside second, but still nearer to the driver, is guarded by a sliding catch on the lever.

Turning to the other controls, the horn button is in the middle of the bottom edge of the centrally placed instrument panel, where it is easily pressed by a finger or knuckle of the left hand. The other small controls also find a place on this panel.

Placed centrally is the large speedometer dial with total and trip mileage recorders as well as a small clock face. On each side in the upper corners of the panel are smaller dials, containing two instruments each, the four being oil gauge, ammeter, fuel gauge and water thermometer.

Mounted on the toe-board, just above the clutch pedal, is a foot-operated switch for the anti-dazzle arrangement. The latter is a little unusual, but very effective. Instead of being dipped, both headlamps are extinguished, and a small Lucas Passlight is brought into play. This is mounted between the headlamps and gives a truly flat-topped beam, which picks up road obstructions a good way ahead but does not annoy other road users. It should also be a boon in fog.

Visibility from the driver's seat deserves mention as being particularly good. So low is the bonnet that, although the seat also is low, both wings can be seen perfectly.

As to maintenance, the Morgan appears to be well arranged. Chassis lubrication nipples are for the most part easily reached, and the same is true of the various engine components. Under the bonnet is a fair-sized tool box, and there is also space for tools, dusters and the like underneath each seat, so that the two cubby holes in the facia board can be reserved for more perishable articles.

An attractive feature is the jacking arrangement. By lifting the carpet on either side, a small trap-door is revealed. When this is opened, access is obtained to the end of a cross-member in which there is a hole. The jack is provided with a horizontal peg which fits into this hole.

Convenient Jacking System.

After attaching the jack in this way, with its foot near the ground, an ordinary spanner is used to turn a hexagon on the top of it. This lifts one entire side of the car very easily, and entirely cuts out the need for grovelling to find a suitable place for the jack.

Although not quickly adjustable in the usual manner, the seat position can be altered without difficulty. The one-piece squab is arranged so that it can be moved forwards or backwards, and the two separate cushions are then placed to correspond with it.

Behind the squab is a large space in which suitcases or other luggage can be carried. Its approximate dimensions will be found in our data panel. Within this space underneath the tonneau cover is also carried the hood. This has a folding frame which can be brought quickly into position. The hood fabric is quite separate and is attached by means of turn buttons on the body and press buttons on the screen.

Side curtains fill the space between the hood and the door tops, which are low to give ample elbow room, but even when these curtains are in use, the occupants are by no means cramped. Moreover, there is sufficient room under the hood for a man of average height to wear a hat in comfort if he wishes.

Altogether, this Morgan 4·4 is a most attractive little car. It is genuinely as pleasant to handle as it is to look at.

(Top) The collapsible hood folds neatly out of sight into the luggage locker. (Above) This photograph of the off side of the engine shows clearly the petrol pump, coil, distributor, dynamo and oil filler. (Right) When erected, the hood and side curtains provide good weather protection without unduly limiting vision.

FIRST RACE VICTORY OF MORGAN 4/4
R. CAMPBELL WINS ULSTER TROPHY RACE AT 53.73 m.p.h.
FASTEST AVERAGE BY A. CONAN-DOYLE (BUGATTI)

Yet another excellent Irish road-race has come and gone. The I.M.R.C.'s Ulster Trophy race was notable for several crashes of a minor nature and for a very high percentage of retirements, for out of twenty-one starters only nine finished the race. The four-mile Ballyclare course is on the whole good, if slower that was expected and ballynarrow in places. Spectators were, in our opinion, allowed to assemble far too close to the road, with inadequate protection.

The race was handicapped on a system of credit laps and given a mass start, with the cars placed in positions in handi-

cap order. Ivo Peters, from the front line, rapidly went ahead in his new 2.6-litre Alfa-Romeo, but Robin Hanson brought his 1½-litre Maserati past him, and Conan-Doyle's twin-cam 1½-litre straight-eight Bugatti and Powys-Lybbe's well known 2.3-litre Alfa-Romeo clung to Peters's tail. Then Hanson left the road about half a mile from the start at a series of difficult bends, the Maser poking the hedge and suffering damage in consequence. On the straight leg Lybbe came up to second place, and after one lap Peters had 10 secs. lead, followed by Lybbe, Doyle, H. B. Prestwich (M.G. Magnette) and Faulkner (M.G. Magnette).

After three-quarters of the race was run R. Campbell of Belfast, driving the Morgan 4/4 for his employer's wife, Mrs. R. E. Parish, because Mr. Parish's Competition Licence had not been forthcoming, was fourth on handicap. He had eight laps credit in thirty-six laps of 149 miles total and had lapped consistently at 53½ m.p.h. The leader at this stage was H. B. Prestwich (single-seater K3 M.G.), winner of the Cork race, who had lapped consistently at 66 m.p.h., doing one lap at 68 m.p.h. Second was Campbell's own J2 M.G., driven by R. Scott, with G. Best's P-type M.G. third. Shortly afterwards Campbell got past Best, as did J. R. Weir (driving Murray-Frame's K3 M.G. Magnette) and Adrian Conan-Doyle (Bugatti). Now it was Prestwich's turn, and five-and-a-half valuable minutes were spent in the pit as a result. The Morgan 4/4 had its chance and won by two minutes at 53.76 m.p.h. Weir, also troubled by mis-firing, managed to snatch second place with his M.G. at 64.26 m.p.h. Prestwich just got home third at 65.33 m.p.h. and Conan-Doyle pipped Wilson's Lagonda Rapier right on the post to get fourth place, averaging the highest speed of anyone at 65.83 m.p.h.

RESULTS
1. R. Campbell (1,120 c.c. Morgan) (8 credit laps), 2h. 9m. 30s., speed 53.73 m.p.h.
2. J. R. Weir (1,087 c.c. Magnette, S.), (2 laps), 2h. 11m. 30s., 64.26 m.p.h.
3. H. B. Prestwich (1,078 c.c. Magnette, S.), (2 laps), 2h. 11m. 53s., 64.07 m.p.h.
4. A. Conan Doyle (1,497 c.c. Bugatti, S.), (1 lap), 2h. 12m. 8s., 65.83 m.p.h.
5. J. L. Wilson (1,104 c.c. Lagonda), (8 laps), 2h. 12m. 9s., 52.66 m.p.h.
6. T. Graham (1,089 c.c. Riley), (8 laps), 2h. 14m. 43s., 59.03 m.p.h.
7. W. McDowell (1,089 c.c. Riley), (7 laps), 2h. 16m., 52.99 m.p.h.
8. M. F. L. Faulkner (1,089 c.c. Magnette, S.), (2 laps), 2h. 26m. 48s., 57.59 m.p.h.
9. A. Powys-Lybbe (2,364 c.c. Alfa), (scratch) 2h. 31m. 59s., 58.87 m.p.h.

I Peters (Alfa-Romeo) at Bally Robert Hairpin. He recorded the fastest lap time, but crashed a mile from the finish.

The Morgan 4-4 in Modified Form
CONTINUED FROM PAGE 7

the earlier Morgans, a fact which was verified by us on the road.

In conformity with the present trend, an air-cooled dynamo is now fitted and this is driven by belt instead of by chain. The ignition distributor, which previously was combined with the dynamo, is now independently driven by skew gears.

Almost alone amongst modern cars the first Morgan four-wheelers had their engines bolted rigidly to the chassis. This has been altered to some extent. There is no attempt to give the extreme flexibility of mounting which is to be found on some cars, but in order to trap the high frequency vibrations, rubber is now interposed between the engine and the chassis frame.

Care has been taken to arrange matters so that there is no metal to metal contact between engine and chassis at the mounting points and the same ap-

plies also to the gearbox. This, it may be recalled, is not attached close up to the engine as in the usual form of unit construction. Between it and the clutch housing there is a large diameter tube which encloses a driving shaft.

The gearbox is thus located appreciably farther back than usual and a short lever mounted directly on it gives all the convenience usually associated only with a remote control, but avoids the complications of that device. An improvement noted in that part of the car is a new brake lever.

Mounted on this most interesting little chassis is a two-seater body of distinctly smart lines. The doors are cut away and each of the two seats has its own pneumatic cushion, but there is a single squab stretching from side to side. This is adjustable and behind it is a space in which can be carried a considerable amount of luggage as well

as the detachable hood and side curtains. A cover is provided for it. Behind that again is a fuel tank with a capacity of nine gallons and fitted with a quick-action filler cap.

In the Morgan, performance is not obtained by means of a highly tuned engine. On the contrary, the power unit is a standard production type, with a single carburetter, but it has the advantage that it is mounted in a car of unusually low weight.

MORGAN MODEL 4-4
ENGINE: Four cylinders; overhead inlet and side exhaust valves; 63 mm. by 90 mm. (1,122 c.c.); tax, £7 10s.
TRANSMISSION: Four-speed gearbox with synchromesh for third and top.
MISCELLANEOUS: Girling brakes; helical springs front and semi-elliptic rear; nine-gallon rear tank.
DIMENSIONS: Wheelbase, 7 ft. 8 ins.; track, 3 ft. 9 ins.; overall length, 11 ft. 8 ins.; overall width, 4 ft. 6 ins.
PRICE: £194 5s.

A FOUR-SEATER MORGAN 4/4

Scope of Popular Four-wheeler Model Increased by Addition of New Body Style. Chassis Unaltered

ALTHOUGH it is not yet possible to describe the Morgan three-wheeler range for 1938, it can be stated that there are to be two four-wheeler models from the famous little factory at Malvern Link. In addition to the two-seater, which has now been on the market for nearly two years, a four-seater body is now available on the same chassis.

Without altering the wheelbase or curtailing the driver's leg room, really sufficient knee space for the rear passengers has been provided. The

(Above) The two-seater model which has gained an excellent reputation and is continued for 1938. (Left and below) Two views of the new four-seater model; the front portion, it will be observed, is identical with the two-seater type whilst the rear seats have been added without undue overhang.

appearance of the front part of the car is the same as the two-seater and the front-seat cushions also are as on that model, there being a separate air cushion for the driver and another for the passenger.

Instead of a bench type squab, however, there are two separate back rests of the bucket seat type, and the passenger's is arranged to hinge forward for access to the rear compartment. The back seat is low although naturally not quite down to the level of the front seats, and the floor space—which is, as usual, divided by the propeller shaft tunnel—is big enough for the passengers to move their feet about for a change of position.

The hood is of the non-detachable type; it folds neatly down to the level of the body sides and is encased in an envelope. From beneath this hood, the rear panel of the body slopes in a straight line interrupted only by a recess into which the single spare wheel fits.

Both the two-seater and the four-seater have a single panel folding windscreen equipped with a twin-bladed wiper, the motor being mounted at the bottom of the screen frame in front of the passenger.

Similarly, both models have an instrument panel with three dials. The central and largest one is a 90 m.p.h. speedometer with trip and total mileage recorders as well as a clock. In the two smaller dials are scales showing water temperature, oil pressure, amperes, and the amount of fuel in the tank. Flanking the instruments are two useful cubby holes and various minor controls are on the instrument

panel. These include the choke, the starter, the ignition key and the lamp switch.

Apart from the latter, there is a foot-operated switch controlling the headlamps and a Lucas FT 27 auxiliary lamp. The headlamps themselves do not dip but are extinguished completely

---

IN BRIEF

ENGINE : Four cylinders ; overhead inlet and side exhaust valves ; 63 mm. by 90 mm. = 1,122 c.c. Tax, £7 10s.

TRANSMISSION : Single dry-plate clutch ; four-speed gearbox with synchromesh for third and top. Ratios, 5, 7, 12 and 17.5 to 1 ; reverse, 22.6 to 1. Final drive by open propeller shaft and spiral bevel.

GENERAL : Girling brakes ; helical front springs and semi-elliptic rear springs ; 9-gallon rear tank.

DIMENSIONS : Wheelbase, 7 ft. 8 ins. ; track, 3 ft. 9 ins. ; overall length, 11 ft. 8 ins. ; overall width, 4 ft. 6 ins.

PRICES : Two-seater, £210 ; Four-seater, not yet announced.

MORGAN MOTOR CO., LTD.,
Malvern Link, Worcs.

---

and the FT 27 is brought into action. It gives a good spread of light over the road surface for some little distance ahead, but does not dazzle other road users. As a fog lamp also it is valuable.

Although there are no alterations to the chassis, a brief description of it will be of interest. The engine, a Coventry Climax, has its exhaust valves at the side and its inlet valves overhead, operated by push rods and rockers. A single horizontal Solex carburetter supplies the mixture and ignition is by coil. The distributor is driven by skew gears, which in turn are operated by the camshaft chain. Within the distributor head there is the usual automatic timing adjuster.

Unlike the arrangement in most modern light cars, the gearbox in the Morgan is not bolted direct to the engine. It is supported on the centre cross-member of the chassis and is connected to the clutch housing by a large tube which encloses a driving shaft.

At every point of support, the engine and the gearbox are separated from the chassis by rubber in the form of bushes or thick washers let into the bearers. This does not give the extremely flexible mounting which is so usual to-day, but it does damp the slight vibrations which even a well-balanced engine generates.

Although the clutch itself is the well-known Borg and Beck, its actuating mechanism is unusual. Fitting inside the tube that surrounds the clutch shaft, there is a cylindrical sliding piece something like a piston without a crown. This bears against the graphite ring which forms the thrust bearing. A peg in the underside of this piston protrudes through a slot in the tube and is connected to the clutch pedal shaft by a push rod and a link.

Behind the gearbox, the transmission is conventional. The chassis and suspension, however, do not comply entirely with that description. Considering the springing first, the front wheels are independently mounted in a manner that is very like that of the Morgan three-wheelers.

Across the front of the frame there are two steel tubes, one above the other. These are carried in a steel pressing and are stiffened by tie rods, each pair of tube ends being separated by a stout spindle that is inclined slightly to give the necessary castor angle for the front wheels.

On the spindle is mounted a steel forging with two phosphor bronze bushes. It can, therefore, slide up and down or turn on the spindle, but it is forced downward by a strong helical spring between it and the top tube end. Formed in one with this forging is a flange to which the brake back-plate is bolted. The steering arm is attached to the forging, as also is the lower end

of an hydraulic shock absorber of telescopic type.

At the rear the suspension is less unusual. It employs two long half-elliptic leaf springs mounted below the axle on each side. The forward end of each spring is pivoted to the frame, the pivot pin being carried in the frame side member and in a bracket above a cross member. At the other end of each spring instead of a shackle there is a trunnion bearing inside the tubular cross member which joins the extreme ends of the frame side members. These, by the way, pass below the back axle.

A novel but useful section is adopted for the side members. There is a vertical web with a flange, top and bottom,

but whereas the upper flange is turned outwards the lower one is turned inwards. It, therefore, serves excellently to support the floorboards at a nicely low level.

Apart from the front "axle" already described, and the tubular cross member at the rear, there are four cross members. These consist of pressings of various sections adapted to their particular position.

As a result of these various features developed from the experience gained in a quarter of a century's manufacture of light three-wheelers, the weight of the complete Morgan 4-4 with two-seater body is appreciably under 14 cwt. In spite of that it is anything but flimsy, as anybody who has driven one knows; it is, in fact, a robust little car with a good power-weight ratio that has helped it to gain many successes already in trials and races.

(Right) The facia board and controls of the new model. With the exception of the separate squabs for the front seats, everything shown in this view is the same on the two-seater model.

(Left) A sketch of the unusual chassis construction which employs "Z" shaped side members on the lower flanges of which the floorboards rest; note the underslung frame and springs. (Below, left) The rear compartment of the new model; the neat semi-concealed hood will be noted. (Below) An under-bonnet view showing the horizontal carburetter, o.h. inlet valve covers and the mounting of the petrol pump and battery.

MORGAN ...   ... STAND 68

The two Morgan 4/4 models. The four-seater (above) is new, whilst the two-seater (right) is already very popular.

Two-seater	£210	0
Two-seater De Luxe ...	£218	8
Two-seater (Special Wheels)	£216	0
Four-seater	£225	0
Exhibition Chassis		

IT is now two years since the Morgan concern entered the four-wheeler field, after a period of very successful three-wheeler production dating from the years before the war. The success which has attended the latest efforts of the factory can be gathered from the fact that the two-seater model on show this year is substantially the same as that exhibited last year, whilst there is now also a four-seater.

The chassis used for both types is identical, and so also is the front part of both cars, but the bench-type squab of the two-seater is replaced on the new model by two separate back rests of the bucket type, that on the passenger's side being arranged to hinge forward to provide an entry to the rear compartment. Although, naturally, not quite so low as those at the front, the back seats are low enough for comfort.

A non-detachable hood, which folds neatly down to the level of the body sides and is encased in an envelope when furled, is fitted, whilst the rear panel slopes in a straight line towards the rear wing tips, but is relieved by a recess into which the single spare wheel fits. On the two-seater, of course, two spares (mounted vertically behind the nine-gallon tank) are provided, thus enabling trials drivers to keep two competition tyres ready for instant use.

In the matter of equipment, too, the Morgan 4/4 is well schemed to appeal to those who like sporting motoring; the windscreen is of the fold-flat type, the facia board

includes a large-dial 90 m.p.h. speedometer with clock inset, the steering wheel is of the spring-spoke type and the four-speed gearbox—which has synchromesh for top and third speeds—is controlled by a pleasantly stubby gear lever.

Of the three examples of the two-seater shown, the model finished in British racing green is the standard product, the cream model with red upholstery is standard except for its special finish, which is available at an extra charge of £8 8s., and the example in blue differs in that special wheels and tyres are fitted; the latter are of 5.5-in. section, as opposed to the normal 5-in. size—an alteration for which trials drivers will readily pay the extra £6 asked in view of the advantage of these bigger tyres both for obtaining a grip on loose and muddy surfaces and for the slightly increased ground clearance.

In its general chassis design the Morgan is built for high performance and good road-holding, as can be seen from the chromium-plated chassis exhibited on the stand. It is powered by a four-cylinder engine with overhead inlet and side exhaust valves, the actual dimensions being 63 mm. by 90 mm. (tax £7 10s.), which gives a capacity of 1,122 c.c., well capable of dealing with the light weight (under 14 cwt.) of the whole car.

Several unusual features characterize the chassis. The front suspension is independent by means of helical springs, the gearbox, instead of being in unit with the engine, is separate and situated amidships and the chassis side members have their upper flanges turned outwards and their lower flanges turned inwards so that they form a most convenient support for the floorboards.

A rear passenger's view of the new four-seater Morgan. Actually, the layout of the instrument board and controls is identical on both models. The louvres along the top of the bonnet are an unusual feature.

No. 1,216.—10 h.p. MORGAN FOUR-SEATER TOURER

SMALL in size and therefore handy on the road, also modestly priced and decidedly economical to run, the Morgan four-cylinder four-wheeler is of sports type in performance and handling. It is unusual among the smaller cars in having independent front wheel suspension, and the chassis design is such that weight has been kept low.

The outcome is a 10 h.p. car which is lively in acceleration, quick on a journey because it holds the higher speeds well, and exceptionally comfortable for this size of vehicle. This open four-seater supplements the two-seater model, and is on the same length of wheelbase. It is of trim and decidedly pleasing appearance.

Useful power is produced by the engine, which is capable of revving freely. Thus the indirect gears can be used to advantage, and they are needed fairly frequently if the best is to be obtained from the car. On the other hand, top is a 5 to 1 ratio, and the flexibility and climbing power afforded is good—indeed, somewhat surprising at times.

Not often in average country is second gear wanted, third being a good gear for the kind of hill which is too much for top, or allowing faster climbing than would be possible on top gear, again, for a spurt of acceleration. Second gear is on the low side, and a rough-surfaced 1 in 4½ to 5 gradient of trials calibre with sharp corners can be taken on it, leaving first as an emergency ratio for the worst sort of gradient, or for restarting on a steep section.

As to general running, it is not a car that suggests a best speed to hold; it keeps up 50 m.p.h. or so readily, and the engine is not much more noticeable at 60, whilst on clear stretches of road the speedometer needle will go round to the 70 region readily.

This speedometer was remarkably close in its readings, being almost dead accurate at 30, appreciably less than 1 m.p.h. fast at 40 and 50, only fractionally more than 1 m.p.h. fast at 60, and showing a highest reading of 80 when the car was being timed for maximum speed on Brooklands track at 78.26 m.p.h. This was with the windscreen lowered. With the screen up, a quarter-mile was timed at 76.92 m.p.h., the speedometer showing 78.

The engine is not altogether quiet, there being mechanical noise under acceleration and at the higher speeds. Exhaust note, however, was virtually absent. Pinking occurred during acceleration.

Outstanding features of the Morgan are the steering and the stability. The steering is finger light, easy even at low speed and when turning round, yet properly firm and accurate, giving the driver the all-important feeling of having direct, responsive control. There is definite caster return, and no more reaction is felt from the front wheels

---

DATA FOR THE DRIVER

10 H.P. MORGAN FOUR-SEATER TOURER.

PRICE, with open four-seater tourer body, £225. Tax, £7 10s.
RATING: 10 h.p., four cylinders, i. over e.; 90 × 63 mm., 1,098 c.c.
WEIGHT, without passengers, 14 cwt. 2 qr. 18 lb. LB. PER C.C.: 1.50.
TYRE SIZE: 4.50 × 17in. on bolt-on perforated pressed-steel wheels.
LIGHTING SET: 12-volt; three-rate charging; 9 amps at 30 m.p.h.
TANK CAPACITY: 8 gallons; approx. normal fuel consumption, 35–38 m.p.g.
TURNING CIRCLE: (L. and R.): 33ft.   GROUND CLEARANCE: 6in.

Overall gear ratios.	ACCELERATION			SPEED.	m.p.h.
	From steady m.p.h. of				
	10 to 30	20 to 40	30 to 50	Mean maximum timed speed over ¼ mile	75.95
5.00 to 1	12.9 sec.	13.8 sec	15.7 sec.	Best timed speed over ¼ mile ...	78.26
7.00 to 1	9.9 sec.	10.4 sec.	11.7 sec.	Speeds attainable on indirect gears (normal and maximum):—	
12.00 to 1	6.2 sec.	—	—		
17.50 to 1	—	—	—	1st	13—21
From rest to 30 m.p.h. through gears ... ... 7.0 sec.				2nd	27—33
To 50 m.p.h. through gears 17.3 sec.				3rd	43—59
To 60 m.p.h. through gears 28.3 sec.				Speed from rest up 1 in 5 Test	
25 yards of 1 in 5 gradient from rest ... ... 5.1 sec.				Hill (on 1st gear) ...	18.76

BRAKE TEST: Mean stopping distance from 30 m.p.h. (dry concrete), 29.5ft.

WEATHER: Dry, hot; wind fresh, E. Barometer: 30.05in.

Performance figures for acceleration and maximum speed are the means of several runs in opposite directions, with two up.

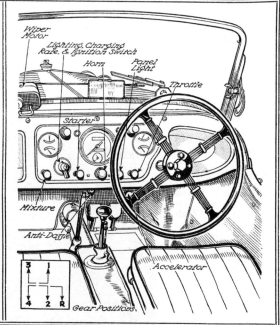

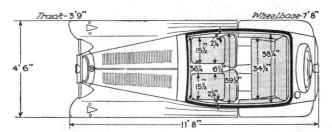

than a slight shake over some road surfaces. It is high-geared steering, needing only 1¾ turns from lock to lock.

Regarding stability, a steadier, safer small car would be practically impossible to find. It goes round corners fast without the least sign of lurching or heeling over, following an accurate course close to the near side. At speed on the straight it is firm and shows almost no trace of pitching motion. Yet the insulation against shock over poor surfaces is striking in this size and type of car, in the back seats as well as the front, even though the springing tends towards firmness rather than softness.

In front the Morgan system of vertically disposed coil springs is employed, with piston-type shock absorbers. At the back the springs are normal half-elliptics with friction shock absorbers.

Handy Size on Busy Roads

The steadiness of the machine contributes much to its good averaging capabilities, besides which it is a size of car overall, with the necessary degree of acceleration, for ready overtaking. Again, it does not occupy much room in narrow lanes, and the driver is placed so that he can see what he is doing.

Girling brakes are used, and, in the usual manner of this type, provide excellent power with only moderate pedal pressure. They act well and safely at speed, and, as the test figure shows, give capital emergency stopping results. The hand-brake lever has a fly-off ratchet, is quite conveniently placed, and effective in holding the car.

Synchromesh is fitted on third and top in the four-speed gear box, second and first being plain. The short lever is firm and moves lightly, and there is an easily operated stop against reverse. Little use of first gear is needed when starting away. Changes can be made quite quickly. Appreciable revving-up is needed to get down to second gear at a fair road speed, but an ordinary double-clutching process usually effects quiet engagement. The gears were noisy, but this matter is receiving attention.

From the first a stranger to the car feels confident in driving it, for the wheel—thin-rimmed and spring-spoked —is admirably placed, and the seat gives just the right

position and support. Also, there is plenty of leg room, with freedom for the driver's left foot when off the clutch pedal. Pneumatic front seat cushions are used over a foundation of coil springs in tension, and the back rests are nearly upright. Although these seats are not specially soft, they do not prove tiring on a long run.

At the back there are foot wells, and, again, leg room is generous. It is a proper back seat for two people, not an occasional one, and the occupants sit well down in the car.

There are cubby holes but not door pockets; an excellent view behind is given by the driving mirror. The instruments are clearly grouped; their lighting at night, by two direct lamps, was rather too bright. Only inside door handles are fitted, and with a side screen up it is not the easiest matter to open the door. A practical point is a soft padded strip placed as an elbow-rest in the cut-away of the doors.

The hood folds neatly and goes up and down easily

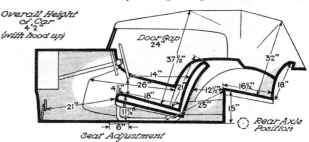

Seating dimensions are measured with cushions and squabs uncompressed.

enough, though there are a good many turn-buttons to deal with in undoing and doing up the hood and tonneau covers. It would be better if all the fasteners were of the quick-action press type. The side screens attach readily, and the protection afforded is very fair. The tonneau cover is an extra.

Cold or hot, the engine is a particularly good starter and soon gains working temperature. It is neat in appearance, and the oil filler and dipstick, and various auxiliaries, are convenient to reach. Battery and tools are under the bonnet. The externally mounted radiator filler is of quick-action type, as also is the petrol filler. The horn note could be stronger. One becomes used fairly quickly to the horn switch being at the centre of the instrument board, where actually it is readily "found." The anti-dazzle is by switching over to a centre lamp, which gives an adequate beam that does not seem to worry other drivers.

A reserve petrol tap is not fitted, but due to the strikingly economical running the range of the tank appreciably exceeds 250 miles. A test totalling more than 1,000 miles indicated an oil consumption in the order of 3,000 m.p.g.

A good view is given of the off-side wing, and the near-side one is just in sight. The windscreen is deep, though the wiper details and mirror get in the way a little. The raised side-screens are indicated.

NEW: A smart drop-head coupe has been introduced on the Morgan 4/4 chassis for the forthcoming season. The hood, as the photographs show, is of especially neat design.

4/4 MORGANS FOR 1939

Prices Considerably Reduced; New Drop-head Coupe Added to Range

FOR a number of reasons the Morgan 4/4 is one of the most individual light cars on the road. Whilst it is not specifically designed for a very high maximum speed, its comfort, good steering, and road-holding properties are such that long journeys can be accomplished with a minimum of fatigue and at really high average speeds. The features responsible for these results are the independent front suspension, high geared and positive steering, low build and high power-to-weight ratio.

The Morgan 4/4 can be obtained with three styles of coachwork, each built on to the same chassis. The prices are as follow: — Two-seater, £199 10s.; 4-seater, £215 5s.; and drop-head coupé, £236 5s. The two and four-seaters show a reduction in price of £10 10s. and £9 15s. respectively.

Dealing first with the new body, this has many practical features. To begin

with, the weight has been kept low so as to maintain a good power/weight ratio, whilst the body space is commodious. The seat width is 44 ins. and the length from the pedal board to the squab is 3 ft. 10 ins. Behind the seat is a good-sized luggage space measuring 3 ft. 6 ins. by 2 ins. by 1 ft. 5 ins. Excellent support is given to the back by having the squab 24 ins. high; the cushions themselves are pneumatic.

Doors, 26 ins. wide, are fitted with windows which have twin sliding glasses. Each panel can be opened to give ventilation either from the front or back of the window. Another point is that the panels do not wind down, thereby leaving the doors free to accommodate elbow rests. Also the whole window frame can be removed by simply undoing two nuts which secure it to the door.

When the hood is raised there is plenty of head room inside, and the

car is very snug and compact. When the hood is folded, it fits away so neatly that it is difficult to detect its presence. To improve silence, the engine is mounted on Silentbloc bushes. Whereas the other models have spoked wheels and 4.50-in. by 17-in. tyres, the coupe has 5.50-in. by 16-in. Dunlop E.I.P. tyres and disc wheels.

Improvements since last year include a strengthened back axle which now has a four-star differential, larger front-wheel spindles and bearings, and a quick-opening oil filler into which a tin can be inserted and left to drain.

Morgan three-wheelers for 1939 will be described in an early issue.

IN BRIEF

ENGINE: 9.8 h.p., four cylinders, 63 mm. by 90 mm.=1,122 c.c. Overhead inlet and side exhaust valves. Tax £7 10s.

TRANSMISSION: Single dry-plate clutch; four-speed gearbox with synchromesh for top and third; gear ratios: 5, 7, 12 and 17.5 to 1. Final drive by spiral bevel.

GENERAL: Girling brakes. Suspension: (front) independent helical, (rear) semi-elliptic. Rear 9-gallon tank.

DIMENSIONS. Wheelbase, 7 ft. 8 ins.; track, 3 ft. 9 ins.; overall length, 11 ft. 8 ins.; overall width, 4 ft. 6 ins.

PRICES: Two-seater £199 10s.; four-seater, £215 5s.; drop-head coupe, £236 5s.

THE MORGAN MOTOR CO., LTD.,
Malvern Link, Worcs.

A good idea of the Morgan 4/4 in "Set Fair" and "Stormy" guise is given by these three pictures of the car tested. The four-seater coachwork makes no discernible difference to the behaviour of the car on the road.

Road Tests of 1939 Models

The MORGAN 4/4 FOUR-SEATER

Road-holding and Cornering Above the Average, Economical Running and a Fine Performance Are Combined in this 205-guinea Car

ANY driver who finds himself in the need of a tonic in the motoring sense will find an excellent prescription in the Morgan 4/4 It is one of those cars which is sufficiently out of the usual run of present-day types to be thoroughly interesting without being so unorthodox as to be disconcerting or unreliable.   In short, the Morgan is a car with that indefinable quality often referred to as "character."

It is not the purpose of a road-test report to describe the mechanical features of a car in detail, but, as many features of the Morgan design play a very definite part in its performance and the way it handles, a brief reference to the various points of the chassis and body layout may well be included when dealing with aspects of the behaviour of the car on the road.

One of the best examples of this relationship between unconventional design and the manner in which the car handles is the matter of cornering and road-holding. In both these qualities the Morgan is quite definitely superior to the general run of light cars: quite how superior may be gathered from the fact that the member of the staff who tested the Morgan—himself a sports-car driver—repeatedly found that he was over-braking for corners.   Many miles were covered before it seemed right and proper to take the car into bends at the speeds it was well capable of maintaining without awkward moments arising.

General road-holding and cornering are co-related qualities in that it is useless for the latter to be good unless road-holding is on a correspondingly high plane;

otherwise the first bumpy corner taken at speed is liable to land the driver into serious trouble. With the Morgan there is no fear of that, for the car sits on the road in a most reassuring fashion.

At low speeds the springing is not so soft as one finds in the normal run of saloons. On the other hand, there is none of that spine-shattering rigidity that one used to experience with sports cars a few years ago. In the Morgan, in fact, one discovers all the good qualities of the old harsh, but effective, suspension with some measure of the comfort of the more elastic but less controllable springing of modern touring cars.

The reasons for these good qualities are not far to seek.   At the front end, independent suspension by means of vertical helical springs is employed. Although the system seems almost too simple to work effectively, the fact that the manufacturers have had 28 years' experience of the design (it was originated on very early three-wheelers), has given them ample time to perfect it.   Built into the design are the long, piston-type hydraulic shock absorbers.

At the rear end of the car conventional semi-elliptic

leaf springs are used; they are mounted on the inside of the chassis side-members, with their rear ends sliding in slots in the rear tubular cross-member. The arrangement gives much greater lateral stability than the conventional type of shackle. Multiplex Hartford friction-type shock absorbers take care of the rebound.

Coupled with these details is a chassis frame which is not only very low (it is underslung at the rear), but is also of special section, which allows an even lower seat-

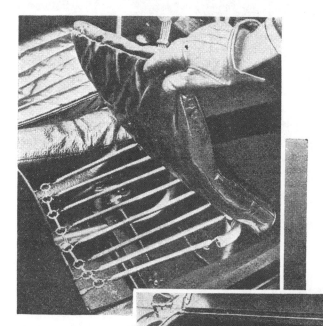

(Above) Spring frames are provided for the front seats, the main tubular frames of which are secured to a cross-member by a screw-down clamp which permits of adjustment. (Right) An under-bonnet view showing the four-cylinder engine, accessible 12-volt battery and the tool locker.

ing position. Actually the side-members are of Z section, with their upper edges turned outwards to serve as a mounting for the body frame and their lower flanges facing inwards, where they carry the platform-type floorboards. Thus the front seats are actually between the side-members.

Steering is moderately high-geared and strikes a nice compromise between the somewhat heavy operation of the ultra-high-geared type and the very easy steering of the wheel-twiddling variety. In terms of wheel movement, 1¾ turns of the steering wheel serve to move the front wheels from full left to full right lock. The system used is the well-known Burman-Douglas design, and a spring-stroke wheel is fitted.

One has only to mention that the braking system carries the name Girling for it to be appreciated that not only are rapid stops a possibility but that the pedal pressure required, although entirely progressive, is very light. When the usual braking tests were carried out

by means of the Ferodo Tapley meter, the road surface, unfortunately, was damp, but, in spite of this, a figure of 93 per cent. was recorded from 30 m.p.h. This is equivalent to a stopping distance of slightly over 32 ft. Obviously on a dry road on which the wheels did not lock, an even better figure could have been recorded. A detail which will be appreciated by sporting drivers is the racing-type spring-off ratchet for the hand brake.

One other point remains to be mentioned in connection with the fine way the Morgan handles—the matter of visibility. No matter what some people may say, it quite definitely *is* a help in busy streets or narrow lanes to be able to see the full width of the front of a car. With the Morgan 4/4 the driver's vision ranges right across from the tip of the front wing on one side to the tip of the wing on the other. In addition, the driver looks through the centre of the screen, all the essential parts of which are cleared by the inverted wiper arms in wet weather.

A car which handles in the manner we have described would be wasted without performance to match; in this case there is no wastage. Unfortunately, Brooklands track was littered with piles of broken concrete at the time of the test and no timed maximum speed figure was obtainable, but, with an accurate speedometer, 75 m.p.h. was registered on a stretch of level by-pass. Under slightly favourable conditions, 80 m.p.h. is obviously within reach.

So far as acceleration is concerned, the figure for the standing quarter-mile of 23.0 secs. speaks for itself. The

(Below) The rear seats are reached in the usual way in cars of this type—by tipping the front seats forward and entering via the front doors. The deep wells alongside the propeller-shaft tunnel provide plenty of leg room.

Morgan is definitely a lively as well as a fast car. As for its capabilities, on the indirect gears, 30 m.p.h. can be reached in second and a mile-a-minute is a possibility in third. The gear change is both fast and easy.

The four-cylinder engine is unusual in that it has overhead inlet and side exhaust valves. It is an engine which does not seem to tire, even when the car is maintained at a consistent mile-a-minute for miles on end. With the latest rubber mounting, it gets on with its job in a very effortless fashion and is quite reasonably sweet.

So much for performance, which, after all, is one of the main things about a car like the Morgan. So far as bodywork is concerned, it should be mentioned at this point that the car selected for test was a four-seater—a model which can strongly be recommended for the driver who does not wish to be restricted to a single passenger.

With some four-seaters distinct sacrifices are made to obtain the extra accommodation, but this hardly applies to the Morgan. The performance figures quoted clearly show that performance, compared with the two-seater, does not suffer to any appreciable extent, and the only other differences are the facts that only one spare wheel is fitted in place of two, and the rear tank is placed under the seat instead of being mounted externally.

Weather Protection.

As for the rear seats themselves, the figures given in the accompanying panel show that they provide plenty of room for two adults. Naturally, the passengers in the back sit rather higher than those in the front—that is inevitable in a low-built car of this type—but they have quite a comfortable ride. They are, moreover, fully protected by the hood (which provides plenty of head room) and the rigid side screens. When not in use, the seats can be covered by a tonneau cover which is supplied as standard and embraces the concealed hood sticks. A separate hood envelope is supplied for use when the tonneau cover is not in position.

From a driver's point of view the Morgan is nicely arranged and gives an immediate feeling of confidence on first acquaintance. There is no need to describe every control in detail, and a single example will give a key to the care taken in the layout. With the left hand gripping the wheel in the most natural position, a slight twist of the wrist brings the knuckles against the horn button; if the hand is allowed to drop, it falls naturally right on the gear lever.

So far as the instruments are concerned, the labelled photograph on this page gives all the particulars.

This automatically brings us to the matter of equipment, and in this respect the Morgan in every way conforms to modern standards. A point worthy of special praise is the head lamps, which are of the Lucas Biflex long-range type, and combine length of beam with an excellent spread of light near the car. Instead of the usual dipping reflector in the near-side lamp, the dipper switch serves to cut out both head lamps and bring a central road light into action. Another point concerning equipment is the fact that an easy jacking system of the Stevenson type is supplied.

As for maintenance, individual greasing nipples are used, but their number is not excessive and the Morgan is obviously not a difficult car for the owner to maintain.

In short, the Morgan 4/4 four-seater is a thoroughly likeable car that will immediately endear itself to the man whose ideas on motoring rise high above mere transport; and at its price of £215 5s., moreover, it represents extremely good value for money.

This worm's-eye view of the Morgan 4/4 shows that despite the low build, there are no low projections to catch when trials hills are being negotiated. Below is the layout of the facia board and controls.

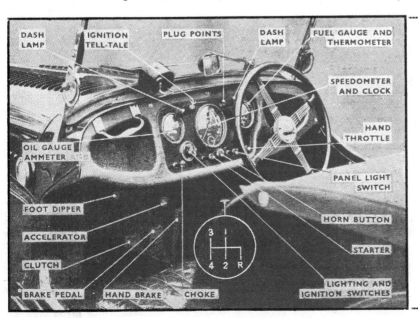

DASH LAMP · IGNITION TELL-TALE · PLUG POINTS · DASH LAMP · FUEL GAUGE AND THERMOMETER · SPEEDOMETER AND CLOCK · HAND THROTTLE · PANEL LIGHT SWITCH · HORN BUTTON · STARTER · LIGHTING AND IGNITION SWITCHES · CHOKE · HAND BRAKE · BRAKE PEDAL · CLUTCH · ACCELERATOR · FOOT DIPPER · OIL GAUGE · AMMETER

DATAGRAPH

ENGINE: Four-cylinder; overhead inlet and side exhaust valves; 63 mm. by 90 mm. = 1,122 c.c. Tax, £7 10s. Power output, 35 b.h.p. at 4,500 r.p.m.

TRANSMISSION: Single dry-plate Borg and Beck clutch; four-speed gearbox synchromesh for top and third. Ratios, 5, 6.7, 11.95 and 19.3 to 1. Reverse, 22.3 to 1. Final drive by Hardy-Spicer propeller shaft and spiral bevel.

GENERAL: Girling brakes; independent suspension by helical springs at front, semi-elliptics at rear; 9-gallon rear tank.

DIMENSIONS, etc.: Wheelbase, 7 ft. 8 ins.; track, 3 ft. 9 ins.; overall length, 11 ft. 7 ins.; overall width, 4 ft. 6 ins.; weight, 14 cwt. 3 qrs. 24 lb. Turning circle, 33 ft.; width across front seats, 39 ins.; width across rear seats, 39½ ins. (between wheel-arches, 34½ ins.); depth of front cushions, 20 ins.; depth of rear cushion, 17 ins.; knee room at rear (max.) 15 ins., (min.) 11 ins.

PERFORMANCE: Maximum speed on road (see text), 75 m.p.h. Standing ¼-mile, 23 secs. Petrol consumption (driven hard), 34 m.p.g.

PRICE: £215 5s.

THE MORGAN MOTOR CO., LTD., MALVERN LINK, WORCS.

NEW MORGAN ENGINE

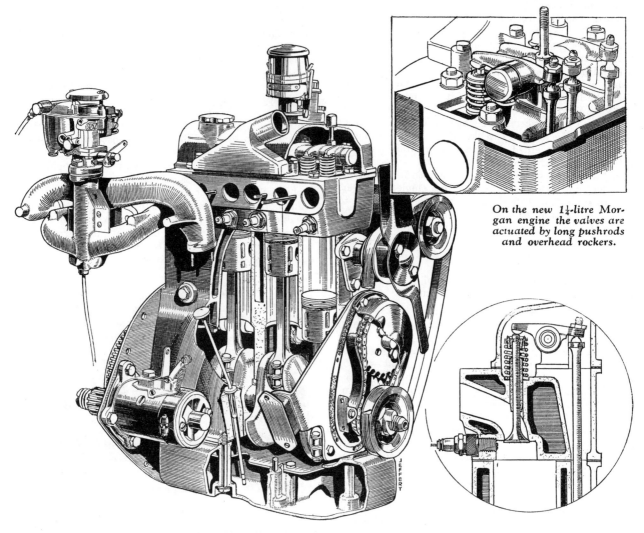

On the new 1¼-litre Morgan engine the valves are actuated by long pushrods and overhead rockers.

A sectional drawing which shows the main constructional details. A Solex downdraught carburetter is used and the compression ratio is 6.8 to 1. The unit develops over 38 b.h.p. at 4,500 r.p.m. (Circle) The combustion chamber is notably compact and turbulence is encouraged by its offset position.

Coupe Model Now Has all Valves Overhead—Obtainable on Other Models for £5 Extra

RUMOURS have been current for some time that the Morgan 4/4 is to be fitted with this or that make of engine in future. Nearest to the truth was the story that a Standard Ten engine was to be used. The fact is that the Standard Motor Co., Ltd., is manufacturing an engine specially for the Morgan Motor Co., Ltd. This new unit has all valves overhead and is now standardized in the coupé Morgan. It can be obtained in the open 4/4 models at an extra cost of £5.

Bore and stroke of this new Morgan engine are 63.5 mm. and 100 mm. respectively. It has a compression ratio of 6.8 to 1 and it will run up to 5,500 r.p.m. Although its power peak is at its maximum at about 4,500 r.p.m. when 38.8 b.h.p. are developed, the curve remains fairly level up to 4,800 r.p.m.

Power output at lower speeds also is good. At 1,000 r.p.m. it is 10.7 b.h.p.; at 2,000 r.p.m. the figure is 23.3 b.h.p., and at 3,000 r.p.m. it is 34.2 b.h.p. At its best the b.m.e.p. is close on 120 lb. per sq. in.

Part of the credit for these results must certainly be attributed to the special design of combustion chamber.

The overhead valves are vertical and in line, but are offset from the centre of the cylinder. In plan, the combustion space is more or less oval and its length is greater than the cylinder diameter, but its width is considerably less.

As the piston reaches the top of the compression stroke gas is deflected into the combustion chamber from that part of the cylinder which is blanked off by the head casting. This gives rise to additional turbulence and the sideways flow into the ends of the chamber probably adds to this effect.

Amongst details which may be noted is the fact that the inlet valves are appreciably larger than the exhausts. The 14 mm sparking plugs have ¾-in. reach, which gives better cooling by providing a larger area of contact with the head casting. The plugs are placed horizontally in the head close to the valves.

Single springs are used on the valves and there is an additional spring at the foot of each push-rod. The overhead rockers are simple forgings and adjustment of valve clearance is by the well-tried method of a ball-ended set-screw in the rocker, the ball fitting into the cupped top end of the push-rod. At the bottom these rods are themselves rounded to fit into the cupped tops of the tappets, which, by the way, are of ample size.

A special shape of cam is used. This permits a clearance of .015 in. and takes up that clearance gradually before the valve starts to open so that quiet operation is obtained. That is assisted in other ways. Owing to the push-rod return springs already mentioned, the valve clearance must always be at the top end.

Any sort of metallic hammering there is prevented by a feature of the lubrication system. Oil is fed along the overhead rocker shaft to each rocker bearing and, through it, to passages drilled at each end of every rocker. Consequently there is always a supply of oil in the clearance between the rocker and the valve stem as well as in the cupped top end of the push-rod. This has a distinct cushioning effect.

Conventional Lubrication System.

For the rest the lubrication system is conventional. Oil is fed to the three main bearings and, through passages drilled in the crankshaft, to the big-end bearings. The cylinder bores and the small end bearings receive their lubricant by splash, the top of each connecting rod being cupped and drilled.

The oil pump itself is of the gear type and is submerged in the sump, which is a large ribbed aluminium casting holding 11 pints. There is a floating gauze-covered intake to the pump so that lubricant is drawn from the cleanest part of the oil near the surface.

To work this pump there is a vertical shaft driven by

ENGINE AND GEARBOX MOUNTING DETAILS.

(Below) Compressed rubber mounting is used behind the clutch casing at two points.

RUBBER

helical gears near the centre of the camshaft. That shaft is continued upwards also to drive the ignition distributor head.

On the other side of the engine there is a down-draught Solex carburetter on a manifold casting which combines the inlet and the exhaust passages. This is, of course, arranged to provide a hot patch near the centre of the inlet portion. An A.C. mechanical fuel pump is driven by the camshaft.

Cooling is arranged on the thermo-siphon principle and there is a two-bladed fan driven by an endless rubber belt from the front end of the crankshaft.

The complete unit is installed in the well-known Morgan chassis in a manner which is generally similar to that followed in the past, but with certain important modifications of detail. The same gearbox is mounted in the identical position, connected as before by a large steel tube to the engine. At its front end this tube has a substantial flange which is bolted to a pressed-steel bell housing enclosing a Borg and Beck clutch.

The principal difference in the mounting is to be found in a more generous use of rubber. At the front there is a pressed-steel bracket or arm each side of the engine, ending in a face inclined at about 45 degrees. Under this face, sandwiched between it and another bracket attached to the chassis frame, there is a block of soft rubber. This is loaded partly in compression and partly in shear.

There are altogether six points of support for the com-

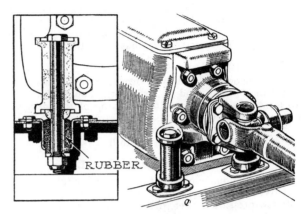

FRONT ENGINE BRACKET

RUBBER

Rubber is used at all six suspension points for the new o.h.v. engine (above). The gearbox is mounted at two points.

(Left) On each side of the engine at the front there is a large rubber pad loaded tangentially and sandwiched between two brackets which are at an angle of 45 degrees.

plete unit, the other four being two under the gearbox and two near the clutch. Each of these consists of a substantial rubber bush in a steel cage and with a bolt through its centre. This rubber also is therefore loaded largely in shear, in accordance with what is known to be the most satisfactory principles.

Lively Performance.

At the present it has not been possible to conduct our complete road test of this latest Morgan, but we have driven one of the coupés for a short distance. It impressed as being probably one of the nicest models which have yet emanated from the Malvern factory. Moreover, it appeared to be remarkably lively and to have fine acceleration.

The generous use of rubber mountings has, no doubt, contributed greatly to the quiet running of the unit and its freedom from vibration. Starting from cold is instantaneous and it appears to warm up very rapidly. No flat spots are apparent, whilst it is possible to tick over very slowly indeed.

For the coupé the price remains unchanged at 225 guineas. All those who have seen the model, whether at Earls Court, at Brighton or elsewhere, are agreed on its attractive appearance. Its comfort is no less satisfactory and we anticipate that a full road test in due course will show that performance also is well up to the standard which has so long been associated with the name of Morgan.

Delayed by

An Experimental 8 h.p.-engined Morgan Sp—
Day be Produced to Supplement the 10 h—
Has Been Neglected

By H

WITHOUT interfering with the present activities of the firm concerned, I was able recently to sample an interesting experimental car—a Morgan 4—4 fitted with an 8 h.p. side-valve engine which was mildly supercharged. It appears that just before the war began Morgan's had built up one of their normal sports two-seaters with this power unit as a try-out, in the way that manufacturers do, and it had sat about the works practically unused for rather more than two years.

Thus one had the unusual and much-appreciated experience for these times of driving a virtually new and spotless car, with the added interest of its being different from any other of outwardly identical type on the road.

It will be remembered that the Morgan four-wheeler as introduced some four years before the war· had an overhead-inlet and side-exhaust valve engine of 1,122 c.c., which, in conjunction with the car's low weight and comparatively small frontal area, gave it a good performance among the 10 h.p. sports types of cars. In *The Autocar* Road Tests that model has been timed at 78.26 m.p.h.

Then, not long before September, 1939, a Standard engine was made available, with overhead valves, specially built for the Morgan, and of 1,267 c.c., though still rated at 10 h.p. The war came almost on top of this development, and only a few cars were actually produced, I believe, with this engine, though it is recalled that at least one car so equipped ran in one or two rallies.

8 h.p., but Just Over One Litre

The 8 h.p. engine experiment dates from about the same time. With the co-operation of Carburettors, Ltd., an Arnott low-pressure blower, driven by a belt, was put on, but in all other respects the car followed normal Morgan lines. The engine size was (in fact is) 1,021 c.c., and thus there was no big drop in actual capacity from the engines that had already been used. The important point gained, of course, had it been possible to put such a model into production, with or without the supercharger, was participation in the 8 h.p. sports class, which since the days of the earlier Midgets and the still earlier Singers of that horse-power has been sadly cold-shouldered.

As I have said, this 8 h.p. experimental Morgan, which came into my hands recently, had, by force of circumstances, been put on one side for a good while. It was clean externally, and did not look neglected, but, for instance, rust formation on the bodies of the sparking plugs seemed to tell a story.

Practical experience of the car, though extending over four or five days, was restricted in mileage to little more than the running afforded by my meeting the car at Oxford as a mutually convenient point, and driving in it to the London district, and taking it back there in due course for return to the works.

Evidence of Miles Against the Clock

Nowadays, with a greatly reduced current background of comparison and no stop-watching of speedometer readings to check accuracy or measure actual performance, one is apt to be more impressed by a show of performance than in times when such things were more relative and in better perspective. Nevertheless, the 8 h.p.-engined Morgan possessed performance of a kind which was not to be explained away by thoughts on those lines. The speedometer I strongly suspected of going too readily up to readings every small sports car owner would like to believe, but the evidence of miles put into a given time was significant, the little car being able to cover the ground at a highly satisfactory pace. No one, I think, could possibly expect more from a production car of this modest rating than the Morgan showed itself capable of providing, and that on the present fuel, or could fairly be disappointed.

The Arnott supercharger, I understand, boosts at about 3-4 lb. per sq. in. It was so quiet as to be undetectable, and has its own oil supply from a small tank under the

(Top left, above, and right) Views from various angles of experimental Morgan tried with a supercharged 8 h.p. engine. neat instrument panel, spring-spoked wheel, and fold-flat type windscreen will be noticed, also the two spare wheels.

o-seater, with Supercharger, Which May One

el. A Size of Small Sporting Car Which

ikers in Recent Years

FIELD

ow) The Arnott supercharger (with Arnott carburettor) does interfere unduly with general accessibility ; oil for it is fed from the small tank seen at the rear of the engine.

bonnet, the level in which had not gone down by more than an inch and a half in some two hundred miles.

The engine used has an aluminium head and a quite high compression ratio for an ordinary production unit. It is, therefore, inherently lively. How much the blower adds to the performance I cannot assess exactly, but its chief value, of course, is in helping acceleration. These two-seaters weigh not more than approximately 14½ cwt., and thus give a small engine a chance.

The car stood in the open all night whilst I had it, and though it is true that the nights had not become really chilly there was no difficulty in starting. A strangler control is retained, and when starting from cold it was best to release this almost as soon as the engine first fired. On each occasion it was a process of driving straight off. No supercharger snags of any kind were encountered. Pinking was moderate, and very possibly less noticeable with the engine blown than if it had not been, by virtue of the better mixing and distribution of the mixture usually obtained, especially at the lower engine speeds, with a supercharger in use.

Superchargers for General Use

Personally, I have never been "anti-supercharger," and I consider that these auxiliaries represent a method whereby the all-important acceleration can be secured from ever-smaller engines, provided that earlier difficulties have been, or can be, overcome. That they have largely been, and that a blower can now safely be put in the hands of the more or less ordinary owner is true, I believe. But another name should be found if what we know as a supercharger is ever to be supplied to the general public. The term carries with it a certain prejudice born of the past, and suggests racing and super sports cars too strongly to the average motorist.

That is a digression. Concerning other qualities of the Morgan, the low build and suspension layout make it a most satisfactorily steady and safe feeling small sports car. The front independent suspension, of vertical-slide and coil spring type, comparatively limited working travel being permitted, is softer in effect than when first used on the car, but undoubtedly shines in the matter of stability. Helped by "quick" steering, the driver can do quite exciting things with this car, and on an ordinary main road scarcely any conscious steering is needed ; finger pressure on the wheel takes the car round bends. Although the drums are not large, the Girling brakes work very well, too. A rev counter would be worth having, more particularly with the blower fitted.

Well "Wound-up"

On the last part of the final journey in the car I was pressed for time, and, letting restraint go briefly, I " wound it up " for the first and only time. It took gradients on the Maidenhead-Oxford route at a cracking pace, not relying for opinion upon the speedometer, which on a useful but level stretch of road on this section I noticed once at the 80 mark. This was surprising—not, for the moment, in the sense of suspecting its veracity, but because I had not appreciated that much more than an easily seen 60 or so was being indicated at that point. An Aircraft-man whom I was able to pick up—the second of his kind during the day, as it happened—enjoyed his ride, apparently, saying that he had never travelled so fast in his life. Although I had not taken particular note of the time myself, he worked out, upon getting out of the car, that we had done nine miles in ten minutes. Thereabouts, anyway.

The engine thermometer was showing a high reading, though I remembered that the Morgan usually did this, which is good, provided that it does not go too far. When I handed the car over, the engine seemed none the worse.

If an 8 h.p. edition can be marketed after the war it should certainly appeal to many of the sports car fans, who appreciate performance and all the other qualities of the type of car concerned, but who must keep costs down.

"TALKING OF SPORTS CARS" (No. 139)

The Morgan 4-4

An Owner's Experiences Compared With Road Test Impressions of the Model

COMING down from the 20 h.p. of the last two sports cars described in the series to exactly half that figure, we arrive this week at the 10 h.p. Morgan 4-4. This, as some readers will probably recall, is not the first time the Morgan four-wheeler has been featured in "Talking of Sports Cars," but it is the first time one of these cars has been described here by an owner.

Wartime Experiences

On the previous two occasions (January 3rd, 1941, and June 26th, 1942), I had been able to make brief trials of examples of the species myself, the more recent one being the model fitted with the specially built 10 h.p. o.h.v. four-cylinder engine of Standard origin, which the Morgan people had adopted as an alternative unit no great time before the war.

The present car is one which, I gather, was new in May, 1940, and which—as recounted by Mr. C. B. Field, who lives near Ringwood, Hants—had a severe crash in the hands of a friend of his. Mr. Field bought the wreckage and turned it into a presentable and service-able Morgan 4-4 once more, to the extent that in the past year he has covered some 12,000 miles with it, on important work, with, one deduces, every satisfaction.

My own fairly recent experiences of the type include the Standard-engined model I tried last year, the other, earlier as already mentioned, and a third example which came into my hands for a brief spell from the works, an experimental car fitted with an 8 h.p. Standard side-valve engine and a blower. Previously to these necessarily limited wartime experiences the last time I had anything to do with a Morgan was in the summer of 1938. This was in connection with a Road Test published in *The Autocar* of August 12th, 1938. The practice appearing to have supporters, I am again including a reprinted version of the performance and specification table which appeared in that Road Test of some four years ago.

Over maximum speed, I am interested to observe the Morgan owner's speedometer figure by a stop-watch-checked instrument, of 82 m.p.h. under favourable conditions, and his assessment of the car's true speed as being about 76 m.p.h. It will be noticed in the table that the car tested in 1938—a Coventry Climax engined model, and also a four-seater, in common with Mr. Field's later-built example—gave a mean timed speed over the ¼-mile of 75.95 m.p.h. That would have been with the windscreen lowered, and as the average of numerous runs, in turn aided and handicapped by the prevailing wind, over different ¼-mile stretches round the Brooklands circuit. With the screen up normally, a favourable ¼-mile was timed at 76.92 m.p.h. on that occasion. The speedometer then showed 78, and its highest reading was 80 during the other runs for speed timing; it was only fractionally faster than 1 m.p.h. on the test car at an indicated 60.

1000-mile Test

That car was given a rather longer test than most of the cars received. I had it in my keeping for a fortnight, and it covered more than 1,000 miles; including a spell in North Devon, where it tackled most of the best-known hills with great aplomb. Bearing also on Mr. Field's remark about a negligible oil consumption, I see that the Road Test stated that an oil "consumption" in the order of 3,000 m.p.g. was suggested by the experiences of the test, in spite of the stiff climbing that was undertaken in the West. I entirely agree, too, with his comment upon the steering feeling "right" for the weight and size of car, and about the car being under full control at all times.

In my opinion, no small car handles better or requires less effort for fast cornering—and the Morgan *can* corner fast. The impression received is that it would never turn over until, on a possible unfortunate occasion, it actually hit something, such as a kerb, and not easily even then. Looking back I should describe the springing that contributed so much to this stability as being on the hard side over some kinds of road surfaces, but the insulation afforded against actual shock on poor surfaces was satisfactory by standards of judgment applied to a small sports car.

Driving Confidence

The steering was decidedly high geared, 1¾ turns of the wheel giving the full lock-to-lock movement. A Road Test comment was: "From the first a stranger to the car feels confident in driving it . . ." It was also remarked that the Morgan readily kept up 50 m.p.h. or so, and that the engine was not much more noticeable at 60. The engine was put down as being not altogether quiet, there being, not unexpectedly, mechanical noise under acceleration and at the higher speeds, though exhaust note was virtually absent.

The brakes (Girling) gave capital results in the test; the experience, I see, of the owner in question is that they require fairly frequent adjustment. The hand-brake lever, by the way, is of the fly-off type, the pawl engaging with the ratchet only when the knob is depressed, and there is synchromesh for third and top. A further Road Test comment, regarding hill-climbing, was that second gear, as it obviously is, was on the low side (12 to 1), a climb being possible on this ratio of a Devon trials hill with acute corners and about 1 in 5 or 4½ maximum gradient. 'This is a better plan, I consider, for a small car than having a higher second and a very low first, on which the engine has frequently to be "screamed" in difficult country.

Now I'll hand over to Mr. Field, remarking finally that he will be interested to try to help over any queries Morgan owners may have, provided that they will send him the customary stamped addressed envelope, and do not mind waiting a little. "V."

❖ ❖ ❖

"The first thing that comes to my mind" (writes C. B. Field) "when comparing a Morgan with any other car is a remark I once heard: 'If God had not made a tree, Morgan could never have built a motor car.' The Morgan I own was purchased new by a friend of mine in May, 1940; in fact, I had eyed it in the showroom for some time before he bought it, but as I was going abroad at the time I persuaded my friend to agree to sell the car to me on my return to England if I still wished to have it, and for this consideration I assigned all purchase rights to him!

Small Car v. Lorry

"When I returned to England I found my friend just out of hospital and the car lying in a garage, very crushed, it having come into contact with a heavy R.A.F. lorry. Incidentally, the poor lorry driver was killed, which shows that the heavy vehicle driver does not always get away with it best of all. I purchased the salvage and commenced rebuilding. No damaged parts were used again, all replacements being made with new parts purchased from Morgan's, their spare part prices being extremely reasonable, in my opinion.

"We pulled the wreckage to pieces, and the main new parts were as follows: Chassis, steering unit, front axle assembly complete, off-side front wing and running board, clutch housing, clutch plate, primary shaft from engine to gear box, engine mounting plates, and a number of smaller items. The car, up to the time of this accident, had completed 3,000 miles. The body, a four-seater open tourer, was smashed away on the off side, also the scuttle; this we rebuilt, using the appropriate tree species, and re-panelled. During rebuilding I fixed all the floorboards with ³⁄₁₆in. Whitworth bolts, with large 'penny' washers on the wood and spring washers on the chassis. I think that this greatly strengthened up the structure, and was well worth while—the makers' practice was to use wood screws only, but these fell out after a while.

"I will pass over the rest of the rebuilding, but would mention one or two points which I consider to be important and peculiar to the Morgan. (1) The torque tube between clutch housing and gear box is considered an integral part of the clutch housing by Morgan Motors, and these parts should not be separated unless machining facilities are available. (2) The front engine mounting brackets should be very carefully located if local stressing of the chassis is to be avoided, since, owing to the thin gauge of the metal, fractures will occur. (3) The front axle tie-rods to the chassis should be of exact length, for the same reason as in Item 2. (4) The two spring-loaded bolts securing the track rods should be mounted the correct way up, that is, with the head of the bolt at the bottom, and the spring on the top surface. This is absolutely essential if wheel wobble is to be avoided.

"The car was finally put on the road in March, 1941, and from that date to February last was run continually, covering 12,000 miles. During the whole of the period it was driven fairly hard, long distances having to be covered periodically, but it always received careful servicing.

Acceleration and Speed

"Concerning performance, the acceleration is extremely good; also the average speeds which can be maintained, hour after hour, are high; a constant 60-65 m.p.h. will not fatigue the car. The maximum speed recorded, against a speedometer checked with a stop-watch, is 82, but this was under favourable conditions, and I would say that the genuine speed of the vehicle is nearer 76 m.p.h. The brakes are extremely efficient, but require fairly frequent adjustment. Road holding is excellent, and the front independent suspension is a great asset in these days of deteriorating roads. Steering is somewhat direct, but feels 'right' for the weight (13½ cwt.) and size of the car, and at no time have I left the car not to be under full control. Petrol consumption, on Pool, appears to be approximately 36 m.p.g. at speeds around 50-53 m.p.h. If these speeds are exceeded the figure drops to about 32 m.p.g. Oil consumption is absolutely negligible.

Morgan and guardian—presumably an "enthusiast dog!" This is the 4-4, which, as described, Mr. C. B. Field rebuilt from virtual scrap after it had been in a bad crash.

"The engine (10 h.p. Coventry Climax), with its unusual feature of overhead inlet and side-valve exhaust, is very sturdily built and trouble-free. Valve clearances retain their settings the whole time between decarbonisings—in my case every 7,000 miles—although this frequency does not appear to be really necessary. All parts are extremely accessible, and I have fitted a Fram oil cleaner (I have one on my Competition A.C. as well), and consider that such an accessory is of very great value. The oil is renewed every 2,500-3,000 miles, but the Fram cleaner keeps it perfectly clean this period, and I am sure it could be made to last longer.

Fitting the Oil Cleaner

"I would mention that when I fitted the Fram, as per Simmonds Aerocessories' instructions, 'hydraulicing,' was noticed in the valve box, to which the return pipe was fitted; also, I could not stop oil seepage from the exhaust valve cover. I therefore removed the return pipe from this position, plugged the hole in the valve cover and fitted the Fram return pipe to the top of the sump oil filler, and since then have had no trouble whatsoever. Colloidal graphited oils should not be used with a Fram cleaner, since the cleaner has then to spend much of its energy in removing the graphite! But it is an easy matter to disconnect the inlet pipe by inserting a blank at the union when running on a colloidal graphite oil—which is an excellent practice and a sound basis for good bearing surfaces.

"It is very important that moving parts on the Morgan's front axle should be well lubricated, and the Newton shock absorbers require rather frequent attention and, I consider, are a weak feature of the car; also the axle has a tendency to distort. Toe-in is ⅛in. and tyre pressure 18-20 lb. per sq. in.

"The gear box is sturdy and very pleasant to operate, the changes being as quick as you can make them, but the teeth are square cut and intermediate gears emit a slight whine, which is not actually unpleasant, but

DATA FOR THE DRIVER	"THE AUTOCAR" ROAD TEST AUGUST 12th, 1938
10 H.P. MORGAN FOUR-SEATER TOURER.	

PRICE, with open four-seater tourer body, £225. Tax, £7 10s.
RATING: 10 h.p., four cylinders, i. over e.; 90 × 63 mm., 1,098 c.c.
WEIGHT, without passengers, 14 cwt. 2 qr. 18 lb. LB. PER C.C.: 1.50.
TYRE SIZE: 4.50 × 17in. on bolt-on perforated pressed-steel wheels.
LIGHTING SET: 12-volt; three-rate charging; 9 amps at 30 m.p.h.
TANK CAPACITY: 8 gallons; approx. normal fuel consumption, 35-38 m.p.g.
TURNING CIRCLE: (L. and R.): 33ft. GROUND CLEARANCE: 6in.

ACCELERATION				SPEED.			
Overall gear ratios.	From steady m.p.h. of						m.p.h.
	10 to 30	20 to 40	30 to 50	Mean maximum timed speed over ¼ mile			75.95
5.00 to 1	12.9 sec.	13.8 sec.	15.7 sec.	Best timed speed over ¼ mile ...			78.26
7.00 to 1	9.9 sec.	10.4 sec.	11.7 sec.	Speeds attainable on indirect gears (normal and maximum):—			
12.00 to 1	6.2 sec.	—	—	1st			13—21
17.50 to 1	—	—	—	2nd			27—33
From rest to 30 m.p.h. through gears			7.0 sec.	3rd			43—59
To 50 m.p.h. through gears			17.3 sec.	Speed from rest up 1 in 5 Test			
To 60 m.p.h. through gears			28.3 sec.	Hill (on 1st gear)			18.76
25 yards of 1 in 5 gradient from rest			5.1 sec.				

BRAKE TEST: Mean stopping distance from 30 m.p.h. (dry concrete), 29.5ft.
WEATHER: Dry, hot; wind fresh, E. Barometer: 30.05in.
Performance figures for acceleration and maximum speed are the means of several runs in opposite directions, with two up.

cannot be said to be up to present-day standards of quietness. The back axle, too, is sturdy and silent in operation. The rear springs, half-elliptic, run through trunnions on the chassis, which should be kept lubricated, and are excellent.

"Then the body: the separately adjustable front seats are extremely comfortable with ample leg room, and the driving position is very good. The back seat is not so comfortable, but, of course, is really intended for emergencies only, and with the hood up the head room is very restricted. The body flexes considerably, which worried me when I first had the car, but such flexing, I think, is probably necessary with so light a frame, and it does not appear to be detrimental to any parts, but joints need watching if rattles are to be avoided over a period of time.

A Year's Wear and Tear

"I completely overhaul my cars every twelve months. From experiences of one year's running the following comments may be of interest:—Engine: the crankshaft and connecting-rod bearings are in perfect condition, and no fault could be recorded by a micrometer reading to three figures. The timing chain required retensioning, which is achieved by the distributor drive housing being machined eccentric. The cylinder bores show slight wear, and I have fitted Cord piston rings to the pistons to absorb this wear (incidentally, I have Cord rings fitted to the A.C., and they appear to be very satisfactory).

Transmission and Body

"The only other signs of wear or matters requiring rectification were: (1) Primary shaft between engine and gear box, which was floating, and in consequence the splines were damaged in the coupling. I renewed the coupling and shaft. The cause of this fault appears a little obscure, but it has been rectified by the insertion of a spacer inside the coupling at the gear box end, which prevents such float occurring. (2) The collar which is sweated to the primary shaft torque tube had become unsweated. This bears directly on my previous remarks concerning this tube. (3) The flexing of the body at the scuttle was rather greater than I like, and the scuttle has been diagonally braced to the chassis with 15 cwt. cable, which has had the effect of greatly increasing the rigidity of the structure.

* * *

"Since compiling the above notes I have covered a further 5,000 miles and no further points have arisen which should be quoted, but I might mention that oil pressure should be 40 lb. per sq. in., and that the fitting of a Fram has no effect upon this pressure except with a cold engine, when the drop in pressure is 4 lb. per sq. in.—i.e., a reading of about 46 lb. instead of 50 lb.

Shock Absorbers

"I have come to the conclusion that the front shock absorbers have no effect at all except at very low speed when braking, when they tend to damp a very slight wheel 'shimmy' which sometimes occurs, I think due to the brake cables not being always at exactly the correct tension. I ran 3,000 miles without the shock absorbers, but have since decided to replace them for the reason mentioned."

The Morgan four-seater that was tested by "The Autocar" in 1938. It is seen on a North Devon hill that will be remembered by London-Barnstaple trial competitors in particular, Kipscombe, on an old short-cut road between Challacombe and Bratton Fleming. Last observed hill of that trial, Kipscombe was never really difficult to a modern car, but had amusement value.

500 MILES IN THE 3-CYLINDER, TWO-STROKE SCOTT-ENGINED MORGAN 4/4

Complete reliability and ability to average very high speed.

THE excellent meeting at Cockfosters last July offered us an excuse to test the Scott-engined Morgan 4/4 over a big mileage, whereas previously the car had only been tried round the Saltaire houses, as it were. That visit to the Scott works and brief trial of the car had endeared us to the idea of three cylinders and the two-stroke cycle, as envisaged by Mr. Cull, Scott's chief engineer, and we had no compunction in asking whether we could take the car down to " Cockfosters." Once again Mr. Cull reminded us that it had been hacking all through the war, but that if we wanted to chance it, we could do so. We did. The first hot day of the year saw us off to Bradford in the Austin to collect our unusual mount. On the journey back to Harrogate we took things steadily and looked around. Oil pressure was noted to remain steady at about 8 lb./sq. in., and the water temperature at about 65° C. Had we but known it, these figures were to remain static throughout a hard and hot 500 miles, save just before we put in a quart of XL, when the oil indication fell away a bit on bends. The first surprise was the way in which the Morgan, as engined by Scott, took Humphrey Bank, outside Harrogate, in top gear, whereas many 4-speed moderns call for 2nd speed to negotiate this notorious hump. The engine seemed disinclined to accept much ignition advance, but, as we noted before, ran beautifully evenly and refused to four-stroke even at idling speed. It commenced commendably on the starter and, indeed, behaved just like any well-mannered Otto-cycle unit.

Starting the long run about mid-day, we got on to A1 after a long hold-up at Spofforth level-crossing and, stopping for lunch, and for tea in congested Stamford, we were in and across London early that evening. The Morgan hadn't been pushed very hard, but had cruised happily at around 50 m.p.h., and we had already noted how its seemingly unburstable engine would run up to the same speed in 3rd gear and how astonishingly well the little car—three up, and luggage—pulled up long hills on the highest ratio. Incidentally, gearbox and axle are, we understand, standard Morgan 4/4, in which case the ratios are 5.0, 6.7, 11.95 and 19.3 to 1.

Next morning the H.215 plugs oiled up in London traffic, so the " softer " C.14s were substituted. These not only stood up to low-speed pottering, but also to subsequent prolonged high-speed cruising, so that the 3SM Scott cannot be considered sensitive about plugs. Incidentally, a record cloudburst proved the practicability of the Morgan hood.

So to Cockfosters. Thereafter the real test commenced. Tea was taken in Barnet, and the Morgan pointed north, still three up, at 6.30 p.m. So fast did it run without effort that the plan of arriving home about midnight seemed unworthy of the car, and the driver decided to improve on this schedule. The engine humming grandly, with that

exhaust purr which had led the paddock marshals at Cockfosters to query : " Is it blown ? " we devoured A1 with the speedometer on the " 70 " mark along all the straights. Aided by high-geared steering, a low-hung chassis, Morgan coil-spring i.f.s., and Girling brakes, an unexpectedly good time was made.

In the first half-hour 20 miles were disposed of, and 7.30 p.m. saw us nearly at Eaton Socon, 46 miles out of Barnet. Another half-hour and another 24 miles were gone, while, as the driver's watch

showed 8.30 p.m., we were at Grantham, 98 miles from where we had started. Exactly 24 miles went by in the next 30 minutes' spell, after which we had a quick drink and rapidly consumed some sandwiches. So consistently did the Morgan make for the North that 24 miles again went by in the next half-hour, and in 60 minutes' running time after our self-imposed stop we had covered 40 miles, which included negotiation of the straight, but congested and signal-controlled main road through Doncaster. A curious phenomenon had by now been experienced. As the oil pressure became unsteady, indicating a falling sump level, the engine " pinked " less and became able to accept rather more ignition advance. The solution appears to be that oil is metered into the fuel by means of a special engine-driven combined fuel and oil pump and,

as the oil supply drops, less oil enters the combustion spaces and the full anti-knock properties of the fuel are temporarily restored. This is borne out by the sudden violent " pinking " which is experienced as the float chamber empties when fuel is exhausted, allowing an excess of oil to be momentarily injected into the engine. This latter happening occurred just beyond Wetherby, after we had left the Great North Road for Harrogate, and so, instead of getting home from Barnet in about four hours, we spent a difficult hour in the dusk, trying to prime a seemingly unprimable pump. However, the fuel tank was found to possess a sensible tap and we were thus able to fill the float chamber, whereupon the engine started easily, and primed its own pump—the C14 plugs were quite happy after the excess-oil trick.

Working things out the next day, we became more and more impressed. Even allowing for the absence of full peace-time traffic, an average of 48½ m.p.h. for three hours' running up the Great North Road calls for a very good car, especially when its capacity is a mere 1,108 c.c. The Scott engine poured out 70 m.p.h. on the " clock "—say, something over 60—for mile after mile, and not only *felt* quite unburstable, but didn't overheat or show any sign of distress at all. After a night in the open in heavy rain, a lot of which came through the bonnet, it started straight away on the starter and was driven rapidly back to Saltaire on those same C14 plugs. If ever it didn't want to start an easily-reached cock in the crankcase was opened, the engine spun on the starter to clear out excess fuel and oil, the cock closed and—off she went. The quart of oil went in after some 450 miles—a consumption of 1,000 m.p.g. from a well-worn two-stroke ! Going down, fuel consumption came out at approximately 27 m.p.g., cruising at 40–50 m.p.h. Including London driving, plenty of stopping and starting, and the *very hard* drive home, the overall consumption of " Pool " was 23½ m.p.g., on an S.U. carburetter adjusted for all-round running and not expressly for economy. As an amusing exercise, before returning the car, we tried a 0-50 acceleration test, using very rough timing, and got 17 sec., including a longish dwell between the change from 2nd into 3rd gear at around 45 m.p.h. In all we covered 510 miles and no water was added throughout.

All of which has convinced us that the 3-cylinder, crankcase-compression two-stroke, 3 SM 78 by 78 mm. Scott engine is a very fine little unit. It develops over 40 b.h.p. at 4,000 r.p.m., but the firm's intention is to obtain more power lower down in the speed range, while offering 30+ b.h.p. at peak speed. The engine will probably be supplied in this form after the war, and it should be excellent for competition work. Those interested, especially from the latter viewpoint, should contact Scott Motors, Ltd., Shipley, Yorks.

The Morgan 4/4

1946 Version has New Engine

TWO versions of the Morgan four-wheeler are now available. These are the open two-seater at £355 (plus £99 15s. 1d. purchase tax) and the drop-head coupé at £395 (plus £110 18s. 3d. purchase tax). Externally these interesting little cars show

MORGAN—DATA

(Letters in brackets refer to footnotes.)

	4/4 Two-seater	4/4 Coupe
Present tax ..	£12 10s.	£12 10s.
Cubic capacity ..	1,267 c.c.	1,267 c.c.
Cylinders ..	4	4
Valve position ..	Overhead	Overhead
Bore ..	63.5 mm.	63.5 mm.
Stroke ..	100 mm.	100 mm.
Comp. ratio ..	7	7
Max. power (A)	40 b.h.p.	40 b.h.p.
at	4,300 r.p.m.	4,300 r.p.m.
Max. torque (A)	61.6 lb./ft.	61.6 lb./ft.
at	2,500 r.p.m.	2,500 r.p.m.
H.P.: Sq. in. piston area (A)	2.04	2.04
Wt.: Sq. in. piston area (B)	82.7 lb.	88.5 lb.
Ft./Min. Piston speed at max. h.p. (A)	2,830	2,830
Carburetter ..	Solex d'dr't.	Solex d'dr't.
Ignition ..	Lucas coil	Lucas coil
Plugs : Make and type	Champion N.8	Champion N.8
Fuel pump ..	A.C.Mechanical	A.C.Mechanical
Oil filter make (by-pass, full flow)	A.C. By-pass	A.C. By-pass
Oil circulation: Galls. per min.	2½ g.p.m. at 3,000 r.p.m.	2½ g.p.m. at 3,000 r.p.m.
Clutch ..	Borg and Beck dry single plate	Borg and Beck dry single plate
1st gear ..	17.1	17.1
2nd gear..	12.1	12.1
3rd gear (S)	7.1	7.1
Top gear (S) ..	5.0	5.0
Reverse ..	22.6	22.6
Prop. shaft ..	Hardy Spicer open	Hardy Spicer open
Final drive ..	Spiral bevel	Spiral bevel
Brakes ..	Girling mechanical	Girling mechanical
Drums ..	8 ins. dia.	8 ins. dia.
Friction lining area	84 sq. ins.	84 sq. ins.
Car wt. per sq. in. (A)	19.3 lb.	20.7 lb.
Suspension ..	Independent front with coil springs ; semi-elliptics with Hartford dampers rear	Independent front with coil springs ; semi-elliptics with Hartford dampers rear
Steering gear ..	Burman-Douglas	Burman-Douglas
Steering wheel..	16 ins. dia.	16 ins. dia.
Wheelbase ..	7 ft. 8 ins.	7 ft. 8 ins.
Track, front ..	3 ft. 9 ins.	3 ft. 9 ins.
Track, rear ..	3 ft. 9 ins.	3 ft. 9 ins.
Overall length ..	11 ft. 4 ins.	11 ft. 4 ins.
Overall width ..	4 ft. 6 ins.	4 ft. 6 ins.
Overall height ..	4 ft. 4¾ ins. (closed)	4 ft. 6½ ins. (closed)
Ground clearance	6 ins.	6 ins.
Turning circle ..	33 ft.	33 ft.
Weight—dry ..	14½ cwt.	15½ cwt.
Tyre size..	4.50—17	5.00—16
Wheel type ..	Spoked disc	Disc
Fuel capacity ..	9 gals.	9 gals.
Oil capacity ..	9 pints	9 pints
Water capacity ..	16 pints	16 pints
Electrical system	Lucas 12-volt c.v.c	Lucas 12-volt c.v.c
Battery capacity	57 amp. hrs.	57 amp. hrs.
Top Gear Facts: Engine speed per 10 m.p.h.	645 r.p.m.	677 r.p.m.
Piston speed per 10 m.p.h.	421 f.p.m.	443 f.p.m.
Road speed at 2,500 ft./min. (piston) ..	59.3 m.p.h.	56.3 m.p.h.
Litres per ton-mile	3,380	3,330

(A) With normal road setting of carburetter etc.
(B) Dry weight. (S) Synchromesh.

no change compared with the 1939 models, but several alterations have been made in the chassis.

Of these, much the most important is the new engine. This, it is true, was in hand at the outbreak of war, and a few Morgans were actually delivered with this unit, but no description of it has yet been published and the following account will therefore be news to most readers.

The New Engine

Made specially for the Morgan Motor Co., Ltd., by one of the largest car manufacturers in Coventry, this engine has all its valves overhead, and is in that respect unlike the previous

power unit of the 4/4. Its general arrangement follows established practice with four water-cooled vertical cylinders forming a single casting with the crankcase, a detachable head in which the vertical valves are operated by overhead rockers and tubular push-rods, and a counterbalanced crankshaft carried in three bearings. These, like the big ends, are of the steel-backed, thin-shell type. The connecting-rods are steel stampings and the pistons are light-alloy Aerolites with split skirts.

In short, the new Morgan engine is conventional and has nothing experimental about it. From our data panel it will be seen that more power is available than was provided by the previous unit. The increase is about 5 b.h.p., or nearly 15 per cent., and this is achieved at a slightly lower crankshaft speed.

As usual, a Borg and Beck clutch is mounted in the flywheel, but the gearbox of the Morgan is not attached directly to the flywheel housing. Instead it is placed almost amidships in the chassis, but it is connected rigidly to the engine by a large tubular mem-

ber which encloses a short driving shaft. This arrangement appears to have several advantages. It places the short, stiff and direct-acting gear lever just where it is wanted. More room is left for the clutch and brake pedals. The propeller shaft is short and therefore is less liable to whip, and the weight distribution is somewhat better.

With synchromesh for top and third, the four-speed gearbox is of the same general design as in 1939, but it is now manufactured in the Morgan factory at Malvern, where a very useful machine shop was organized early in the war to produce high-precision parts for aircraft and other purposes.

Behind the gearbox, the transmission system is conventional, and so is the suspension, except that the semi-elliptic springs have no shackles. Instead, the rear ends slide in trunnions carried in the ends of a tubular cross-member of the frame. Hartford Multiplex frictional shock absorbers control the action of the springs.

At the front, there is independent suspension of each wheel and, although the main features have been used by the Morgan company for 35 years, a brief description may not be out of place here. Across the front of the frame are two parallel steel tubes, diagonally braced and well spaced one above another. Joining each pair of outer ends is a vertical steel rod on which is a sliding piece with the road wheel spindle forming part of it. The wheel, therefore, is free to slide up and down this rod and to swivel round it for steering purposes. Above the sliding axle and surrounding the vertical rod, there is a helical compression spring which takes the load and provides the necessary resilience. Beneath the slider there is a short compression spring to take rebound.

That is the general scheme, but one

ROBERTS

SIMPLE.—The Morgan chassis includes the well-proved Morgan system of I.F.S. which now incorporates a steering damper. An unorthodox note is struck by the remotely mounted four-speed gearbox.

COVERED. — The 1¼-litre four-cylinder Morgan is offered with very neat coupe body which is convertible to entirely open form. Weighing only 15½ cwt. it offers the driver over 50 b.h.p. per ton.

or two detail improvements have been made since it was last in production. These relate both to the suspension and to the steering qualities. In the former, there has been some adjustment of the spring characteristics, particularly with regard to the rebound springs, and this has effected such improvement that it is no longer necessary to use shock absorbers at this end of the Morgan.

More obvious to the eye is the addition of steering dampers. Between each sliding axle and its top spring there is a saw-steel leaf with bronze thrust washers suitably riveted to it. The other end of this spring leaf is anchored to the chassis side. By this means a certain amount of friction is provided at the steering head, and at the same time, the spring is relieved of any twisting effect which might arise when the sliding axle turns for steering. As a result, it has been found that all tendency to wheel wobble has been eliminated.

One of the outstandingly obvious features of the Morgan 4/4 is its low build. This is due largely to the particular form of its chassis frame. Apart

from the fact that it passes below the rear axle and is also lower than the front wheel centres, the pressed-steel side members are of an unusual section, with the top flange turned outwards but the lower flange turned inwards towards the middle of the chassis. Consequently the floor boards (by the way they are boards and not steel pressings) rest on the lower flange instead of being above the side members. This places them only 7½ ins. above the ground level and so permits the rest of the body to be correspondingly low.

Girling Brakes

One or two of the mechanical features must be noted before turning to the bodywork. The brakes are Girlings of the mechanical type, and the hand control has a spring off ratchet, as commonly preferred for competition work.

A simple screw-type jack is provided and has an arm or peg which can be inserted into a hole at either end of the central cross-member of the chassis frame. Access to this member is given by trap doors in the floor. In this way, either side of the car can be lifted.

Both bodies have certain features in common. For instance, there is the neat tail which carries two spare wheels, and there is the low bonnet with its top as well as its sides louvred. Behind the seats, in both cases, too, there is a sizeable space for luggage.

For the open two-seater there is a hood which stows away completely into the luggage space. The windscreen can be folded down on to the scuttle if desired. Both doors have cut-away tops and are hinged well forward, almost at the bonnet edge, so as to give easy

access, and there is a hand grip on the facia just above the near-side cubby hole.

In the coupé, both doors are hinged at the back and carry two-piece sliding windows which permit an opening at the front edge or the back or at both, according to the sort of ventilation desired. In hot weather the complete window assembly can be removed quite easily and stowed in the back of the car. Inside, the doors are recessed to form elbow rests and this does increase the effective width of the body, of course. The head folds down neatly into the luggage space and the car is just as smart when open as when closed.

Whereas the two-seater has a wire-mesh "stoneguard" front to the radiator cowl, the coupé has a grille of vertical slats. Both models are equipped with a pair of Lucas fixed-reflector head lamps and a Lucas Passlight, the foot-operated dipping switch being wired so as to divert current from the latter to the former or vice versa.

Altogether these two Morgan models are good examples of the sort of car which, in the opinion of many, is all too rare on the British market. They are roadworthy and sturdily built, yet light and certainly not under-powered. In short they combine the English cult of the light car with the equally English preference for a vehicle with its own individual and distinctive characteristics.

The three-wheeler chassis is continued as a four-seater with side-valve four-cylinder engine at 933 c.c., and as a sports two-seater with similar engine of 1,133 c.c. In both cases a three-speed gearbox is used with worm gear and final drive by chain. Prices are £205 plus £57 13s. 10d. and £245 plus £68 16s. 1d. respectively.

31

LATEST MORGAN

Individual Small Sports Car Again in Production

TO renew acquaintance with the 10 h.p. Morgan 4-4 is a pleasant proceeding, because the car is quite different from anything else on the market, and has an appeal entirely its own. The design is deceptively clever, for it presents straightforwardly simple solutions of features which are basically desirable in a sports car of the kind.

For instance, the chassis is low built, with a rigid type of independent suspension in front, and frame members slung beneath the axle at the rear. These side members are of Z-section and the floorboards, which act as stiffeners, are carried upon the bottom flange; hence the height of the seat cushions is not raised by wasted space, and the centre of gravity is as low as it can be. Moreover, the weight distribution tends to keep the weight well inside the wheelbase, which makes for stability and the necessarily accurate steering, and the underneath part of the car is quite flat and free from projections, which helps to reduce wind resistance.

Nice To Handle

By the tenets of the sports car enthusiasts the Morgan 4-4 should be a nice car to handle, and in practice this is so. On entering the drop-head coupé, for example, the driver finds himself sitting well down inside what appears to be a high-sided body, but the forward visibility is good because the bonnet is not high above the ground. The steering is fairly quick and of the kind which is held on to a curve; that is to say, it does not oversteer. The car feels extremely safe at speed and can be placed accurately. The suspension is a nice blend of stability with comfort—the ride is not over-hard, but an "all in one piece" feeling is evident, and there is no suggestion of sponginess.

There is plenty of life in the engine, which is capable of giving the car round about 75 m.p.h. as a maximum. All the best eggs are not on the top of the power basket, so to speak, as the engine pulls well at the lower speeds, and comfortable top-gear touring can be had as well as maximum acceleration with full use of the gear box. The gear change is a quick, snappy one, as the sports driver would wish. The brakes are powerful, and can confidently be used at speed. The car may not be so quiet generally as the modern family saloon, but the subdued noise which it does make is pleasantly mechanical and rather pleasing than otherwise to the enthusiastic ear. Add to these features a decidedly graceful and quite individual appearance, which is essentially practical, and you have a fair picture of the appeal of the car. It is not a luxury vehicle, but a lively and satisfying small car for the fan who drives for the sake of driving, enjoying every minute of it.

Of the Morgan 4-4 two styles will be available, a drop-head coupé at £395, plus £110 18s 3d purchase tax, and an open two-seater

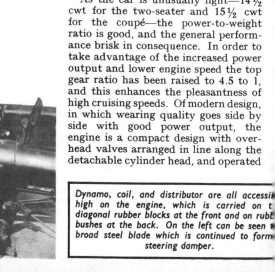

at £355, plus £99 15s 1d purchase tax. In the main no considerable changes have been made in the design, with the exception of improvements in the front suspension and in the steering, which will be described later. The main difference between the new series and earlier models is the adoption of a new engine, which was incorporated in a few cars in 1939. This engine is specially made for the Morgan Motor Co, Ltd. by the Standard Motor Co, Ltd, and gives about 15 per cent more power at slightly lower engine revolutions, as it has a fairly long stroke. Rated at 9.99 h.p. it has four cylinders of 63.5 × 100 mm (1,267 c.c.) and develops about 40 b.h.p. The compression ratio is 7 to 1.

As the car is unusually light—14½ cwt for the two-seater and 15½ cwt for the coupé—the power-to-weight ratio is good, and the general performance brisk in consequence. In order to take advantage of the increased power output and lower engine speed the top gear ratio has been raised to 4.5 to 1, and this enhances the pleasantness of high cruising speeds. Of modern design, in which wearing quality goes side by side with good power output, the engine is a compact design with overhead valves arranged in line along the detachable cylinder head, and operated

Dynamo, coil, and distributor are all accessible high on the engine, which is carried on t[...] diagonal rubber blocks at the front and on rub[...] bushes at the back. On the left can be seen [...] broad steel blade which is continued to form[...] steering damper.

4-4

MORGAN 4-4 SPECIFICATION

Engine.—9.9 h.p., four cylinders, 63.5 x 100 mm (1,267 c.c.). Push-rod-operated overhead valves, three-bearing counterbalanced crankshaft, steel connecting rods, steel-backed shell bearings. Aerolite split-skirt aluminium alloy pistons. Pressure lubrication with AC filter, fan-assisted pump water cooling. Solex down draught carburettor, AC mechanical fuel pump. 9-gallon rear tank. Compression ratio 7 to 1. Maximum b.h.p. 40 at 4,300 r.p.m.

Transmission.—Borg and Beck single-plate clutch. Separate four-speed gear box with enclosed drive from clutch. Synchromesh on top and third. Overall gear ratios: Top, 5.0, third, 7.1, second, 12.1 and first, 17.1 to 1. Hardy Spicer open propeller-shaft to spiral bevel final drive.

Suspension.—Independent front with coil springs, and half-elliptic rear with Andre dampers.

Brakes.—Girling mechanical in 8 in drums.

Tyres and Wheels.—Two-seater: 4.50 x 17 in on spoked disc wheels. Coupé: 5.00 x 16 in on disc wheels.

Steering. — Burman-Douglas, with spring-spoked wheel.

Electrical Equipment.—Lucas 12-volt with constant voltage control.

Main Dimensions.—Wheelbase, 7 ft 8 in. Track, 3 ft 9 in. Overall length: Two-seater, 11 ft 4 in; width, 4 ft 6 in; height, 4 ft 4½ in. Coupe, length, 11 ft 7½ in; width, 4 ft 6 in; height, 4 ft 6½ in. Ground clearance, 6 in. Turning circle, 33 ft. Weight: Two-seater, 14½ cwt. Coupe, 15½ cwt.

light alloy type with split skirts. The distributor head of the ignition is driven by a vertical shaft and is placed conveniently high at the side of the detachable cover over the valve gear. The electrical equipment is Lucas 12-volt with a 57 amp-hour battery. At the front of the engine is a triangulated belt drive for the fan and water impeller unit and the dynamo. Carburation is by a down draught Solex fed from the 9-gallon rear tank by an AC mechanical pump.

At its front end the engine is mounted in the frame on diagonally placed rubber blocks. At the rear is a laterally placed beam with flexible rubber cushions at its extremities. In unit with the engine is a Borg and Beck dry single-plate clutch enclosed in a housing. An interesting point of difference between the Morgan and other cars is that the gear box is not integral with the engine. Instead it is carried separately some distance back in the frame, which secures certain advantages. The first is that the open propeller-shaft is shortened and is less liable to whip. The second is that the

This photograph shows how compactly the hood folds down on the Morgan 4-4 coupé. The sliding windows above the doors are detachable. Two spare wheels are a feature.

through rockers and push rods from a side camshaft.

The four water-cooled cylinders are combined with the crankchamber in a single casting. The crankshaft is counterbalanced and is carried in three steel-backed main bearings. Steel connecting rods are used, and the pistons are the Aerolite

For enthusiasts and competition work. The Morgan 4-4 open two-seater. The screen will fold flat, the doors are hinged well forward and allow quick entry, and behind the seats is ample space for luggage and equipment.

LATEST MORGAN 4-4

continued

Seen here are the spring-spoked steering wheel, the remote gear lever for snappy changing, the large-dial speedometer in the neat instrument panel, and the capacious cubby holes. This is the two-seater.

There is a speedy air about the coupé, the low build of which suggests stability. Complete weather protection is obtained in the closed position.

short stiff gear lever comes in just the right place for the driver's hand, and the third is that more room is made available for the pedals on the low floor. The drive from the clutch back to the gear box is completely enclosed. Synchromesh is provided on top and third gears.

Of the pressed-steel banjo type of construction, the rear axle is orthodox, but the frame and the half-elliptic rear springs pass beneath instead of above it, so that the sides of the low-built frame are straight. The rear springs are anchored on normal eyes at the front ends, but the rear ends pass through sliding trunnion blocks contained in a tubular cross-member. This arrangement is less liable to sidesway than shackles are when they become worn. It is to be noted that special-tread tyres can be carried for competition work. The two spare wheels are carried at the extreme rear of the frame, and the twin batteries are mounted low just forward of the rear axle, which improves weight distribution.

Interesting I.F.S.

A most interesting feature of the design is the independent front suspension. Vertically placed in the front is a steel pressing with a stout X bracing from corner to corner. At the top and at the foot of this structure is a transverse steel tube, arranged so that the two tubes lie parallel to one another but some distance apart. The outer ends of the two tubes, which extend almost to the full track of the wheels, are joined by vertical steel rods, and these combine the dual duties of guides for the suspension and swivels for the steering. The stub axle of each front wheel is formed with a vertical sleeve on its inner end, and the vertical guide passes through the sleeve. Above and below the sleeve is a compression coil spring surrounding the vertical guide. The upper spring carries the

suspension load and the lower one checks rebound.

In this manner a very simple form of independent suspension is obtained, and one in which caster angle does not alter with spring deflection. Two material improvements have been incorporated : a variation in the characteristics of the springs themselves, particularly in the rebound spring, has gained better riding to the point where it is no longer necessary to fit front shock absorbers. The second change is the provision of a simple type of steering damper, which introduces a slight amount of steadying friction and also prevents steering movement from tending to wind or unwind the coil springs. The damper on each side consists of a spring steel blade anchored at one end to the frame and running diagonally forward and outward to the vertical guide. The blade is pierced so as to surround the guide and at this point bronze thrust washers are riveted to it. These thrusts are placed between the base of the suspension coil spring and the top of the steering swivel. The effect is to eliminate any tendency towards wheel wobble.

Girling brakes are fitted and are operated through a combination of links and cables. They are self-compensating. The hand-brake lever is mounted just in front of the gear box, in a very convenient place. The ratchet device is of the competition type.

Cruciform front cross-member with horizontal tubes above and below, forming the basis of the independent front suspension. The stub axle swivels slide on the vertical guides at the extremities, and their movement is governed by coil springs.

As regards the bodywork, the coupé is a decidedly smart-looking car. It is a two-seater, but has considerable space behind the front seats and within the folding hood for the accommodation of luggage. It is a fairly high-sided body, though low in build relative to ground level. The wide doors are hinged at their rear edges, and are surrounded by sliding glass windows in chromium-plated frames. When desired the complete frame can be unbolted and stowed away in the back of the car; the head folds neatly down into the luggage space.

The open two-seater is a slightly different style, designed with an eye upon competition work. The doors are hinged at the front and well forward to give quick access. The hood can be stowed complete in the luggage space, and the windscreen can be folded flat. On both cars there are louvres in the top of the bonnet as well as in the sides. The coupé has a vertical slot grille in the front of the clean-cut radiator, but on the two-seater a wire-mesh stoneguard is fitted. Both cars have Lucas fixed-reflector head lamps and a Lucas pass light on a front cross bar.

A workmanlike appearance has been achieved in the "home-built" body, and a suitably stark effect obtained by the visible exhaust system, twin spare wheels behind a large ex-M.G. fuel tank and the abbreviated wings.

Morgan 4-4

A 1947 Chassis With "Home-made" Two-seater Body

IT is surprising how many people successfully build a presentable body for their cars. Last week an Avon Standard Special owner described his post-war efforts in this direction. Now an enthusiast whose name will not be unfamiliar, R. de Yarburgh-Bateson, tells us what he and friends have recently done in this direction, but with the difference that he has been working on a new Morgan 4-4 chassis, after becoming tired of waiting for delivery of a complete car under present conditions. Having expressed himself in some detail in *The Autocar* some time ago on the æsthetics of sports car outline he feels it to be necessary to offer an apology for the finished result, but at all events he has provided himself with a usable car and, as he remarks, it is traditional in character among those who consider that cars should still look like cars. It is not every architect, as Yarburgh-Bateson is by profession, who could obtain as practical a result in car body building as his Morgan represents.　　VIZOR.

•••••••••••••••••

"IT may be that to tell the story of JLB 460 is the like of writing the biography of a three-year-old child, so undeveloped is the *character* of the car concerned, yet the tale may give encouragement to others, who are determined to counter the frustrations of the present time with positive action (writes R. de Yarburgh-Bateson, M.A., A.R.I.B.A.).

"Release from the Forces emphasized the need for some form of personal transport to satisfy business and recreational requirements. It had been hoped that a new H.R.G. would fill the gap, but post-war prices and the addition of purchase tax ruled the idea out of court. For some while second-hand cars were sought, but it soon became evident that a good second-hand car cost as much as or more than a cheaper form of new car. Rightly or wrongly it was argued that a new car should prove more reliable, would have new tyres and cost less in upkeep. Thus was the new car field examined for a suitable open car in the price range up to £500 maximum. Perhaps fortunately the range was very small and final choice lay between the TC M.G., the Morgan 4-4 and the Singer Roadster. The last-mentioned was ruled out as the performance was not quite of the type required, although having the alternative advantage of more room and other well-known Singer qualities. The M.G. attracted very much, but just had not sufficient leg-room. The Morgan had sufficient leg room and had a form of i.f.s. which should have all the bugs ironed out of it. It was, moreover, a nice looking little car, lighter than most and possessed of reasonably high performance. So Morgan it was . . .

Send Something !

"After the inevitable wait of nine months the price of the two-seater had risen £50 and the prospect of delivery seemed as remote as ever. In despair a letter was written to the company begging them to deliver something, be it only an incomplete car. The resultant offer of a chassis was accepted without delay. Innocence argued that there was nothing to building a body but erecting a framework and affixing thereto a few side panels of suitable material. Innocence was not aware that the quoted chassis price of £345, included mudguards, instruments, windscreen, petrol tank and so forth, but did not include the assembly of those parts or the provision of a bulkhead between engine room and cockpit. Anyone who has attempted the construction of a car body will agree with me when I say that the key to success lies in the building of a bulkhead which is the right shape and sufficiently strong. If you get this wrong, you'll never get the complete car right.

"In April, 1947, a lorry delivered the very naked chassis together with an assortment of loose parts stuffed into two cardboard boxes or strapped to the chassis. Friends rallied round and a gallant and respected 12-50 Alvis towed the Morgan to the scene of its dressmaking, the while the owner sat precariously on the chassis keeping his stern out of reach of the front universal joint and steering via the unfixed steering column, which seemed to be very, very long and liable to break at any minute! Less than a mile of the King's Highway had been covered in this manner when a Proctor on a "mechanical pony" halted the procession of Free Englishmen and demanded to know whether we had a licence to tow. Regrettably we had not heard of such a thing and it was in vain that we protested that the Morgan, admittedly unlicensed, could in no sense be described as a 'mechanically propelled vehicle.' However, we had evidently touched some streak of compassion, for we were allowed to proceed on the dual understanding that we were going 'only round the corner' and that we should on no account be guilty of committing so heinous a crime again.

Reliability a First Need

"From study of the mechanical data and of the pre-war Road Test reports of the Morgan 4-4 with a smaller engine of different manufacture it was thought that the standard car should have a good performance but would not shine particularly in 1,500 c.c. competition classes, where it gave away too much capacity. As business requirements demanded reliability, performance must be sought by other methods than super-tuning and undesirably high compression ratios necessitating the use of benzole. The obvious answer was to try to save an appreciable amount of weight as compared with the standard car. Furthermore, the standard

TALKING OF SPORTS CARS

——— continued ———

cruising speed of 62 m.p.h. at a piston speed of 2,500 feet per minute could then be increased to approximately 68 m.p.h. by raising the overall gear ratio by fitting oversize (5.50 by 17in) tyres on the rear wheels.

"Since the overall weight of the production two-seater is exceptionally low for a British car it was certain that some cunning and a degree of self-discipline would be necessary to eliminate unnecessary avoirdupois from the specification. However, I was more than fortunate in having J. Keeping and W. A. Hill to form the body-building confederacy. It is less than fair to say here that without Keeping's skill and craftsmanship and Hill's unfailing encouragement when morale slumped with evening fatigue, the task would never have been completed without professional assistance.

"The work was done in a small mews garage at week-ends and in the evenings, and took approximately six months. Most of the purchases had to be made before office hours in the morning or during lunchtime. Sometimes there was difficulty in getting materials, and such things as screws and nuts and bolts were sometimes lacking at vital moments and the work was held up. A portable electric hand-drill proved invaluable and I shudder to think of the number of drills that I broke through brute force and ignorance. It is strange, too, how often the drill seemed to arrive at the most awkward spot, where the nut could not be fitted or the rivet was too short to reach!

Enter Puffington

"Not long after the work had started bureaucracy decided to 'lend a hand' and a Customs and Excise official arrived at my office with the demand that the *full* purchase tax must be paid before the car was put on the road. This was not paid without some demur, but the alternative is prosecution, so discretion won. Insult was added to injury when I was forced to register as a motor car manufacturer in order that the payment could reach the Treasury via the correct channels. This involved the filling in of numerous completely irrelevant forms in triplicate.

"The form of construction decided upon was to build up the main bulkhead with aluminium angles scientifically disposed, filled in with fire-resisting plywood faced with Duralumin, and the use of Duralumin gusset plates at junctions. The bulkhead behind the seats was similarly constructed, but is of more simple character. Elsewhere a light aluminium angle frame is built up with gusset plates. Great care was essential to ensure the necessary degree of rigidity, both laterally and in the fore and aft direction. At each stage Hill applied his own special test before the next was attempted. This test involved the placing of his own rear end upon the part to be tested, raising his feet off the ground and remarking with evident satisfaction, 'Look, you can sit on it!'

"At the rear it was decided to discard the standard petrol tank, which was too

wide to fit conveniently into the projected body contour, and to use a J.2-type M.G. tank of greater capacity. It was not easy to provide a mounting for this, but Keeping devised an ingenious inverted cradle made of angle iron, which we had welded by a nearby garage, which also welded a sort of quadrapod; this carries the rear mudguards and forms the back cross-brace of the body proper, to which the petrol tank is also strapped.

No Doors

"The external skin is composed of anodised aluminium sheets with felt and riveted to the main frame. There are no doors, as they were not thought to be essential with so low a car, and their incorporation would have introduced endless problems in the avoidance of body weave and rattles. As it has turned out, anyone except the aged or crippled can get in or out with consummate ease, except when the hood is up, but it is a simple matter to undo the front hood "lift-the-dots" before entry or egress. The lack of doors makes the cockpit much warmer than it would otherwise be. The thing to aim at with a no-door body is that one can step straight on to the floorboards from the pavement—i.e., the front edge of the seats must be some way behind the lower edge of the facia board.

"Internally, the upholstery is leathercloth attached loosely to plywood. The cutaway sides are padded with sponge rubber and covered with leathercloth. The passenger seat is a pan-type bucket seat with aircraft-type back squab and Dunlopillo cushion. The driving seat is finished similarly, but is made of plywood as it was necessary to lower the seat more than was possible with a metal standard bucket seat. The tunnel over the propeller-shaft provided some difficulty, as part had to be detachable to give access to a grease nipple on the rear brake cable and another hole was necessary to lubricate the front universal.

"To save weight and because the shape did not suit the projected body contours very well the mudguards supplied with the chassis were not used and standard non-swivel cycle-type guards are used instead. These suffer from the disadvantage that rather a lot of mud is thrown up on to the screen. The rear guards end somewhat high up so horizontal fins are fitted to the top of the rear

'dumb-irons' in order that the poor fellow following is not smothered with spray.

"The cellulose spraying was done professionally, as it was thought better not to spoil the ship for a ha'porth of tar and the proper facilities were not available. Incidentally, it seems that anodised aluminium requires treatment with a liquid called de-oxygene before cellulose can be made to stick to it, which is worth remembering when buying the sheets intended for the external skin, if this is to be cellulosed.

"So far the car has run less than 800 miles and is still being run with an eye on the rough spots. The weighbridge read 13 cwt when the car was weighed 'slightly wet,' i.e., with water, oil and a couple of gallons of Pool. There have been few teething troubles with the body, although the chassis flexes much more than was expected and the rubber strip at the rear of the bonnet tends to come adrift, being only stuck.

Considerable Adjustment

"As the chassis left the works without road test, it is perhaps not surprising that a great deal of adjustment has been required to brakes, steering, gear box and clutch. The only mechanical failure so far has been a fractured front wheel stud, which dropped into the brake drum and caused some little concern at the time. The guarantee covers the cost of such work only if carried out at the manufacturer's works, which are unfortunately inaccessible in these days, so the cost must be added to the total expenditure, which has worked out at roughly the same as the standard job. Purchase tax was extracted at £114, which is the agreed figure for the standard Morgan 4-4 two-seater.

"In conclusion and upon a personal note: as the author of an article in *The Autocar* entitled 'Appearance' I must admit that JLB 460 has a slightly 'bogus-vintage' appearance, of which I should certainly disapprove in a 1947 production car. However, the car is traditional in character and was constructed with very limited technical facilities and skill, which ruled out expensive panel beating and two-radius curves. The result is an essentially honest non-streamlined machine, and that, I think, is not unsatisfying in itself."

The push-rod o.h.v. engine of 1,267 c.c. with which the latest Morgan 4-4 is fitted. Coil and distributor are carried high, it will be noticed, a good feature for trials work.

THE MORGAN 4/4 RANGE

Trim Two- and Four-seat Models Substantially Unchanged

THE Morgan 4/4 will appear at the Motor Show in substantially unchanged form, but readers will recall that several notable innovations were included in the design when production was resumed after the war. The most notable was the new power unit made especially for the Morgan Motor Co., Ltd., by The Standard Motor Co., Ltd. This, a 1,267 c.c. four-cylinder, with push-rod-operated o.h.v., develops 40 b.h.p. which gives a lively performance to a car which, in two-seater form, has a dry weight of only 14 cwt.

The chassis design is straightforward

and businesslike, but possesses a number of unusual features. One is that the gearbox is not in unit with the engine, but is situated in the centre of the chassis and connected rigidly to the power unit by a tubular member which encloses a short driving shaft. By this means the propeller shaft is kept commendably short and it has been possible to place the stubby gear lever just where it is wanted without recourse to complicated operating mechanism. In addition, the absence of a gearbox in the usual place provides increased foot room. In other respects the transmission system is conventional.

The frame has the side members arranged with their upper flanges outwards and their lower flanges inwards, the latter serving to provide a support for the wooden floorboards. At the rear, the side rails pass beneath the back axle and are carried on semi-elliptic springs which slide in trunnions at the rear.

At the front, the simple but efficient form of independent suspension, pioneered and developed by the Morgan concern right from earliest days, is retained. The system embodies sliding axles and coil springs, the arrangement including main and rebound springs with Newton telescopic hydraulic shock absorbers. An ingenious detail of the front layout is the incorporation of a simple form of friction steering damper which inhibits any tendency towards wheel wobble.

Choice of Style

Three types of coachwork are available, all produced in the Morgan works. One is an open two-seater, the trim "competition" appearance of which is emphasized by its disappearing hood, cutaway doors and twin spare wheels at the rear. Behind the seats is a useful compartment for luggage.

The coupé follows similar general lines, but with the accent on comfort. The head folds down into the luggage space behind the seats to produce a smart open-car appearance and the windows in the doors are unusual in that they incorporate sliding glass panels, but can be removed in a few minutes, complete with their frames, rather in the manner of side screens, and stowed in the car when not in use.

The four-seater is noteworthy for the fact that the passengers in the rear, thanks to the clever chassis layout, enjoy an unusually low seating position, the floor in the rear actually being at the same level as at the front. In other respects, the general arrangement is similar to that of the two-seater except for the provision of one spare wheel instead of the pair provided on both the two-seater and coupé models.

MORGAN 4/4 TWO-SEATER DATA

Engine Dimensions:		Transmission —contd.	
Cylinders	4	Prop. shaft	Hardy Spicer
Bore	63.5 mm.	Final drive	Spiral bevel
Stroke	100 mm.	**Chassis Details :**	
Cubic capacity	1,267 c.c.	Brakes	Girling mechanical
Piston area	19.6 sq. ins.	Brake drum diameter	Front: 9 ins. Rear: 8 ins.
Valves	Overhead	Friction lining area	82 sq. ins.
Compression ratio	7 : 1	Suspension, front	Independent (coil)
		Suspension, rear	Semi-elliptic
Engine Performance:		Shock absorbers	Front: Newton hydraulic
Max. b.h.p.	40		Rear: Hartford friction
at	4,300 r.p.m.	Wheel type	Spoked disc
Max. b.m.e.p.	125	Tyre size	4.50 x 17
at	3,550 r.p.m.	Steering gear	Burman
B.H.P. per sq. in. piston area	2.04	Steering wheel	16 ins.
Peak piston speed ft. per min.	2,830	**Dimensions :**	
		Wheelbase	7 ft. 8 ins.
Engine Details:		Track, front	3 ft. 9 ins.
Carburetter	Solex downdraught	Track, rear	3 ft. 9 ins.
Ignition	Lucas coil	Overall length	11 ft. 4 ins.
Plugs: make and type	Champion N8	Overall width	4 ft. 6 ins.
Fuel Pump	AC Mechanical	Overall height	4 ft. 4¼ ins. (closed)
Fuel capacity	9 gallons	Ground clearance	6 ins.
Oil filter (make, by-pass or full flow)	AC By-pass	Turning circle	33 ft.
Oil capacity	9 pints	Dry weight	14 cwt.
Cooling system	Thermo-siphon and fan		
Water capacity	16 pints	**Performance Data :**	
Electrical system	Lucas 12-volt C.V.C.	Piston area, sq. ins. per ton	28.0
Battery capacity	57 amp.-hours	Brake lining area, sq. ins. per ton	117
		Top gear m.p.h. per 1,000 r.p.m.	16.0
Transmission :		Top gear m.p.h. at 2,500 ft./min. piston speed	61.0 m.p.h.
Clutch	Borg and Beck	Litres per ton-mile, dry	3,400
Gear ratios : Top	4.72		
3rd	6.70		
2nd	11.4		
1st	16.1		
Rev.	21.33		

NOTE. The above particulars apply to the two-seater. The d.h.-coupe specification differs in the following respects:—Overall length, 11 ft. 7¼ ins.; overall height (closed) 4 ft. 1¾ ins.: dry weight, 15 cwt.; tyre size, 5.00 x 16 ; wheel type, disc. The four-seater differs as follows:— Overall length, 11 ft. 7 ins.; overall height (closed), 4 ft. 6½ ins.; weight, 14½ cwt.

Morgan Plus Four

The coupé version of the Plus Four has removable sliding windows and a disappearing hood.

THE current Morgan 4-4 is well known; it has had many successes in trials, and recently won the 1,100 c.c. class in the Production Car Race at Silverstone. It is the product of a firm which primarily became famous for the unique Morgan three-wheel car. As might be expected, therefore, the new Plus Four is a direct descendant of the 4-4, and retains most of the unique features of that original design. The Plus Four, however, has a four-cylinder engine 85×92 mm (2,088 c.c.) which is built by the Standard company, and adapted from the well-known Vanguard. Rated at 18 h.p. this engine develops 68 b.h.p. at 4,300 r.p.m. and has a compression ratio of 6.7 to 1. It has overhead valves operated by push-rods, a special arrangement of valve springs, a three bearing counterweighted crankshaft, and centrifugally cast wet cylinder liners which are replaceable.

One of the features of Morgan design is that the gear box is not bolted straight on to the back of the engine, but is mounted almost centrally in the car, and connected to the plate clutch by a jack shaft which is enclosed within a stout Elektron tubular casing and bell housing. This casing makes the engine and gear box into one unit, but the components are some distance apart. There are several excellent reasons for this arrangement. It gives a good distribution of weight, it allows a short direct acting

The Morgan i.f.s. now has longer swivels, softer springs, automatic lubrication and telescopic dampers.

gear lever to be very conveniently placed for snappy gear changing, rightly preferred by the sports car driver, it considerably shortens the length of the open propeller-shaft running to the rear axle and so avoids propeller-shaft whirl, and it allows plenty of room for the pedals to be set low down and well forward.

The long unit is flexibly rubber mounted in the frame at the front and at the tail of the gear box. The gear box itself is particularly robust, and gives four speeds with synchromesh on all except first. The clutch pedal is linked to a short lever, which in turn carries a link, adjustable in length by a turn buckle, attached to a sleeve sliding in the tunnel of the bell housing. The clutch pad is carried on the front of the sleeve. This device gives a straight line movement to the clutch withdrawal or engagement.

Another Morgan feature is the frame. This consists of deep side members of Z cross-section. The bottom flanges of the Z face inwards, and to them the flooring of the car is attached. The arrangement allows the floor to be much lower than is usual. The gear box in fact is above the floor instead of below it. In the new car the general layout of this type of frame is retained, but there are several major improvements in stiffness. In place of channel section cross members, five box section members are employed. The side members now curve gently inwards towards the front. The bulkhead structure is of sheet steel and greatly increased in rigidity. Some sheet steel valances are inserted between the structure and the front end.

It is interesting to record that the particular form of independent front suspension used on Morgan cars was originally patented by Morgans some 40 years ago, so it can certainly be said to have stood the test of time. The system is based upon using upper and lower tubular cross members which are spaced well apart and are continued outwards to carry stationary swivel pins. These tubes are diagonally braced together and give a light but strong structure which is sprung weight. Sliding up and down on each swivel pin is a sleeve which carries each stub and steering axle. Above the sleeve and around the pin is a coil compression spring, and below the sleeve a shorter rebound spring.

In the latest design there are some improvements. By inclining the swivels

very slightly inwards at the top it has become possible to increase the vertical length of the pins and allow longer and softer springs to be used, with consequently improved comfort of suspension. Another point is that the sliding sleeves of the swivels are now arranged for automatic lubrication. The driver presses a valve on the facia, and a small dose of engine oil is forced under pressure to these bearing surfaces. An interesting small feature of the design is the use of a wide blade of spring steel which encircles the swivel pin below the compression spring and prevents the spring from influencing the steering. The blade runs diagonally backwards to the side member, and helps to stiffen the suspension structure fore and aft. Rubber bushes are used in the steering connections to take care of changes in alignment during rise and fall of the suspension. Girling double-acting telescopic hydraulic dampers control the front suspension. Half-elliptic rear springs are used, and the tail ends of these are not fitted with shackles, but pass through trunnion blocks, whereby side play is lessened. Piston-type Girling dampers are used at the back.

Latest Type Brakes

The brakes are the latest type of Girling full hydraulic four wheel, with two leading shoes, and pedal acting direct on the master cylinder. The drums are nine inches in diameter. The hand brake is independently mechanically operated and the lever has the racing type of catch. Dunlop tyres of larger size, 5.25 ×16in, than on the previous 4-4, are mounted on pressed steel four-bolt wheels with wide base rims.

Three types of body are standardized, open two-seater, open four-seater and drophead coupé.

These bodies are coachbuilt, and follow on the general lines of the Morgan 4-4. But the width of the body across the seat has been increased by 2in, and the width across the pedal ramp by 2in. Also the leg room is 2in more. Appearance is enhanced by a longer bonnet and a radiator slightly higher at the base and with a chromium-plated grille. The two-seater is a most attractive and purposeful looking sports body, with a concealed hood, and two spare wheels and tyres carried at the back. The coupé is a smart little car with a concealed top, and sliding side windows which can be detached easily. Prices are: Plus Four two-seater £510 plus purchase tax £142 8s 4d, total £652 8s 4d. Drophead coupé £565, plus purchase tax £157 13s 10d, total £722 13s 10d.

The Plus Four handles admirably, steers well and holds the road excellently at speed. The engine never feels to be working hard, and considerable gradients can be climbed effortlessly on top gear. And when the gears are used the acceleration is remarkable and very pleasant. The car does not feel front heavy, nor is it inclined to snake. The suspension may be a trifle hard at low speeds by modern standards, but it is all that could be desired at speed. The Plus Four is indeed a small sports car with an immense urge.

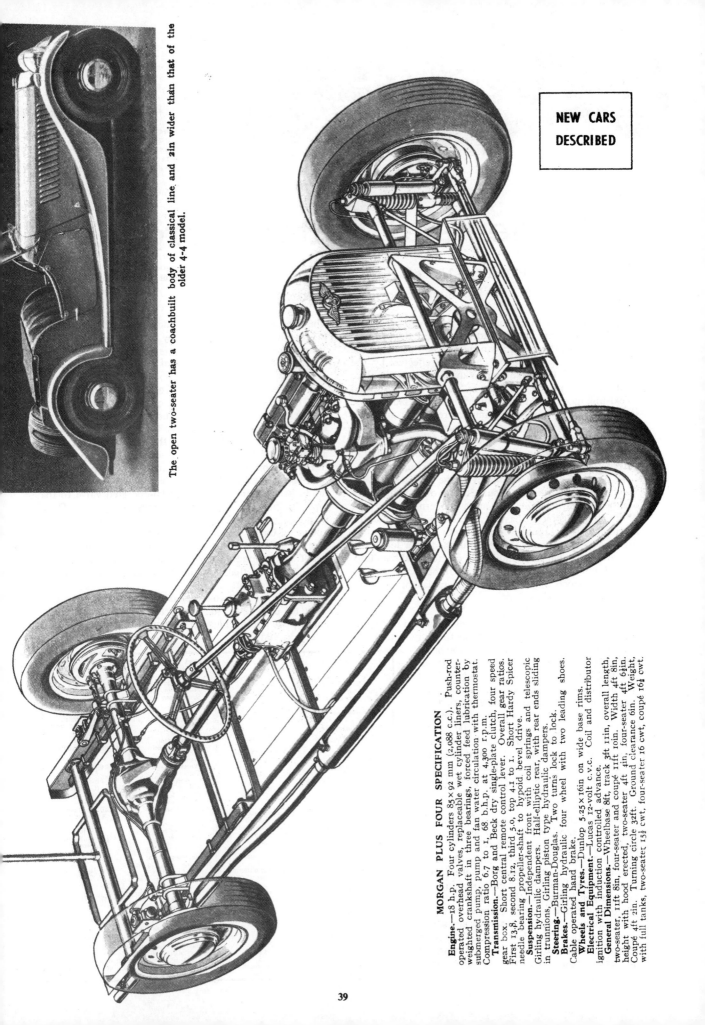

The open two-seater has a coachbuilt body of classical line and 2in wider than that of the older 4-4 model.

MORGAN PLUS FOUR SPECIFICATION

Engine.—18 h.p. Four cylinders 85×92 mm (2,088 c.c.). Push-rod operated overhead valves, replaceable wet cylinder liners, counter-weighted crankshaft in three bearings, forced feed lubrication by submerged pump, pump and fan water circulation with thermostat. Compression ratio 6.7 to 1, 68 b.h.p. at 4,300 r.p.m.

Transmission.—Borg and Beck dry single-plate clutch, four speed gear box. Short central remote control lever. Overall gear ratios. First 13.8, second 8.12, third 5.0, top 4.1 to 1. Short Hardy Spicer needle bearing propeller-shaft to hypoid bevel drive.

Suspension.—Independent front with coil springs and telescopic Girling hydraulic dampers. Half-elliptic rear, with rear ends sliding in trunnions, Girling piston type hydraulic dampers.

Steering.—Burman-Douglas. Two turns lock to lock.

Brakes.—Girling hydraulic four wheel with two leading shoes. Cable operated hand brake.

Wheels and Tyres.—Dunlop 5.25 × 16in on wide base rims.

Electrical Equipment.—Lucas 12-volt c.v.c. Coil and distributor ignition with induction controlled advance.

General Dimensions.—Wheelbase 8ft, track 3ft 11in, overall length, two-seater, 11ft 8in, four-seater and coupé 11ft 10in. Width 4ft 8in. Height with hood erected, two-seater 4ft 4in, four-seater 4ft 6½in. Coupé 4ft 2in. Ground clearance 6in. Turning circle 32ft. Weight, with full tanks, two-seater 15½ cwt, four-seater 16 cwt, coupé 16¼ cwt.

PLUS FOUR.—Features of the high-performance 1951 Morgan are the mating of a 2.1-litre engine and 4-speed synchro-mesh gearbox, the assembly being mounted in a widened frame with improved suspension and hypoid rear axle.

1951 CARS

Bigger and Better Morgans

New Plus Four Models have Standard Vanguard Engine, Softer Suspension and Sturdier Chassis

WITH an increase in maximum power of no less than 70 per cent., and an added weight of the order of only 1 cwt., the Morgan enters a new performance class for 1951. The change has been effected by the adoption of a 2.1-litre Standard Vanguard engine in place of the 1¼-litre power unit (also of Standard origin) fitted to earlier models. Apart from this most notable increase in power/weight ratio, the manufacturers have aimed at retaining the essential character of this small sports car and, apart from minor alterations for those with eyes to see, there is little to distinguish the new Plus Four model, in external appearance, from the 4/4 which it supersedes.

In point of actual fact, however, the changes go very much deeper than the mere substitution of one engine for another of larger size and more modern design and, although the distinctive basic layout remains unaltered, the entire chassis has been re-designed with the dual object of giving added sturdiness to withstand the higher loads and of providing enhanced standards of comfort and handling. In addition, there is a slight increase in passenger accommodation which makes for a considerable improvement in comfort and convenience.

* * *

In the Plus Four, the Vanguard engine is used in normal form apart from slight modifications to the induction and cooling systems which do not affect the power output of 68 b.h.p. at 4,000 r.p.m. This output, in a car weighing approximately 14½ cwt. dry in two-seater form, coupled with moderately-high gearing, gives outstanding performance factors. To quote only two, the top gear road speed at a piston speed of 2,500 feet per minute works out at 76.1 m.p.h. (compared with 61 m.p.h. previously), whilst the litres per-ton-mile figure in top gear is now the unusually high one of 4,710 (as opposed to the 3,280 of the 4/4 model).

Thus, an outstanding top-gear performance may be expected—and was, in fact, experienced, in a short run we were privileged to make in one of the new models.

The chassis side members pass, as before, beneath the rear axle. Since the introduction of the original three-wheeler model in 1911, the Morgan has always been notable for the use of independent front suspension of the type employing vertical coil springs and sliding axles. On the Plus Four model, the same system is employed except that the main coil springs are now 3 ins. longer, to give greater

wheel movement and a softer ride, whilst the geometry of the layout has been improved by inclining the assemblies at an angle of 2 degrees to the vertical. In addition, the Girling telescopic dampers are of a larger size than those previously used.

With the sliding-axle type of front suspension, considerable importance attaches to adequate lubrication of the sliding members if the system is not to stiffen up in action. In the past, grease nipples have been relied upon as the means of lubrication but, on the new model, a semi-automatic arrangement has been adopted. The upper ends of the suspension spindles are connected by copper piping to a metered two-way union adjacent to the dash, this union being connected via a pedal-operated valve to the pipe leading to the engine oil-pressure gauge. Thus, momentary pressure on this pedal opens the valve and allows oil under the full engine pressure to flow into the pipes and thence to the suspension units. In practice, one "shot" every hundred miles or so is sufficient to provide all the lubrication that is required by both suspension and steering movements.

The price of the two-seater is £510, which, with a purchase tax of £142 8s. 4d., gives a total of £652 8s. 4d.; the coupe price is £565, plus purchase tax £157 13s. 10d., total £722 13s. 10d.

Engine Dimensions:			Chassis Details:		
Cylinders	...	4	Brakes	... ...	Girling all hydraulic
Bore		85 mm.			(2 LS on front)
Stroke		92 mm.	Brake drum diam.	...	9 ins.
Cubic capacity		2,088 c.c.	Friction lining area		105 sq. ins.
Piston area		35.2 sq. ins.	Suspension:		
Valves		Overhead (push rod)	Front	... ...	Coil and slide I.F.S.
Compression ratio		6.7	Rear	... ...	Semi-elliptic
			Shock absorbers	...	Girling tubular
Engine Performance:			Wheel type	...	Dunlop pressed steel
Max. power	...	68 b.h.p.	Tyre size	... ...	5.25 × 16
at	...	4,000 r.p.m.	Steering gear	...	Burman
Max. b.m.e.p.	...	128 lbs./sq. ins.	Steering wheel	...	17-in. spring spoke
at	...	2,500 r.p.m.	**Dimensions:**		
B.H.P. per sq. in. piston area	...	1.93	Wheelbase	... ...	8 ft. 0 ins.
Peak piston speed			Track:		
ft. per min.	...	2,410	Front	... ...	3 ft. 11 ins.
			Rear	... ...	3 ft. 11 ins.
Engine Details:			Overall length	...	11 ft. 8 ins.
Carburetter	...	Solex downdraught	Overall width	...	4 ft. 8 ins.
Ignition	...	Coil	Overall height	...	3 ft. 10 ins. (hood up.
Plugs: make and type		Champion L10			4 ft. 4 ins.)*
Fuel pump	...	A.C. mechanical	Ground clearance	...	6 ins.
Fuel capacity	...	11 gallons	Turning circle	...	34 ft.
Oil filter (make, by-pass or full flow)	...	Fram by-pass	Dry weight	...	14½ cwt. (2-str.,
Oil capacity	...	1 gallon			approx.)
Cooling system	...	Pump, fan and thermo-stat			
Water capacity	...	9 pints	**Performance Data:**		
Electrical system	...	Lucas 12-volt	Piston area, sq. in. per ton	...	48.4
Battery capacity	...	51 amp./hr.	Brake lining area, sq. in. per ton	...	145
Transmission:			Top gear m.p.h. per 1,000 r.p.m.	...	18.3
Clutch	...	Borg and Beck s.d.p.	Top gear m.p.h. at 2,500 ft./min. piston speed	...	76.1
Gear ratios: Top	...	4.1			
3rd	...	5.4			
2nd	...	8.0	Litres per ton-mile, dry	...	4,710
1st	...	13.5			
Rev.	...	13.5	*Dimensions given are for the 2-str. Overall lengths of the 4-str. and coupé models are 11 ft. 10 ins., whilst overall heights are: 4-str., 4 ft. (hood up, 4 ft. 6¼ ins.), coupé, 3 ft. 11 ins. (hood up 4 ft. 2 ins.).		
Prop. shaft	...	Hardy Spicer			
Final drive	...	Hypoid			

The Autocar ROAD TESTS

The low straightforward lines of the Morgan coupé are combined with ample weather protection which includes sliding side windows and a three-position head.

DATA FOR THE DRIVER

MORGAN PLUS FOUR

PRICE, with coupé body, £565, plus £315 7s 9d British purchase tax. Total (in Great Britain), £880 7s 9d.

ENGINE : 18 h.p. (R.A.C. rating), 4 cylinders, overhead valves, 85 × 92 mm, 2,088 c.c. Brake Horse-power : 68 at 4,200 r.p.m. Compression Ratio : 6.7 to 1. Max. Torque : 112 lb ft at 2,300 r.p.m. 19 m.p.h. per 1,000 r.p.m. on top gear.

WEIGHT (running trim with 5 gallons fuel) : 17 cwt 0 qr 0 lb (1,904 lb). Front wheels 47 per cent ; rear wheels 53 per cent. LB per C.C. : 0.91. B.H.P. per TON : 80.0.

TYRE SIZE : 5.25—16in on bolt-on steel disc wheels.

TANK CAPACITY : 11 English gallons. Approximate fuel consumption range, 22-26 m.p.g. (12.8-10.9 litres per 100 km).

TURNING CIRCLE : 33ft (L and R). Steering wheel movement from lock to lock : 2 turns. LIGHTING SET : 12-volt.

MAIN DIMENSIONS : Wheelbase, 8ft 0in. Track, 3ft 11in (front) ; 3ft 11in (rear). Overall length, 11ft 10in ; width, 4ft 8in ; height, 4ft 4in. Minimum Ground Clearance : 6in.

ACCELERATION

Overall gear ratios	From steady m.p.h. of		
	10-30 sec	20-40 sec	30-50 sec
4.1 to 1	9.9	9.0	9.5
5.6 to 1	6.5	6.3	7.4
8.1 to 1	4.4	5.1	—
13.8 to 1	—	—	—

From rest through gears to :—

	sec		sec
30 m.p.h.	4.6	60 m.p.h.	17.9
50 m.p.h.	11.3	70 m.p.h.	28.0

SPEEDS ON GEARS :

(by Electric Speedometer)	M.p.h. (normal and max)	K.p.h. (normal and max)
1st	18—24	29—39
2nd	35—46	56—74
3rd	58—69	93—111
Top	85.5	137

Speedometer correction by Electric Speedometer :—

Car Speedometer		Electric Speedometer m.p.h.
10	=	10.0
20	=	19.0
30	=	28.0
40	=	37.0
50	=	45.0
60	=	56.0
70	=	64.5
80	=	72.0
90	=	83.0
95	=	85.5

WEATHER : Dry, cold ; wind gusty. Acceleration figures are the means of several runs in opposite directions. Described in " The Autocar " of September 29, and October 20, 1950.

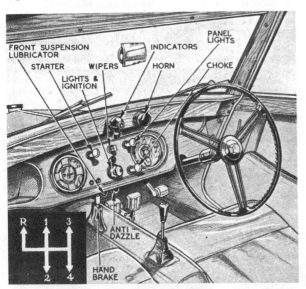

FRONT SUSPENSION LUBRICATOR — INDICATORS — PANEL LIGHTS
STARTER — WIPERS — HORN — CHOKE
LIGHTS & IGNITION
R 1 3 2 4 — ANTI DAZZLE — HAND BRAKE

No. 1428 . . MORGAN PLUS FOUR COUPÉ

A RECIPE that is almost startling has been adopted for the Morgan Plus Four, first seen at last autumn's London Show. This is a car of little greater overall size than the former Four-Four model which was current for a good many years, and therefore it is a small car in all but the engine, which, by special arrangement between the manufacturers concerned, is the Standard Vanguard overhead-valve unit of just over 2 litres. The normal three-speed gear box of the Vanguard is replaced, however, by a four-speed box.

Weight is low and even though no attempt is made by the Morgan Motor Co., of Malvern Link, Worcestershire, to extract additional power from the engine they now use, the power-to-weight ratio of the Plus Four in b.h.p. per ton is right out of the ordinary. As a result, it has remarkable acceleration, a high cruising speed, and a wide range of potent performance on top gear. Its ability to cover ground rapidly, even over roads such as those of England, with their many deterrents to high-speed travel, is equalled by very few cars, though that is not the whole picture of this car.

Indeed, the Morgan is unique in some important respects. The basic design is simple and it forms a car of distinctly sports type, which, it must be emphasized, does not provide by any means everyone's form of motoring, and which is not to be judged on family saloon standards of comfort and quietness. But it does contain a very definite appeal to those who appreciate high performance with reasonable economy, in a compact size of car.

The suspension is firm to the point of harshness over some kinds of surfaces, there is a good deal of mechanical noise when the car is driven hard, and it is relatively stark as regards one or two items of equipment which have come to be regarded as normal in these times. Above all, however, it *goes*, in the full sense of that phrase. It gets up very quickly indeed to about 65 m.p.h. and does not want much road in which to see 70-75, around which figure it can be kept apparently indefinitely, with no sign of heat or falling oil pressure. The ultimate maximum on level ground is above 85 m.p.h. true speed.

Its extreme handiness makes it ideal for narrow roads and town traffic. Journeys can be made in outstandingly good time owing to the vivid acceleration and high natural speed and the way in which it can utilize every legitimate traffic opening with safety. The engine can be felt to some extent, there being a period of hardness around 50 m.p.h. in particular. The impression is soon gained that it can be driven really hard with impunity, to give average speeds

The front end treatment is in the traditional style with nothing "built-in." The radiator filler cap is external, the central pass light is mounted on a "badge bar," and the licence holder is on the left side of the two-piece bonnet in the usual Morgan position.

A hinged flap can be fitted as an optional extra, enabling a quantity of extra luggage to be carried. To keep the flap horizontal, two wires (on the inside of the flap) hook on lugs fitted just below the top of the wings.

ROAD TEST . . . . continued

of exceptional merit. On suitable roads 56.5 m.p.h. was averaged over all but 50 miles; 55.5 m.p.h. over rather more than 40 miles, part of the latter run being considerably affected by traffic at one stage; whilst 54 miles were put into one hour on another familiar route.

Only slight pinking occurred even on low-octane fuel, and no running-on was experienced. Exhaust note is not at all marked; there is "pobbling" in the silencer when throttling back at medium speeds. No suggestion exists of under-gearing on the 4.1 to 1 final drive ratio, yet on top gear the range is from as low as 7 m.p.h. up to the capacity indicated by the ability to climb a hill of 1 in 6½ gradient (approximately 16 per cent), complicated by an appreciable bend, on top gear throughout at a minimum speed little below 30 m.p.h. Only a select band of cars of exceptionally favourable power-weight ratio has gone over this hill usefully on top gear during many years of its inclusion in *The Autocar* Road Tests.

It follows that a drop below third gear is seldom actually necessary for acceleration or climbing purposes, or even in congested traffic, although there is much amusement value, from an enthusiastic driver's viewpoint, to be had from free use of the gear box, with 40 m.p.h.-plus available on second gear and comfortably nearly 60 on third. There is great climbing power for really severe gradients. The gear change is an extremely good one, with a rigid, stubby central lever which has a short travel; snap movements are possible, although there is synchromesh. A positive stop prevents unintentional engagement of reverse, the lever having to be lifted slightly in neutral before that position can be selected. The gear box is mounted separately from the engine, a now unusual construction.

Rock-firm stability enables remarkable liberties to be taken in fast cornering, though with enterprising handling methods tyre squeal can be produced even with pressures recommended for fast driving. The front suspension is fundamentally the Morgan system current during many years, utilizing a small-diameter coil spring of considerable depth at each side, in conjunction with telescopic hydraulic dampers. It has none of the softness and certainly not a trace of the roll characteristics associated with most present-day coil spring independent front suspensions.

The steering is high geared; it is heavy at low speed but becomes lighter as the speed rises. There is noticeable understeer and the car has to be pulled fairly vigorously round the faster and more acute bends. The steering has strong self-centring action out of a right-angle corner and a light wheel hold is found best on the straight. At speed there is an unusual "feel" of slight lateral movement, probably arising in the driver's mind from movement of the scuttle structure. Slight lost motion in the steering of this particular car—which had had a hard life, including participation in the Land's End Trial—may have influenced the impressions on which that comment is based. The fact that to obtain the best from it the car has to be "driven" to some extent is no detriment in enthusiastic eyes. The car in question was understood to have covered more than 10,000 miles, an unusual figure for cars submitted to these tests.

Braking Confidence

The Girling hydraulic brakes achieved all that was asked of them during a great deal of fast motoring; they needed fairly heavy pedal pressure for maximum results, but proved dependable. The hand brake is of the fly-off pattern and was found by at least one driver among the test team to be placed rather too far forward for maximum convenience.

The driving position suited a variety of drivers fairly satisfactorily, although some form of fore-and-aft adjustment is desirable for the one-piece back rest, the absence of such mechanism being somewhat surprising. The neat spring-spoked wheel is at a good angle and some slight adjustment of seating height is possible, as the two separate cushions

A useful luggage space is provided behind the seat and the flush inside door trim gives increased elbow clearance.

The head folds down neatly and fixes on dowels projecting above the back of the seat. The chromium framed side windows reduce draught quite effectively.

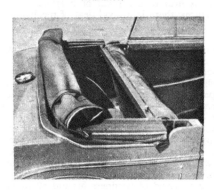

The head mechanism allows the front half to be rolled back in the "de ville" position, an unusual feature for a small car.

The traditional wing treatment combined with a fairly deep side valance in front effectively shields the body, but leaves the wheels entirely accessible. A central quick action petrol filler cap is mounted above the spare wheel.

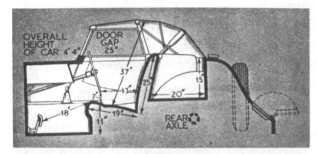

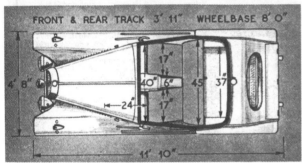

Measurements in these scale body diagrams are taken with the driving seat in the central position of fore and aft adjustment and with the seat cushions uncompressed.

have pneumatic upholstery which can be inflated suitably. As it was, an average height driver could barely see the left wing. There is plenty of leg room; there is no space for the left foot to the left of the clutch pedal, though a place can be found for it between the clutch and brake pedals. Heel-and-toe operation of brake and throttle pedals is possible. Instruments include an engine water thermometer as well as an ammeter, oil pressure gauge and clock, though not a rev counter, and they are sufficiently illuminated at night without causing glare.

It is a coupé model that has been sampled, as distinct from the open two- and four-seaters that are also available. The head goes up and down easily and can be used with the front part of the head rolled back; in the fully folded position it naturally detracts from the limited enclosed luggage space behind the seat. Luggage capacity can be supplemented externally by a tray hinged down from the tail, this arrangement being optional in place of the second spare wheel that is normal equipment. Wood cappings of pleasing appearance are used in the interior. The coupe has sliding windows and, in the manner of this style of body, leftward vision is rather seriously restricted at road junctions, whilst rearward visibility, through a small rear window, cannot be described as good, especially in view of the fact that with the type of side windows used the driver cannot put his head out to see astern. Nor is the mirror view comprehensive. It would be a distinct advantage if the doors were lockable, but it is not easy to contrive effective locking in conjunction with sliding windows.

The head lamp beam is useful and the anti-dazzle system

is to switch out both head lamps with transfer to a centrally mounted third lamp. This gives a satisfactory spread, but not much length of beam; operation of the dip switch involves a rather awkward movement of the left leg. The horn note is higher pitched than usual and proves penetrating without being unpleasant; both it and the manually returnable traffic signals are operated by switches placed centrally above the facia, where they are convenient enough once one has become accustomed to the now unusual positions. A valuable provision is a foot-operated control to the left of the dip switch whereby the front suspension can be lubricated via the engine oil pump, from the sump supply, while running. Engine starting from cold was quick, and in temperatures around 50 deg F the choke control could be put out of action quite quickly. Oil consumption was negligible.

The Morgan Plus Four has many of the advantages of the often lamented older type of sports car, and certainly offers all the benefits that are so frequently argued for by motoring enthusiasts as deriving from a very favourable power-weight ratio. It feels rugged and suggests that it can take rough going staunchly, even though not so comfortably as a more softly sprung car; and clearly it has a real value for trials and sports car competitions of the kind open to private owners.

It has faults of both omission and commission as seen through eyes accustomed to the entirely modern plan of car; but none of them is of a character to prevent its being great fun to drive, and to some large extent they can be forgiven. It is not difficult to believe that the keen minority of owners whom such a car interests would become very fond of it because of its fundamentally honest outlook and achievements. Certainly a great respect was felt for the Plus Four after one particular day of fast motoring towards the end of the testing, during a trial totalling more than 1,000 miles, of which half was covered in two days. Few machines, irrespective of price, could run away from it on a journey, and such performance is not easily bought today at the basic price of the latest Morgan; some accompanying sacrifices are perhaps inevitable.

The space under the bonnet is well filled by the 2-litre engine. To the right of the extremely accessible distributor and the coil is the crankcase breather pipe, and above the bell housing, on the bulkhead, is the front suspension pressure lubrication system. A carburettor air cleaner is not fitted.

The Motor Continental Road Test No. 5C/51

Make: Morgan   **Type:** "Plus Four" 2-seater
Makers: Morgan Motor Co. Ltd., Pickersleigh Road, Malvern Link, Worcs.

Dimensions and Seating

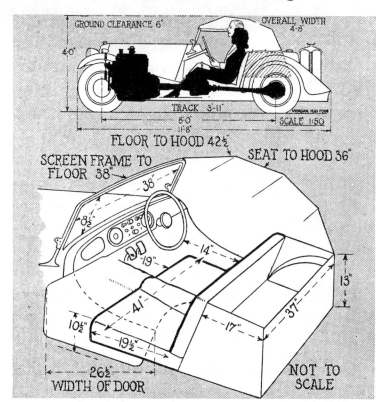

GROUND CLEARANCE 6"
OVERALL WIDTH 4-8
4-0
TRACK 3-11
5-0
11-8
SCALE 1:50
MORGAN PLUS FOUR

FLOOR TO HOOD 42½
SEAT TO HOOD 36"
SCREEN FRAME TO FLOOR 38
38
8½
19"
14
13"
41
10½"
19½"
17
37"
26½
WIDTH OF DOOR
NOT TO SCALE

In Brief

Price, £535, plus purchase tax, £298 14s. 6d. equals £833 14s. 6d.
Capacity .. .. 2,088 c.c.
Unladen kerb weight.. .. 16 cwt.
Fuel consumption .. .. 25.6 m.p.g.
Maximum speed .. .. 84.7 m.p.h.
Maximum speed on 1 in 20 gradient .. .. ..77 m.p.h.
Maximum top gear gradient 1 in 7.7
Acceleration:
10-30 m.p.h. in top.. .. 7.8 secs.
0-50 m.p.h. through gears.. 9.9 secs.
Gearing:
18.4 m.p.h. in top at 1,000 r.p.m.
76 m.p.h. at 2,500 ft. per min. piston speed.

Specification

Engine
Cylinders 4
Bore .. .. 85 mm.
Stroke .. .. 92 mm.
Cubic capacity .. .. 2,088 c.c.
Piston area .. .. 35.2 sq. in.
Valves .. .. Push-rod O.H.V.
Compression ratio 6.7/1
Max. power .. .. .. 68 b.h.p.
.. .. 4,200 r.p.m.
Piston speed at max. b.h.p. 2,540 ft. per min.
Carburetter .. .. ..Solex downdraught
Ignition.. .. .. .. Lucas coil
Sparking plugs .. 14 mm. Champion L10
Fuel pump .. .. A.C. Mechanical
Oil Filter .. .. Fram

Transmission
Clutch .. .. .. Borg & Beck s.d.p.
Gearbox .. Set back behind engine
Top gear (s/m) 4.1
3rd gear (s/m) 5.4
2nd gear (s/m) 8.0
1st gear.. .. .. .. 13.5
Propeller shaft ..Hardy Spicer, open
Final drive .. .. Hypoid bevel

Chassis
Brakes.. .. Girling hydraulic, 2 l.s. front
Brake drum diameter .. .. 9 ins.
Friction lining area .. .. 105 sq. in.
Suspension: Front ..Coil and slide I.F.S.
Rear .. .. Semi-elliptic
Shock absorbers: Front .. Telescopic
Rear ..Girling piston-type
Tyres .. .. Dunlop, 5.25-16

Steering
Steering gear .. .. .. Burman
Turning circle.. .. .. 33 feet
Turns of steering wheel, lock to lock 2¼

Performance factors (at laden weight as tested)
Piston area, sq. in. per ton 36.1
Brake lining area, sq. in. per ton .. 108
Specific displacement, litres per ton mile 3,500
Fully described in "The Motor," October 18, 1950.

Test Conditions

Mild, showery weather with strong cross wind. Smooth concrete surface (Ostend-Ghent motor road, Belgium) dry during acceleration tests. Standard grade Belgian pump fuel.

Test Data

ACCELERATION TIMES on Two Upper Ratios

	Top	3rd
10-30 m.p.h.	7.8 secs.	5.4 secs.
20-40 m.p.h.	7.9 secs.	5.2 secs.
30-50 m.p.h.	7.7 secs.	5.8 secs.
40-60 m.p.h.	8.2 secs.	7.3 secs.
50-70 m.p.h.	11.3 secs.	—
60-80 m.p.h.	19.9 secs.	—

ACCELERATION TIMES Through Gears
0-30 m.p.h. .. .. .. 4.0 secs.
0-40 m.p.h. .. .. .. 6.5 secs.
0-50 m.p.h. .. .. .. 9.9 secs.
0-60 m.p.h. .. .. .. 14.1 secs.
0-70 m.p.h. .. .. .. 19.7 secs.
0-80 m.p.h. .. .. .. 33.2 secs.
Standing Quarter Mile .. .. 19.5 secs.

MAXIMUM SPEEDS

Flying Quarter Mile
Mean of four opposite runs .. 84.7 m.p.h.
Best time equals .. 85.7 m.p.h.

Speed in Gear
Max. speed in 3rd gear .. 68 m.p.h.
Max. speed in 2nd gear .. 47 m.p.h.
Max. speed in 1st gear .. 28 m.p.h.

WEIGHT
Unladen kerb weight .. .. 16 cwt.
Front/rear weight distribution .. 49/51
Weight laden as tested .. 19½ cwt.

INSTRUMENTS
Speedometer at 30 m.p.h. .. 2% slow
Speedometer at 60 m.p.h. .. 3% fast
Speedometer at 80 m.p.h. .. 4% fast
Distance recorder .. .. 1% fast

FUEL CONSUMPTION
34.0 m.p.g. at constant 30 m.p.h.
32.5 m.p.g. at constant 40 m.p.h.
29.5 m.p.g. at constant 50 m.p.h.
27.5 m.p.g. at constant 60 m.p.h.
24.0 m.p.g. at constant 70 m.p.h.
20.0 m.p.g. at constant 80 m.p.h.
Overall consumption for 461 miles, driving fast, 18 gallons=25.6 m.p.g.

HILL CLIMBING (At steady speeds)
Max. top gear speed on 1 in 20 .. .. 77 m.p.h.
Max. top gear speed on 1 in 15 .. .. 72 m.p.h.
Max. top gear speed on 1 in 10 .. .. 62 m.p.h.
Max. gradient on top gear .. 1 in 7.7 (Tapley 285 lb./ton)
Max. gradient on 3rd gear .. 1 in 5.4 (Tapley 410 lb./ton)
Max. gradient on 2nd gear .. 1 in 4 (Tapley 545 lb./ton)

BRAKES at 30 m.p.h.
0.95g retardation (=31¾ ft. stopping distance) with 100 lb. pedal pressure
0.62g retardation (=48¼ ft. stopping distance) with 75 lb. pedal pressure
0.37g retardation (=81 ft. stopping distance) with 50 lb. pedal pressure
0.18g retardation (=167 ft. stopping distance) with 25 lb. pedal pressure

Maintenance

Fuel tank: 11 gallons. **Sump:** 11 pints, S.A.E. 30 Summer, S.A.E. 20 Winter. **Gearbox:** 2½ pints, S.A.E. 90 gear oil. **Rear axle:** 2½ pints S.A.E. 90 hypoid oil. **Steering gear:** S.A.E. 140 gear oil. **Radiator:** 11 pints (2 drain taps). **Chassis lubrication:** By grease gun every 1,000 miles to 3 points. Use steering lubricator pedal in cockpit every 100 miles. **Ignition timing:** Static 2° b.t.d.c. **Spark plug gap:** 0.032 in. **Contact breaker gap:** 0.012 in. **Valve timing:** I.O., 10° b.t.d.c.; I.C., 50° a.b.d.c.; E.O., 50° b.b.d.c.; E.C., 10° a.t.d.c. **Tappet clearances (cold):** Inlet, 0.010 in., Exhaust, 0.012 in. **Front wheel toe-in:** 0-⅛ in. **Camber angle:** 2°. **Castor angle:** 4°. **Tyre pressures:** Front 18 lb., Rear, 18 lb. **Brake fluid:** Girling crimson. **Battery:** 2 in series, 6-volt 57 amp.-hr. **Lamp bulbs:** 12-volt. Side and number plate, 6 watt, head 36/36 watt. Stop/tail 24/6 watt.

Ref. B/21/51.

The MORGAN "Plus Four" Two-seater

A Simple and Moderately-priced Sports Car of Vivid Performance

WEATHERPROOF —Effective and quite easily erected by one person, the all-weather equipment matches the speedy lines of the Plus Four Morgan.

IT has for many years past been the proud claim of the Morgan Motor Company that their cars were faster than anything else obtainable at the same price. Costing rather more than preceding models from the factory at Malvern, but also performing very much better than its predecessors, the latest "Plus Four" Morgan proved on a recent 1,900-mile, 11-day road test that the "fastest at the price" claim of its manufacturers remains very fully justified.

Sporting two-seater cars, built to a price limit which keeps them within reach of a large and reasonably youthful public, are an established part of Britain's range of car types. Emphasis on performance at a moderate price means that, inevitably, touring car luxury and carrying capacity are sacrificed to a greater or less extent. But, given acceptance of this bartering of spaciousness for speed, the open two-seater Morgan is a car which can give immense pleasure to the right sort of owner.

Effective Ingredients

The ingredients which go to make up the "Plus Four" are simple and well known. An engine which propels the six-seater Standard Vanguard saloon (of 900 pounds greater unladen weight than the Morgan) at nearly 80 m.p.h., untuned save for elimination of any throttling by a carburettor silencer. A four-speed synchro-mesh gearbox which has already proved itself on sporting cars of much greater weight. A compact and low-built chassis, the layout and independent front-wheel suspension of which represent developments of previous Morgan. designs. Finally, a body which is just the right size and shape for accommodating two people and a reasonable quantity of luggage.

The finished product, first and foremost, provides the outstanding performance on the road which is its *raison d'etre*. It accelerates in an exhilarating manner which whisks it effortlessly past ordinary traffic, acceleration from a standstill to 50 m.p.h. for example taking less than 10 seconds and 70 m.p.h. being reached after only another 9.8 seconds. It also reaches usefully high maximum speeds when required, as witness the two-way mean speed of 84.7 m.p.h. recorded, with hood and sidescreens erected, during our performance tests in Belgium, but acceleration and hill climbing are the car's finest features. So far as a "best" cruising speed can be defined, we would put it at a genuine 70-75 m.p.h. for long or short journeys.

Speed is of limited use on busy roads without the backing of powerful brakes, and whilst it was not possible to extend our test into Alpine territory it can safely be said that the Girling hydraulic brakes of the Morgan will meet all normal demands. They are given a good deal of work to do, but check the car with a squeal of tyres in response to moderate and well-graduated pedal pressures, in a dead straight line save at a morning's first application in wet weather, when a front brake sometimes proved liable to grab. For parking, there is a handbrake lever with the sports car "fly-off" pattern ratchet, but the effectiveness and accessibility of this were not truly worthy of the car.

A vital contribution to the car's sporting character is made by the four-speed synchro-mesh gearbox which, unusually, is located some distance behind the engine. The extremely short gear lever which projects from the top of the gearbox is ideally placed near to the steering-wheel rim, and although it is possible to beat the synchro-mesh, the change works excellently whether treated in a normal fashion or "snatched" during some contest of speed. Giving very comfortable speeds of 20, 35, and 55 m.p.h., with much more in reserve if required, the gears are really useful for intensive motoring—although it should be emphasized that the engine retains normal touring flexibility right down to 10 m.p.h. in top gear, and can take the car over quite astonishingly steep hills in that gear. The problems of insulating gearbox heat and noise from the interior of the car seemed to have been quite adequately overcome on the test car, despite the unusual proximity of this unit to the driver.

Desirable Property

Given acceleration, speed and braking performances of a very desirable nature, the less easily defined qualities of general steadiness and controllability on the road are what really make a car desirable, acceptable or disappointing. Covering rather more than 500 miles in the Morgan during the first 24 hours after collecting it from the works, and another 1,400 before parting with it, those of our staff who drove and rode in the car were unanimous in putting it in the desirable category—this in spite of showery weather conditions which might have been thought ill-suited

LOW BUILT—Only 48 ins. in height, the Morgan is clean-lined and has such competition features as accessible twin spare wheels and a large snap-action petrol filler.

TAILORED—Comfortable and well protected from the elements, the driving position is excellent, a detail open to criticism being, however, the remote location of secondary instruments.

to open-car motoring, and of an appreciable number of points of detail criticism.

Essentially, the Morgan has the "alive" character on the road which in an era of soft suspension and slow-to-respond steering is called "old fashioned." Considerably more flexibly sprung than its predecessors, and giving its passengers ample insulation against shock on any but the very worst surfaces, the chassis nevertheless does follow the contours of the road more precisely than do many of its contemporaries. In relation to the character of the car, of which reasonably firm springing is a natural part, our main criticisms of the suspension would be that the rear shock absorbers did not match the telescopic units fitted into the front suspension in ability to resist bouncing on awkward surfaces negotiated at high speed, and that at just 58 m.p.h. there was a perceptible front-end shake on the test car. Our testing period in Belgium was unfortunately brief, but although the firmly sprung car was lively when rushed over pavée surfaces, it did not give the impression that it would suffer from regular use on rough going.

Prompt Steering Response

The same "alive" character which distinguishes the car's riding is to be noted in the steering. There is no marked oversteering or understeering characteristic to attract comment, but rather a measure of balance, of prompt but not exaggerated response to steering wheel movements, which takes most of the conscious effort out of fast driving. There are imperfections; in the form of a rather unexpected springiness of the steering linkage which, feeling like slight lost motion, allows gusty side winds to induce wander of the car on straight roads; and in the form of castor action so progressive that considerable effort is needed to get full lock on a hairpin corner. But, overall, the standard of easy controllability provided by the quick and reasonably reaction-free steering is very good.

Strictly sporting is the non-adjustable driving position, and for alert driving very comfortable also. The floor is the lowest part of the car, and although set well above floor level the driving seat also is very low, but there is a good forward view over the long bonnet. The way in which the floor is set low between the chassis side members means that entry to the car is not as easy as it might be, but once entered the cockpit is really comfortable, air-cushion seats giving support under the knees, and the backrest being upright and properly

shaped. Instinctively, a driver feels a part of the car, and although a stranger is at first apt to find rather a lot of knobs and corners against which to bruise himself, consciousness of these is soon lost in appreciation of such details as rubber padding on top of doors cut away to form elbow rests of just the right height.

Luggage-carrying capacity is available in the back of the car, sufficient to meet the needs of most sports-car owners and protected from the elements by a tonneau cover, and there is also a glove compartment on the facia panel. For weather pro-

UNCONCEALED—Easy access is available to the 2.1-litre o.h.v. engine, which with downdraught carburetter and thermostat-controlled hotspot is notably quick to warm up after a start from cold.

tection, two sidescreens which are easily mounted on the doors combine with the raked fold-flat windscreen to make the car very reasonably draught free—there is no trace of the common open car trouble of exhaust fumes sucked forwards into the cockpit. The hood is very weatherproof and not unduly slow to erect, a loose canvas panel (which can serve as full-length tonneau cover if the car is parked) being secured by press-studs over a light-looking but apparently quite sufficiently strong folding frame.

Experience showed that a quite surprising amount of hood-down motoring was possible even in showery weather, since with the car in motion rain is thrown over the heads of the driver and passenger. Further, the presence of wide running boards as part of the car's effective mudguarding layout means that an elbow projecting through the flaps provided in the side-screens does not become wet as it does in so many low-built sporting cars. Owners of earlier types of Morgan will, incidentally, appreciate the considerably

greater foot and elbow room made available by the new chassis.

Maintenance work would appear to be relatively simple on this car, the most vital parts of the sliding-pillar front suspension system having oil ducts from the engine and receiving lubrication when a pedal in the cockpit is pressed at recommended 100 mile intervals. Apart from being of simple design, the car gives easy accessibility to engine components.

Other running costs should be low in spite of the generous dimensions of the engine, high gear ratios and low car weight being valuable contributors to fuel economy. The figures for mileage per gallon quoted on our data page (25.6 m.p.g. overall) are creditable in themselves, but certain comparative interest attaches to results obtained on a 500-mile circuit of the Welsh mountains at fractionally over 30 m.p.h. running average speed: with a ten-minute change-over of jets and choke tube made before the start, at some very slight sacrifice of maximum speed but not seemingly of acceleration, and with a considerable amount of coasting indulged in, 38.6 m.p.g. was recorded in a long-distance petrol consumption contest.

With either the normal carburetter settings used for obtaining the figures published on our data page, or the economy settings installed temporarily to suit a particular competition, the engine was unhesitating in response to the throttle almost immediately after it had been started from cold. The actual start from cold was less immediate than on many cars which we test, but seemed entirely dependable and unaffected by overnight parking in exceptionally heavy rain.

Our overall impression of the Morgan is indicated by the fact of our running up more than double the conventional Road Test mileage during the modest period for which it was in our hands. It has shortcomings, but they are of the kind which do not seem terribly important when one is driving an open car, the vivacious character of which makes the use of it a potent rejuvenating tonic.

FOUR MONTHS WITH A MORGAN "4/4"

ON December 15th last year I went down to Malvern to collect a Morgan "4/4". Not until the little blue two-seater was handed over—a pair of those excellent Bluemel number-plates bolted on—did I know that I had missed a "Plus Four" and would have to be content with one of the 10-h.p. models, now virtually obsolete.

This model was introduced on the eve of war and not much has appeared in print about it, although quite a number are now in use. To recap briefly, the "4/4" appeared early in 1936, as Morgan's first four-wheeler, and sold readily at £225, to those who wanted an M.G., but couldn't abide hexagons. The engine was a 34 b.h.p. 1,122 c.c. i.o.e. Coventry-Climax and, following good showing at Le Mans, a 1,098 c.c. 45 b.h.p. "Le Mans Replica" was listed, with Solex or S.U. d.d. carb., and Lucas or Scintilla vertical magneto. It was recognisable by its cycle-type front wings, sloping tail, aero-screens, big tank, etc., and it weighed about 13½ cwt. dry. A few of these were built in 1936, but by mid-1939 the ordinary model had a 63.5 by 100 mm., 1,267 c.c. 40 b.h.p. Standard o.h.v. engine. The chassis, with its coil-spring vertical-slide i.f.s., underslung ½-elliptic back springs and cable Girling brakes, remained virtually unaltered for fourteen years with the exception of the price, which, abetted by p.t., soared to £556. Mine weighs almost exactly 14½ cwt.

The present "Plus Four" is bigger, and different in various ways, and its Vanguard engine will, alas, not shoe-horn into the former 7 ft. 8 in.-wheelbase chassis.

There was snow on the hills behind the factory when I took delivery, and the first stop was to have a liberal dose of Smith's "Bluecol" put in. Then slowly over to Cheltenham to cover the R.A.C. Championship Trial. Meeting the photographer at the station he insisted on planting a vast suitcase in the back compartment, and as the sidescreens are rather casually stored therein I erected them hastily in self defence. Some days later, when snow blew about my face so that I could hardly see, I reluctantly put up the hood; so severe has the past winter and spring been that it has since been furled only for a day! This seems to be the place to remark that, rigged thus, protection is good on the move, except where the rather oddly-contrived sidescreens part company with the hood, but that rain collects on the seats if you park and visibility is akin to that from the driving-slot of a tank.

I drove home over sheet-ice, with showers of road-grit shot-blasting the enamel, but it seems to have stood up well and the Morgan still looks the "pretty little car" that an old lady proclaimed it when I inquired the way of her in Cheltenham on the first day of ownership.

Running-in during that ice-bound era wasn't easy, but I tried religiously to keep the revs. down even when the back wheels spun. The car had a particularly unhappy "childhood," especially when ice froze into ridges that made motor-cycling impossible and motoring at more than 10 m.p.h. likewise. The racketing experienced in 30 unavoidable miles must have been the equal of a dozen Cape Rallies stretched end to end, but nothing broke or fell off, in contrast to a Scammell lorry we overtook, temporarily converted into a five-wheeler.

After 700 miles I drained the sump and refilled with Castrol XL, at the same time having the front-suspension slides greased again—Malvern had more or less advised carrying a grease-gun in the cubby hole and attending to these two nipples at every red traffic light, if wear was to be avoided. N.B.—They actually specify every 500 miles, which I've done pretty conscientiously, either with one of those beautiful old Enots guns or the toy-affair from the tool-roll; the "Plus Four" has one-shot engine-oil lubrication here. The back spring trunnions call for similar attention, but do not retain the grease very well. After just under a month's driving I oiled every moving part I could reach, and noted that everything seemed intact except that the pedal-rubbers had fallen off. It was some time after this that a dunderheaded lead-foot in a Vanguard couldn't find his brakes and sailed into the Morgan's tail when she was stationary in a city traffic jam. I got off with a dented back wing, Mr. Vanguard with a pithy lecture.

As the engine loosened up I drove faster, finally deciding that the happiest cruising speed was between 50 and 60 m.p.h. and 70 about the comfortable maximum. I have no performance figures to offer, but there seems to be as much speed in third as there is from a TD M.G. and very useful lower-end acceleration. Road-holding is excellent; the suspension softer than pre-war "4/4-ists" seem to expect; the brakes good if fairly frequently adjusted (at least, thrice in 6,000 miles), which is simplicity itself. Corners can be taken really fast with not a trace of roll. Starting wasn't exactly instantaneous in cold, damp weather, but is now O.K. Pleasantly high-geared steering, very good Lucas lamps with a sensible central pass-lamp for "dim," a good clutch, and effective quick-action fuel tank filler and well-padded seats occur as credit-points. The body is best dismissed as "adequate."—I shuddered at the bare wood planks that serve as a floor. The seats are unadjustable, the two cubby holes rather too shallow, the batteries are buried beneath the screwed-down three-ply "floor" of the luggage space and this floor is smitten by the back-axle far too frequently, even at low speeds over main-road "bumps" that appear harmless. The general construction, however, seems good, as nothing much has fallen off in 6,000 miles. The fly-off hand-brake, pleasant to use, flips-off at the wrong moments and on full-lock the off-side front wheel fouls the valance.

Fuel consumption is a bright point. The average, over the last 2,500 miles of almost equally-divided fast main-road and traffic driving, has been 34.4 m.p.g. and one lucky gallon took us 37 miles. But the engine (7 to 1 compression-ratio) protests almost continually at the stuff for which our present rulers charge 3s. 7¼d. a gallon and call petrol. Redex was put in while running-in. As to oil, half-a-gallon of Castrol XL was added in 4,112 miles and then the sump was drained and refilled with evil-smelling Mobiloil "Arctic" which, I'm told, acts as a detergent. (The makers recommend sump-draining every 4,000 miles.) With this thin oil, the same 60 lb./sq. in. pressure shows at normal speeds when warm, but consumption is perhaps a trifle heavier. The filler in the valve cover isn't very easy to pour into.

Mileage to date is nearly 6,200, in 19 weeks. During that time the car has taken the rough with the smooth, literally, has occasionally carried four persons (? yes, two small children will fit in the luggage space!) and has only failed me on three occasions—the first time was when, after 3,400 miles and a pleasing run in company with an exactly similar "4/4" encountered by chance, a mysterious "short" in the distributor reduced speed to a crawl, to disappear as mysteriously after a new rotor arm had been fitted. The steering has developed the usual "play," one dash lamp bulb has ceased to function, and the second temporary disablement was when petrol flooded from the d.d. Solex, due, I discovered on calling at the Marylebone Road service depot, to loss of the J-jet. I also discovered the price of this innocent little bit of brass! The third failure has laid the car up and thus given me time to pen these notes—some teeth have stripped from the constant-mesh pinions of the Moss gearbox. I have never been very happy with this box, which has been noisy, the gears difficult to engage from rest and working so stiffly as to mar the pleasure of using the remote-control change. No doubt it is one of those unlucky chances which happen in even the best engineering shops—even B.R.M.'s. That Malvern had no spares in stock and the Moss Gear Co., Ltd., only second-hand ones rather rubbed the salt in. Incidentally, like a vintage car, the Morgan has a separate gearbox; the ratios are 16.14, 11.42, 6.7 and 4.72 to 1.

This snag apart, the "4/4" has proved a willing and useful companion. It has had a minimum of servicing during this four months hard—just the usual greasing, cleaning of the A.C. by-pass oil filter, setting of c.b. and plug gaps, and checking of oil and water levels—and no leakage of either fluid has been evident. The 4.50-17 Dunlops have not had so much as a single puncture and the treads are still very good, apart from a suggestion of i.f.s. scrub on the front ones. The recommended pressure is 18/20 lb., but I prefer 22-24 lb./sq. in. The tappets have not required adjustment. The twin spare wheels, nine-gallon fuel tank, fold-flat screen (for fog or frost) and snug, easily-erected hood are amongst the points which appeal when embarking on long journeys at short notice.—W. B.

4,000 MILES WITH A PLUS FOUR

Experiences with the Latest Morgan as a Hard-Used Staff Car

AT Earls Court last year the Morgan Plus Four, with 68-b.h.p. engine in an 8-ft. wheelbase chassis, was an exciting newcomer. On July 2nd this year MOTOR SPORT took delivery of one for editorial use. By September 2nd the 4,000th mile rolled up on the odometer as the writer was ambling along the pleasant lanes near Winchfield, Hants. In other words, the Morgan had been in almost continual hard use, although down at Malvern, while they maintain that the Vanguard engine does not need running-in, they also consider that until it has been driven 5,000 miles it hasn't really settled down. When that mileage has been covered they recommend removal of the head for a decoke and a light valve-grind.

When I took delivery from the factory this blue two-seater had done only 19½ miles. In spite of the aforesaid assurances I drove it below 35 m.p.h. on the long run home and below 40 m.p.h. for the next 300 miles, subsequently keeping to 45 m.p.h. until the sump had been drained and refilled with 11 pints of Castrol XL, after 566 miles. The Pool was also freely laced with Redex or Carburol during this period.

Initial impressions were that improvements over the earlier " 4/4 " were legion—more room in the body, better sidescreens, a single but deeper and lined cubby-hole, the latest Lucas double-dipping headlamps and separate fog-lamp (the latter swiped, alas, at Silverstone), bigger tyres, and infinitely better brakes. On the older car I had been conscious that the i.f.s. slides needed frequent greasing ; on the Plus Four you merely tread on a little button every 50 miles or so and engine oil is pumped to these hard-worked components. The oil-gauge flicks back 25 lb./sq. in. to reassure you that oil is going where you want it to ; the front tyres also bear visual indication that this is so !

The 2,088-c.c. Vanguard engine, which satisfactorily fills the under-bonnet space, certainly endows the car with a very usable performance. The acceleration, even in the 4.1 to 1 top gear, is impressive, particularly from 30-60 m.p.h., making you " king of the traffic hold-ups," and 40 m.p.h. on the speedometer comes up in second gear (8 to 1), 60 m.p.h. in third gear (5.4 to 1). I have not tried for absolute screen-down maximum speed in top, but 65-70 m.p.h. is a happy cruising gait, with lots more to come. The engine pulls away well on the highest ratio from a mere 20 m.p.h., although so pleasant is the change on the Moss gearbox, of a type which the Plus Four shares with the 3½-litre Jaguar, that the driver is encouraged to use freely the lower ratios. The Morgan is about the only car to retain " vintage " location of its gearbox remote from the engine, and consequently the rigid little central lever is absolutely to hand, yet works *sans* any lost motion, being a joy to use. All the changes are brisk ; the slowest is from second to third.

Another " vintage " merit is the absence of roll when cornering fast—and this Morgan can be taken round very fast indeed, without its Dunlops emitting more than a very occasional " yelp." This good roadholding, coupled with " quick " steering (1¾ turns, lock-to-lock), produces excellent averages, in the order of 45m.p.h. over give-and-take secondary roads in the wet. The driver sits a thought too low, but both front wings, certainly both sidelamps and their reassuring indicator-windows, are visible, although the central rear-view mirror and wiper rather obstruct the near-side view when cornering. The steering is light, with ample castor action, and transmits only a minor degree of return motion ; I am disappointed, however, that it has already developed over 2 in. of lost-motion.

The Plus Four encourages hard driving, so it is good to find the Girling hydraulic brakes (2LS at the front) really first class. Apart from emitting a shriek before their linings bedded-in, they have done everything good brakes should do. And, with no attention of *any* sort, after 4,000 fast miles they are still adequately powerful, although the pedal goes down further than it did originally, of course. The hand-brake is a trifle too far forward, its ratchet doesn't grip and it doesn't hold the car on hills, but I like the fly-off action.

In spite of being driven fast and doing its very fair share of traffic work, the Morgan is proving commendably economical : in towns 23 m.p.g., and 26 m.p.g. on long, wide-throttle runs. This is with the middle setting of three variants which can be had for the Solex carburetter ; using the economy setting and, doubtless, a light throttle-foot, Joe Lowrey achieved an incredible 38.6 m.p.g. in the recent Cheltenham Rally.

The engine starts readily, even fiercely, with only partial choke. It runs too cool (55-60 deg. C., rising to 75 deg. in London). With a 6.7 to 1 compression-ratio it is very reasonably free from pinking even on straight " Pool." So far no adjustments, not even plug-cleaning, have been needed. It idles roughly, however, on its rubber mountings, conveying to the separate gearbox its impatience to be off. Oil pressure is a healthy 50 lb./sq. in. idling, rising to 75 lb./sq. in. at speed. The Fram filter appears to keep the lubricant in good condition, while consumption is about 1,200 m.p.g.

No car is perfect and the Plus Four's weaknesses are its hard suspension, so that you need a good constitution if you are to hurry over secondary roads, in spite of the adequate upholstery in the cockpit, and a chassis that seems a bit hard-put to cope with bad roads. Over certain surfaces the scuttle floats noticeably and the body gets racked about a good deal, so that frequent tightening of the knobs which retain the sidescreens and the spare-wheels clip is necessary, for example. This may be somewhat accentuated because whereas the recommended tyre-pressure is 16-18 lb./sq. in., I thriftily prefer 20-22 lb. Incidentally, this 16½ cwt. car is generously shod with 5.25-16 Dunlops, which naturally show little wear so far. And *two* spares are provided !

After 1,350 miles the clutch refused to free and, although conscious that racing drivers do not need this component, I spent 11/- having things " adjusted " at local garages before discovering that a vital operating lever had been bent over. However, Malvern had the engine out, a stronger lever installed, and the car back on the road in under six hours—a good

Continued on page **83**

[MOTOR SPORT *copyright*

STAFF CARS—The Morgan Plus Four and the MOTOR SPORT *Jupiter, photographed at Silverstone after the M.C.C. Meeting, and just before leaving for the B.O.C. International Speed Hill-Climb at Cheltenham.*

The 4-4 Morgan, here seen as a Show car in light finish, changed little from its first introduction in 1936 except for the substitution of a Standard for a Coventry Climax engine.

A TALE OF TWO MORGANS

EXPERIENCES WITH A 4-4 AND THE LATEST PLUS FOUR MODEL

THERE is still much controversy as to what constitutes a sports car, but where the four-wheeled Morgan products are concerned, I do not think there can ever have been any doubt.

True, in the very first days of this make the famous three-wheeler was conceived as an economy runabout. But this popular tricar soon appeared in sporting forms, including a certain very stark single-seater with big air-cooled V-twin engine affected by a well-known motoring journalist before the Kaiser war (it was called "Jabberwock") and the rather similar car with which H. F. S. Morgan raised the cyclecar hour record to just under 60 m.p.h. at Brooklands in November, 1912. Thereafter there was always a sports model in the Morgan range.

I have never owned a three-wheeler Morgan—more's the pity !—and it is with the later 4-4 and current Plus Four cars with which this article deals.

The first of these Morgans with which I had intimate contact was a 1949 4-4, and there was little question but that this was a sports car. It had room for two persons, but two only, sitting on low cushions above the planking floor. It had an appearance rendered rakish by reason of the low build, plenty of louvres along bonnet top and sides, a slab rear tank neatly concealed beneath a flowing rear panel and behind this panel two upright-mounted spare wheels. Of luggage space there was a quite generous cavity behind the seat, with its own tonneau cover and beneath the hood if this were erect, but otherwise forming a stowage space for the hood cover and its frame in fine weather. The new 4-4 was obviously a car intended primarily for sport, whether that was interpreted as driving in rallies, trials or speed events, or merely going away with a friend and a minimum of luggage on a lengthy journey. The single-pane screen would fold flat on to the scuttle and that was obviously more of a concession, in a ten horse-power car, to fresh air and fun than to maximum speed.

Diligent search reveals that *The Autocar* road tested a Coventry Climax-engined 4-4 on August 12, 1938, or, more accurately, published on that day the findings of a test extending over more than 1,000 miles. The tabulated figures

show a mean ¼-mile speed of 75.95 m.p.h., the best ¼-mile reading being 78.26 m.p.h., with absolute maxima on the indirect gears of 21, 33 and 59 m.p.h. respectively. Acceleration from rest to 50 m.p.h. occupied 15.7 sec, and to 60 m.p.h. 28.3 sec. Fuel consumption was assessed as 35-38 m.p.g. In short, the new Morgan had performance characteristics to appeal to a large number of open car lovers, particularly as, in that day and age, the price was a modest £225. Moreover, these data applied to a four-seater version which, with a trim coupé, had been added to the original two-seater.

The 4-4 soon made a big circle of friends and scored notable successes in rallies and in trials, its ground clearance of six inches being less of a hazard under the latter conditions than might be supposed, because the bottom of the car is

smooth and free from obstructions. The exhaust pipe is up beside a side-member safely out of the way. I use the present tense deliberately, for the same applies to the current Plus Four Morgan.

Indeed, so successful in competition did the 4-4 prove, and so popular was it with sporting drivers, that the Morgan company decided to run at Le Mans. Their cars did well, but not sensationally, and the outcome of this racing venture was that a Le Mans Replica model was added to the range. It was distinguishable by its cycle-type wings at the front, sloping tail housing a big fuel tank, and aero windscreens. The engine was a 1,098 c.c. Coventry Climax unit with downdraught Solex or S.U. carburettor to choice, and coil ignition replaced by a Lucas or Scintilla vertical magneto, again to choice. This engine was claimed to give

The Vanguard engine as installed in the Plus Four. It is positively mounted in the frame and has a pronounced slope downwards to the rear.

Although it has been softened, the telescopic i.f.s. remains substantially as it always has been.

A TALE OF TWO MORGANS: continued

45 b.h.p. and the weight was kept down to about 13½ cwt dry. Some of these Le Mans Replica models are still active today.

Just before the outbreak of war the supply of the inlet-over-exhaust Coventry Climax engines began to dry up and Morgans were forced to seek an alternative power unit. The choice fell on a Standard Ten engine, known to be exceedingly durable, and specially endowed with a push-rod overhead-valve head. These units were delivered, after test, from the Coventry factory of Standard to the works under the shadow of the Malvern Hills where the 4-4s were assembled, still almost entirely by hand even to the final brush-finish on the bodies. The car had remained almost unmodified since its inception in 1936 and with its newfound 63.5 x 100 mm (1,267 c.c.) engine, for which 40 b.h.p. was claimed at 4,300 r.p.m., it had a performance not dissimilar to that of its Coventry Climax-powered forerunner. The new engine, however, developed more power low down in the speed range and was smoother to drive behind.

The post-war example of which I have had experience settled down very nicely to a cruising speed of about 55 m.p.h. and was good for a speedometer 70 m.p.h. at any time. The roll-free cornering and quick, positive gear change were ever a delight, and to these pleasures were added a fuel consumption of 35 m.p.g. and quite good brakes, although the latter required

rather frequent taking-up of the cables if they were to retain their full efficiency. The ride was on the hard side, but softer than on the earlier cars, or so I was told by people who had tried both. The front sliding members of the i.f.s. called for frequent doses from a grease gun if rapid wear was to be avoided, but under-bonnet accessibility was excellent, with a useful well for tools in the scuttle. The twin batteries remained where Morgan had originally stowed them, by the fuel tank, and for this reason were difficult of access.

The Standard engine took lots of punishment cheerfully but showed its dislike of trying to digest Pool petrol on a compression ratio of 7 to 1 by loud pinking. Its valve cover polished up nicely and an AC filter kept the oil (I used Castrol XL) commendably clean. The filler in the valve cover was not altogether convenient to use, however. Pressure was healthy; 60 lb per sq in at speed.

As I have said, the Morgan 4-4 was purely and simply a sports car. There was comfortable room for two normal-sized adults, who were separated by a padded tunnel. Weather protection was reasonable without being superlative, but the hood frame looked a thought Heath Robinson and could tie itself into the sort of knots which that gentleman loved if you attempted to erect it too hastily. There was really nowhere to rest one's clutch foot but, as if to compensate, the action of the fly-off hand brake was admirable. Good, too, was the fuel range of well over 290 miles, ensured by a nine-gallon tank; nor did the mechanical fuel pump ever give any trouble.

Eventually it was time to replace the trusty 4-4 with another car and a Plus Four was luckily available.

Real Power

The differences were pretty vivid. In the first place, here was *real* performance, allied to greater comfort and really fine Girling hydraulic 2LS brakes.

I believe that as the source of Coventry Climax engines had dried up, so had the stream of o.h.v. Standard Tens begun to ebb. Morgans again had to look for something else and, after contemplating using a Ford Ten power unit, they decided to depart from the 1½-litre class in which they had so long been represented and bring out a new car with a Standard Vanguard engine.

The Vanguard engine is installed in absolutely standard form (no pun intended!) except that, as it sits at a different angle in the Morgan from that which it adopts in the saloon Vanguard, the

carburettor flange has to be altered to keep the gasworks upright. To the engine is mated a Moss gear box with ratios of 13.5, 8.0, 5.4 and 4.1 to 1. It remains in the now-rare "separate" location.

There is little point in labouring the differences in specification between the old 4-4 and the current Plus Four, for these have been described in *The Autocar* fairly recently and were evident at Earls Court. When I say that there is now *real* performance I refer to truly vivid acceleration, even in top gear; and to a maximum speed of a genuine 80 m.p.h. with the screen erect. Weather elimination has been considerably improved and on many days the interior of the car is really too stuffy when the rigid side curtains and snug hood are up; the Heath Robinson hood frame remains but seems to resist abuse. The same wooden floor, comfortable seats and fly-off hand brake are there, but now I have one large lined cubby-hole for gloves and handbag instead of two rather inadequate small ones. There is now room, too, for my clutch foot between the brake and clutch pedal.

M.P.G.

The economy of the 4-4 seems to be reflected in the Plus Four in spite of its 2,088 c.c. engine. At all events, I get about 26 m.p.g. without trying particularly to save fuel, and using the middle setting in the Solex carburettor and not the economy setting.

The suspension gives a very hard ride compared with other contemporary cars but this is, after all, a sports car. Perhaps in consequence, I have had some trouble with broken spring dampers and a broken suspension rebound spring, in a mileage of 7,500. A clutch lever has also broken and I have met other Plus Four owners who have also experienced these troubles.

One very much appreciated and rather fascinating feature is the automatic oiler for the front suspension slides, which saves all the bother with a grease gun. One irritating matter is that the clip which secures the twin spare wheels has to be done up very tight if it is not to work loose, causing the tyres to assume an out-of-true shape.

Wherever I park the Plus Four it attracts favourable comment on account of its racy appearance. Whatever the "blower brigade" may say, I maintain that this is the kind of car that appeals to a very large proportion of the world's buyers who have any use at all for a sports car.

WINIFRED HOLBROOK.

A coupé version of the Morgan Plus Four, this particular car being that which was the subject of a Road Test by *The Autocar* in the spring of 1951.

A YEAR WITH A MORGAN PLUS-FOUR

ON the scorching day of July 2nd, 1951 I took delivery at Malvern Link of the Editorial Morgan Plus-Four two-seater, KAB 303 (bought incidentally, at full list price plus purchase tax), and on the not-much-less-scorching day of July 2nd, 1952, when it attained its first birthday in my hands, the mileage recorder read 15,645 miles.

After 4,000 miles I set down my experiences of the Morgan in these pages, but as so much interest centres on the Plus-Four, until recently the least expensive sports car on the British Market (a price increase shifted this distinction to the TD M.G., by a matter of less than £5) some further remarks may not come amiss.

I have enjoyed using my shiny-blue two-seater very much, even if owners of those vintage cars for which I myself have such a warm affection are apt to refer to the Morgan as my " boy's racer," while conceding that it makes an apt background for my pre-war B.A.R.C. badge and blue Bugatti Club pennant. The chief reasons for this enjoyment are the car's lively performance, its dependable starting, and the pleasure derived from driving "something different" and an open car at that. Taking these qualities in order, by *lively performance* I mean acceleration, safe quick-cornering, and an easy cruising speed of the 65-m.p.h.-order. I have not timed the true performance but, while a contemporary records 85.7 m.p.h. as the Plus-Four's maximum speed, the MOTOR SPORT example is reluctant to exceed a speed of 80 m.p.h. Incidentally, as delivered, the throttle did not open fully when the accelerator was on the floor !

Take it then, as a nice compliment to the car's accelerative ability (I would not willingly change to a car with less), its very good Girling brakes and its pleasantries of gear-change, road-holding and quick steering that I do not object to speeds which seem less than those realised by other scribes—speedometer readings of 40 in 2nd, 60 in 3rd and 80 in top being about as much as the engine can comfortably stand.

Dependable starting ?—yes, quick to fire and to open-up from cold without displays of asthma or hay-fever. Not *quite* so quick now as a year ago, but dependable, which I appreciate and give thanks for to Messrs. Standard, Lucas, Solex and Champion; and none at all to the purveyors of Pool petrol !

Other pleasures—would take too much space to detail, but the acceleration, particularly useful through traffic at the end of a jading day, is amongst the more notable. The screen has been folded-flat but once—at the request of an 18-year-old fanatic—and with both it and the side-screens permanently erect, you sit sufficiently low not to be unduly wind-swept. The hood is excellent (except for visibility-impairment) and useful, too, to drape over the seats when the car is parked. It has worn well, having only recently acquired one slight slit.

The car has not been exactly trouble-free, for after only 1,350 miles a clutch-operating lever broke and at 1,750 miles the off-side steering damper snapped, followed at 1,970 miles by fracture of its fellow. The clutch lever was replaced by Morgan's and no further trouble has been experienced, although a lot of free-play has developed since. The steering dampers were replaced by their Aldershot agent, but after another 6,000 miles the new near-side damper broke, likewise a suspension rebound spring. To date the off-side damper has held together and absorbs wheel wobble providing its attachment bolts are kept really tight and cobbles and bad pot-holes are avoided. The steering is undoubtedly the weakest feature of the Plus-Four. With both dampers broken it is impossible to control the violent wheel shimmy which occurs below about 40 m.p.h. and with only one damper working this shimmy is liable to return at awkward moments and in any case undue return-motion and steering kick is transmitted, accentuated by a lack of rigidity in the region of the scuttle. Apart from damper failure, the drop-arm has tried to detach itself from the steering box, and after a year's use there is 5 in. of free-play at the steering-wheel rim. I suspect that when larger wheels and tyres were specified for the Plus-Four, a layout which had sufficed for the 4/4 became unduly stiff and that to counteract this the castor-angle was reduced, placing undue reliance on the essentially-flimsy dampers. These dampers consist of strips of steel depending from the frame side-members and having attached to them bronze rings which encircle the steering tubes. The rings rise and fall with the suspension and so the arms have to flex, and eventually break. When my first pair broke I heard that improved dampers were on the way but was disappointed to find that, apart from a step in the arms, they were as before. After his excellent performance in the 1951 Alpine Rally Dave Price experienced this trouble but a French garage cured it by cutting new ones from saw-steel. Another solution has been given to me by the Irish competition driver C. S.

Porter and as his letter will interest Morgan enthusiasts I reproduce it below—

Sir,

I have owned a Plus-Four Morgan for just over a year, during which time it has covered 19,000 hard miles.

Apart from covering over 30 miles per day to and from business, I have competed in practically every speed event in Ireland (and several in Scotland) during the past twelve months, gaining at least one 1st and several places in various races and hill-climbs, and also having some success in trials during the winter. During that time the head has been removed twice for decoking, and " tuning " consisted of removing windscreen and spare wheels and fitting the slightly larger jet recommended by the makers. Lamps and mud-guards were left in position, and in this trim the car was timed at approx., 96 m.p.h. over the measured distance in the Handicap Race at Dundrod, and finished at an average of approx. 68 m.p.h. using pump fuel. Oil consumption is still negligible. Road-holding is all that could be desired, and the car is very comfortable, provided recommended tyre pressure (16/18 lb.) is not exceeded.

Needless to say, there were one or two " snags," but how many new models are free from them ? I broke three steering dampers (and after all, it is asking a lot from thin sheet steel to expect it to bend indefinitely *without* breaking) before curing the trouble by drilling four holes in the broken portion, and joining it to the chassis bracket between two pieces of "Balata " flat belting. No trouble since (I find one damper quite sufficient) and if any "sufferer " wants further details, I shall be glad to oblige. The other alteration I made concerned the engine mountings, which allowed the unit to wobble like a jelly, especially at low speeds. After being deprived of a place in one of the Irish races, due to excessive engine movement cutting the top radiator hose, I decided that the mountings would have to be altered, and am now using Jeep front mountings, and Morris Commercial rears. Engine movement is now negligible, so much so that I can use a steel pipe from manifold to silencer, instead of flexible tubing (a constant source of exhaust leaks). In my opinion, the " wobbly engine " is just another Americanism which has (unfortunately) established itself in most British cars. Surely a well-designed engine does not require large lumps of rubber to insulate it from the chassis ?

Altogether a most satisfactory little car, and the best value for money in its class.

I am, Yours, etc.,

Killinchy.   C. S. PORTER.

The fact remains that the steering does not feel exactly taut, the flimsy track-rod, wear at the various joints and movement of the steering box on the chassis contributing to this state of affairs. The car *might* pass a race-scrutineer, but certainly the amount of play which has developed will have to be seen to. The transmission, too, gives evidence of some " wear and tear."

Peter Morgan told me that tyres last about 12,000 miles and after 15,645 miles I am in possession of two bald spares, about to be Blue Peter retreaded, one well-worn and one not-too-bad back tyres, and two fair tyres on the front wheels—which is where motor traders and those who respect mobile coppers put their better covers ! To Mr. Dunlop's credit there has been only one puncture, an unlucky nail quite early on. Oh, and the comic jack folded over and jammed up, just as a correspondent told us it would ! The Girling brakes have already received honourable mention but I do so again, for they remain powerful, if squeaky, yet have been bled only once and adjusted only once over the entire mileage. Likewise, the Newton and Girling dampers have never been serviced, nor the Solex carburetter dismantled.

The Standard Vanguard engine blew its head gasket for no apparent reason after 9,800 miles. I say " for no apparent reason " but the aforesaid steering shimmy caused chassis flexion and that resulted in a radiator leak at 3,165 miles and constant topping-up of a steaming header tank with cold water probably took its toll. I changed the gasket myself on Christmas Eve, rather cowed by the present price of gasket sets, getting the local garage to grind-in the valves at the same time. The 10,000th mile showed up crossing Staines Bridge on New Year's Day. The carbon wasn't excessive but suggested odd mixture distribution. The Champion L 10s were cleaned at the time and are still in use. The engine certainly wobbles alarmingly on its rubbers, but the only ill-effect has been to slide its flexible exhaust piping off, which a garage replaced without needing new

CONTINUED ON PAGE 54

JOHN BOLSTER *Tests*

THE MORGAN "PLUS-FOUR"

A Lively Sporting Two-Seater which Possesses Vivid Acceleration, First-class Road-holding and a 90 m.p.h. Maximum

IT is often suggested nowadays that the individually "hand made" car is on the way out. Such machines, we are told, can no longer compare with the superb creations of the vast mass-production combines. It is perfectly true that some of the smaller firms are having considerable difficulty in keeping their costs within bounds, and it is consequently hard to justify their wares on a basis of value for money. Nevertheless, there is one sports-car, which comes from a factory of moderate dimensions, and which gives more performance per pound sterling than anything else on the market. That vehicle is the Morgan "Plus 4".

The typical British sports 2-seater, of around 1½-litre capacity, is quite a pleasant conveyance, though excessive weight is a common fault. When driving these machines, one is apt to feel that an extra half-litre or so on the engine, and a couple of hundredweights pared off the chassis, would make a great improvement to the pleasure of driving. That is exactly what the Morgan Motor Co. have done, and the result comes right up to expectations. They provide a car that looks, to the casual observer,

like a "ten horse" job, but under the little bonnet they secrete 18 sprightly quadrupeds. What a surprise for the boys, for unless they have paid at least double the price of the "Plus 4", the only view of it that they will ever see is two spare wheels receding into the distance!

Quite how the thing is made for the money it is not easy to see, but when I visited the Morgan works recently, and drove off in a "Plus 4", I decided that it should have a week of the hardest possible motoring. In that way, I figured that if the design had any weaknesses, I would assuredly find them out. So, from the outset, I placed my right foot firmly on that little pedal, and there it remained whenever conditions permitted.

Many were the highways and byways that saw the rapid passage of the small blue motor, and the Boreham and Brands Hatch circuits were lapped to the best of my ability. Also, as a change from doing the Dunlop shareholders a bit of good, London was twice traversed from end to end. There were already 17,000 miles on the clock when I took over, including some distin-

guished performances in rallies, but when I returned to Malvern, the machine was still as lively and rattle-free as a newly run-in example. Admittedly, a week is not a sufficient period for a reliable assessment of wearing qualities to be made, but I was able to form the impression that the latest Morgan is a tough little car.

I do not know whether the Standard Vanguard engine receives any special tuning, but in conjunction with the four-speed gearbox, and a well-chosen axle ratio, it sends the "Plus 4" along to some purpose. This is a genuine 90 m.p.h. car, my fastest "one way" speed being 92 m.p.h.; but much more important is the reserve of power at normal cruising speeds. As an example, a certain main road hill I know will, if approached at 70 m.p.h., bring the average small sports-car down below 60 m.p.h. The "Plus 4", however, will accelerate strongly all the way up, finishing at a full 80 m.p.h.

The handling qualities are interesting. The car corners fast without any roll, and feels perfectly happy when flung through the curves at racing speeds. It has no vices whatever, and the authentic four-wheel drift technique is within its compass. It sticks to bumpy roads like a leech, and no bouncing or wheel lifting is ever apparent. The exceptionally high-geared steering gives a fine feeling of mastery, and it would be a poor driver indeed who did not find himself quickly at home behind the wheel.

Less travel is allowed on the suspension than is usual these days, and consequently the ride is a good deal harder than is fashionable. If rock steadiness and controllability are your first consideration, you will fall in love with the Morgan, but if you like a boulevard ride, it is not the car for you. The suspension is certainly softer than on previous cars of this make, but it is still firmer than with other i.f.s. systems. No gyroscopic effects mar the behaviour of the steering.

sticks fold away neatly, without encroaching unduly on the luggage space. It would be fair to say that saloon-car standards of comfort are provided with the hood up, and entry is not unduly difficult by sports-car standards.

Z-Section Frame

The general construction is somewhat unusual. The chassis frame is of "Z" section, and carries the rear springs within the rear portion, which is as wide as the track permits. The forward anchorage of the flat semi-elliptics is on Silentbloc bushes, and at the back, they slide in trunnion blocks that locate inside a sturdy tubular cross member. The drive is on the Hotchkiss system, as the torque reaction is taken through the spring leaves.

In front, a light tubular structure is bolted to the frame, and this car-

ries the vertical suspension guides which are, in effect, also the king pins. Helical springs take the weight and rebound, and the telescopic hydraulic dampers are double-acting. The steering swivels are connected by a track rod, and a separate cross rod goes to the Burman Douglas steering box. If the geometry lacks theoretical perfection, there is certainly no perceptible fault. An important feature, for smooth working and long life, is the pressure lubrication system. This suspension layout is a refined version of the original Morgan design, which has appeared on these cars for more than 40 years.

The Standard Vanguard engine is rubber mounted. It is a sturdy four-cylinder unit, of just over 2-litre capacity, with vertical overhead valves, and a counterbalanced crankshaft. It is very accessible for servicing.

Gear Lever Just Right

At the rear of the unit a most unusual arrangement is employed, for the Elektron bell-housing develops into a long tube, which carries the gearbox right back amidships. This brings the lever exactly where it is wanted, but, more important, it gives a very short propeller shaft, which is consequently entirely free of vibration or whirling.

The hydraulic brakes are powerful and responsive, which is most

MULTUM IN PARVO: (Left) The 2,088 c.c. Vanguard engine, compactly housed in the Morgan chassis, results in brisk all-round performance without stress.

DECIDEDLY SPORTING: The Morgan "Plus Four" follows classic sports-car lines.

There is ample room for two on the bench type front seat, but the position of the gearbox precludes the carrying of another passenger. The driving position is really first class. The floor is secured to the bottom web of the frame, which is only about 6 ins. above the road. Consequently, one's feet are well down below the level of the seat, and one sits up to one's work as in the better continental cars. The short gear lever, working straight through the lid of the box, is ideally situated, so that the left hand falls straight on to it.

Sitting well down inside the body, one is well protected by the shallow screen. The hood gives very good weatherproofing, in conjunction with the rigid sidescreens. The supporting

The Morgan "Plus-Four"—*continued*

desirable with such a lively car. If they are used continuously with great ferocity, they become less progressive, as is usual with 2.L.S. designs. I did not succeed in provoking serious fading, however. The "fly off" hand brake acts on the rear drums, and is powerful enough to lock the wheels.

Severely practical in appearance, this car makes no concession to the modern, streamlined trend. It looks neat and workmanlike, and several of my friends admired it very much, because it provided such a contrast to the fat and bulbous vehicles that abound nowadays. It would indeed be difficult to imagine two more utterly different shapes than the somewhat angular "Plus 4" two-seater, and the saloon that the Vanguard engine generally propels.

The latest Morgan is a machine of exceptional personality that combines a fine performance with road-holding and controllability of a very high order. It may not be everybody's car, but if you like it, you will like it very much indeed. At today's prices, it represents quite remarkable value, and for those who prefer to take their motoring neat, without air-conditioning, radio, or built in cocktail cabinets, it is quite a proposition.   J. V. B.

SPECIFICATION AND PERFORMANCE DATA

Car Tested: Morgan "Plus 4" sports 2-seater, price £565 (plus £315 7s. 9d. P.T.).

Engine: Four cylinders 85 mm. x 92 mm. (2,088 c.c.). Pushrod operated overhead valves. 68 b.h.p. at 4,300 r.p.m. 6.7 to 1 compression ratio. Solex downdraught carburetter. Lucas coil and distributor.

Transmission: Borg and Beck clutch. 4-speed Moss gearbox with short lever directly in top of box, ratios 4.1, 5.4, 8.0, and 13.5 to 1. Hardy Spicer propeller shaft. Salisbury hypoid axle.

Chassis: Z section, underslung at rear. Independent front suspension by stub axles sliding upon extended king pins against helical springs. Semi-elliptic rear springs with Silentbloc bushes and sliding trunnion blocks. Girling hydraulic dampers all round. Pierced disc wheels, fitted 5.25 in. x 16 in. tyres. Girling 2 L.S. hydraulic brakes in 9 in. drums.

Equipment: 12-volt lighting and starting. Speedometer, ammeter, water temperature, oil pressure, and fuel gauges.

Dimensions: Wheelbase, 8 ft. Track, 3 ft. 11 ins. Overall length, 11 ft. 8 ins. Turning circle, 30 ft. Weight as tested, 15½ cwt.

Performance: Maximum speed, 90 m.p.h. Speeds in gears, 3rd 72 m.p.h. 2nd 46 m.p.h. Standing quarter-mile, 19¾ secs. 0-50 m.p.h., 9⅝ secs. 0-60 m.p.h. 12⅘ secs. 0-70 m.p.h. 19 secs.

Fuel Consumption: Driven hard, 23 m.p.g.

MORGAN PLUS FOUR—continued from page **51**.

piping. It uses very little oil, being topped-up with Castrol XL when I think of it; the chassis is regularly greased and the gearbox and back-axle topped-up with Castrol lubricants. The engine functions as well as ever but runs too cool and its early promise of economical running has deteriorated to around 20/23 m.p.g. The fuel pump seems to be getting a bit weary, for it now needs more than a gallon to prime it if the tank runs dry ; and the hand-primer doesn't help.

Some people say that a 2-litre engine in a 16½-cwt. car calls for a higher back-axle ratio than 4.1 to 1 and it would be an interesting experiment, particularly as a Plus-Four has been known to give nearly 39 m.p.g. with the economy carburetter setting and restrained driving. On the other hand, the present arrangement endows the Morgan with " 30/98 " top-gear-pulling characteristics (which seems to have led Mr. Laurence Pomeroy into believing that there are only three forward speeds !) pleasant to experience, notwithstanding the excellent gear-change of the Moss four-speed box. Black mark, however, to Mr. Moss for providing an oil dip-stick requiring pliers for its removal ! Which reminds me, the fly-off hand-brake is too apt to fly-off and a wing-stay came adrift after 4,800 miles.

No electrical failures have been experienced bar early demise of the dashlight and stop-lamp bulbs, the original fan-belt is in use, all the instruments work well although the Smith's clock believes that *tempus fugit*, and generally, the Morgan has stood up staunchly to hard work at the hands of an impulsive driver, and still looks smart, especially when given a Lifeguard polish.

Remember that at £535 this is one of the least expensive sports cars, that it really can find its way through traffic and cover the ground, and that essentially it is for those who enjoy servicing a car as much as driving it and any criticisms I have aired will, I hope, be seen in a proper perspective. Certainly I enjoy the Plus-Four, regard it as practical fast transport as well as a means of relaxation after long-duration pen-pushing, and am not changing it for anything else at present.

I could write much more about it but this seems to cover most of the impressions I have of the car, read in conjunction with an earlier article which appeared in MOTOR SPORT last October. Let me conclude, therefore, by saying that I have always liked the idea of a sizable power unit in a lightweight car and that the Morgan Plus-Four fully bears out the enjoyment to be derived from such a formula.

—W. B.

ROAD and TRACK ROAD TEST No. F-5-52
Morgan-Plus 4

SPECIFICATIONS

Cylinders	4 in line	Curb Weight	1880 lbs
Valve System	pushrod, ohv	Weight, front	880 lbs
Compression ratio	6.7:1	Weight, rear	1000 lbs
Horsepower	68 at 4200 rpm	Weight as tested	2660 lbs
Bore and Stroke	3.35x3.62	Wheelbase	96 in.
Displacement	2088 cc i	Overall length	140 in.
Steering lock to lock	2⅛ turns	Overall width	56 in.
Turning circle	37 feet	Seating Cap.	2 Pass.
1st gear	13.5:1	Transmission	4 speed
2nd gear	8.0:1		
3rd gear	5.4:1		
4th gear	4.1:1		
List price	$2395		

PERFORMANCE

Test condition   2300 ft. alt., cool, clear, moderate winds.

Flying ¼ mile	81.4 mph
Fastest one way	84.1 mph
32% Grade, 1st gear	24 mph
Standing ¼ mile	21.2 secs.

TAPLEY READINGS

Pulling power	Gear	mph
450 lbs per ton	1st	26
360 lbs per ton	2nd	32
261 lbs per ton	3rd	34
170 lbs per ton	4th	38

SHIFTING POINTS

2nd gear	23 mph
3rd gear	42 mph
4th gear	57 mph

Deceleration Rate
(Coasting)

30 lbs per ton at	10 mph
50 lbs per ton at	30 mph
117 lbs per ton at	60 mph

ACCELERATION THRU GEARS

0-30 mph	4.43 secs.
0-40 mph	7.50 secs.
0-50 mph	11.35 secs.
0-60 mph	17.10 secs.
0-70 mph	27.45 secs.

SPEEDOMETER CORRECTION

Speedometer	Actual
30 mph	28.5
40 mph	37.3
50 mph	47.8
60 mph	58.0
70 mph	69.2
80 mph	79.9

Fuel Consumption

At a Steady	Miles per gal.
20 mph	29.5
30 mph	28
40 mph	26.5
50 mph	22.5
60 mph	19
70 mph	15.5

The Morgan factory at Malvern Link, England, is a very small place—even by the most modest British standards.

If a Detroit tycoon ever saw the size of the factory, he would "blow his top." And if he counted the number of employees (which turns out little more than a half dozen cars per month) he would throw up his hands in horror. He'd never believe it.

But small plants like these (Morgan, Frazer-Nash and the rest) are by no means exceptions in England. And they are the backbone of British enthusiast motoring.

To give you an idea of the way their production line works, there is one Morgan employee in particular who is worth mentioning. He is the man who has hand-painted (with a brush, mind you) every Morgan to leave the factory in over twenty years.

You probably remember that Morgan has been turning out specialist's sports cars for a long time—since 1911, in fact. And the elder Morgan and his son to this day are familiar sights in British competition.

Price of Morgan Plus Four now includes bumpers which were originally an optional extra.

Until 1936, the Morgan specialty was its world famous three-wheeler . . . which was powered by various motorcycle engines, and more recently by the small Ford 10. However, in '36 a normal four-wheeler was put into production, using at first the Coventry-Climax engine and later a 1267 cc Standard. It was, of course, the Morgan 4/4. Tho not very many of these cars reached the public, this model was continued until 1951, when the Plus Four was introduced. It was (and is) powered by a bigger engine and uses a longer, stronger chassis, tho it is only slightly over 100 pounds heavier. (The three-wheeler, incidentally, was discontinued some time back, but due to hysterical demands on the part of British enthusiasts, the popular little vehicle is again in limited production.

Steve Wilder, a transplanted (to Manhattan Beach, California) Bostonian, graciously offered his Plus Four to the staff for testing. Ever since this car was announced and displayed in this country last year, more orders have poured in than the factory could fill. So dealers haven't been anxious to furnish test cars. Naturally, Road and Track jumped at Steve's generous offer.

BOB DEARBORN REPORTS

There's a big argument nowadays, between MG and Morgan owners—about the relative merits of their cars. I don't want to get in the middle, because as far as I can see the argument will never be resolved—the two cars are so different. However, a simple summing of the two sports machines would be that the MG is neater handling while the Morgan has more performance, due to its better weight/horsepower ratio.

The Morgan feels like a sports car, if you know what I mean. When you seat yourself way down into this little bomb, fire up the engine, glance out over the long, louvered hood, slip and solid-feeling gear lever into first, and mash on the throttle, you get away from the mark in true sporting fashion—with a jolting roar. The car sits flat on corners too, but right here the Morgan and I come to a parting of the ways.

I took Steve's car down my favorite mountain road. It's my own private testing ground and I've driven quite a few cars thru it, to try out their handling qualities. I must say that the Morgan is the only imported car I've ever driven thru this twisting course that has had me really worried. The tail end was *always* out on corners and never twice in the same way.

Another thing that bothered me was the steering. There was excessive play in the steering wheel which keeps you from setting

The Morgan's tandem spare wheel arrangement gives it a distinctive sports car flavor.

Clean-cut American, Steve Wilder, shows how tail breaks loose with over-inflated tires.

a true course in a corner and which throws you all off when you try to correct. And on a straight high speed run the car demands an awful lot of driving. It tends to wander.

Much of this fault may be attributable to Steve—as he will point out in his following remarks. As far as I know the front wheels were never aligned in 14,000 miles of racing and hard driving (the kind of driving only a very young and very ardent enthusiast can do) and the steering gearbox was never adjusted. Further, Steve had changed to larger tires on the rear and at the time I breezed thru the aforementioned hills, I was carrying twenty-eight pounds of air in the tires. Later we discovered that cornering ability was improved 100% when we lowered the pressure to twenty pounds.

It's really unfair to judge all Morgans by this particular car. I suspect that Steve's car, with proper tire sizes and pressures, some attention to the front wheel alignment and balance, and an adjustment to the steering gearbox, would give the kind of handling we've heard the Morgan has.

Still, I didn't warm to the Plus Four the way many of my friends have. As far as I could see, it is a car of many idiosyncrasies, which would take a lot of getting used to. I had difficulty in getting in and out of the car, and once seated I was entirely too close to the wheel to be able to handle the car comfortably. Maybe you won't be bothered, but with my 250 plus pounds and over six feet of height, I was uncomfortable. My elbows stuck out because I was too close to the steering wheel and this was particularly annoying when the side curtains were in place. There's a wooden beam which the back of the driver's seat rests against. If

Ideally, the windshield wiper motor should be relocated to give driver more knuckle room. A tachometer would be a welcome addition.

this were repositioned (and it shouldn't be too difficult) I would be a whole lot happier about owning one of these cars.

On the other hand, Morgan's idea of pneumatic seat cushions is really sparkling. The car has a fairly stiff and firm ride, but the driver is unaware of this because the air in the cushions absorbs practically all road shock. Negatively, the girl who rides with me, jotting down results of road tests, said that the passenger seat-back kept pushing her forward—and she felt cramped. The interior of the Morgan is quite "chummy" to say the least—if you are larger than average.

But with all this, the Morgan is a real sports car, and one of the last of a great breed. Sports cars today are getting sleek,

quiet, and refined. They are softer riding, and more comfortable. But if you buy a Morgan, you will know that you are the owner of a genuine sports car in the traditional sense. You may put up with some inconveniences, but you'll have a barrel of fun.

OWNER'S IMPRESSIONS

Since March 7th, my Morgan has carried me solo from Boston to Florida and back . . . and then to California. At the Sebring 12-hour race Gus Ehrman and I had a trouble-free run and won 1st place in our class (2000-3000 cc). The car has also provided miscellaneous around-town and Sunday driving. Having driven it over 13,000 miles, I feel that the car is thoroly good.

Good (tho not ideal) for the sort of trips I was taking . . . driving over 750 miles per day occasionally; good for rushing around thru mountainous country for the sheer fun of it; good for rallies and hill-climbs; yet good for puttering thru city traffic. For a small sports car its power-weight ratio is fine. With quick gearbox work you can keep up with (and usually beat) the De-

All engine accessories are fully accessible when the very light Morgan hood is lifted.

troit iron in acceleration. However, for "big-time" competition (i.e., road racing) the advertised 68 hp at 4200 rpm just isn't enough for the 1900 pound curb weight (call it 1850 pounds in racing trim). In the 1930-3000 cc class you are left rather far behind the Ferrari, Aston Martins and Frazer-Nashes.

The traditional Morgan independent front suspension features kingpins sliding within nearly vertical tubes, around which are the coil springs—two per side, an upper and a lower one. The telescopic shock absorbers are mounted in front of this at a slightly skew angle. The ride of the Plus Four seems to be a shade stiffer than an MG TD but softer than a TC. The final drive is Hotchkiss (hypoid), the only point of interest being that the leaf springs are unshackled. Mounted with rubber bushings at the front, the main leaves pass straight thru slots in the tubular cross member at the rear of the frame. This sliding joint requires greasing every 500 miles—a shorter distance than is recommended for any other fitting except the sliding kingpins—which receive engine

No modern sports car has more businesslike, traditional lines than the Morgan Plus Four.

Owner Wilder jauntily extends little finger and with extreme matador-like grace deftly erects the Morgan's removable-fabric top.

oil at 50 mile intervals, if the driver remembers to push the button on the floorboard.

The car's unusual suspension results in a cornering ability par excellence, as well as giving the driver the added assurance of remaining nearly level while cornering. The rear wheels will break loose if you try hard. It is difficult to avoid over-correcting for this as the tail seems to swing back with great alacrity to the opposite side. I think a track rod and larger shock absorbers would be useful at the rear, but in lieu of making these changes, I have been experimenting with the tire pressures. In front I now run 25 psi in 5.25 x 16 tires, at the rear 20 psi in 5.50 x 16 tires. Cornering ability is improved over previous pressure settings. In regard to replacement, I wish now I'd kept the stock 5.25's or gone to 5.00 x 16 all around.

Adjacent to the fascinating front end is a major weakness in the design, the Burman cam steering box. Ever since the car was delivered, there has been substantial play in the steering, tho I am now told this can probably be adjusted out. Rack and pinion steering would be a welcome improvement on future models. The tie-rod is mounted with rubber bushings which adds nothing to a solid feel but prevents road shocks from reaching the driver.

The four-wheel Girling hydraulic brakes (two leading shoe in front) are of large size, tho the brake fade has appeared; the first time while driving very vigorously on California's twisting Route #1. However, I suspect grease on the linings had a bit to do with this and the two subsequent fadings. Unlike old soldiers, my brakes seem to be dying (of abuse, not old age).

When in the cockpit, one immediately notices the low seating position which contributes to the much better than usual protection from the wind. The doors are very comfortably edged with a leatherette-covered strip of foam rubber. The equally comfortable pneumatic seats cannot be temporarily

(Continued on page 83)

The MORGAN 'PLUS FOUR'

Three Versions of an Inexpensive Fast Car Continue Without Major Changes

SPORTING CONVERTIBLE.—Sparkling performance and full weather protection for two people are offered by the 2.1-litre drop head coupé Morgan.

FOR 1953, the Morgan Motor Co., Ltd., continue to offer their 2.1-litre " Plus Four " sports model in two-seater, four-seater and two-seater convertible coupé forms. Combining good road holding with a power-to-weight ratio which is quite unique amongst cars of comparable price, these models have scored a notable series of successes in rallies and other sporting events during the past two years.

The rubber-mounted power unit of the Morgan comprises a Standard Vanguard engine, the power output of which is quoted as 68 b.h.p., specially mated to a sturdy four-speed synchromesh gearbox. One of the unique features which this model has inherited from past Morgan practice, is the use of a large-diameter steel tube to position the gearbox some distance back from the engine and clutch; this layout permits a short and rigid gear lever to be ideally positioned, there being no need for a remote gear control, and no long propeller shaft to induce vibration at high speeds.

A chassis frame with Z-section side members allows the floor level to be lowered in the manner usually associated only with front-wheel-drive cars, and in conjunction with relatively firm suspension ensures roll-free cornering.

The four wheels are independently sprung, by a modern version of the familiar Morgan layout, using coil springs and near-vertical slides, and underslung half-elliptic springs with sliding-trunnion ends locate the hypoid-geared rear axle; a point which will be appreciated by those who do their own routine maintenance work is a simple one-shot oiling system for the i.f.s., leaving only four grease nipples and two accessible oil-can points requiring regular attention on the front and rear suspension and the steering mechanism.

The low-built two-seater open body, which at a price of only £565 (excluding British Purchase Tax) has proved very popular, is of classic style, offering good all-weather equipment and useful luggage capacity. A drop-head version of the two-seater, with sliding glass windows, offers increased internal body width. The range is completed by a four-seater tourer which is surprisingly comfortable and good-looking in view of the modest dimensions of the chassis.

Sample performance figures recorded during our Road Test of a two-seater model last autumn were: 0-50 m.p.h. in 9.9 secs.; 30-50 m.p.h. using top gear in 7.7 secs.; a maximum speed of 84.7 m.p.h.; and an overall fuel consumption of 25.6 m.p.g.

A number of detail refinements have been incorporated into Morgan " Plus Four " cars during the past year. Improvements in the steering dampers, and stronger front suspension springs, may be mentioned as examples. Also, an alternative final drive ratio of 3.73 is now available to order at an extra cost of £10, this offering faster cruising than the usual 4.10 ratio at the expense of slightly abated top gear acceleration.

MORGAN " PLUS FOUR "

ENGINE.—Dimensions: Cylinders, 4; bore, 85 mm.; stroke, 92 mm.; cubic capacity, 2,088 c.c.; piston area, 35.2 sq. ins.; valves, pushrod o.h.v.; compression ratio 6.7/1. **Performance:** Max. power, 68 b.h.p. at 4,200 r.p.m.; max. b.m.c.p., 128 lb./sq. in. at 2,000 r.p.m.; b.h.p. per sq. in. piston area, 1.93; peak piston speed, ft. per min., 2,530. **Details:** Carburetter, Solex 32 B10 downdraught; ignition, Lucas coil; plugs (make and type), 14 mm. Champion L10; fuel pump, AC mechanical; fuel capacity, 11 galls.; oil filter, Purolator by-pass; oil capacity (including filter), 12 pints; cooling system, pump, fan and thermostat; water capacity, 11 pints; electrical system, Lucas 12-volt; battery capacity, 51 amp. hr.

TRANSMISSION.—Clutch, Borg and Beck 9A6-G; gear ratios: Top, 4.1 (optional 3.73); 3rd, 5.4 (optional 4.9); 2nd, 8.0 (optional 7.28); 1st, 13.5 (optional 12.3); rev., 13.5 (optional 12.3); prop. shaft, Hardy Spicer, open; final drive, Salisbury hypoid bevel.

CHASSIS DETAILS.—Brakes, Girling hydraulic; brake-drum diameter, 9 ins.; friction lining area, 121 sq. ins.; suspension: front, coil and slide i.f.s.; rear semi-elliptic; shock absorbers, front; Girling (telescopic); rear, piston; wheel type, steel disc; tyre size, 5.25 by 16; steering gear, Burman worm and nut; steering wheel, 17-in. spring-spoke.

DIMENSIONS.—Wheelbase, 8' 0"; track: front, and rear, 3' 11"; overall length, 11' 8" (coupé and 4-seater, 11' 10"); overall width, 4' 8"; overall height (windscreen), 3' 10" (coupé, 4' 2" over roof); ground clearance, 6"; turning circle, 34'; dry weight (2-seater), 15 cwt.

PERFORMANCE DATA.—Piston area, sq. in. per ton, 47.0; brake lining area, sq. in. per ton, 161; top gear m.p.h. per 1,000 r.p.m., 18.3 (optional 20.2); top gear m.p.h. at 2,500 ft./min. piston speed, 76.0 (optional 83.5); litres per ton-mile, dry, 4,570 (optional 4,130).

LIGHT AND LOW.—The layout of the low-built chassis, with its coil spring i.f.s. and underslung semi-elliptic rear springs, is visible in this photograph. The gearbox is set back some distance from the engine, but forms part of the same rubber-mounted unit assembly, and the chassis illustrated has provision for mounting twin spare wheels directly on the tail of the frame.

"... fifteen minutes concentrated work with a shovel ..."

Winter Odyssey

A Morgan Plus Four shakes the sand out of its shoes and gets some snow on its boots.

By Denys Peterson

TO the exile in Egypt, Christmas in England seems a highly desirable goal; and to one who has experienced two full years of stifling heat under a merciless blue sky, the prospect of a winter holiday is one of unusual attractiveness. To add an even keener edge to my anticipation were the facts that my previous assignment had been for three years in Austria, for whose lovely mountains and valleys I yearned, and that I am the possessor of a Morgan Plus Four drophead coupé of 1951 vintage who was as tired as I was of the eternally flat, dusty, boring desert highways of Lower Egypt. In fact, all the ingredients for a perfect holiday were there: all that remained was to combine them to the best possible advantage.

After a careful survey of all the available means of trans-Mediterranean transport, my choice fell for reasons of economy on the Jugoslav State Steamship Line *Jugolinija*, which was prepared to convey myself, my baggage, and the 850 kilograms of *Putzi II* to the shores of Europe for the astonishingly small sum of £45 sterling, in the somewhat odd division of £30 for me, eating three meals a day, and £15 for Putzi, eating nothing at all. These Jugoslav boats are little freighters of 3,000 tons, carrying up to 12 passengers as a sideline. Their rates are over 100 % lower than those of the fast 11,000-ton passenger liners which operate from Genoa, Naples and Venice. The ships are comfortable and well appointed—every cabin with a private bath—but they suffer from the basic trouble of cargo boats in that their movements are dictated by the available freight.

However, from Alexandria, they guarantee to land you either at Venice, Trieste, or Rijeka (the pre-war Fiume), and as these ports are only about 200 kilometres distant by road, the maximum probable lateral deviation is insignificant when compared with the total axial distance to be travelled.

As it so happened M/N. *Skopje* sailed only two days behind schedule and landed Putzi and me on the quayside of Trieste at noon on December 13, along with 5,000 bales of cotton from the Nile, 15,000 cases of oranges from the Lebanon, and 20 tons of garlic from Syria—which mercifully had travelled in strict seclusion in the strong-room. We parted with affection, and Putzi, crammed to the roof with assorted luggage and with a pair of eight-foot hickory skis strapped on outside, stormed out of the dock gates, clearly as eager as I was to sample once again the qualities of Italian roads and high-octane fuel.

Administrative Setback

We were not bound directly for Britain, but had a date in Vienna and an appointment in Geneva—somehow one cannot imagine a "date" in staid Geneva, and an "appointment" in Vienna could scarcely be really serious. However, in Trieste at the very start we had a bad check to our plans. The little Free State is under Allied tutelage and, together with other doubtful blessings of Anglo-Saxon culture, the English week-end is firmly established. December 13 was a Saturday, alas, and, at the very moment of our docking, officialdom had already placed its feet on the mantelpiece until Monday morning. Hence no permit to cross the Russian Zone of Austria in order to reach Vienna was to be had, and the delay of two clear

Mediterranean regained—the coast line between Rijeka and Opatija.

n the Arlberg-
...asse between S.
...nton and Inns-
bruck.

days would be too great with Christmas but 12 days away. I knew my Russians too well to risk the transit without a "grey card" in my pocket, diplomatic passport notwithstanding, and so the visit to Vienna receded in the nostalgic limbo of the might-have-been. Still, all was not lost, and a little violent cabling made Innsbruck and not Vienna a port of call.

A quick study of the map and a little searching of my memory assured me that the best way to Innsbruck ought to be via Udine, Cortina d'Ampezzo, and thence along the old South Tyrol highway to Fortezza and the Brenner, so, with this project in mind, we took off along the magnificent coast road from Trieste to the Italian frontier proper at Monfalcone. But Putzi was plainly furious at having been denied Vienna and so, on a particularly lonely stretch of road, she quietly, malevolently, and irrevocably burned out her ignition coil—about the only foreseeable spare with which we were unprovided. . . . By the time I had hitch-hiked back to Trieste, acquired another at an astronomical lira figure, returned and fitted it, things didn't look so good, and Innsbruck uncomfortably distant. But Putzi, during her period of enforced contemplation, had apparently repented of her ill-humour and decided that in any case it wasn't fair to take it out on me, and she snored along to Udine at a steady 120-125 k.p.h., taking her corners as sweetly and gracefully as a contented Morgan will.

Impasse

I had no snow chains and, indeed, on the 1951 Morgan dropheads it is impossible to fit them (an oversight since remedied on the 1952 models), but with 68 b.h.p. on tap from the 2-litre Vanguard engine, a delicate throttle toe, and plenty of easily changed gears, I was pretty confident of being able to surmount any reasonable hazard that might lie ahead. But again, Fate, or what you will, stepped in, and at dusk, at the foot of the first serious ascent at Pieve di Cadore, I saw the ominous sight of a line of stationary traffic ahead. Inquiry revealed that an incautious *autotreno* driver had skidded on the first hairpin, jack-knifed his trailer, and overturned, neatly sealing off the whole of the roadway. Local talent assured me that all would be well in an *oretta*, but I knew these Italian "little hours" of old, and I saw no future at all in the situation. Without any hesitation whatsoever, I turned Putzi in her tracks before more traffic could silt up behind and headed back down the pass on the long and dreary

150-kilometre detour through Trento and Bolzano. Before, during, and after Trento road conditions became appalling. There had been a good deal of slushy snow during the day which the wheels of the heavies had worn into deep ruts. This, with the coming of night, had frozen solid. To make matters worse, a thickish mist had descended, against which headlights were worse than useless; and it was bitterly cold. Driving in those ruts was a nightmare, for the Morgan, with her 9-in. ground clearance aft, was continually bottoming on the centre bank, and any attempt to leave the "tramlines" was to court disaster. Over and over again, I blessed the hypoid back end with the prop. shaft *inside* the car, where it could come to no harm. I made the market square of Bolzano at one-thirty in the morning, nearly dead on my feet, but relieved and triumphant at being there.

I felt, though, that I was in no fit state to tackle the Brenner then and there, comparatively easy pass though it is, and so I turned into the ever-open Hotel Griffone for the luxury of a hot bath and an hour or two of sleep. By six o'clock, a good deal recovered and in the best of spirits, I was once again under way, and, as we climbed the foothills of the Alps, it was clear that for once the gods were with us, for the rising sun discovered a cloudless sky and a perfect day, with a surface of level packed snow on which to travel. Putzi positively sang up the slopes, executing neat and dazzling "christies" on the bends, and, soon after eight, was chuckling quietly at the frontier officials, who were very gratifyingly surprised to see us at that early hour. "*Che bellina!*" exclaimed the Customs man, pointing at Putzi. "*Aber schon ist der Wagen!*" they said on the Austrian side. "Yes," I thought, "beautiful indeed!" as I brought her to rest outside the Arlbergerhof at 9 a.m. on the dot.

Building-in Warmth

I spent the whole day in Innsbruck, feeling my way back into that glorious *Gemutlichkeit* which makes Austria "home" for evermore to those who have lived there and learned to love her. Putzi spent the day in a workshop being fitted with an interior heater, for the horrifying experiences of the previous evening and night had convinced me that I could not hope to enjoy a long trip through a European winter without one, with my blood nicely thinned out by the Egyptian sun. Although it meant losing a whole day on schedule, thus risking my appointment in Geneva, and driving to the Swiss border by night, the delay was well worth while, for the whole character of the ride changed as I felt the pervading and grateful warmth blowing up from under the scuttle. It was the first interior heater I had ever had in 20 years of motoring—but I'll never be without one in future. Warm and relaxed, rather than hunched and shivering, one's reactions are immeasurably improved, and a much higher psychological safety factor is available. I had feared drowsiness as a result of interior heating, but I was amazed to discover that the exact reverse was the truth.

Traction to Spare

Putzi now had another passenger aboard, but she didn't seem to resent the extra weight at all as she pounded up the long, long Tyrolean valley towards the forbidding barrier of the Arlberg. I thought the pass would probably be too much to ask of any car on a winter's night, and I intended to avail myself of the train service through the tunnel which cuts off the worst of the road. But, alas, there were no more trains that night, and so over the top or nothing it had to be. "Can we do it?" I anxiously asked at S. Anton. They looked at the car without enthusiasm and shrugged. "You can try," they said. But, of course, from the outside, the Morgan is a deceptive little car—it could so easily be a "ten" (and was, not so long ago). I had faith, but even I doubted as we gingerly assailed that first frightful hairpin at Moserkreuz. I need not have worried. Putzi, with two up, with four heavy suitcases, with every available cranny crammed with impedimenta, and with no snow chains, sailed over S. Christoph with traction to spare, albeit the snow walls on either hand stood a foot and more proud of her little roof. Superb vehicle! My running log shows that she did the 189 km. from Innsbruck to Schaan in four and three-quarter hours, which included a coffee in Bludenz and the crossing of the Liechtenstein frontier after Feldkirch—an average of just under 40 k.p.h.

Bed in the pocket principality of Liechtenstein was sheer delight. Just try the Hotel Risch in Schaan sometime, preferably after a long drive through snow and darkness at more than ten below, and you will know what I mean!

The next stretch through Zurich to Berne was mere child's play despite the thawing slush, and the following day's run for lunch in Geneva scarcely more than a perfunctory potter. Saturday teatime to Tuesday lunch, with 1,250 km. on the clock, with two Alpine passes and three frontiers behind, driving mostly in the dark, although by no means near Monte-Carlo standard, was not too discreditable, we felt. Actual driving time had been just under 26 hours, giving a running average throughout of just over 47 k.p.h.

Business in Geneva satisfactorily disposed off, Putzi was pushed on to Auxerre (how she enjoyed the N-6!) and then allowed to rest.

Winter Odyssey - - - - - - -

On the following day Putzi took us faultlessly to Paris for lunch, posed for a photograph before the Louvre, and then hustled on to Dunkirk, protesting a little at the pave in the Pas de Calais, and delivered us at the Ferry Dock with time to burn.

On the way from Dover to Bexhill, her final destination, Putzi broke her fanbelt bang outside the Standard service station, and was highly amused when I promptly produced a spare from her own tool locker. "Well, of course," she said, "if I'd only known you had *that* on board——"

While in England I took the opportunity of driving Putzi down to her ancestral home at Malvern Link, where she received a great welcome and the company demonstrated that they mean what they say in the foreword to the Instruction Book— "our interest in every Morgan continues until the car is is scrapped." They remembered Putzi as an individual, and they treated her as such. Peter Morgan asked what criticisms I had after two years of desert use, and I told him candidly. In every case I mentioned, since 1951 a "mod." had already been developed. Steering dampers, which are comparatively fragile can now be replaced in half an hour without dismantling the front suspension; the clutch thrust pin has been strengthened;

"Putzi securely lashed to the after well deck."

an aircleaner is now fitted to the Solex downdraught carburetter; the cooling properties of the radiator have been improved; the doors have been sealed against dust penetration by rubber sponge strips, and the wheels are now slotted for snow grips. These were exactly the criticisms I had found to make. Without further ado, Putzi was trundled into the shops and modified to 1952 standards, and I drove her away with an even increased respect for the integrity of her makers, and a complete confidence in the marque as such. We then celebrated her partial renaissance by leaving Malvern just before four, having tea in Cheltenham, dinner in Oxford, and being safely at home on the Sussex coast well before midnight, in spite of all a miserable English winter night could do to stop us.

After a very pleasant sojourn in the land of our fathers, we faced the prospect of the journey back, the sadness of which was to be palliated by a week's ski-ing in the Austrian Alps, and one foggy night (we didn't *choose* it: it chose us) we set out again for Dover. Well as I know Sussex, by the time I reached Rye I was utterly baffled, and hadn't a clue as to where the road was. As I sat gloomily at the wheel wondering

The old port of Dubrovnik, on the Dalmatian coast of Jugoslavia, where the M/N Skopje called.

what on earth to do for the best, a lighted bus thundered past, the magic word "Folkestone" on its destination board. I ripped Putzi into action, tore off up the road after the bus and when it pulled into Rye station yard I asked the driver's permission to follow him through to Folkestone. This he readily gave, and we made the trip in splendid time—he was less than five minutes late on schedule.

In Folkestone I found another bus which piloted me to Dover. A big "thank you" to those two drivers: without their skill and expert local knowledge I could certainly never have reached the port that night. On the other side of the Channel, when we finally reached it hours late, things were no better regarding the fog, but rather worse in general, as the road was covered with "verglas." After a somewhat apprehensive start from Boulogne at 11 a.m. though, by dint of much local bus following, I managed to reach Chateau Thierry for bed— 275 soul-searing km. from the coast. The next morning the fog was as thick as ever, and Geneva, at 450 km. distance, seemed to be quite out of the question. But yet another bus got me to Troyes and after that the fog cleared and the treacherous "verglas" gave way to good honest snow on which Putzi was by now quite at home.

Clear Passage

Thus, contrary to all expectation, we stood on the frontier at La Cure by eight p.m. Neither the French nor the Swiss authorities evinced the slightest desire to leave their offices in order to examine Putzi's nether extremities in search of her chassis number, etc.—which was not surprising as the thermometer stood at 15 below and a keen breeze was blowing. Putzi, thus trusted and enfranchised, sailed down the Col de la Givrine in an exalted mood, her tail end pleasantly but not alarmingly adrift, her normal marked degree of understeer completely nullified by the smooth snow surface. We finished up in Geneva in grand style with a beautiful broadside, neither of us in the least weary.

But on the following day all was not well, as fountains of hot water from the radiator testified. "Gasket," I thought, notwithstanding the fact that she continued to fire on all four cylinders and didn't seem to drink her water at all. However, undue pressure in the radiator can be but one thing and so, reluctantly, off came her head. Gasket trouble it certainly was, but the burn was so slight and so curiously situated that although it could let the compression *out*, it could not let the water *in* on the induction stroke.

All this delayed us for some hours, of course, and we only reached Konstanz that night, crossing in the morning on the ferry to Friedrichshafen in order to take the longer though easier road through Germany to Lindau rather than that serpentine affair that leads through Nafels to Buchs and is far too narrow for comfort when there is snow about. I can recommend this northern route to anyone finding themselves in Switzerland and wishing to reach Austria in a hurry—a very natural reaction. Putzi then further distinguished herself by climbing the Arlberg Pass from *west* to *east* without chains, a vastly more difficult feat than her earlier performance on this pass, and one which the gendarme in Stuben village below the first hairpin swore couldn't be done at all. But we did it.

Up at S. Christoph, 5,450 ft. above sea-level, I had a glorious five days of quite perfect sunny weather with wonderful sport, hissing down the long gleaming open

Innsbruck for breakfast: Putzi on her way down the snowy Brenner Pass.

slopes over crisp dry snow; sunbathing (and getting burnt) with the ground temperature 10 below, a fantastic experience. Putzi got a 15 minute tickover each day just to keep her in form, but apart from that was allowed to sleep in peace in the open air, heavily drugged with antifreeze.

Off to Austria

On the closing night of my stay the beautiful weather broke, and I awakened in the morning to find no Putzi—just a big white heap. Fifteen minutes concentrated work with a shovel revealed her to sight though, and she started on the button without demur. Once the snowplough had been through and opened up the pass we slithered off, Vienna-bound at last, the Russian permit safely clipped into my passport.

Vienna offered its eternal charm, of course, and so completely demoralized Putzi that she would only fire on three cylinders at speeds below 50 k.p.h., although she went the whole hog when driven faster. This odd tendency defeated me, and completely baffled two electricians, who could find nothing wrong. The third found it by accident—a tired contact-breaker spring that had lost its temper. By no means obvious—but oh, how understandable!

At last a melancholy telegram from the shipping agency ordered us south: "Skopje" lay at the quay in Rijeka and would not be denied. So regretfully we left our beloved Austria through that most lovely of all her provinces, Carinthia. Heads high, but a tear suspiciously and uncomfortably near, we re-embarked for Egypt.

Now here we are steadily pounding down the Adriatic, me snug in my cabin, Putzi lashed down to the after well-deck. She has 7,500 proud km. on her clock, and I have my running log to con over to bring back happy memories of the astounding exploits through fog and darkness, through snow and ice, of Putzi, the magnificent Morgan.

Queer ideas of holidays these English have—or have they?

MORGAN Plus 4 TOURER

Photographs by Rolofson

Sparse dash is neat but lacks essential tachometer. Note instrument cluster.

From the rear, and with the top folded, the Plus 4 is clean-lined.   But should it rain, the Morgan might well hide its head.

Arguments pro and con on classic styling may rage on forever, but there is no denying that one of the greatest charms of the imported sports car is its ability to bring back memories of the past, with the added advantage of greatly reduced depreciation to keep the argument on a firm dollar and cents basis.

Less controversial is the question as to whether there is a demand for a genuine sports car offering extra passenger accommodation. The Morgan Plus 4 tourer, with seats for four, is such a car, and its classic styling and brisk performance leave no room for doubt as to its claim to the title "sports car."

One of the problems associated with small 4-seater sports cars is the provision of a neat appearing top with full headroom for all passengers. In the Morgan the rear seat is over the rear axle and as a result, the rear passengers sit slightly higher than those in front. This in turn requires a high top that inevitably looks rather odd. But a sports car owner usually buys a car such as this to enjoy the benefits of open-air motoring, and the top is inevitably folded at every reasonable opportunity. When the rear seat is unoccupied, the tonneau cover gives the Plus 4 the unmistakable air of a smaller replica of one of the great old Bentleys at Le Mans.

The Bentley illusion is further heightened by the firm ride, the quick steering and the flexibility of an engine large enough to do the job. Yet, the smooth acting, four-speed transmission is a joy to use and gives the Morgan a dual personality. Driven conservatively, the car has no trouble keeping up with traffic; driven briskly, the performance is more than satisfying.

There is also an open two-seater model and a two-seater convertible for those who do not need the extra seats.   ●

The four seater model is a rarity in the United States although it has been in constant production. Note single spare tire.

The body styling has been altered slightly. At the rear, two exposed spare wheels maintain the traditional appearance, and the somewhat angular two-seater is unchanged up to the scuttle. In front, however, a new cowl replaces the plated radiator, and the headlamps are faired into the mudguards, which extend farther forward than before. There may be a fractional reduction in wind resistance, but the greatest gain is in rigidity. The new front end stiffens up the chassis and suspension assembly, to the benefit of roadholding.

The driving position is just about ideal. The seat cushions and squabs give exactly the right support, and the high tunnel over the gearbox stops the passenger sliding into the driver's lap on

JOHN BOLSTER TESTS

THE MORGAN PLUS-FOUR

With TR2 Engine Sports Two-Seater can Reach 100 m.p.h. and has Exceptional Acceleration

An interesting and quite recent development among sports cars is the provision of extremely high performance in vehicles of moderate price. Several cars now exist which bring a genuine 100 m.p.h. maximum within reach of the man who, formerly, had to be content with the non-performing type of sports model. The Morgan has always been a formidable contestant in rallies by virtue of its exceptional acceleration and controllability. Now, the adoption of the Triumph TR2 engine has added 100 m.p.h. motoring to those assets, and at £585 this is the cheapest car which can encompass "the full ton".

I have covered many enjoyable miles in previous Morgans, but the fastest of them would not exceed 92 m.p.h. It was thus with a feeling of anticipation that I journeyed recently to Malvern with the object of trying out the latest model. To put all doubts at rest, let me say, straight away, that against the stop-watch, timed in both directions, the car *does* achieve 100 m.p.h. It needs a long run to get the last 2 or 3 m.p.h., but the Morgan is now definitely in the exclusive 100 m.p.h. class. Incidentally, the speedometer read 5 m.p.h. *slow* at maximum speed.

However, I anticipate. At the works I was able to examine the cars in course of construction. As before, the frame is straight with Z section members, which pass beneath the rear axle. The cross members are tubular, and the floor-cum-undershield is attached to the bottom flange of the chassis. The underslung rear springs are located by

Silentbloc bushes in front, and slide in trunnion blocks behind.

The independent front suspension is of time-honoured Morgan design. The stub axles slide up and down on extended king pins against helical springs and are controlled by Girling telescopic dampers. There is still a single-piece track rod ahead of the wheel centres, but it is now of larger diameter, and the steering gearbox is entirely new. It is of cam and sector type and operates a transverse drag link.

Another typical Morgan feature is the mating of the engine and gearbox. The Elektron bell housing is connected by a tube to the front anchorage of the box, so that it is brought right back amidships. A short, vertical lever on the lid of the gearbox is thus perfectly placed for the driver's hand. An extension shaft connects the clutch with the gearbox primary shaft, and an open Hardy Spicer propeller shaft takes the power to the hypoid axle.

fast bends. The particular car which I was using was one for the American market, and consequently it had left-hand drive. This brought the central gear lever under the right hand, which suited a personal preference of mine. The car also differed from the domestic version in having a special grade of upholstery, flashing indicators, and a spot-lamp.

All the controls work very nicely. The clutch is dead smooth, but cannot be made to slip; nor do the rear springs "wind up", as happens with many modern cars. The gearbox has synchro-mesh on the three upper speeds, and the ratios suit the characteristics of the engine perfectly. That short, rigid lever allows exact control of the gears, and is a delight to use. The hand brake lever is of the proper "fly-off" type, and is powerful in action.

The steering is very "quick", requiring only two turns from lock to lock, and one can "feel" the front wheels, as in

ACCELERATION GRAPH OF THE MORGAN PLUS-FOUR

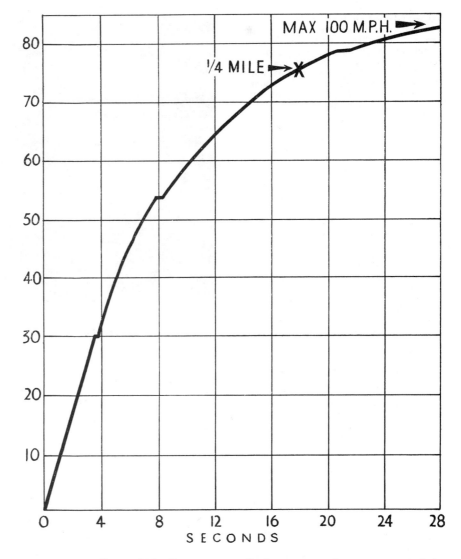

a good vintage car. I thought it was rather on the heavy side, though I am informed that it would probably become lighter with use. A foot-operated lubricator keeps the front suspension and steering parts well oiled.

On the road, the car covers the miles with delightful ease, and I found myself putting up some exceptional averages under give-and-take conditions. The acceleration is very good indeed, the 0-60 m.p.h. figure of 10.8 secs. being somewhat remarkable for a fully equipped 2-litre. Above 75 m.p.h. the acceleration curve begins to flatten out, no doubt due to wind resistance, but 90 m.p.h. comes up fairly quickly, at which speed the engine does not seem at all highly stressed.

Understeering Characteristics

The handling characteristic is an understeering one, and the car can be drifted by the judicious application of power. The behaviour on wet roads is excellent, and one can slide deliberately under perfect control. Fast cornering not only appears safe to the onlooker but feels safe to the occupants, and there is virtually no roll. The ride is considerably harder than is fashionable nowadays. The car is firm and steady and travels smoothly on reasonable surfaces, but the more severe bumps are definitely felt. Nevertheless, it rides more comfortably than any previous Morgan, principally due to the improved bracing of the front end.

The brakes are powerful in normal use, and are smooth and responsive in action. Really hard driving, however, including frequent heavy braking from near the century mark, may cause some lack of progressiveness to be noticeable. Serious fading does not occur, but a slight tendency to pull or grab gives a gentle hint that things are warming up. The brakes quickly return to normal, and no noticeable wear took place during my test.

I have previously commented on the comfort of the seats, and this is aided by the very low floor, which allows one to sit in a natural position. With the sidescreens in place, the driver and passenger are well protected, and the slight burble of the exhaust is carried away on the wind, so one covers the ground in effortless ease. The hood is effective, cosy, and easy to erect, but, like most of its kind, it does magnify engine noises somewhat. I do not say that the car is then unusually noisy, but the delightful silence of the open vehicle is lost. I have no doubt that a little extra padding, or the use of carburetter intake silencers, would overcome this slight criticism. An owner who wished to make long journeys with the hood up could easily have this work carried out.

Large Luggage Space

Behind the seats there is a large luggage space. This could well form a comfortable seat for one medium-sized child or two small ones, which renders the Morgan an attractive proposition for the young family man. Accessibility for adjustments and maintenance is far above the average, which will appeal to the enthusiast who likes to do his own work. A useful tool kit is carried under the bonnet, ready for use.

A rather remarkable feature of my test was the fuel economy of the Morgan. This was actually some 9 m.p.g. better than the previous model of the

NINETY B.H.P. is delivered by the 2-litre TR2 engine fitted in the car tested. The large-bore twin SU carburetters are standard.

same make which I tested, in spite of a 10 m.p.h. improvement in maximum speed! The figure given in the data panel was taken during some extremely hard driving, and any normal user could rely on averaging at least 35 m.p.g. The combination of an efficient engine in a light car, pulling a high gear ratio, has worked once again.

In spite of this high gearing, the machine is very flexible. It will pull strongly away at 15 m.p.h. on top gear, and can, in fact, remain in that ratio nearly all day. What a pity, though, not to use that lovely little gear lever!

The Morgan is an attractive car in the vintage tradition. It makes little attempt to emulate the smooth lines and soft ride of the typical modern vehicle, but for sheer controllability and fierce acceleration it ranks very high by any standards. There are a few little details that I would like to alter if I were ordering one—for instance, I think the steering wheel is half an inch too close to the facia panel—but such personal whims can be easily satisfied in a hand-made sports model like this. Above all, the car has been greatly improved without losing its essential character, and I am sure it will make many new friends for this old-established name.

SPECIFICATION AND PERFORMANCE DATA

Car Tested: Morgan Plus Four Sports two-seater. Price £585 (£829 17s. 6d. with P.T.).

Engine: Four cylinders 83 mm. x 92 mm. (1,991 c.c.). Pushrod operated overhead valves. 90 b.h.p. at 4,800 r.p.m. 8.5 to 1 compression ratio. Twin S.U. carburetters. Lucas coil and distributor.

Transmission: Borg and Beck 9 ins. single dry plate clutch. Four-speed Moss gearbox with short central lever directly on top of box. Ratios: 3.72, 5.1, 7.3 and 12.5 to 1. Short open Hardy Spicer propeller shaft. Salisbury hypoid rear axle.

Chassis: Z section, underslung at rear. Independent front suspension by stub axles sliding upon extended king pins against helical springs. Cam and sector steering. Semi-elliptic rear springs with Silentbloc bushes and sliding trunnion blocks. Girling hydraulic dampers all round, front telescopic type, rear piston and lever. Pierced disc wheels fitted 5.25 x 16 in. tyres. Girling 2 L.S. hydraulic brakes in 9 in. drums.

Equipment: 12-volt lighting and starting. Speedometer, rev. counter, clock, water temperature, oil pressure, and fuel gauges.

Dimensions, etc.: Wheelbase, 8 ft. Track, 3 ft. 11 ins. Overall length, 11 ft. 8 ins. Turning circle, 30 ft. Weight, 16 cwt.

Performance: Maximum speed, 100 m.p.h. Speeds in gears: 3rd, 78 m.p.h.; 2nd, 52 m.p.h.; 1st, 30 m.p.h. Standing quarter mile, 17.9 secs. Acceleration: 0-30 m.p.h., 3.6 secs.; 0-40 m.p.h., 5.2 secs.; 0-50 m.p.h., 7.4 secs.; 0-60 m.p.h., 10.8 secs.; 0-70 m.p.h., 14.6 secs.; 0-80 m.p.h., 23.8 secs.

Fuel Consumption: Driven hard, 31.6 m.p.g.

DIMENSIONS

A *Overall height, 4 ft. 4½ ins.*
B *Clutch pedal to seat, 1 ft. 8 ins.*
C *Steering wheel to seat cushion, 6 ins.*
D *Height of seat, 9½ ins.*
E *Squab to steering wheel, 1 ft. 4 ins.*
F *Seat to roof, 3 ft. 0½ in.*
G *Height of boot, 1 ft. 2 ins.*
H *Length of boot, 1 ft. 8 ins.*
I *Wheelbase, 8 ft.*
J *Overall length, 11 ft. 8 ins.*
K *Overall width, 4 ft. 8 ins.*
L *Width at elbows, front seat, 3 ft. 4 ins.*
M *Width of seat cushions, 1 ft. 3 ins.*
N *Width of seat back, 3 ft. 6 ins.*
O *Width of boot, 3 ft. 1 in.*

OFFICE: Large, easy-to-read instruments are provided on the well-planned facia panel of both left-hand and right-hand drive models.

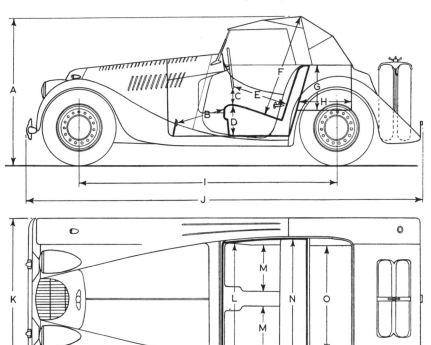

A NEW 2½-LITRE SPORTS-RACER?

IT is not unlikely that a famous British sports-racing car will make its appearance later in the season with a 2.5-litre engine. First race will probably be the Nürburgring "1,000 kilometres", to be followed by the Tourist Trophy.

INTERNATIONAL DATE FOR AINTREE

THE Winfield Joint Committee have transferred their International date to Mrs. Topham and, on 2nd October, the B.A.R.C. will organize the event on the new Aintree circuit. This has been done with the full cognizance of the R.A.C., and although the W.J.C. regret having to make the transfer, a variety of difficulties have forced them to do so. There will, however, be consolation for Scottish enthusiasts in the fact that the W.J.C. will stage a National meeting at the Charterhall circuit on 4th September, and the transfer of the International date has been made without prejudice to the Winfield Joint Committee's organizing of an International meeting next season.

NEW LONDON MAP

"MOTORING About London" is a handy up-to-date map published for the Dunlop Co. by Geographia Ltd. at a price of 4s. 6d. It gives the through-town routes officially recommended by the M.O.T., with main, connecting and ring routes picked out in distinctive colours.

Small, compact and purposeful, the Morgan is one of the few remaining adherents to this type of bodywork. Wide doors make for easy entry and exit—with the hood down. The large fuel filler cap is situated in the centre at the top of the rear-mounted tank. Twin spare wheels are rigidly mounted on an extension of the chassis frame.

The Autocar ROAD TESTS

No. 1531:

MORGAN PLUS FOUR SPORTS TWO-SEATER

THERE are very few manufacturers who have concentrated on sporting cars with such singleness of purpose as the Morgan company. It is true to say that there has never been a non-sporting Morgan. Ever since the first Four-Four was produced in 1936 it has been the policy of the company to build cars which will accelerate from rest to, say, 60 m.p.h. and come to a standstill again in the shortest possible time. A fair top speed has been the result, and in sporting events, where a good power-weight ratio has told, the Morgan has frequently been successful.

In 1951, for an increase in weight of only 22 per cent, the 1,267 c.c. engine—also of Standard manufacture—was replaced by the 2,088 c.c. Vanguard engine, giving an increase in b.h.p. of no less than 70 per cent in conjunction with a redesigned chassis frame. Now the 68 b.h.p. Vanguard engine has been replaced by the 1,991 c.c. Triumph TR2 unit with its 90 b.h.p., the maximum power has been increased by a further 32 per cent without any increase in weight, and the Morgan has joined the select company of 100 m.p.h. cars.

Those are stages in the development of the Morgan from a lively sporting car to a definitely potent machine. The likeable robust character of the car is still there, however. Minor styling changes have been made around the front—concessions, only, to the modern trend—but the car remains a survival of the off-the-peg competition car of the 'thirties and what, to many people, is the best type of sports car. There are slight crudities, possibly, and certain refinements to which the somewhat spoilt modern motorist is accustomed are lacking. Fundamentally, however, this recipe of an excellent power-weight ratio and a simple chassis gives reliability without high stresses. The extraordinary performance is proof that the ingredients are right.

Within a very short space of moving away from rest a driver strange to it becomes at home in this Morgan, which gives the driver complete confidence. One of the outstanding features is the sheer joy an enthusiastic driver gets from handling it. The suspension is independent in front by the sliding stub axle system first used in principle by Morgans in 1911, and by leaf springs at the rear. Though the vertical coil

Unfamiliar frontal treatment has now submerged the Morgan radiator, and the former external filler cap has disappeared beneath the bonnet, in keeping with the modern trend. The Lucas "Flame thrower" lamp on the car tested is not a standard fitting.

springs in the front suspension were lengthened by 3in when the chassis was redesigned and strengthened for the Vanguard engine, the ride is still stiff and firm. In spite of this, the car does not tire the crew; on two 300-mile journeys undertaken during the test period very much the reverse was found.

The chassis and bodywork give the impression of being sturdy and on rough surfaces there is no tell-tale sideways movement of the scuttle. The cam and sector steering which has replaced the type used on the previous models is light, sensitive and accurate. There is none of the feeling of having to "steer" the car along fast, straight stretches; one needs only to hold the thin, notched wheel rim lightly in the fingers and the car does the rest. The steering is sensitive to road "feel," yet transmits very little shock.

On fast, open bends it is necessary only to bear on the wheel towards the corner, rather than to steer the car round; there is a slight understeer, a good point with a car of this type. As only two turns are required from lock to lock, even slight movements of the steering wheel are transmitted to the road wheels. On sharper corners the Morgan holds the road beautifully and one finds oneself looking forward to the twisting bends of a familiar route, for the pleasure of dealing with them without a reduction in speed and free from the slightest signs of roll.

Doubts Dispelled

It is difficult to believe the comparative accuracy of the speedometer, so quickly does the car gather speed, and, until the instrument had been checked against the electric speedometer, its truthfulness was seriously doubted. This suspicion was proved to be unfounded, however, and 80s and 90s so frequently seen in this car are, in fact, near to being genuine. The cruising speed is limited only by road and traffic conditions and, on suitable roads, an indicated 90 m.p.h. can be reached quickly and held for as long as conditions allow.

With the car's excellent power-weight ratio it is to be expected that the acceleration should be good, as indeed it is. That the 100 m.p.h.-plus test maximum, reached within approximately 1¼ miles, was no flash reading is shown by the fact that an indicated top reading of 105 (a true 102 m.p.h.) was reached on the road with hood and sidescreens in position and two in the car. This speed was reached during the actual testing with only the driver in the car; the windscreen had been removed and the passenger side of the cockpit was covered by the tonneau cover.

The manner in which the Morgan covers long distances is most impressive. A very familiar run of 268 miles—normally reckoned as a day's march—was completed in 5 hr 35 min and included a stop for petrol and a 15-minute stop for food.

The "control room." All the instruments needed by the discriminating driver are there. Oil pressure gauge, ammeter, fuel gauge and water thermometer are grouped to the left of a central panel which has the speedometer to the right. On later examples than the car tested, the revolution counter, to the extreme right, has black figures on a white dial to match the other dials.

This, admittedly, was by night, but the average of about 50 miles in each hour is an indication of the car's capabilities. During this and other runs it was found that all but the fastest cars were overtaken, and even those left the Morgan behind only when they were driven with an enterprise seldom seen.

Hill-climbing, too, is inspiring. The famous Porlock, in North Somerset, was climbed lightheartedly in second gear, the revs building up to over 4,000 between the hairpins. In the West Country, also, a 1 in 5½ climb was taken from a standing start at the foot; by the half-way mark the engine was pulling happily in top gear, which it continued to do for the remainder of the ¼-mile climb. In traffic the car's progress is swifter than most. Its compact size, good visibility and brisk acceleration make it possible to take advantage of every gap.

The four-cylinder o.h.v. engine, with its compression ratio of 8.5 to 1 and output of almost 45 b.h.p. per litre, is smooth and gives the impression of having very little work to do at all normal road speeds. The engine is not particularly quiet, though what noise there is—mostly from the valve gear —is not troublesome. The exhaust note is surprisingly subdued for a car of this nature. In built-up areas there is no back-echo when driving between houses and at high speed it is quiet, as heard by a bystander, except for a shrill whistle.

Gear Change

The clutch is smooth and light in operation and was well able to stand up to full-throttle gear changes and the fierce initial getaway when the acceleration test figures were being taken. The synchromesh on the example tested was worn and was easily over-ridden; the car in question, though not its engine, had covered 16,000 miles of strenuous driving, which included the recent R.A.C. Rally. The position of the short central gear lever is ideal and one tends to use third speed rather more than is strictly necessary because of the pleasant nature of the gear change and the acceleration available. Actually, the car will pull away easily in top from 15 m.p.h. and will climb any main road hill comfortably in this gear. Gear box noise is confined to a pleasant hum. A vibration period occurred on the overrun in third gear at about 40 m.p.h., though over only a small range.

A certain amount of criticism may be directed at the brakes, which, for a car with such a fine performance, need to be very good. Though they were well able to stop the car quickly when necessary, the pedal had a peculiarly "dead"

The seats are comfortable and good support is given by the one-piece back rest. On current production models the "dished" steering wheel is replaced by one with flat spokes and the column is lengthened. The central pad between the seats is not standard.

feeling and a considerable amount of pressure was required when the full stopping power was needed. During the main road period of the test they would pull up the car in a straight line from 75 m.p.h. with the driver's hands off the steering wheel. After the performance figures had been taken, however, they tended to pull over to the right, though there was no increase in pedal travel.

One of the outstanding impressions on sitting behind the wheel is of the lowness of the car; one can touch the road comfortably. The seats are located between the frame members, the floorboards resting on their lower flanges. Though it is felt that the seat itself might be slightly higher, both front wings are visible. As a result one can aim the long, almost level bonnet with great accuracy, and in traffic the car is ideal. Entry to the cockpit calls for some degree of nimbleness, though one soon gets accustomed to it.

No adjustments are provided for either the separate seat cushions or the one-piece back rest, though it would be an easy matter to "tailor" the driving position for an individual driver with chocks of wood. The fly-off hand brake lever is short and centrally placed; in the "off" position it is rather far forward and might be slightly inconvenient for a short

driver to reach. The hand brake holds the car adequately on both up- and down-grades and is fully up to "stop-and-restart" conditions of trials and rallies.

Two large dials in a central panel contain a grouped ammeter, oil pressure, and fuel and water temperature gauges to the left, and speedometer to the right; the latter dial includes total and trip mileage recorders and a small inset clock. To the right of the facia is a revolution counter, which is slightly obscured by the steering wheel. Lamp, ignition, starter, horn, panel and fog light switches are grouped in the centre of the facia. It is felt that the horn button tends to be cluttered up by other switches and might well be moved to a better position. A small open locker is placed to the left, opposite the passenger.

The twin windscreen wiper blades clear an adequate area and the motor is located below the scuttle. The non-variable instrument lighting is too bright and tends to dazzle the driver; a rheostat would be a welcome addition. The double-dip head lamps are adequate, though to use the full performance at night on a strange road it was desirable to supplement them with the non-standard driving lamp fitted to the car tested.

MORGAN PLUS FOUR SPORTS TWO-SEATER

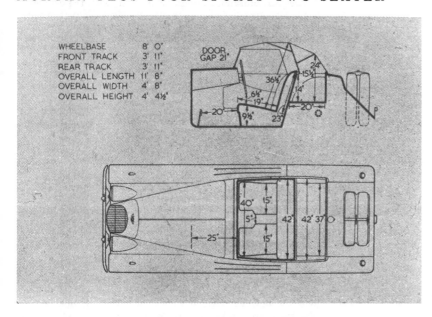

WHEELBASE 8' 0"
FRONT TRACK 3' 11"
REAR TRACK 3' 11"
OVERALL LENGTH 11' 8"
OVERALL WIDTH 4' 8"
OVERALL HEIGHT 4' 4½"

DOOR GAP 21"

PERFORMANCE

ACCELERATION: from constant speeds. Speed, Gear Ratios and time in sec.

M.P.H.	3.72 to 1	5.1 to 1	7.3 to 1	12.5 to 1
10—30	—	5.5	4.0	2.9
20—40	8.4	5.4	3.9	—
30—50	8.4	5.9	4.6	—
40—60	8.6	6.1	—	—
50—70	9.6	7.3	—	—

From rest through gears to:

M.P.H.	sec.
30	3.5
50	9.0
60	13.3
70	17.5
80	24.5
90	35.9

Standing quarter mile, 18.5 sec.

SPEED ON GEARS:

Gear		M.P.H. (normal and max.)	K.P.H. (normal and max.)
Top	(mean)	96.3	155.0
	(best)	102.0	164.2
3rd		63—80	101—129
2nd		42—54	68— 87
1st		24—32	39— 51

SPEEDOMETER CORRECTION: M.P.H.

Car speedometer	10	20	30	40	50	60	70	80	90	100	105
True speed	11	20	30	39	50	58	68	77	87	97	102

TRACTIVE RESISTANCE : 20 lb per ton at 10 M.P.H.

TRACTIVE EFFORT :

	Pull (lb per ton)	Equivalent Gradient
Top	258	1 in 8.8
Third	350	1 in 6.3
Second	483	1 in 4.6

BRAKES :

Efficiency	Pedal Pressure (lb)
87 per cent	135
54.3 per cent	100
31.5 per cent	50

FUEL CONSUMPTION :
30 m.p.g. overall for 760 miles (9.4 litres per 100 km.).
Approximate normal range 26—33 m.p.g. (10.9—8.6 litres per 100 km.).
Fuel: First grade.

WEATHER : Dry; light to fresh breeze. Air temperature 42 degrees F.
Acceleration figures are the means of several runs in opposite directions.
Tractive effort and resistance obtained by Tapley meter.
Model described in *The Autocar* of September 29, 1950.

DATA

PRICE (basic) with two-seater body, £585. British purchase tax, £244 17s 6d. Total (in Great Britain), £829 17s 6d.
Extras: Heater, £8 12s.

ENGINE: Capacity: 1,991 c.c. (122 cu in).
Number of cylinders: 4.
Bore and stroke: 83 × 92 mm (3.27 × 3.62in).
Valve gear: Overhead; push rods.
Compression ratio: 8.5 to 1.
B.H.P.: 90 at 4,800 r.p.m. (B.H.P. per ton laden 88.6).
Torque: 130 lb ft at 2,600 r.p.m.
M.P.H. per 1,000 r.p.m on top gear, 21.

WEIGHT (with 5 gals fuel): 16¾ cwt (1,876 lb).
Weight distribution (per cent): F, 49.3; R, 50.7.
Laden as tested: 20¼ cwt (2,276 lb).
Lb per c.c. (laden): 1.14.

BRAKES: Type: F, Two-leading shoe. R, Leading and trailing.
Method of operation: F, Hydraulic. R, Hydraulic.
Drum dimensions: F, 9in diameter; 1¼in wide. R, 9in diameter; 1¼in wide.
Lining area: F, 39.8 sq in; R, 39.8 sq in (78.3 sq in per ton laden).

TYRES: 5.25—16 in.
Pressures (lb per sq in): F, 19; R, 19 (normal). F, 24; R, 24 (for fast driving).

TANK CAPACITY: 11 Imperial gallons.
Oil sump: 12 pints.
Cooling system: 16 pints.

TURNING CIRCLE: 33ft (L and R).
Steering wheel turns (lock to lock): 2.

DIMENSIONS: Wheelbase: 8ft 0in.
Track: F, 3ft 11 in; R, 3ft 11in.
Length (overall): 11ft 8in.
Height: 4ft 4½in (hood erected).
Width: 4ft 8in.
Ground clearance: 7in.
Frontal area: 7¼ sq ft (approximately).

ELECTRICAL SYSTEM: 12-volt; 54 ampère-hour battery.
Head lights: Double dip; 36-36 watt bulbs.

SUSPENSION: Front, independent; coil springs and sliding stub axles. Rear, half-elliptic springs.

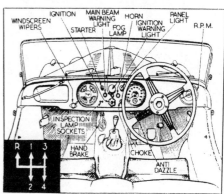

The good lines of the car are in no way spoiled when the hood is erected. The rear window is of non-cracking plastic to avoid damage when the hood is stowed. The lower parts of the sidescreens are hinged flaps to allow for hand signalling. No traffic indicators are fitted.

ROAD TEST

The driving position is, in general, very comfortable by enthusiast driver standards; both the seat cushions and the back rest give ample support and after a long journey there are no signs of stiffness or soreness. As so often in this type of car where there is a large shaft tunnel (in the Morgan this contains the gear box) there is nowhere to rest the left foot when it is not operating the clutch. One is forced either to hold the foot poised just above the pedal or to rest it flat on the floor by bending the knee—neither of which positions is particularly comfortable. The dip switch is placed on the toe board above the shaft tunnel.

Close to the dip switch is another foot-operated plunger; this operates a one-shot lubrication system for the sliding stub axles of the i.f.s. Depressing the plunger allows engine oil, under pressure, to reach the suspension units; a momentary reduction in the reading on the oil pressure gauge indicates that this supply is taking place.

Though no wet weather was encountered during the test period it is felt that the weather protection would be adequate. The hood frame stows neatly behind the seats and the hood cover is separate. After a "practice run" it can be erected in two or three minutes. The sidescreens are rigid and are held securely to the doors by knurled thumb-screws; a small key is provided to tighten these. Wind noise is fairly considerable with the hood up, though it does not billow unduly. A certain amount of rattle is caused by the forward edges of the sidescreens against the windscreen frame.

There is more luggage accommodation than is usually available in a small two-seater and this space is protected by the hood. When the hood is stowed a neatly fitting cover clips over the luggage compartment and a separate cover is supplied to fit over the passenger seat if it is unoccupied. In general the quality of the weather equipment is good and, in the closed state, the interior of the car is warm if a little draughty. Visibility from beneath the hood is adequate though it is difficult to see traffic lights from close up.

An asset of this type of bodywork and general layout is the extreme accessibility of the engine and auxiliaries. Though the radiator cap is no longer externally mounted on the radiator shell it is readily reached by lifting the two-piece bonne Carburettors (twin S.U.s), dynamo, distributor, dipstick, oil cleaner, and so on are all easily reached; from the point of view of the type of person who is likely to own this car, it is a joy to maintain. Two six-volt batteries, connected in series, are mounted on either side of the hypoid bevel rear axle, beneath the floor of the luggage compartment. It is necessary to remove two screws to lift the floorboards out and check battery and rear axle levels.

The only parts requiring frequent attention with the grease gun—every 500 miles—are the rear spring slides. Apart from these there are six points requiring grease at intervals of 3,000 miles and a further nine at 5,000-mile intervals. Hand tools, jack, pump and starting handle are stowed in a compartment on the bulkhead, beneath the bonnet. The jack, which lifts the entire side of the car, is particularly neat and quick in operation. The seat cushion on the side to be raised is removed and a small plate is found which covers a hole in the floorboards. The jack is lowered through the hole and a peg on the body of the jack is inserted in a hole in a cross member; the whole operation takes less than two minutes.

Fuel consumption throughout the test (with the exception of the abnormal conditions prevailing when the performance figures were taken) averaged 30 m.p.g., with a maximum of 33 m.p.g. obtained during a main road journey. A minimum of 26.6 m.p.g. was obtained while hill-climbing in North Devon and Somerset. Oil consumption was slightly high, four pints being used in 1,008 miles. Part of this consumption may be attributed to over-generous use of the suspension one-shot lubrication system.

Generously Cooled

Starting from cold is good; the engine fires almost at once. It takes some time to warm up, however, and intermittent use of the choke control is required for up to two miles. In normal running conditions the water temperature, in air temperatures up to 50 deg, seldom rose above 65-70 deg C, which suggests that the engine may be over-cooled. There was a flat spot at the lower end of the range, which had some effect on the acceleration figures from the lower speeds in top and third gears.

The Morgan with the engine now fitted is a specialist car with a wonderful performance. It does not pander to the creature comforts and, in exchange for a slightly Spartan outlook on the part of the driver, it will give him real pleasure. Its ability to cover the ground is outstanding and it is a joy to drive however long the journey. Though one or two criticisms have been directed at the particular car tested it must be remembered that the Morgan is not a quantity produced car in the true sense; it can hardly be said that any particular example is "standard." The points criticized are there, but one forgets most of them in enthusiasm for the performance. And it should be borne in mind that though by successive increases in engine size and output for a given total weight a brilliant straight road performance must inevitably result, the steering and chassis development — with the possible exception of the brakes — have kept pace with the performance, and the cornering and handling qualities are excellent.

Pre-war accessibility: the Triumph TR2 engine could not be much more accessible, a state of affairs which should gladden the heart of the most enthusiastic owner-mechanic. Spare plugs are carried in a rack on the shelf to the left, at the back of which is the tool compartment, not shown in the photograph.

MORGAN PLUS FOUR

. . . and more!

photographs by Rolfson

THERE ARE no two ways about it. The new Morgan with the 1991 cc Triumph TR-2 engine is a true sports car in the "grand tradition", and not even the most fastidious purist will be disappointed in driving it. Short on comfort, long on performance, this agile two-seater is sure to be a car to reckon with in sports competition during the coming year.

The Morgan company has had a reputation for producing a sporting breed of 4-wheelers since 1936, but their quantity has always been meagre, not exceeding a few hundred cars per year. In 1951 the com-

pany began using the 2088 cc Vanguard engine in their car, yielding 68 bhp, but now, switching to the very reliable TR-2 engine, horsepower has been upped to 90 with no increase in weight, and the car becomes a very tempting package with its $2595 price tag.

There is little change in the outside appearance of the new Morgan, and its low, rugged lines are retained along with the unique characteristic of two rear-mounted spare tires. The grille has been altered (but not necessarily improved) by curving the top section back into the hood, and the hood itself is copiously louvered along its top and sides. The wheels are still the same disk type with small holes cut out, and their replacement with wire wheels, shortly to be offered as an optional extra, would definitely brighten up the car's overall character.

On the inside, not many concessions have been made to comfort. The seating arrangements consist of nothing more than a straight-across back and two unattached cushions placed on wood; and since nothing is adjustable, *you* have to fit the car instead the other way around. The floor is, however, cut down low on each side of the transmission, and leg-room is ample for any size person. The dash is of dark varnished wood, with the instruments grouped in three large dials, and a small, open glove compartment is placed on the passenger's side. For bad weather, side curtains clip on, and the top, the canvas for which is not attached to the frame but clips on all around when the frame is erected, is surprisingly weatherproof. Windshield wipers are electric, and the motor to run them has been moved under the hood instead of being dash-mounted as before. Doors are cut low and open from the rear, and with top and curtains up, getting in and out is not an easy proposition until the correct "technique" is mastered.

One of the first impressions that nearly everyone seems to gain about the car is that it is strongly reminiscent of the old MG TC—but with lots of muscle. The chassis is now extremely rigid, and the suspension

Morgan instruments are legible and now include a tachometer.

The 2-litre Standard TR-2 engine has wet cyl. sleeves.

(coil springs and sliding stub axles in front; semi-elliptics in rear) gives a ride which can only be described with kindness as "firm". However, as a result, the car handles with astounding precision and accuracy, and the driver is never without a feeling of complete control. As an added fillip, there is a one-shot, foot-operated lubrication system which allows engine oil, under pressure, to reach the sliding stub axles of the i.f.s.

Our bright red test car was loaned and driven by its owner, Mel Chaitlin, physical director at the Beverly-Wilshire Health Club, who having taken delivery only a week earlier, was kind enough to have stayed up late nights putting miles on the car before our roadtest. At the beginning of testing, however, the Morgan had only 1127 miles on the odometer, and the engine, though running smoothly throughout, still seemed tight. Consequently the best top speed run (100 mph on the nose) would doubtless improve after a few more thousand miles. In deference to the tight engine, only two top speed runs were made (top up and curtains in place), but the engine showed no signs of overheating at any time. The 0-60 acceleration average was a more-than-commendable 10.8 sec, which should enable the Morgan to please its owner at the average stop-light encounter. The four-speed gearbox is free and easy to handle, and the speed of shifting is limited only by the driver's technique. Strangely enough, the tachometer is "red-lined" at 4500 rpm, but the engine's peaking point is 4800 rpm. With the engine's capabilities in mind, the suggestion might be ventured that the tach be "yellow-lined" at 4500 and "red-lined" at 5000 rpm. The indicated rpm at 100 mph was only 4600. Speedometer readings were refreshingly accurate throughout the speed range, never indicating more than three mph over actual speed. Quietness is not one of the car's virtues, but engine and exhaust noise does not reach an objectionable degree, and the most noticeable sound at speed is a carburetor whistle that makes the car resemble a barreling tea-kettle.

Inevitably, the Morgan will be compared to the Triumph TR-2, since the engines are identical. The TR-2 tested in March 1954 had a test weight 150 lbs greater than the Morgan; it also had a 4-speed gearbox *with* overdrive. Although the TR-2's top speed was about 3 mph faster, the Morgan's 0-60 time was less by 1½ secs, and the standing quarter times were virtually the same, as was gas consumption. The Triumph costs about $100 less and offers a little more in the way of comfort, but the Morgan looks and feels a little more like the classic conception of the old-time sports car. The safest thing to say is that the coming year should provide some exciting competition in Class E! ●

Appearance is unusually neat with top up.

ROAD AND TRACK ROAD TEST NO. F-2-55

MORGAN TR ROADSTER

SPECIFICATIONS

List price	$2595
Wheelbase	96.0 in.
Tread, front	47.0 in.
rear	47.0 in.
Tire size	5.25 - 16
Curb weight	1940 lbs
distribution	48.5/51.5
Test weight	2260 lbs
Engine	Triumph 4 cyl.
Valves	pohv
Bore & stroke	3.27 x 3.62 in.
Displacement	121.5 cu in.
	(1991 cc)
Compression ratio	8.50
Horsepower	90
peaking speed	4800
equivalent mph	98.0
Torque, ft/lbs.	116.5
peaking speed	3000
equivalent mph	62.6
Mph per 1000 rpm	20.9
Mph at 2500 fpm	86.5
Gear ratios (overall)	
4th	3.73
3rd	5.24
2nd	7.38
1st	12.85
R & T performance factor	49.7

PERFORMANCE

Top speed (avg.)	98.4
best run	100.0
Max speeds in gears—	
3rd (5000)	74
2nd (5000)	53
1st (5000)	30
Shift points from—	
3rd (4500)	67
2nd (4500)	48
1st (4500)	27
Mileage	28/32 mpg

ACCELERATION

0-30 mph	4.0 secs
0-40 mph	5.5 secs
0-50 mph	7.9 secs
0-60 mph	10.8 secs
0-70 mph	15.1 secs
0-80 mph	21.2 secs
0-90 mph	29.9 secs
Standing ¼ mile —	
average	18.3
best	18.1

TAPLEY READINGS

Gear	Lbs/ton		Mph
1st	590	at	27
2nd	480	at	35
3rd	340	at	44
4th	245	at	52
Total drag at 60 mph, 117 lbs			

SPEEDO ERROR

Indicated	Actual
10	12.8
20	21.8
30	30.1
40	39.2
50	49.0
60	59.2
70	68.0
80	77.6
90	89.0

Morgan TR Roadster
Acceleration through the gears

ROAD and TRACK

SECONDS

A businesslike silhouette has always been a feature of the Morgan. The pierced wheel discs help brake cooling

NEW MODEL FROM MALVERN

Morgan 2-seater Tourer with Ford Engine

A NEW and cheaper model from the Morgan Motor Co., Ltd., a very long established manufacturer of sports cars, is added to the range for 1956. Basically similar to the other models in chassis design and external appearance, the new Morgan—to be known as the 10 h.p. Series II—will cost £638 12s 6d, including purchase tax, and is therefore more than £200 cheaper than the more potent TR2-engined car.

The chassis frame is similar to that used for the Plus Four models—the main side members, which curve inwards at the front, are a deep Z cross section, joined by rigid box section cross-members. The flooring of the body is attached to the bottom flanges of the chassis members. The well-known Morgan independent front suspension is employed and this, together with the low centre of gravity, provides the excellent road-holding qualities for which the make is famous. The system uses upper and lower tubular cross-members which are spaced well apart, and are continued outwards to carry stationary swivel pins. These tubes are diagonally braced together and provide a strong and light structure which forms part of the sprung weight. A sleeve which carries the stub axle slides up and down each swivel pin. Above the

sleeve and round the pin is a coil compression spring, and below the sleeve a short rebound spring. Rear suspension is by half elliptic leaf springs, carried inboard of the frame members. Telescopic dampers are fitted front and rear.

The standard 1,172 c.c. side valve Ford engine and three-speed gear box unit are flexibly mounted in the frame, and the use of the combined engine-gear box unit has given slightly more space between the seats. On the Plus Four models, a separate gear box is fitted and this is placed some distance from the engine.

In its untuned condition the Ford engine is claimed to develop 36 b.h.p. at 4,400 r.p.m. with a compression ratio of 7.0 to 1. The new Morgan will certainly appeal to the enthusiast, who, if not satisfied with the already quite lively and adequate performance of the production car, can take advantage of the very many aids to greater acceleration and maximum speed that are available for this particular power unit.

The steel panelled, two-seater body is built in the Morgan works and the only noticeable difference between the new model and the existing Plus Four two-seater is the sloping tail, which is recessed to accommodate the single spare wheel. A single piece windscreen with easily

detachable frame is provided, and a hood and side screens form part of the equipment. The one-piece back rest of the seats is adjustable.

The TR2-engined version of these taut little cars, which are so popular in the U.S.A., is continued unchanged. Three types are available with the TR2 engine, the two- and four-seater tourers and the two-seater coupé. A coupé and a four-seater tourer fitted with the Standard Vanguard engine complete the range.

SPECIFICATION

Price.—£450, U.K. Purchase Tax £188 12s 6d. Total in United Kingdom £638 12s 6d.

Engine.—Number of cylinders—4. 63.5mm × 92.5mm (2.5in × 3.64in), 1,172 c.c. B.H.P. 36 at 4,400 r.p.m. Compression ratio 7.0 to 1. Side valve.

Clutch.—Single dry plate, hydraulic operation.

Gear Box.—3-speed and reverse ratios: Top 4.4, 2nd 8.25, 1st 15.07, reverse 19.71 to 1.

Rear Axle.—Hypoid—ratio 4.4 to 1.

Suspension.—Front, independent, vertical coil; rear, half elliptic.

Tyres.—Size 5.00 × 16in.

Petrol.—Tank capacity—8 galls.

Dimensions.—Wheelbase 8ft; track 3ft 11in; overall length 12ft; width 4ft 8in; turning circle 33ft. Dry weight 1,430lb (12¾cwt).

The lines are trim and businesslike, and there is good visibility from the driving seat. New treatment of the rear panelling is very neat

Make: Morgan

Type: 4/4, Series II

Makers: The Morgan Motor Co., Ltd., Pickersleigh Road, Malvern Link, Worcs.

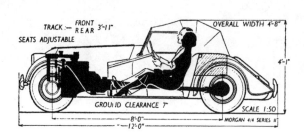

TRACK:— FRONT 3'-11" REAR
SEATS ADJUSTABLE
OVERALL WIDTH 4'-8"
4'-1"
GROUND CLEARANCE 7"
SCALE 1:50
8'-0"
12'-0"
MORGAN 4/4 SERIES II

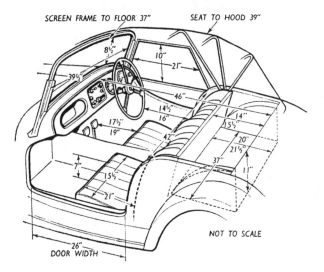

SCREEN FRAME TO FLOOR 37"
SEAT TO HOOD 39"
8½"
10"
21"
39½"
46"
14½"
16"
14"
15½"
17½"
19"
42"
20"
21½"
7"
37"
11"
15½"
21"
26"
DOOR WIDTH
NOT TO SCALE

WEIGHT

Unladen kerb weight	.. ..	13¾ cwt.
Front/rear weight distribution..		48/52
Weight laden as tested	.. ..	17 cwt.

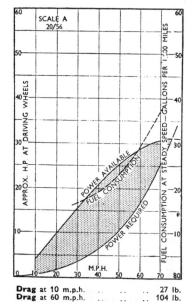

Drag at 10 m.p.h. .. .. .. 27 lb.
Drag at 60 m.p.h. .. .. .. 104 lb.

Specific Fuel Consumption when cruising at 80% of maximum speed (i.e. 60.2 m.p.h.) on level road, based on power delivered to rear wheels .. 0.86 pints/b.h.p./hr.

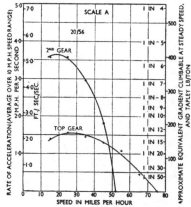

Test Data

CONDITIONS. Weather : Warm, dry, slight breeze (temperature 62-64 °F., barometer 30.0-30.1 in. Hg). Surface : Smooth dry tar macadam. Fuel : Premium.

INSTRUMENTS.

Speedometer at 30 m.p.h.	.. ..	7% fast
Speedometer at 60 m.p.h.	.. ..	3% fast
Distance recorder	.. ..	2% slow

MAXIMUM SPEEDS

Flying Quarter Mile

Mean of four opposite runs ..	.. 75.3 m.p.h.
Best time equals	.. 76.3 m.p.h.

"Maximile" Speed (Timed quarter mile after one mile accelerating from rest)

Mean of four opposite runs ..	.. 74.1 m.p.h.
Best time equals	.. 75.0 m.p.h.

Speeds in Gears

Maximum speed in 2nd gear ..	52 m.p.h.
Maximum speed in 1st gear ..	27 m.p.h.

FUEL CONSUMPTION

60.0 m.p.g. at constant 30 m.p.h.
52.0 m.p.g. at constant 40 m.p.h.
43.0 m.p.g. at constant 50 m.p.h.
33.5 m.p.g. at constant 60 m.p.h.
27.0 m.p.g. at constant 70 m.p.h.

Overall consumption for 745 miles, 21.2 gallons, =35.1 m.p.g. (8.04 litres/100 km.)

Fuel tank capacity 8 gallons.

ACCELERATION TIMES Through Gears

0-30 m.p.h.	.. .. ..	6.4 sec.
0-40 m.p.h.	.. .. ..	10.3 sec.
0-50 m.p.h.	.. .. ..	16.0 sec.
0-60 m.p.h.	.. .. ..	26.9 sec.
0-70 m.p.h.	.. .. ..	47.8 sec.
Standing Quarter Mile	.. ..	23.0 sec.

ACCELERATION TIMES on Two Upper Ratios

	Top	2nd.
10-30 m.p.h.	13.5 sec.	5.6 sec.
20-40 m.p.h.	13.2 sec.	6.2 sec.
30-50 m.p.h.	14.7 sec.	8.9 sec.
40-60 m.p.h.	17.2 sec.	—
50-70 m.p.h.	31.2 sec.	—

HILL-CLIMBING (at steady speeds)

Max. gradient on top gear	1 in 13.5 (Tapley 165 lb/ton)
Max. gradient on 2nd gear	1 in 6.3 (Tapley 350 lb/ton)

BRAKES at 30 m.p.h.

0.98g retardation	..	(=31 ft. stopping distance) with 110 lb. pedal pressure
0.96g retardation	..	(=31½ ft. stopping distance) with 100 lb. pedal pressure
0.77g retardation	..	(=39 ft. stopping distance) with 75 lb. pedal pressure
0.51g retardation	..	(=59 ft. stopping distance) with 50 lb. pedal pressure
0.21g retardation	..	(=143 ft. stopping distance) with 25 lb. pedal pressure

Maintenance

Sump: (incl. filter) 5½ pints S.A.E. 20. **Gearbox:** 1¾ pints, S.A.E. 80 E.P. **Rear Axle:** 2 pints, S.A.E. 90 E.P. **Steering gear:** S.A.E. 90 E.P. **Radiator:** 12 pints (1 drain tap). **Chassis Lubrication:** By grease gun every 2,000 miles to 2 points and every 5,000 miles to 7 further points. Use steering lubrication pedal in cockpit every 150 miles. **Ignition timing:** 5° B.T.D.C. **Spark Plug gap:** 0.025 in. **Contact breaker gap:** 0.014-0.016 in. **Valve timing:** Inlet opens 3½° B.T.D.C. and closes 56½° A.B.D.C. Exhaust opens 47½° B.B.D.C. and closes 12½° A.T.D.C. **Tappet clearances:** (Cold) Inlet and exhaust 0.0115-0.0135 in. **Front wheel toe-in:** ⅛-³⁄₁₆ in. **Camber angle:** 2°. **Castor angle:** 4°. **Tyre pressures:** Front 16 lb., Rear 16 lb. (increase to 19 lb. front and 18 lb. rear for fast driving). **Brake fluid:** Girling High Temp. **Battery:** 12 volt, 32 amp./hr. Ref. B/12/56.

The MORGAN 4/4 Series II

An Attractive Open Two-seater with Good Handling Qualities and Notable Economy at a Very Modest Price

LOWERED bonnet and scuttle, compared with the Plus Four, give a very sleek appearance to the traditional Morgan outline of the new 4/4 Series II, but even a tall driver remains well-protected by the windscreen and has a good view through it.

A T £713, including purchase tax, the Series II Morgan 4/4 is not only the cheapest open two-seater at present on the market, but sells at some £200-£300 less than the normal run of current sports cars.

Introduced at the Earls Court Show last autumn, it represents a welcome attempt to cater for a type of motorist who has been largely neglected since the war, namely the driver whose leanings are all towards a sports car, but whose resources are on a scale appropriate only to a popular family saloon of 10 h.p. or thereabouts. Modestly, its makers call it a tourer and, to the extent that its performance is frankly not in the same class as that of the 2-litre Morgan Plus Four and other sports cars of similar category, that description is appropriate. This small Morgan does, however, offer all the handling qualities expected of a sports car, plus a most attractive-looking body in the modern-traditional style.

In standard form, with the Ford Anglia power unit untuned, it offers a maximum speed of 75 m.p.h., a rest-50 m.p.h. acceleration figure of 16 sec. when carrying two people and some test instruments, and a most frugal appetite for fuel; the 4/4, in fact, goes down on the short list in *The Motor* road test records as a car which reached 60 m.p.g. (at 30 m.p.h.) in the constant-speed consumption tests; its overall figure recorded over a distance of 745 miles was 35.1 m.p.g., this covering a good deal of the distinctly hard driving inevitably associated with a Road Test.

Two points are worth emphasizing at

In Brief

Price: £475 plus purchase tax £238 17s. equals £713 17s.

Capacity		1,172 c.c.
Unladen kerb weight ...		13¾ cwt.
Fuel consumption	...	35.1 m.p.g.
Maximum speed ...	...	75.3 m.p.h.
"Maximile" Speed	...	74.1 m.p.h.

Maximum top gear gradient 1 in 13½

Acceleration:

10-30 m.p.h. in top	...	13.5 sec.
0-50 m.p.h. through gears		16.0 sec.

Gearing: 16.8 m.p.h. in top at 1,000 r.p.m.; 27.8 m.p.h. per 1,000 ft. per min. piston speed.

this point: one is that the choice of an Anglia engine and gearbox (with a high-ratio rear axle) not only contributes very materially to keeping down the initial cost to the very competitive figure quoted, but means also that the owner has at his disposal the advantage of Ford service in price and availability anywhere in the world; the other is that tuning kits for these engines are readily available at moderate cost so that, having purchased the car in standard form, buyers have great scope for subsequent tuning.

At a later date, it is hoped to carry out a supplementary test showing what can be

done in this respect. Here, however, remarks must be confined to the standard product. In this state, the car will cruise happily at a true 65 m.p.h., regaining this speed fairly readily after a check. Right up to the maximum—as, indeed, at any other part of the range—the unit is free from vibration periods but acceleration tails off appreciably over the last 10 m.p.h. of the speed range.

In second gear, 52 m.p.h. is possible before valve bounce sets in and 45 m.p.h. may be regarded as the easy maximum for normal use, with 50 m.p.h. available when maximum acceleration is required. Undoubtedly, a four-speed gearbox would be an advantage for opportunist overtaking on winding or busy roads, but the cost of departing from the complete Ford engine-gearbox unit would have entailed a disproportionate increase in the cost of the car.

Docile Engine

There is the fact, too, that the Anglia engine has good low-speed torque and the Morgan will trickle along very happily at 1,000 r.p.m. (approximately 17 m.p.h.) in top and accelerate away quite readily. The exhaust becomes "healthy" in the manner of this type of car as the revs. rise, but the noise level does not reach the point of irritation or embarrassment.

Starting from cold is easy and the initial warming-up period does not last long. A

PLACED well forward in the chassis, the Ford Ten engine is easy of access for routine maintenance; there is a useful tool-box on the scuttle. Passing through the centre of the scuttle is the remote-control gear linkage.

SEEN here on its native heath, the 4/4 Series II reveals built-in headlamps, ventilated disc wheels, fixed windscreen and louvred bonnet. Product of a company whose founder is still active, the latest Morgan retains the effective sliding-axle and coil-spring i.f.s. used since pre-World War I days.

bonnet hinged down the centre gives good access to all the points normally requiring attention, but a minor annoyance is a dipstick on the right-hand side and an oil filler on the left. The model tried, with a mileage of 9,000 behind it, used some oil, but the consumption was not excessive—actually 3 pints in 750 miles.

The clutch is one after the enthusiast's heart, taking up the drive positively without need for any undue finesse in engagement. In conjunction with an unusual but effective gear-change mechanism, it assisted in providing the sort of quick concise gear changes which delight the keen driver. As those who read the original descriptions of this model will recall, the lower portion of the ordinary Ford central gear lever is retained and is linked by a simple yoke to a horizontal rod running backwards into the cockpit, the rod passing through a flexible bearing which allows some angular movement as well as a push-pull action. The horizontal rod is suitably cranked and terminated in a normal gear lever knob, the arrangement being such that movements across the gate are achieved simply by moving the knob to the appropriate side, actual engagement being by a push-pull motion. Once one obtains the knack of using the gear lever in this manner (and resisting any temptation to impart a twisting action as called for by some Continental designs) the Morgan arrangement is entirely straightforward and positive. The only snag of the arrangement is that the normal gear lever positions are reversed laterally.

Responsive Steering

The handling qualities of the Series II 4/4 may be summed up by saying that they are entirely in keeping with the sleek appearance of the car. The steering is high-geared (2½ turns from lock to lock) but not heavy, and there is a quick response to the wheel which is most satisfying. Unlike some cars where this applies, there is no call for constant attention on changing cambers or in gusty cross-winds, neither is there any objectionable reaction through the wheel on bad roads. Fast cornering produces no appreciable roll and the car has no violent understeer or oversteer qualities which need to be learnt. Neither, in fact, has it any objectionable tricks on wet roads.

In common with all other Morgans from the early days (and that phrase means well pre-World War I in the case of this marque), the Series II 4/4 has independent front suspension by sliding axles and coil springs, but the spring rate has been very considerably lowered on this model to give a ride which, whilst firm by modern touring-car standards, is nevertheless much softer than on former models. The result is a very comfortable ride and good road holding, the only fault being a tendency for the springs to bottom on bad potholes. The rear suspension is well matched but, in common with all cars which have an underslung frame at the rear, downward movement of the axle is positively restricted by the frame and the contact between the two can be felt if a hump is taken at high speed.

As will be seen from the figures on the data page, the brakes are both light and progressive, and are, in fact, the sort of brakes which one very soon comes to take absolutely for granted. The hand brake is of the pistol-grip type, mounted under

SEATS are shaped to give lateral support, aided by the projecting propeller-shaft tunnel. The controls are simple and generally well placed, and the unusual gear lever operation is soon mastered.

the facia where it is out of the way but fairly easy to reach and conveniently near to the gear lever. Its action is adequate rather than powerful.

The other controls are nicely disposed for easy operation and a strange driver rapidly feels at home. As with most cars of this kind with a very low floor and a somewhat pronounced propeller shaft tunnel, the driver's left foot almost inevitably rests on the clutch pedal. The smaller switches are all very neatly and logically arranged in a central panel, two particularly good points being that the lighting switch is both handy and unmistakable and that sockets are provided for an inspection lamp. On the other hand, the manufacturers have fallen into the all-too-common fault of placing the speedometer on the extreme edge of the board where only the driver can see it, the passenger being given a good view of the ammeter, fuel and oil gauges which do not interest him or her at all.

The horn button is unusually placed, on the right of the board where it is exceptionally convenient for knuckle operation without the driver's hand leaving the wheel. Also commendable is a small pedal somewhat resembling a dipper switch which serves to lubricate the front suspension from the engine lubrication system, the supply being metered so that the manner in which the system is operated does not affect the quantity of lubricant supplied. Apart from this, there are only nine grease nipples and they need attention only at long intervals so that lubrication maintenance is cut to a minimum.

Thanks to the low floor level, and in spite of a scuttle and bonnet line 2½ in. lower than on the Plus Four Morgan, both driver and passenger sit well in the car and even a tall driver looks through the

SNUG all-weather protection is provided by the hood, once it has been rather laboriously erected, and apart from blind spots on the rear quarters permits quite adequate vision. Headroom is ample.

centre of the fixed screen. There is, moreover, ample headroom for a soft felt hat to be worn with the hood erected. The seat cushions are pneumatic and the squab, which rests on an adjustable rail at the top and has a two-position base, gives ample support for the shoulder blades. Good sideways location is provided by the body sides and the propeller shaft tunnel so that both occupants are well positioned for fast cornering.

Weather Protection

Rather laborious to erect, the hood nevertheless provides very snug all-weather protection. The side-screens, which may be left in position with the car open or closed, have the usual signalling flaps which might with advantage be made deeper. With the hood up, some slight agility is required to enter or leave the car which is, however, no worse than most of its type in this respect.

It goes without saying that vision is good with the car open and the view along the long bonnet flanked by the faired head-lamps and wings is impressive. With the hood erected, vision also reaches an acceptable standard apart from somewhat blind rear quarters.

As with most cars with this style of coachwork, luggage accommodation is not over-generous, the space behind the seats taking one moderate-sized suitcase and not much else. When this space is in use, moreover, there is no convenient spot for stowing the side-curtains. Inside the cockpit, stowage for oddments is limited to a cubby hole on the passenger's side, but a useful trough for tools and the like is provided under the bonnet.

Limited accommodation is something which many sporting motorists are very willing to tolerate, however. Smart in appearance, inexpensive to buy and run, steering and holding the road in sporting fashion, and with 75-m.p.h. performance which can be further improved by engine tuning if required, the Morgan 4/4 will undoubtedly appeal not only to young people acquiring their first new car, but also to many others whose tastes are not easily met within their financial resources.

Mechanical Specification

Engine

Cylinders	...	...	...	...	4
Bore	...	...	...	...	63.5 mm.
Stroke	...	...	...	...	92.5 mm.
Cubic capacity	...	...	...	1,172 c.c.
Piston area	...	...	...19.64 sq. in.
Valves	...	...	...	...	Side
Compression ratio	...	...	...	7/1
Max. power	...	...	...	36 b.h.p.
at	...	...	...	...	4,400 r.p.m.
Piston speed at max. b.h.p. 2,670 ft. per min.
Carburetter	...	...	Solex downdraught
Ignition	...	...	...	12-volt coil
Sparking plugs	...	...	Champion L10
Fuel pump	...	...	...	AC Mechanical
Oil filter	...	...	...	AC By-pass

Transmission

Clutch	...	...	...	Single dry plate
Top gear (s/m)	...	...	...	4.44
2nd gear (s/m)	...	...	...	8.91
1st gear	...	...	...	17.29
Propeller shaft	...	...	Open Hardy Spicer
Final drive	...	...	Salisbury hypoid
Top gear m.p.h. at 1,000 r.p.m.	16.8
Top gear m.p.h. at 1,000 ft./min.
piston speed	...	...	...	27.7

Chassis

Brakes	...	Girling hydraulic, 2 l.s. front
Brake drum diameter	...	...	9 ins.
Friction lining area	...	...	87.7 sq. in.
Suspension:
Front	...	Independent, vertical coil
Rear	...	...	Semi-elliptic
Shock absorbers:
Front	...	...	Armstrong telescopic
Rear	...	...	Armstrong piston-type
Tyres	...	5.00-16 Dunlop tubeless

Steering

Steering gear	...	...	...	Cam gear
Turning circle (between kerbs):
Left	...	...	...	33 feet
Right	...	...	...	32 feet
Turns of steering wheel, lock to
lock	...	...	...	...	2¼

Performance factors (at laden weight as tested):

Piston area, sq. in. per ton	23.1
Brake lining area, sq. in. per ton	103
Specific displacement, litres per
ton mile...	2,460

Fully described in The Motor, October 5, 1955.

Coachwork and Equipment

Bumper height with car unladen:
  Front max. 19 in., min. 9¾ in. (with o'riders)
  Rear max. 18 in., min. 8 in.

Starting handle	... ... Extra
Battery mounting	... Under luggage boot
Jack	... ... Screw type
Jacking points	... ... One each side

    on cross-member in front of seat.

Standard tool kit: Jack, pump, grease gun, screwdriver, pliers, tyre levers, adjustable spanner, 2 box spanners and tommy bar, 4 double-ended spanners, tyre valve tool, wheel-nut spanner.

Exterior lights: Two headlamps, 2 side lamps, 2 stop/tail lamps, number plate lamp.

Direction indicators	... ... Extra
Windscreen wipers	... Dual-blade electric
Sun vizors	... ... Nil

Instruments: Speedometer (with trip), oil gauge, ammeter and fuel gauge.

Warning lights	... ... Ignition and

    headlamp main beam

Locks: with ignition key	... Ignition switch
with other keys	... ... Nil.
Glove lockers	... ... One
Map pockets	... ... Nil
Parcel shelves	... ... Nil
Ashtrays	... ... Nil
Cigar lighters	... ... Nil
Interior lights	... Instrument dials
Interior heater	... ... Extra
Car radio	... ... Extra

Extras available: Starting handle, flashing direction indicators, interior heater, overriders for front bumper, wheel trims, screen washer, leather upholstery, non-standard colours, high-compression engine, rev. counter.

Upholstery material	... P.V.C. plastics
Floor covering	... ... Rubber
Exterior colours standardized	... Three
Alternative body styles	... ... Nil

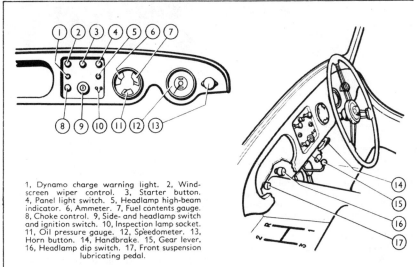

1, Dynamo charge warning light. 2, Windscreen wiper control. 3, Starter button. 4, Panel light switch. 5, Headlamp high-beam indicator. 6, Ammeter. 7, Fuel contents gauge. 8, Choke control. 9, Side- and headlamp switch and ignition switch. 10, Inspection lamp socket. 11, Oil pressure gauge. 12, Speedometer. 13, Horn button. 14, Handbrake. 15, Gear lever. 16, Headlamp dip switch. 17, Front suspension lubricating pedal.

MORGAN PLUS 4 —TR3 ENGINE

THE Morgan Car Company of Malvern, Worcestershire, have been building cyclecars and sports cars for over forty years, and it is to their credit that up to the present day they have not allowed outside design trends to influence the essential practicability of their own products. There are few companies with such a single mindedness of purpose—they have always built sporting motor cars, and each succeeding model has shown improvement over the last, whilst still retaining basically the same concept. The front suspension, which is an independent system, was patented by the Morgan Company forty years ago. Although the suspension gives a harsh ride, the road holding of the car is justification of their continuance to use this type of suspension.

The car tested was fitted with the TR3 engine, and the only visible difference between the TR2 engine and the TR3, as fitted, is the larger SU carburetters (H6) and the inlet manifold. The adoption of this engine variant gives even better acceleration than hitherto, but with, unfortunately, some sacrifice in economy of fuel consumption. Used as the car is intended, that is flat out through the gears and as fast in top as conditions allow, we did no better, or worse, than 21 mpg.

FAST THROUGH THE BENDS

There are very few sports cars that I have driven that are capable of cornering with such a feeling of safety, and if the car is provoked to such an extent that the back does break away, it is quickly checked by a slight movement of the steering wheel. The steering is extremely sensitive and accurate, and on fast open stretches of road one gains the impression that the car steers itself. On fast winding roads, only a gentle pressure is needed on the wheel to change the direction of the car without any reduction in speed whatsoever. There is a slight tendency to under-steer, and the car can be drifted under power. I had the opportunity of driving the car in torrential rain, and I found myself going through corners at speeds much higher than I would have driven certain contemporary sports cars. The windscreen wipers under such circumstances proved quite adequate, and though they look ridiculously small, clear an adequate area of the low windscreen.

When I collected this car I had never before driven a Morgan, but it was not long before I had put 50 miles into the hour. This car soon makes friends, and I found myself at home in it after only a few miles of motoring. By most standards it is not a really comfortable motor car, but the thrill of driving a car so well mannered is worth the slight discomfort of a harsh ride. The seating, however, is particularly good, and gives support to the driver and passenger in an upright position. The seat cushions are below the chassis side-members and this, together with the high tunnel, prevents both driver and passenger sliding about on fast bends.

The centrally mounted gear lever is in a convenient position for the left hand, and

Ian Walker looks at home in the TR3-engined Morgan. Product of one of the oldest-established British motor manufacturers, the car has a simple specification yet a maximum of over 100 mph

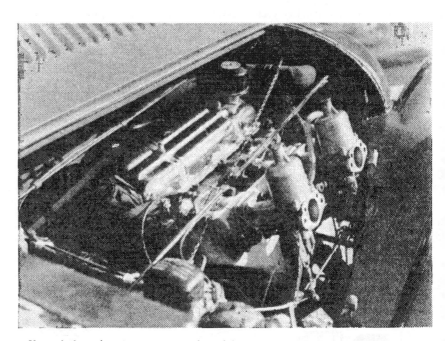

Unusual these days is a two-piece, hinged-down-the-centre bonnet. The well-proved Triumph TR3 engine with two large SU carburetters is truly accessible. This gives more power than the TR2, yet fuel consumption under fast conditions was 21 mpg.

there is a very short travel when changing gear. I had the feeling that the car was over-geared (3.73 to 1) and I feel a much better acceleration and top speed would have been gained by using the alternative ratio of 4.1 to 1. The clutch is quite light in operation, and well able to stand up to really fierce acceleration. One criticism I would mention is that there is nowhere to rest the left foot when not operating the clutch, owing to the shaft tunnel, but I expect with usage this would not be noticed unduly. Also, I feel that the body could be wider to give more " elbow room."

The brakes are very powerful, but require a fairly heavy pedal pressure. No fade occurred whatever during our tests, but there was a tendency to pull after braking from maximum speeds. After a short while, however, the brakes returned to normal. The handbrake is a fly-off type mounted on the left-hand side of the clutch housing. The weather protection provided is quite adequate and very quickly erected, the whole of which stows neatly away behind the seats, still leaving plenty of space for luggage. The hood frame is a very light tubular structure, and the hood cover is separate

CONTINUED ON PAGE 83

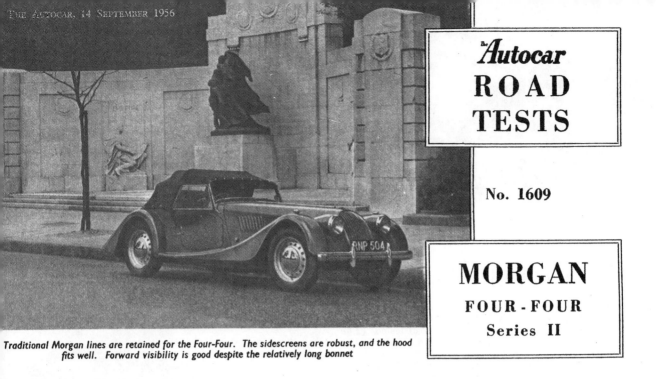

The Autocar
ROAD TESTS

No. 1609

MORGAN
FOUR-FOUR
Series II

Traditional Morgan lines are retained for the Four-Four. The sidescreens are robust, and the hood fits well. Forward visibility is good despite the relatively long bonnet

AT the last London Show the Morgan company were welcomed back into the narrow ranks of manufacturers producing what might be called an economy sports car; that is, a car of unquestionably sporting character with an inexpensive engine capable of giving an acceptable performance without using much fuel. Before the war the Morgan Four-Four and a smart three-wheeler were turned out in limited numbers at the attractive little factory in Malvern, Worcestershire. After the war, production of similar models continued until the Plus Four, with Standard Vanguard engine, was introduced and the three-wheeler and Ten-engined sports car were dropped.

The introduction of the Triumph TR2 engine presented an opportunity to give the Plus Four more power and, at the same time, bring it within the 2-litre class for competition work. Partly as a result of very many successes, primarily in rallies, the Plus Four has become widely known. Now there are three basic chassis—the Plus Four with Vanguard or Triumph engine, and the new Four-Four Series II with a 1,172 c.c. Ford engine—the subject of this test. The Plus Four may be obtained as a two- or four-seater tourer or two-seater coupé, while the Four-Four is available only as a two-seater tourer.

At 14 cwt the Ford-engined car is 3 cwt lighter than

its more powerful counterparts, and 1½ cwt lighter than either the Ford Prefect or Anglia, from which the power unit is derived. The engine and gear box are fitted in standard form as supplied by Ford, and thus the acceleration is superior to that of the Ford saloon only in proportion to the reduction in weight and frontal area. However, the extra performance is well worth having—50 m.p.h. is reached in 18sec, compared with 21.8 for the Prefect, and the Four-Four is 9.5sec quicker to 60 m.p.h. than the Ford. Top speed is approximately the same for both cars, the Morgan being slightly faster when the hood is up. The overall top gear ratio of both cars is almost the same, but the substantially larger wheels of the Morgan step up the gearing, so that at maximum speed the Four-Four is not over-revving.

The acceleration figures are not exciting, but the company has probably been wise in its decision to keep down initial cost in this type of car, in part by installing the engine in production form. There are several tuning kits available—special cylinder heads, and carburettor and manifold conversions, for example—which owners can buy and fit for themselves, according to the dictates of their pockets. Thus the relatively high overall gearing in top, resulting from the larger rolling radius, is an advantage,

The simple facia layout is businesslike. The speedometer is in the right-hand dial, and minor instruments in the dial on the left of the steering column. Switches are laid out neatly in a central panel

So that the hood can be removed completely, there are fasteners round the rear quarters as well as across the screen, making lowering and raising rather laborious. There is no luggage locker in the tail

MORGAN FOUR-FOUR . . .

for owners can enjoy the fruits of extra power without engine speed being excessively high at 70 m.p.h. or more.

Since the Ford Prefect was fully road-tested (*The Autocar*, December 17, 1954) first and second gear box ratios have been lowered, with the result that the Morgan has a second gear ratio of 8.9 to 1 instead of the 8.2 fitted to earlier Prefects. Even with the larger road wheels the Morgan would have been better with the former higher ratio, for maximum speed is under 50 m.p.h. and few owners would regularly exceed 40, in second. As a result, when one wishes to accelerate after being held up behind other traffic travelling in the 30s, a shortcoming of the intermediate ratio is revealed.

Top speed and acceleration are comparable with those of small family saloons when studied on the impersonal data recorded by the stop watch, but the difference in handling characteristics between the two types of car ensures an improvement in journey times. On smooth roads the road-holding of the Four-Four is particularly good. Quite sharp corners can be taken at speeds that are astonishingly high even for a sports car. On bumpy surfaces the car tends to hop at the rear, disturbing the predetermined line through the corner.

Provision is made for a starting handle, and the side lights are mounted on the top of the wings where they can be seen from the driving seat. The number plate is mounted above the bumper where it does not interfere with the airstream under the car

The independent front suspension is by sliding pillar and coil springs—a system used by the company from its early days before the 1914-18 war. Half-elliptic leaf springs are used at the rear. Vertical travel of the road wheels is restricted, hence the hopping-about tendency on bad surfaces, but on British main roads the taut character of the suspension can be enjoyed to the full. Again on bumps there

is a noticeable tendency for the rear to "bottom" on its axle stops, but the construction of the car as a whole is so obviously strong that this is of little account.

With only two and a half turns from lock to lock and a turning circle of 33ft, it will be realized that the steering is sensitive, yet it is not in the least heavy. The degree of self-centring is good, and on the straight the car holds a clean line at speed, almost regardless of wind direction or strength.

The brakes are not merely adequate for the car but sufficiently good to stand the extra calls made on them by an owner who undertakes engine tuning. In normal driving, light pedal pressure produces a firm response, and heavier pedal pressure at high speed slows the car quickly without pulling to either side. They are brakes that can be used with equal confidence in the wet or the dry.

The back axle, of Salisbury manufacture, is of the hypoid type. Although the engine is firmly mounted it is smooth, and no vibrations are therefore caused by any mechanical components. The scuttle shakes perceptibly, primarily because of the firm suspension. The silencer, not of Ford manufacture, permits the emission of appreciable noise. The sound is not sufficient to annoy the occupants, but one's passage through built-up areas is made evident to the local inhabitants.

The modest total price, with tax, of £713 17s, is matched in attraction by the fuel consumption and the accessibility of the mechanical components for home servicing. Driven quietly, 41.2 m.p.g. was obtained on a long run. To enable this consumption to be fully appreciated, it should be explained that the word "quietly" is used here relatively to the character of the car—using a cruising speed of 40 to 50 m.p.h., being sparing with use of the throttle, yet passing slower traffic in the ordinary way. Even when the Four-Four is driven hard it gives more than 35 m.p.g. In addition to the financial considerations, this fuel consumption gives a range of 300 miles or even more on the contents of the eight-gallon tank.

The bonnet opens on either side, with the hinge running down the centre line. The engine is mounted well forward, with the result that the clutch housing and gear box are within the long underbonnet area. Accessibility is, therefore, of the order dreamed about by impecunious drivers with a mechanical bent. A minor snag is that the dipstick is on the opposite side of the bonnet from the oil filler cap, the engine being designed by its manufacturers for cars which have one-piece bonnets.

The coachwork is traditional, and although attractively smooth and purposeful in appearance, it has shortcomings. Although officially designated as a tourer, little provision has been made for luggage. There is a large tray under the bonnet, in which some parcels could be carried in addition to the tools, but for ordinary luggage there is only a narrow "slit trench" behind the seats; there is no locker in the tail. Although the hood may be removed entirely, in Britain's unsettled climate it is more likely to be folded down in dry weather, with the result that luggage space is still further reduced. This Road Test was the first occasion on which the test equipment, in addition to the two occupants, could not be carried in the luggage space provided, one rather bulky item being accommodated in the free space under the bonnet.

The pneumatic seat cushions are comfortable, and the backrest, in one piece, is shaped so that neither driver nor passenger slide about. There is not a great amount of room for the driver's right elbow, and it is not possible to straighten the arms, although the steering wheel is close to the facia. The instruments are arranged in two large dials which can be seen easily through the three-spoked wheel. The speedometer is on the right with total and trip mileage recorders, and the oil pressure and fuel gauges and the ammeter are grouped on the left. There is no rev counter. Within a neat panel in the centre of the wooden facia are the ignition and lighting switch, and knobs for the starter, choke, wipers and a spare for use with a fog lamp. To the left of these is an open glove compartment.

The pedals are well placed, in such a way that heel-and-toe gear changes can be made easily, but there is no room for the driver's left foot away from the clutch, nor is it easy to bend the knee sufficiently to rest the foot on the floor on the driver's side of the pedal.

The forward position of the power unit in the chassis requires a rather unusual layout of the gear-change mechanism, but the result is quite delightful, and enables snappy changes, appropriate to the character of the car, to be made. The lower portion of the original Ford gear

lever is retained, and this is linked to a horizontal rod which passes through the scuttle into the cockpit, with a flexible bearing to accommodate angular movement in addition to the normal fore-and-aft action.

The control knob is moved to the left or the right and engagement becomes a simple pull-and-push operation. The change between top and second, which is the one most used, is a straightforward quick push down into the lower ratio, and the natural action of returning to top is to rest the thumb against the facia as a reaction point, with the fingers pulling the lever knob backwards over its very short travel. The linkage used means that the normal gear lever positions are interchanged, with the two upper ratios away from the driver. The long linkage and flexibility of the scuttle produces small tremors at the gear knob at high speeds when the road surface is bumpy.

Even with the hood up, forward visibility is good, as there is no beetle-browed effect, thanks to the fairly high screen and low seating position. The rear corners are rather blind, and as no indicators are fitted on the standard

Accessibility of the engine and other components is excellent, even the clutch and gear box being housed in the under-bonnet compartment. Gear selection is effected by distinctly remote control, but the mechanism is nevertheless positive. There is a capacious tool tray running across the bulkhead which may supplement parcels space

model, unless requested as an optional extra, some manœuvres may be found tricky in heavy traffic conditions. A certain amount of rain water gets into the cockpit, particularly when the car has been left standing, but the fit of sidescreens and hood is generally good. The sidescreens are solidly built, and derive extra security from a mounting system which, unfortunately, calls for the use of a special tommy bar housed in the glove locker.

To lower or raise the hood is laborious, as there are many fasteners to be handled individually, and when the

Covers for the luggage and passenger compartments are available as optional extras. They give a thoroughly tidy appearance to the car when the hood is down

hood is wet its tightness makes this more difficult. With the hood removed the luggage compartment and the passenger seat can be enclosed with tonneau covers which are available as optional extras. A heater may be had at additional cost.

The main criticism of the bodywork is the difficulty of entry and exit, particularly for a fairly tall driver. One expects a car of this type to have shortcomings of this sort, but the Morgan suffers particularly from the narrow gap between the steering wheel and the right side of the seat backrest. Of course, entry and, to a lesser extent, exit are easier when the hood is down. The bodywork as a whole seems robust, and rattles on the car tested were limited to some scuttle shake. Even the side screens, which can often be troublesome on sports cars generally, did not vibrate.

The car does not suffer abnormally from wind noise, and with the car open the screen gives good protection against buffeting by the wind. There is a back draught—common to sports cars—when the car is in its open form, which, in cool weather, makes a scarf or some other protection for the back of the neck desirable.

The Four-Four is a creature of compromise. Main items on the debit side are performance which is not exciting in standard form, difficulty of getting in and out, the laborious hood mechanism and the lack of accommodation for luggage. On the credit side are low price, fuel economy, handling of a high order, the ease with which engine power could be increased, and the accessibility of those parts subject to routine attention. In recent years there has been little to satisfy the motorist who wants an economical sporting car at relatively low initial cost, and the Morgan Four-Four Series II fills just that gap.

MORGAN FOUR-FOUR Series II

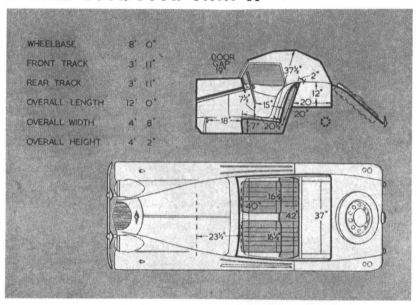

WHEELBASE	8' 0"
FRONT TRACK	3' 11"
REAR TRACK	3' 11"
OVERALL LENGTH	12' 0"
OVERALL WIDTH	4' 8"
OVERALL HEIGHT	4' 2"

Measurements in these ¼in to 1ft scale body diagrams are taken with the driving seat in the rearmost of the two alternative positions and with the seat cushions uncompressed

DATA

PRICE (basic), with two-seater sports body, £475.
British purchase tax, £238 17s.
Total (in Great Britain), £713 17s.
Extras: Heater £11 11s plus £5 15s 6d purchase tax.

ENGINE: Capacity: 1,172 c.c. (71.55 cu in).
Number of cylinders: 4.
Bore and stroke: 63.5 × 92.5 mm (2.5 × 3.64 in).
Valve gear: side valve.
Compression ratio: 7 to 1.
B.H.P.: 36 (gross) at 4,400 r.p.m. (B.H.P. per ton laden 42.35).
Torque: 52 lb ft at 2,500 r.p.m.
M.P.H. per 1,000 r.p.m. on top gear, 16.8.

WEIGHT (with 5 gals fuel): 14 cwt (1,568 lb).
Weight distribution (per cent): F, 46.4; R, 53.6.
Laden as tested: 17 cwt (1,904 lb).
Lb per c.c. (laden): 1.62.

BRAKES: Type: Girling. F, two-leading shoe, R, leading and trailing.
Method of operation: Hydraulic.
Drum dimensions: F, 9in diameter; 1¾in wide. R, 9in diameter; 1¾in wide.
Lining area: F, 44 sq in; R, 44 sq in (103.5 sq in per ton laden).

TYRES: 5.00—16in.
Pressures (lb per sq in): F, 18; R, 18 (normal).

TANK CAPACITY: 8 Imperial gallons.
Oil sump, 5¼ pints.
Cooling system, 12 pints.

TURNING CIRCLE: 33ft (L and R).
Steering wheel turns (lock to lock): 2¼.

DIMENSIONS: Wheelbase: 8ft.
Track: F, 3ft 11in; R, 3ft 11in.
Length (overall): 12ft.
Height: 4ft 2in with hood erected.
Width: 4ft 8in.
Ground clearance: 7in.

ELECTRICAL SYSTEM: 12-volt; 32 ampère-hour battery.
Head lights: Double dip; 36/36 watt bulbs.

SUSPENSION: Front, independent, coil springs. Rear, semi-elliptic.

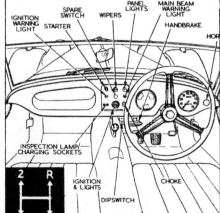

PERFORMANCE

ACCELERATION: from constant speeds. Speed Range, Gear Ratios and Time in sec.

M.P.H.		4.44 to 1	8.91 to 1	17.29 to 1
10—30	..	—	6.65	—
20—40	..	15.1	7.2	—
30—50	..	15.5	—	—
40—60	..	19.2	—	—

From rest through gears to:

M.P.H.		sec.
30	..	6.9
50	..	18.0
60	..	29.4

Standing quarter-mile, 23.5 sec.

SPEEDS ON GEARS:

Gear			M.P.H. (normal and max.)	K.P.H. (normal and max.)
Top	(mean)		70.5	113.45
	(best)		70.7	113.85
2nd	..	..	40—48	64.4—77.2
1st	..	..	20—28	32.2—45.1

TRACTIVE RESISTANCE: 30 lb per ton at 10 M.P.H.

TRACTIVE EFFORT:

	Pull (lb per ton)	Equivalent Gradient
Top ..	165	1 in 13.5
Second..	355	1 in 6.2

BRAKES:

Efficiency	Pedal Pressure (lb)
91 per cent	85
54 per cent	50
23 per cent	25

FUEL CONSUMPTION:
35.6 m.p.g. overall for 665 miles (8.0 litres per 100 km.).
Approximate normal range 34.8—41.2 m.p.g. (8.2—6.8 litres per 100 km.).
Fuel, First grade.

WEATHER: Dry, light diagonal breeze.
Air temperature 60 deg F.
Acceleration figures are the means of several runs in opposite directions.
Tractive effort and resistance obtained by Tapley meter.
Model described in *The Autocar* of October 7, 1955.

SPEEDOMETER CORRECTION: M.P.H.

Car speedometer	..	..	10	20	30	40	50	60	70	72
True speed	..	..	9	18	28	38	48	57	67	68

Continued from page 48

from it. The two side screens are secured to the doors by knurled frame screws. When the hood is stowed, a small cover fits over the luggage compartment.

The engine installation and auxiliaries are very accessible via the two-piece bonnet. Engine maintenance, therefore, is a very easy matter. On top of the bulkhead is mounted the fuse boxes, wiper motor and spare plug carrier, and built into the top of the bulkhead is the jack and tool kit stowage. The body is very well made and has a good paint finish. There is one spare wheel carried almost vertically behind the petrol tank in place of two as previously.

The Morgan is a hand-built specialist sports car with an all-round performance of a very high order. The Morgans' successes in all forms of motor sport are evidence of its worth, and in the right hands is virtually unbeatable in driving tests. In exchange for some concession to luxury and comfort, the car will give a great thrill and considerable pleasure to drive. Furthermore at a total cost of £893-17-0 is the least expensive car available that will exceed 100 mph.

SPECIFICATION AND PERFORMANCE DATA

PRICE : £595 0s. 0d. plus £298 17s. 0d. PT.

ENGINE : Four cylinders in line.
1991 cc.
Bore 83 mm.   Stroke 92 mm.
8.5 to 1 compression ratio.
90 bhp at 4800 rpm.
Twin SU type H6 carburetters.
Oil capacity 10 pints.

TANK CAPACITY : 11 gallons.

CHASSIS FRAME : A special feature of the car is the chassis which is a patented design. The side-members are deep Z shape, arranged to give ample steering lock together with maximum width. This arrangement also permits a low floor at the same time saving weight.

There are five cross members of boxed or tubular section. The front end is easily detachable and follows usual Morgan practice.

CLUTCH : Borg & Beck single dry plate.

GEARBOX : Four speed Moss Gearbox. The gears are changed by a short lever fitted direct to the top of the box, which is connected to the engine by a large electron casting forming the clutch housing.

BRAKES : Girling hydraulic with two-leading shoe. operating on four wheels. The handbrake by cable with compensated linkage.

SUSPENSION : The front wheels are independently sprung—a patented Morgan system. Girling double acting tubular type shock absorbers are fitted to the front springs. The rear springs are semi-elliptical with Silentbloc bushes fitted at both ends. Control is by Armstrong hydraulic dampers.

IGNITION : Coil and distributor with induction-operated advance and retard mechanism.

DIMENSIONS : Wheelbase 8 ft. Track 3 ft 11 in. Overall length 12 ft. Overall width 4 ft 8 in. Ground clearance 7 in.

WEIGHT : 16½ cwt.

PERFORMANCE : Maximum speed 105 mph, Third 80 mph, Second 60 mph, First 40 mph. Standing quarter mile—17.1 seconds.

ACCELERATION

THROUGH GEARS			TOP GEAR		
0–30	..	3 seconds	30–40	..	2.9 seconds
0–40	..	4.4 ,,	40–50	..	3.3 ,,
0–50	..	7.2 ,,	50–60	..	4.2 ,,
0–60	..	10 ,,	60–70	..	5.0 ,,
0–70	..	13 ,,	70–80	..	5.5 ,,
0–80	..	17.5 ,,	80–90	..	8.0 ,,
0–90	..	27.4 ,,			

FUEL CONSUMPTION :

Driven hard—21 mpg.
Cruising   —28 mpg.

ALL PERFORMANCE FIGURES TAKEN WITH SCREEN ERECT AND TWO OCCUPANTS.

"pit-stop," and there has been no recurrence of the trouble since.

Alas, after 1,750 miles the off-side steering damper was seen to have broken and when, about 250 miles later, its fellow went the same way, the car became unsteerable at under 40 m.p.h., due to chronic wheel wobble. This, in turn, racked the radiator and started a tiny leak (cured more or less with one small tin of "Never-leak"). I needed the car and put up with this irritating complaint for a further 2,000 miles, but the police took too great an interest (on one occasion we were "arrested" by no fewer than five mobile cops who wanted to know, couldn't I see my front wheels ?—I couldn't, of course, with those excellent front wings in place !) So Morgan's supplied new dampers and Archers, of Aldershot courteously fitted these wafer-thick affairs in 1½ days, for a charge of £1 18s. 6d., discovering at the same time a broken near-side rebound spring. Now the Plus Four and I can go to town again. But I await redesigned dampers with some impatience.

While on "snags," let me say that a bonnet bracket has broken despite gentle treatment, the screen wiper gets so hot you can't lay a hand on it and an evil-smelling chewing-gum runs out (however, it goes as well as ever !), the choke sticks and its wire has pulled out, a wing stay has come adrift, and the silencer joints have blown somewhat (lovely noises, though !). Those, however, are the total mishaps to a car which has had to give maximum service with a minimum of attention. And, after all, you must expect a few "bugs" from a new model.

The fact remains that the Plus Four is very good fun to drive, being remarkably handy in traffic, able to hold a speedometer 65 m.p.h. indefinitely, and possessing very good acceleration, cornering stability and brakes. These are qualities that melt the miles.

With hood and side bits up it defeats the worst weather, save for a leak round the wiper-motor mounting bolts and, although you then get pretty warm, the driver can signal *via* the screen flaps. There is good stowage space behind the seat, which, by the way, is non-adjustable. The Lucas lamps are excellent, the horn sensibly penetrating, the triple rear lamps are appreciated, there is comfortable parking space for your clutch foot *between* the pedals, the screen will fold down, the long, well-louvred bonnet enhances the very pleasing appearance of this low-hung, well-finished car, and, although it unnerves me, so far the accelerator cable hasn't broken. Further good points : excellent panel lighting (but a horrid red light when the headlamps are undipped !), a "real" dashboard, excellent leather upholstery, very accessible dip-stick, good snap-open fuel filler, an 11-gallon tank and in-built jacking. The batteries are rather tucked away, one spare wheel has to be removed to grease the back spring trunnions, and the oil filler cap is rather cruel to the fingers. But these are minor grumbles and I am genuinely glad to forsake the editorial chair for the driving seat of this game little Morgan with the big engine.—W. B.

MORGAN ROAD TEST

(Continued from page 56)

adjusted fore and aft, nor up and down, altho when driving alone, the passenger's seat cushion may be placed upside down upon that of the driver's. Incidentally, this improves visibility past the right front fender considerably. Fortunately, the Morgan fits me pretty well.

About the steering wheel, the less said the better. It is non-adjustable, the diameter of the rim is uncomfortably small to grip, and wrapping it with tape is out because the windshield wiper motor is already provokingly close (2⅛" from the wheel).

The transmission is mounted unusually far back in the cockpit and is connected to the clutch by a universal-jointed shaft. Being well covered with insulating material, there is no significant increase in gear noises, while the shift lever is in an ideal location due to a Meccano-like extension gadgetry. The shifting pattern is similar to that on the MG except that reverse is obtained by lifting up, then left and forward.

An outstanding weakness of the car, if it is to be driven hard thru corners, is the soft steel used in the wheels. Caton's Plus Four lost a wheel at Pebble Beach when the nuts pulled right thru.

This is one of the few sports cars I've seen that looks well with the top up, but despite its good looks, the all-weather equipment provides only *minimum* protection.

The engine's only highlights are wet sleeves and a bore-stroke ratio of .924:1. It has the low compression ratio of 6.7:1, only 20 degrees valve overlap, yet it propels the car in a most spectacular fashion, with the snap and vigor that an MG driver always wants but never has. How? Shucks, they've cheated. It's just big (2088 cc, 127 cu in.).

Altho I've suffered considerable difficulty with the starter shafts (the first one bent and the second broke), both were replaced for free by the Lucas people. Other than this, the engine seems to have enough reliability to warrant hopping-up.   •

SCI
ROAD TEST:
THE MORGAN TR3

IT'S LONG been an axiom among students of racing that the first cars of a new concept are invariably beaten by the more highly developed products of an older school. Grand Prix cars got through this stage back in 1934, when the radical new German machines were being trounced by the classic Alfa P3's. Since then each year has seen more converts to the scientific approach to car design, but somewhere there has always been a cart-sprung, loose limbed veteran showing those whippersnappers how it should be done.

Due to its unique road conditions, England has been the traditional stronghold of the classic sports car. With the HRG "gone modern" in a big way, the Morgan remains the sole representative of a superseded era. Some may quibble that independent front suspension takes it out of this class, but the Morgan system has remained substantially unchanged for forty years and even today is "independent" in name only. Though Production Class E has seen the

arrival of many promising newcomers, such as the Triumph, Doretti, and Arnolt-Bristol, a sharply-tuned Morgan will still lead the way to the line.

Since many prospective Morgan owners may have racing in mind, then, we were particularly fortunate in being able to test a car that had been prepared for this purpose at the Morgan works in Worcestershire. As an entry for Sebring, 1956, the TR3 engine on this car had been cleaned up, tuned and balanced within stock specifications, at an additional cost of $270. In Florida it was rolled in practice with minor consequences which have since been rectified, and it now being used daily and in competition by Joe Ferguson, Jr., Vice President of the eastern importers, Fergus Imported Cars, Inc.

The 1956 versions of the Plus Four Morgan have been lightened by fitting one angled spare wheel at the back instead of the old double vertical arrangement, and rubber-bushed shackles have finally replaced greased sliding trun-

BELOW: Rear of cockpit can hold little beside top and side curtains except when canvass is in position for moist weather. Wooden floor can be lifted for access to twin six volt batteries and Salisbury hypoid rear axle.

Beneath that long louvered hood lies the jolting TR-3 mill that will tackle 6000 rpm and then some without a sound of complaint. Ample room around the four-barrel makes tuning a pleasure.

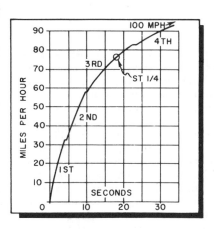

nions at the backs of the underslung rear leaf springs. Armstrong instead of Girling shocks are now used all around, with tubulars at the front to control the short travel of the compact sliding pillar suspension. In 1955 these Mogs started coming through with front brake drums a quarter of an inch wider than the old 1.5 inches, to try to bring the stopping power into line with the increased speed provided by the hot TR2 engine. Brakes are still by far the weakest point of the car in racing, however, and the modern competition seldom gets ahead until they go.

It's odd, but the above criticism is a strong tribute to the Plus Four, since by production sports car standards the brakes are quite good. Pedal feel is firm and progressive, and pulls the car down smoothly and in a straight line. Our ten-stop test showed a lessening of power after four or five stops, but not to a dangerous amount, and full recovery was rapid. In all other important respects the TR3 Morgan is a snorting, fire-breathing road machine, ready and willing to take far greater risks than you will have the nerve to. Marketing a car of such capabilities at a base price of $2655 requires a few sacrifices here and there, and Morgans have shown great integrity and courage by letting the axe fall on the driver and passenger. This is rare in a day when Genuine Leather and polished walnut are frequent cover-ups for skimping under the skin.

Forthright in all respects, the Morgan at once informs you that it has definite ideas about seating and wheel position. A very positive and deliberate latch opens the door from the rear, and hinges placed well forward make the most of the available space. The floor is recessed very deeply between the Z-shaped frame rails, and in spite of the lowness of the car the seating position is almost chair-like. This complicates getting in, but the toughest job is getting out with the top and side curtains up.

Simple pneumatic cushions over angled plywood boards comprise the seat cushions proper, while the single-piece seat back is shaped and padded over a similar base. Nothing is adjustable, and the most that can be said for this is that it contributes a lot to the strength of the coachbuilt

Spare for the Morgan is conveniently carried in a well just behind gas tank which holds 13 gallons.

Cockpit arrangement. Seating attitude is bolt upright on pneumatic cushions. Panel is complete, and readable.

TR-3 engine is equipped with two big bore SU carbs, and enlarged ports for better breathing at high revs. Good torque in the low ranges gives sharp acceleration in all gears.

body. A big Brooklands wheel sits near-vertically in the driver's lap and close to his chest, and has the precise shape and feel that marks that pattern. The seating position is upright and alert, with most of the spinal load carried by the pneumatic cushion. This is not ideal but somehow avoids becoming unbearable during long stints at the wheel. You simply get used to it.

Sideways positioning is not too good, and we appreciated the seat belts on this car. The fixed legroom is naturally close for a six-footer, and elbow room is at a minimum with the curtains up but fine when the padded door cutaways are free. Big, well-spaced pedals mean positive control but no room for the left foot, which usually rests flat on the floor. The handbrake is a good quick-release type, on the passenger side of the wide gearbox housing.

Instruments are big and readable, both by day and night, and rally purposes are well served by a trip recording speedometer on the navigator's side. There is no map light, though, and only one open compartment for loose objects. Pull-out switches at the center control the cowl-mounted wipers and other accessories, while the non-cancelling directional signal switch is at the left.

Ideal for competition in that it can be removed entirely, the heavy-weight top snaps down over a simple tube framework with sturdy Dot and twist-type fasteners. The rear window is big, minimizing the rear quarter blind spots, and at speed the only top fault is a tendency to lift up and out above the side curtains. The latter are clear, stiff, and unusual in that they bolt in place from the outside, which promotes corrosion but eliminates protruding elbow-knockers in the narrow cockpit. Except for the one defect above the draft sealing is very good, and even in the absence of a heater on this car we were warmed on chill evenings by heat from the engine and center-mounted gearbox, which, however, may not be quite so welcome in the summer.

(Continued on page 88)

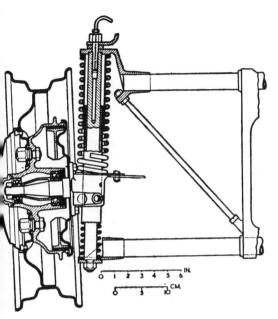

Front suspension consists of coil springs, vertically sliding spindles. Kingpins are carried between outer ends of upper and tubular cross-bars.

...ff springing keeps Morgan clinging fast, and flat, through ...ht bends. This factor coupled with the car's excellent ...celeration, makes it a tough customer on short courses.

...ide curtains and top are positioned by Dot and twist fasten-...rs. All, except the crossbows can be removed for competition ...unning. Note size of rear window for good rear view.

SPECIFICATIONS

POWER UNIT:

Type	four cylinder, in line
Valve arrangement	Overhead, in line
Bore & Stroke (Engl. & Met.)	3.27 x 3.62 in. (83 x 92 mm)
Stroke/Bore Ratio	1.11 to 1
Displacement (Engl. & Met.)	121.5 cu: in (1991 cc)
Compression Ratio	8.5 to 1
Carburetion by	Two 1⅝ in. SU sidedraft
Max. bhp @ rpm	100 bhp @ 5000 rpm
Max. Torque @ rpm	118 lb. ft. @ 3000 rpm
Idle speed	900 rpm.

TOP SPEED:

Two-way average	100 mph
Fastest one-way run	100 mph

ACCELERATION:

From zero to	Seconds
30 mph	3.6
40 mph	5.8
50 mph	8.0
60 mph	11.2
70 mph	14.9
80 mph	20.5
90 mph	30.4
Standing 1/4 mile	18.1
Speed at end of quarter	76 mph

SPEED RANGES IN GEARS:

I	0-36
II	2-58
III	5-82
IV	12-100

SPEEDOMETER CORRECTION:

Indicated	Actual
30	32
40	42
50	51
60	61
70	70
80	79
90	89
100	99

FUEL CONSUMPTION:

Hard driving	22 mpg.

BRAKING EFFICIENCY (10 successive emergency stops from 60 mph, just short of locking wheels)

1st stop	65
2nd	65
3rd	65
4th	60
5th	58
6th	55
7th	60
8th	52
9th	55
10th	55

DRIVE TRAIN:

Transmission ratios Rev	3.44
I	3.44
II	1.98
III	1.40
IV	1.00
Final drive ratio (test car)	3.75
Other available final drive ratio	4.10
Axle torque taken by	rear leaf springs

CHASSIS:

Wheelbase	96.0 in.
Front Tread	47.0 in.
Rear Tread	47.0 in.
Suspension, front	Independent, coil and sliding pillar
Suspension, rear	Solid axle, leaf springs, underslung frame
Shock absorbers	Armstrong tubular front, lever-type rear
Steering type	Cam and sector
Steering wheel turns L to L	2
Turning diameter	33 ft.
Brake type	Girling hydraulic, 2 LS front
Brake lining area	121 sq. in.
Wheel studs	four
Tire size	5.25 x 16 (5.50 x 16 on test car)

GENERAL:

Length	155.0 in.
Width	56.0 in.
Height (top up)	52.5 in.
Weight, test car	1940 lbs.
Weight distribution, F/R	48/52
Weight distribution, F/R with driver	47/53
Fuel capacity—U. S. gallons	13.2

RATING FACTORS:

Bhp per cu. in.	0.823
Bhp. per sq. in. piston area	2.99
Torque (lb-ft) per cu. in.	0.976
Pounds per bhp—test car	19.4
Piston speed @ 60 mph (std.)	1750 ft/min.
Piston speed @ max bhp	3010 ft/min.
Brake lining area per ton (test car)	125 sq. in.

Morgan

(Continued from page 86)

MG owners know what the behind seat trunk room is like and know that it can hold a surprising amount when the top is up. Two twist catches allow the wooden floor to be lifted for quick access to the twin six-volt batteries and the Salisbury hypoid rear axle.

You may have gathered by now that the creature comforts are on the slim side, though starkly honest, and the ride of the Plus Four has the same raw attitude. It tackles big bumps with a leaping, bounding motion which yet avoids the discomfort of true pitching. Our car was fitted with Michelin X tires, which can be run effectively at very low pressures and were thus of great help in lessening the effect of small ripples on the stiff Morgan suspension. The frame is unusually stiff for a classic suspension layout, but small vibrations still give the body a hard time and search out all potential rattle sources. Generally the ride is hard but reassuring in that its response is always consistent.

To the enthusiastic driver, though, it's all more than worthwhile when he wrings the Plus Four out through every variety of bend and finds it clinging tight, flat and fast. There is very little roll and no unwelcome dip at either end, thanks to the stiff springing. This also led us to expect, in combination with a slightly rearward weight bias, an oversteer on corners, but in fact the Morgan understeers very powerfully at most speeds. This is accounted for by the front suspension geometry, which is such that the wheels lean out with the car on corners, and also by the fact that the front end is much stiffer than the rear and thus assumes more of the overturning couple in spite of a low front roll center.

Steering

Steer characteristics is a function of *relative* front-rear cornering powers, and on an *overall* basis the Morgan ranks as one of the stickingest cars we have tested. Steering is not ideal, with two inches of play at the rim and a strong caster action that verges on heaviness, but it is fast and free from excessive road reaction. Understeer plus heaviness means that the Morgan will go wherever you have the strength to point it. The rear end just follows along and never tries to get out of hand, though bumpy surfaces can catch it off balance. We tried tire pressures from 23 to 30 pounds, and the only penalty of the lower figure was a slight amount of tire howl. Wheel response is instantaneous and predictable, and the close-up driving position is well matched to the requirements of the job. At higher speeds there is just enough surplus power available to allow honest drifting, which rounds out the Plus Four's range and confirms it as tops in handling.

Stiff rear leaf springs have further benefits when used with a Hotchkiss drive, as demonstrated by the TR3 Morgan, which bats off from a standing start without a trace of axle hop, wind-up or judder. Either a chirp or momentary wheelspin, according to taste, and away you go. Clutch pedal travel is short, and the engagement is smooth yet solid, remaining that way through all our tests. The gearbox setup is one of the Morgan's unusual features, in that the clutch housing and transmission are separated by some nineteen inches of cast tube and splined clutch shaft. The box thus rests at the forward edge of the seats and that short handy lever goes right down into the works without the aid of remote controls. Since the gear layout and casing are substantially the same as those used in the Jaguar, the unit is more than strong enough and has good ratios.

Easy control is provided by the direct lever, and the travel is so short that at first you are not sure of being in gear. Second gear synchromesh can easily be faulted, but the top two gears are better. Competition security is provided by a block for the lefthand reverse that can only be overcome by lifting the lever.

Engines

Few engines have so quickly established themselves in stock competition as the Triumph TR series, and the latest TR3 version has undergone enlargements in port and carburetor size to make full use of the high revs it can reach. The engine in this "Sebring" car was smooth and solid up to the 6000 rpm that we were permitted, and it felt ready to tackle more. Very good torque in the low ranges gave that "wall-climbing" feeling no matter what gear you were in. Acceleration through the gears as recorded is very quick, though the low-speed times were marred slightly by the bigger-than-normal tires fitted for long distance competition. The use of a straight pipe also prevents judgement of noise, but the standard Morgan has the pleasantly sharp sound of the early TR2 Triumphs. This machine had a delightful shriek over 5000 revs, appreciation of which, however, was not widespread. We love it, and it matched the car's personality perfectly.

Out on the road the Morgan is well within its limits at 75 or 80 and tracks very well with a light hand on the wheel, while wind noise is moderate for a body of this shape. Controlled by a firewall dimmer switch, the headlights are as usual adequate up to around 65 mph. When on a trip you must remember to press the foot-operated engine oil supply to the front suspension every fifty miles or so, and only eleven other greasing points require attention.

Engine accessibility recalls one of the admitted glories of a bygone age. Everything's handy and a cinch to work on. That long, louvered hood is best viewed from the driver's seat, though, where we guarantee it will give the meekest of chauffeurs an anticipatory thrill. It's no ruse, for the Morgan knows its purpose in life and has been at it a lot longer than most of these upstarts. Just tell it you're the boss, and you'll have made the sincerest of friends.　K.E.L.

MODERN version of the well-loved Morgan 4/4 has an 1,172 c.c. Ford engine. The word modern is, as John Bolster says, relative, but there remains much dignity in the classic lines of the car, which Morgan enthusiasts would not have otherwise.

Very wisely, the 1,172 c.c. Ford 100E motor has been chosen. Not only is this highly advantageous as regards initial cost and maintenance, but all the numerous accessories for increasing the power of this unit are available for purchase as finances permit. "My" Morgan had an Aquaplane aluminium cylinder head and twin S.U. carburetters. The power unit is mounted right at the front of the unusually long bonnet, and the Ford gearbox is operated by a remote control, which is similar to that of some front-wheel-drive designs.

In spite of its 8 ft. wheelbase, the Morgan is considerably lighter than the car to which this engine is normally fitted, and it has a smaller frontal area. It also has much larger wheels, which have the same effect as fitting a "higher cog" to the axle. Thus, one may confidently anticipate a higher maximum

JOHN BOLSTER TESTS
THE MORGAN 4/4, SERIES II

OF recent years the name Morgan has become associated with a 100 m.p.h., 2-litre speed model, noted for its acceleration and roadholding. There is a definite market for such a machine, but it is a little too ambitious for the many young people who are launching out with their first sports car. In the past, the Morgan 4/4 was right up their street, and so the decision has been taken to produce a modern version of this smaller model. The word "modern" is relative. The front end of the new Morgan is profiled to some extent, and the headlamps are built-in. Nevertheless, the separate mudguards, running boards, and narrow body with cutaway doors, are nostalgic of an earlier era. Your dyed-in-the-wool "Morganatic" would not have it otherwise, and to him this alliance of vintage and modern will appeal strongly.

The chassis of the Morgan is virtually the same as it has always been. The Z-section members pass beneath the rear axle, and are curved inwards towards the front. There, they are attached to a structure of tubes and pressings that carries the special form of independent suspension that all Morgans have had since 1910. In brief, the stub axles are allowed to slide up and down on what are, in effect, greatly extended king pins. As always, helical springs are the suspen-

I.f.s. has been a feature of the Morgan since as long ago as 1910. Here John Bolster puts the sturdy little car through its paces in the course of his road test.

★

sion medium, but various refinements have been added at different times during the last half century. These include telescopic dampers, and a little pedal that gives a spot of hot engine oil to the hard working steering-cum-suspension pivots. A simple form of damper insulates the stub axles from the twisting moment generated by the winding and unwinding of the helical springs, and the present cam gear steering box is a great advance on the earlier model.

speed and better acceleration figures, even without any tuning of the standard engine.

On taking one's seat, the long tapering bonnet stretches invitingly into the distance, and one remembers the thoroughbred sports cars of one's youth. The controls are well placed, but there is a lack of space for resting the left foot. The push-and-pull gear lever is unconventional, but presents no problems. Purists may regret the adoption of an "umbrella-handle" brake.

Perhaps the most endearing feature of the performance is the surprisingly effortless running of the car when cruising at over 70 m.p.h. There is no sensation of strain, and the fuel consumption remains surprisingly moderate. On the good roads of Southern England, the ride is very reasonable, but the deeper undulations of some of the Midland highways caused my head to hit one of the hood sticks on occasion. The roadholding is

LONG, graceful lines of the Morgan, although in the older idiom, appeal to an enthusiastic minority and can scarcely be denied by even the most dyed-in-the-wool modern.

excellent, and the steering is quick enough to kill any incipient skid. Very bumpy roads cause obvious flexing of the light frame, but this has much less effect on controllability than would be expected. The cornering power is exceptionally high, and if there is a very slight oversteering tendency, it yet seems to be just the right compromise for a car of this type. The tyres fitted to the test car were rather noisy when a sliding technique was employed, but the brakes are entirely adequate for the performance.

As supplied, this attractive little car had one serious disadvantage. Second speed of the standard Ford gearbox is really too low, in spite of the large road wheel, and one constantly bemoans the lack of a gear for overtaking. Proprietary gear sets are available which would overcome this trouble, and it is understood that a new heavy duty version is just out. With second gear raised to give an easy "60" instead of a doubtful "50", the car would be transformed.

The timed maximum speed of 80.3 m.p.h. is good, and will be entirely adequate for the majority of owners. However, the test engine was only moderately tuned, and there is more to come for those so inclined. With a fairly radical conversion, such as the Elva overhead inlet valve arrangement, the machine would certainly exceed 90 m.p.h. The speedometer read 8 m.p.h. fast at 80 m.p.h.

Although it is of sporting aspect, the 4/4 is entirely suitable for everyday transport. With the hood and side-screens in position, I used it as a town carriage, and I found that it was less noisy when closed than are some sports two-seaters. The hood sticks fold neatly into the rear of the body, and though the fabric is separate, it does not take long to stretch it into place. The rear compartment, under a small tonneau cover, is not particularly large, but can carry a useful quantity of luggage, or a child sitting sideways on a cushion.

The bonnet is of the classic type, with a hinge down the centre. The forward mounting of the engine brings the gearbox into the bonnet space, and the accessibility is really excellent. This is important, for the small sports car is generally owned by the type of driver who enjoys doing his own work, and the maintenance of the 4/4 should be well within his powers.

The Morgan 4/4, Series II, is a highly individual type of sports car that is peculiarly British. Though its attraction would be incomprehensible to a Continental, it has its passionate devotees in this country and, curiously enough, in America.

N.B. The car as tested is now catalogued as the Competition model. It is also available with rev. counter, price £531 (£797 17s. with P.T.) or as the Standard model with unmodified Ford engine at £475 (£713 17s. with P.T.).

SPECIFICATION AND PERFORMANCE DATA

Car Tested: Morgan 4/4, Series II, sports 2-seater, price £518 (£778 7s. with P.T.).

Engine: Four-cylinders, 63.5 mm. x 92.5 mm. (1,172 c.c.). Side valves, 40 b.h.p. at 5,000 r.p.m., 8 to 1 compression ratio. Twin S.U. carburetters. Coil and distributor ignition.

ACCELERATION GRAPH

Transmission: Single dry-plate clutch. Three-speed gearbox synchronized on two upper gears, with remote control, ratios 4.44, 8.91, and 17.29 to 1. Open propeller shaft. Hypoid rear axle.

Chassis: Z-section frame passing under rear axle. Independent sliding pillar-type front suspension with cam gear steering, helical springs and telescopic dampers. Semi-elliptic rear springs with piston-type dampers. 5.00-16 ins. tyres on bolt-on disc wheels. Girling hydraulic brakes.

Equipment: 12-volt lighting and starting. Speedometer, oil pressure and fuel gauges, ammeter.

Dimensions: Wheelbase, 8 ft.; track, 3 ft. 11 ins.; overall length, 12 ft.; width, 4 ft. 8 ins.; turning circle, 32 ft. Weight, 13 cwt.

Performance: Maximum speed 80.3 m.p.h. Speeds in gears, 2nd 48 m.p.h., 1st 26 m.p.h. Standing quarter-mile 21.4 secs. Acceleration: 0-30 m.p.h. 5.2 secs., 0-50 m.p.h. 12.8 secs., 0-60 m.p.h. 20.2 secs.

Fuel Consumption: 35 m.p.g.

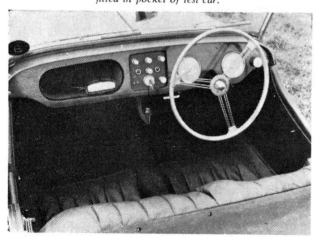

COCKPIT is adequate, if slightly "basic" by modern standards. Gear change is by an unconventional "push-pull" lever beneath the facia. Map reading light was fitted in pocket of test car.

BOTH engine and gearbox share under-bonnet space in the Morgan 4/4. Test car was the Competition model, with Aquaplane head and twin S.U. carburetters. It is also available with unmodified Ford engine.

Removal of traditional extra spare tire and slight reshaping of fuel tank have not materially altered Morgan's good lines: it "looks like a car."

ROAD TEST MORGAN 4/4

WHAT is a British company thinking of, to export to America a classic, fierce looking sports car, complete even to running boards, but with an 1172 cc engine? Does it expect big sales, or perhaps a movement to do away with the envelope body, as suggested in this month's Letters to the Editor?

To understand, it helps to know that Morgan is a company so small as to be almost unbelievable by our standards, and that it has a long history of having built strange vehicles for a limited, but apparently ever-loving, clientele. The description and Classic Road Test on the 3-wheeled 1939 Super Sports (March issue) may explain.

Now, of course, Morgan uses the Triumph TR-3's engine in its higher-priced, higher-performing cars. The 4/4 Series II is intended primarily for what Britons call the home market, and the reasons are economic: it costs a lot to buy a car in England, and it costs even more to run it. Gas rationing is another factor making the Series II a particularly attractive package on its home ground.

The Series II's engine is that of the Ford Anglia, a strong little side-valve 4. In England, the sky's the limit for this engine; the modest "speed" equipment on the test car consisted of an aluminum "Aquaplane" head giving 8.00:1 compression, plus 2 S.U. carburetors unencumbered by air cleaners, and aided by exhaust headers. Without the kit, the base price is now $2195. One can, of course, buy a Series II in its simplest form and go on, as funds permit, to the modifications.

Along with the Ford engine comes its gearbox, also sturdy enough but limited to 3 forward speeds and forced, because of its far-forward location, to use a strange remote control lever which seems to hang from the dash. On the positive side of the ledger, both linkage and the gearbox itself are easily reached beneath the pleasingly long, center-hinged hood. If you bear left as you move the lever through its positions, which are reversed from those of former American floor shifts, clashing ceases to be a problem. The drop-off in rpms as you shift from 2nd to 3rd is a serious hindrance, whether you're poking through traffic or running a road test. The

The standard engine of the $2195 Series II is the Anglia's.

Headers, S.U. carburetors, aluminum head on the modified car.

PHOTOGRAPHY: POOLE

Large white horn button can be seen through wheel spokes.

Extraordinary handling makes up for a lack of cubic inches in this uncompromising classic

test figures and graph bear out what could be expected when adjacent overall ratios differ so sharply as 8.25 and 4.44.

The car handles superbly, with some easily predictable understeer despite the lightness of the front end. Morgan continues to use a form of independent front suspension adopted by it in 1910 (!) with only relatively minor modifications. Coil springs and stub axles are used, the latter moving up and down on what are really large kingpins. This combination of functions makes all the more desirable the partially automatic type of chassis lubrication: a foot pedal shoots hot engine oil to the pivots.

Steering and road-holding are of such a pleasing nature in the Series II that only a super-abundance of enthusiasm should ever get you into a bad spot. Such situations are best avoided, since there's no great margin of power to help you recover.

The ride is unquestionably stern, but unpleasant in one aspect only. There is so little space for rear axle movement, thanks to the frame's underslung configuration, that a fairly ordinary dip can bring forth a spine-jarring crack from behind.

Inside the car, Spartan characteristics are much in evidence. No springs adorn the seat cushions, which sit not too firmly on wood bases and are so light that the passenger's seat, if not occupied and if no tonneau cover is used, can easily become airborne at higher speeds. A deeply contoured seat back gives the feel of bucket seats. Your left foot rests on the clutch pedal, whether you like it or not, and you'll have to handle any problems of reach by your own methods, for neither steering nor seats are adjustable. A tachometer is an extra. A dash-mounted horn is suitable for knuckle or fingertip use. The handbrake is adequate but awkward.

Storage space is limited to the small well behind the seat, and must be shared with the side curtains when they are not erected. We expected these and the top to be sketchy in their protection, in keeping with other parts of the car, but were agreeably surprised. Curtains and the top itself are not a struggle to install or remove; the top fabric is separate from the frame, but easy to handle.

Like the Fiat 1100 (page 18, this issue) the Morgan offers many compensations for its tiny engine. There is no question that driving a higher-powered car is more fun when one has an opening in traffic, and can be more restful on a trip, particularly when cruising rather than being pushed to its utmost. Yet both the Fiat and the 4/4 Series II do remarkably well in the smoothness-for-size department. There is also a certain smug satisfaction in getting a lot out of little; Americans might find it more enjoyable than they suspect. ●

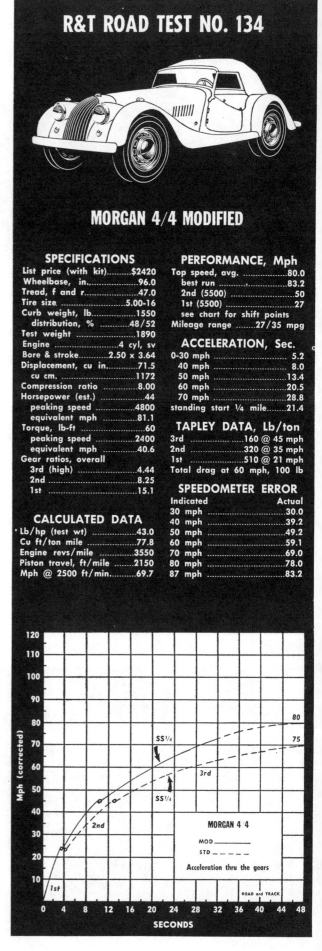

R&T ROAD TEST NO. 134

MORGAN 4/4 MODIFIED

SPECIFICATIONS

List price (with kit)	$2420
Wheelbase, in.	96.0
Tread, f and r	47.0
Tire size	5.00-16
Curb weight, lb.	1550
distribution, %	48/52
Test weight	1890
Engine	4 cyl, sv
Bore & stroke	2.50 x 3.64
Displacement, cu in.	71.5
cu cm.	1172
Compression ratio	8.00
Horsepower (est.)	44
peaking speed	4800
equivalent mph	81.1
Torque, lb-ft	60
peaking speed	2400
equivalent mph	40.6
Gear ratios, overall	
3rd (high)	4.44
2nd	8.25
1st	15.1

CALCULATED DATA

Lb/hp (test wt)	43.0
Cu ft/ton mile	77.8
Engine revs/mile	3550
Piston travel, ft/mile	2150
Mph @ 2500 ft/min.	69.7

PERFORMANCE, Mph

Top speed, avg.	80.0
best run	83.2
2nd (5500)	50
1st (5500)	27
see chart for shift points	
Mileage range	27/35 mpg

ACCELERATION, Sec.

0-30 mph	5.2
40 mph	8.0
50 mph	13.4
60 mph	20.5
70 mph	28.8
standing start ¼ mile	21.4

TAPLEY DATA, Lb/ton

3rd	160 @ 45 mph
2nd	320 @ 35 mph
1st	510 @ 21 mph
Total drag at 60 mph, 100 lb	

SPEEDOMETER ERROR

Indicated	Actual
30 mph	30.0
40 mph	39.2
50 mph	49.2
60 mph	59.1
70 mph	69.0
80 mph	78.0
87 mph	83.2

MORGAN 4/4

MOD ———

STD – – – – –

Acceleration thru the gears

ROAD and TRACK

A more closely cowled radiator grille identifies the Plus Four models for 1958, the open versions also having the wider body seen here. The wire wheels are an optional extra on all types.

An improved MORGAN range

Wider Plus Four Open
Models and a
Competition Version
of the 4/4

FOR 1958 the current Morgan range is being continued, with minor improvements to the Plus Four and an additional Series II 4/4 model in the shape of a Competition version.

In frontal appearance, the Plus Four models have been altered slightly by extending the cowl downwards 3 in. and curtailing the depth of the grille by a like amount, thus giving an even more squat appearance.

Less noticeable at a glance, but of greater actual significance, is a useful increase in the body width of the open Plus Four models. This has been achieved by extending the body sides outwards in relation to the wings and running boards (as is already done on the coupé), the effect being to increase the width at the screen by 2 in. and over the seats by 4 in., the

coil-spring front suspension which the Morgan company pioneered 40 years ago and a robust but unconventional chassis frame with Z-section side members which permit the floor boards to rest on the lower flanges of the "Z" and give very low seating; the frame is underslung at the rear.

The Series II 4/4 model is of similar general design, but the 2-litre engines and separate gearbox of the Plus Four are replaced by a 1,172 c.c. Ford Anglia engine and three-speed gearbox unit. This model, which was introduced two years ago, caters for the driver with sports-car leanings but strictly limited resources. Selling at nearly £150 below the price of the Plus Four two-seater, this model showed a mean speed of 74.1 m.p.h., a 0-50 m.p.h. acceleration time of 16.0 sec. and overall fuel consumption of 35.1

m.p.g. when tested in untuned form by *The Motor*.

In response to the demand for a tuned version, the Series II 4/4 can now (as recorded in this journal three weeks ago) be obtained in Competition form with an Aquaplane aluminium-alloy cylinder head giving an 8/1 compression ratio, stronger valve springs, special inlet and exhaust manifold, two S.U. carburetters and a rev. counter. The result is to increase the power output from the standard 36 b.h.p. at 4,400 r.p.m. to 40 b.h.p. at 5,100 r.p.m. and is stated to increase the maximum speed by some 10 m.p.h.

Prices of these latest Morgan models appear in the usual price panel on page 264, but it should be noted that all models can be obtained with wire wheels if required, at an extra cost of £32 10s. plus purchase tax.

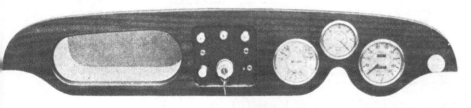

A newcomer is the Morgan 4/4 Competition model, with an Aquaplane cylinder head and other tuning on the 1,172 c.c. Ford engine. The facia panel of this model has three dials comprising (*left*) ammeter, fuel gauge, oil pressure gauge, tachometer (*centre*) and speedometer (*right*.)

internal measurement at the latter going up from 41 in. to 45 in. The value of this substantial increase is particularly apparent when the hood and sidescreens are in use.

In other respects, the Plus Four models are unchanged. There are six models in this range, namely the two-seater, the four-seater and the drophead coupé, each offered with the choice of either the 2,088 c.c. four-cylinder Standard Vanguard engine developing 68 b.h.p. or the 1,991 c.c. Triumph TR3 version with its output of 100 b.h.p. and three-figure maximum speed.

Despite a recent minor increase in prices, these models continue to represent very good value on a speed-for-money basis and the availability of an open four-seater edition is notable. Unusual features of the specification include the vertical

Make: Morgan **Type:** Plus Four (Triumph TR3 Engine)

Makers: Morgan Motor Co., Ltd., Malvern Link, Worcs.

Test Data

World copyright reserved ; no unauthorized reproduction in whole or in part.

CONDITIONS : Weather : Mild, dry, little wind. (Temperature 48°F., Barometer 30.3 in. Hg.) Surface : Smooth concrete (Ostend motor road). Fuel : Belgian premium-grade petrol (approx. 95 Research Method Octane rating).

INSTRUMENTS
Speedometer at 30 m.p.h.	accurate
Speedometer at 60 m.p.h.	5% fast
Speedometer at 90 m.p.h.	4% fast
Distance recorder	1% fast

WEIGHT
Kerb weight (unladen, but with oil, coolant and fuel for approx. 50 miles) .. .. 16¾ cwt.
Front/rear distribution of kerb weight 50/50
Weight laden as tested .. .. 20½ cwt.

MAXIMUM SPEEDS
Flying Quarter Mile
Mean of four opposite runs .. .. 100.3 m.p.h.
Best one-way time equals .. .. 101.1 m.p.h.
"Maximile" Speed. (Timed quarter mile after one mile accelerating from rest.)
Mean of four opposite runs .. .. 100.3 m.p.h.
Best one-way time equals .. .. 101.1 m.p.h.
Speed in Gears
Max. speed in 3rd gear .. .. .. 73 m.p.h.
Max. speed in 2nd gear .. .. .. 50 m.p.h.
Max. speed in 1st gear .. .. .. 30 m.p.h.

FUEL CONSUMPTION
45 m.p.g. at constant 30 m.p.h. on level.
41½ m.p.g. at constant 40 m.p.h. on level.
36½ m.p.g. at constant 50 m.p.h. on level.
31½ m.p.g. at constant 60 m.p.h. on level.
26 m.p.g. at constant 70 m.p.h. on level.
22½ m.p.g. at constant 80 m.p.h. on level.
Overall Fuel Consumption for 1,171 miles, 42.1 gallons, equals 27.8 m.p.g. (10.2 litres/100 km.)
Touring Fuel Consumption (m.p.g. at steady speed midway between 30 m.p.h. and maximum, less 5% allowance for acceleration) 27.1 m.p.g.
Fuel Tank Capacity (maker's figure) 11 gallons.

STEERING
Turning circle between kerbs :
Left .. .. 30¾ feet
Right .. .. 32 feet
Turns of steering wheel from lock to lock 2⅛

BRAKES from 30 m.p.h.
0.93 g retardation (equivalent to 32½ ft. stopping distance) with 115 lb. pedal pressure.
0.80 g retardation (equivalent to 37½ ft. stopping distance) with 100 lb. pedal pressure.
0.61 g retardation (equivalent to 49½ ft. stopping distance) with 75 lb. pedal pressure.
0.39 g retardation (equivalent to 77 ft. stopping distance) with 50 lb. pedal pressure.
0.17 g retardation (equivalent to 175 ft. stopping distance) with 25 lb. pedal pressure.

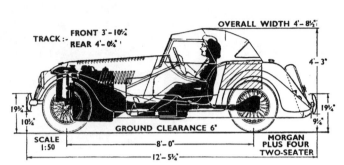

TRACK :- FRONT 3'-10¼" REAR 4'-0¼"
OVERALL WIDTH 4'-8½"
4'-3"
19¼" 10¼"
19¼" 9¼"
GROUND CLEARANCE 6"
SCALE 1:50
8'-0"
12'-5¼"
MORGAN PLUS FOUR TWO-SEATER

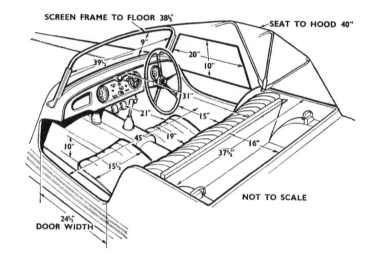

SCREEN FRAME TO FLOOR 38½"
SEAT TO HOOD 40"
9"
39½" 20" 10"
31" 15"
21" 45" 19" 16"
10" 37½"
15½"
24½" DOOR WIDTH
NOT TO SCALE

ACCELERATION TIMES from standstill
0-30 m.p.h.	3.2 sec.
0-40 m.p.h.	4.6 sec.
0-50 m.p.h.	6.8 sec.
0-60 m.p.h.	9.7 sec.
0-70 m.p.h.	13.3 sec.
0-80 m.p.h.	19.1 sec.
0-90 m.p.h.	28.5 sec.
Standing quarter mile	17.5 sec.

ACCELERATION TIMES on upper ratios
	Top gear	3rd gear
10-30 m.p.h.	7.5 sec.	4.8 sec.
20-40 m.p.h.	8.0 sec.	5.4 sec.
30-50 m.p.h.	8.3 sec.	5.5 sec.
40-60 m.p.h.	9.4 sec.	5.9 sec.
50-70 m.p.h.	10.0 sec.	7.3 sec.
60-80 m.p.h.	12.3 sec.	
70-90 m.p.h.	22.0 sec.	

HILL CLIMBING at sustained steady speeds
Max. gradient on top gear .. .. 1 in 7.8 (Tapley 285 lb./ton)
Max. gradient on 3rd gear .. .. 1 in 5.5 (Tapley 405 lb./ton)
Max. gradient on 2nd gear .. .. 1 in 3.8 (Tapley 565 lb./ton)

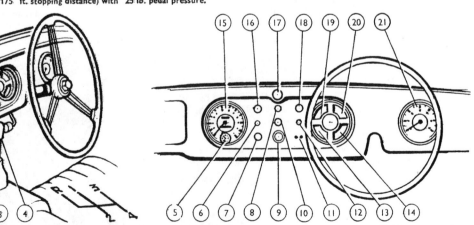

1. One-shot king-pin lubrication pedal. 2. Handbrake. 3. Headlamp dip switch. 4. Gear lever. 5. Clock. 6. Dynamo charge warning light. 7. Choke control. 8. Starter Switch. 9. Ignition and lights switch. 10. Foglamp switch. 11. Charging or inspection-lamp points. 12. Headlamp mainbeam indicator lamp. 13. Water thermometer. 14. Fuel contents gauge. 15. Speedometer with distance recorder. 16. Windscreen wipers control. 17. Horn button. 18. Panel light switch. 19. Ammeter. 20. Oil pressure gauge. 21. Rev. counter.

The Morgan Plus Four Two-seater

(with Triumph TR3 Engine)

Classic elegance goes with functional simplicity. The optional wire wheels lower the m.p.h. per 1000 r.p.m. by about 3%.

A Modern Vintage Sports Car with Vivid Acceleration

THERE was a time, not many years ago, when a sports car was a vehicle which sacrificed comfort, warmth and silence to the more fundamental ideals of performance and a behaviour on the road which gave pleasure to its owner in the mere act of driving. Times have changed, bringing greater comfort with increases in performance which have not always been matched by improved handling, yet in the case of the Morgan two-seater the original definition still holds remarkably good.

It should not be deduced from this that no progress has been made since the first four-wheeled Morgan was marketed in 1936 with the same basic design as today's car. Rather has an essentially sporting but inexpensive machine been developed to modern standards of roadworthiness and performance, without losing sight of the original purpose. Prices, of course, have increased everywhere, but the latest Triumph-engined Plus Four at a total of £969 is the cheapest 100 m.p.h. car made in Britain; in handling it is above average for its class; and in through-the-gears acceleration up to 80 m.p.h. it is a match for competitors costing up to double the price.

Nevertheless, to many a driver accustomed to modern comforts, first impressions of the Morgan will inevitably be of rather Spartan simplicity, a view which may not be finally abandoned until he embarks upon a journey prepared for the pure fun of driving. Cockpit dimensions have been increased considerably since the old days, but the car remains a carefully tailored two-seater. The door openings are a minimum space to climb through, rather than an invitation to flop easily into an armchair. Once inserted, the driver finds himself unexpectedly comfortable on an air-cushion seat (placed on a wooden base that cannot be felt), wide enough for the hips but narrow enough to keep him firmly in place on fast corners. No allowance for different lengths of leg is provided, but the back rest is adjustable for rake between a fairly upright setting and one which is much too upright for most tastes. Mounting the gearbox well back from the engine, in such a position that the short gear lever is directly on top of it, firmly divides the cockpit into two rather narrow slots. As a result the driver's left foot can find a resting place only on the clutch pedal or on the floor between it and the brake pedal, practicable in daylight but not at night when a foot is also wanted for a dipswitch high up on the bulkhead.

Visibility is of the low-slung sports-car type—a driver of moderate height, sitting willy-nilly close up to the steering wheel, can just keep an eye on the separate side-lamp on the nearside front wing. Sideways and rearwards, the view tends to be restricted by rather scratchable plastic windows and a small hood which there is every encouragement to fold and put away. In any but rainy weather, especially if a heater is fitted to warm the feet, a properly coated enthusiast is likely to get the most enjoyment out of his car by running with the hood removed and sidescreens in place.

Pleasure in Precision

Driving pleasure is unquestionably the Morgan's purpose. The pleasure of going fast is part of it, but perhaps more important is a feeling of mastery over any situation which comes with controls designed without frills for their particular job. First among these is the steering, by a spring-spoked wheel which is close to the driver and close to the facia. By the standards of today the effort it requires is large, increasing with the amount of lock applied, on account of strong castor action. The car is naturally straight-running, making unnoticeable the half-inch or so of free play at the rim when the wheel is centred, and on the slightest turn there is no lost

In Brief

Price (including wire wheels as tested)
£677 10s. plus purchase tax £340 2s. equals £1,017 12s.
Price with disc wheels (including purchase tax) £968 17s.

Capacity	... ...	1,991 c.c.
Unladen kerb weight	...	16¾ cwt.
Acceleration:		
20-40 m.p.h. in top gear	...	8.0 sec.
0-50 m.p.h. through gears		6.8 sec.
Maximum direct top gear		
gradient	... ...	1 in 7.8
Maximum speed	...	100.3 m.p.h.
"Maximile" speed	...	100.3 m.p.h.
Touring fuel consumption	...	27.1 m.p.g.

Gearing: 19.7 m.p.h. in top gear at 1,000 r.p.m. (disc wheels, 20.2 m.p.h.); 33.5 m.p.h. at 1,000 ft./min. piston speed (disc wheels, 32.7 m.p.h.)

The front number plate (unlike the rear one) is mounted well clear of the ground, and allows plenty of cool air to reach the sump.

a one-shot oil system operated from the cockpit every 100 miles or so, equal stress is laid in the owner's manual on the need to apply an occasional spanner or screwdriver to parts which may work loose in ordinary motoring.

This does not by any means suggest frailty in the vital components. Remarks about the positive steering and handling apply also to the other controls. Out of a selection of performance figures which are partly attributable to a powerful engine in a light car, can be picked some really startling times which are almost equally due to the robust and effective transmission. In the files of *The Motor* road-test reports, the 6.8 sec. recorded by the Morgan to accelerate from standstill to 50

Real engine accessibility is possible with the side-opening bonnet. Air cleaners have to be omitted for lack of space.

A fair quantity of luggage can be carried, although not under lock and key. The cockpit is tailor-made for serious motoring in close - to - wheel style.

motion or suggestion of sponginess whatever. The description "precise" takes on a new meaning under these conditions which can be forgotten on more ordinary vehicles, and by those who appreciate precision the heaviness is soon forgiven.

Steering control is not the only tradition to be flaunted, for steering behaviour is in keeping with the very "vintage" equal weight distribution between front and rear wheels. There is, in the accepted sense, neither under- nor oversteer, the car going exactly where it is pointed under all conditions, up to the point where the rear wheels begin to slide. On the debit side, reaction from rough roads can be felt through the steering wheel, as it can through the suspension.

The fact that the I.F.S., which locates each front on a coil-sprung sliding pillar, is the same in general layout as the suspension first used on three-wheeled Morgans in 1910, is a tribute to the designer. It would be idle to pretend that springs of such short travel come anywhere near absorbing bumps as might be expected of a 1958 car. In the primary object of keeping the wheels on the road, and the car on a proper line, however, they do a good job. A very British sports car, the Morgan needs a very exceptional British road to throw

it off balance. Stiffly sprung and firmly damped, its roadholding is outstanding and it remains one of the very, very few vehicles (including cars built for racing) which corner with *no* appreciable roll. Pushed beyond the limit, the rear wheels break away controllably, with adequate warning to a competent driver that this is going to happen.

On the aforementioned roads of Britain the ride may be politely described as lively, although in immediately post-war days it would have probably excited little comment. The air-cushion seats are a useful compensation, but on really poor surfaces such as those encountered in Northern France and Belgium *en route* to the Jabbeke highway, one is strongly reminded that the greatest progress in modern, soft suspensions has been the virtual elimination of pitching. The nose of the Morgan bobs up and down in manner now almost forgotten, and an occasional big bump can send the springs on to the stops.

For the soft-bred modern motorist who may find this criticism rather daunting it is only fair to observe that the makers of the Plus Four acknowledge and intend that the car shall have an individual character. Thus, while the importance is stressed of lubricating the front suspension pillars (by

m.p.h. has been beaten only by two sports-racing cars, of $3\frac{1}{2}$ litres and $5\frac{1}{2}$ litres respectively. The vital fact is that this test involved three violent operations of the clutch and two of the gearbox, neither of which (nor the rear axle) showed any sign of protest against decidedly abnormal treatment. The clutch, let in suddenly at 2,500 r.p.m., took up without slip (momentary wheelspin sufficing for take-off) and without judder, yet was reasonably light to disengage. The gearbox, although the synchromesh is barely effective enough even for leisurely gear-changing, could be snatched from first to second with open throttle, and from second to third at just below 5,000 r.p.m. with only a slight lift of the right foot. Movement of the lever is light and positive, with a rather ineffectual spring-loading to guard the reverse position.

In contrast to the transmission arrangements, braking is adequate but no more. In terms of friction lining area per ton of car it is certainly better than adequate, and the brakes showed no fading tendency, but they were prone to occasional grabbing, and the high proportion of effort on the front wheels could cause them to lock at low speeds on a very slippery surface. The fly-off type handbrake is powerful enough

Hood and sidescreens serve adequately to keep the rain out, and less so to exclude draughts.

for use in manoeuvring (rally driving tests, for example) as well as parking. It is, however, too far forward on the passenger's side of the transmission to be really convenient, and on the test car the ratchet was inclined to slip.

Little comment is called for on the very well-known Triumph 2-litre engine, which is now of TR3 specification, developing 100 b.h.p. A penalty of the Morgan remote-gearbox arrangement is that no overdrive unit can be fitted, but light weight enables the engine to pull a high direct top gear and show good fuel economy. On any British premium-grade petrol it starts and warms up quickly in cold weather, and pinks a little only under the kind of treatment a sports car with a good gearbox is unlikely to receive.

The engine is noisy, the more so because the Plus-Four's narrow bonnet necessitates removing the air cleaners so that loud hissing from the twin carburetters accompanies every opening of the throttle. Noise, in fact, is one of the features of the car an owner simply has to get used to; the bulkhead transmits most of that coming from the engine compartment, the gearbox makes a considerable whine in the indirect ratios (especially reverse), and with the hood and sidescreens in place there is more noise from the buffeting of the wind. Exhaust noise, however, is moderate enough

for fast driving not to arouse public displeasure.

As mentioned earlier, there is a good deal to be said for driving, when possible, with the car open. Draught-proofing is usually exiguous on a sports car, and the method of attachment of the sidescreens prevents their being draught-proof, although they effectively keep out the rain. Traditional styling, however, means that wide wings prevent mud being thrown up under the sidescreens. The hood is entirely detachable, with a flexible rear window and quarter-lights, so that it can be folded up and stowed compactly in the generous luggage well behind the seats. Folding or putting up the hood takes only a couple of minutes, and unlike some types in which the hood and frame are integral it can be easily handled by one person. Discouragement to casual kerbside larceny (and occasionally to a forgetful owner in a hurry) is provided by flaps on the sidescreens secured on the inside, so that the door can only be opened after unbuttoning two or three studs of the hood.

The instruments and minor controls are functional and on the whole well arranged.

It is questionable whether, even on a car with a rev. counter, the speedometer should be so far from the driver's line of sight, but the layout places ammeter, oilpressure gauge, water thermometer and fuel gauge directly in front of him. The horn button is at the top of the instrument panel, near enough to be touched with a hand still on the steering wheel. Flashing direction indicators and a recirculating interior heater are optional extra components, the latter occupying a space above the passenger's feet.

As befits a fast car, the headlamps throw a long, penetrating beam, while the horn note resembles that of a continental lorry, with effective results. There seems to be no explanation for extremely short windscreen wiper blades.

Taken as a whole, minor criticisms of the Plus-Four might appear rather forbidding; in detail it undoubtedly lacks some of the refinements of the mass-produced saloon of today. To this the complete answer is that a relatively small body of motoring enthusiasts is still prepared to exchange central-heated luxury for driving that is fun and, incidentally, fast.

Specification

Engine
Cylinders	4
Bore	83 mm.
Stroke	92 mm.
Cubic capacity	1,991 c.c.
Piston area	33.5 sq. in.
Valves	Pushrod o.h.v.
Compression ratio	8.5/1
Carburetters	Twin horizontal S.U.
Fuel pump	AC mechanical
Ignition timing control	Centrifugal and vacuum
Oil filter	AC full-flow
Max. power (gross)	100 b.h.p.
at	4,800 r.p.m.
Piston speed at max. b.h.p.	2,900 ft./min.

Transmission
Clutch	9 in. Borg and Beck s.d.p.
Top gear (s/m)	3.72
3rd gear (s/m)	5.1
2nd gear (s/m)	7.3
1st gear	12.5
Reverse	12.5
Overdrive	No
Propeller shaft	Hardy Spicer open
Final drive	Hypoid bevel
Top gear m.p.h. at 1,000 r.p.m.	19.7 (disc wheels, 20.2)
Top gear m.p.h. at 1,000 ft./min. piston speed	32.7 (disc wheels, 33.5)

Chassis
Brakes	Girling hydraulic, 2 l.s. front
Brake drum internal diameter	9 in.
Friction lining area	121 sq. in.
Suspension:	
Front	Sliding pillar and coil spring i.f.s.
Rear	Semi-elliptic leaf and rigid axle
Shock absorbers	
Front	Armstrong telescopic
Rear	Armstrong lever
Steering gear	Cam gear
Tyres	5.60—15 tubed (disc wheels, 5.25—16 tubeless)

Coachwork and Equipment
Starting handle	Yes
Battery mounting	In rear, under luggage compartment
Jack	Stevenson screw type
Jacking points	One each side through floor
Standard tool kit: 2 box spanners, 3 d/e spanners, adjustable spanner, pliers, screwdriver, contact point gauge, tyre pump, grease gun, tool roll.	
Exterior lights	2 head, 2 side, 2 tail, 1 number plate
Number of electrical fuses	Two
Direction indicators	Extra, flashing type
Windscreen wipers	Electric, non-parking
Windscreen washers	Extra
Sun vizors	None
Instruments: Speedometer with decimal trip distance recorder, rev. counter, oil pressure gauge, ammeter, water thermometer, fuel gauge.	
Warning lights: Dynamo charge, headlamp main beam, indicators when fitted.	

Locks:	
With ignition key	Ignition
With other keys	None
Cubby holes	One in facia
Map pockets	None
Parcel shelves	None
Ashtrays	None
Cigar lighters	None
Interior lights	None
Interior heater	Extra Smith's recirculating type
Car radio	Extra, Radiomobile
Extras available: Heater, tonneau cover, luggage grid, rear bumper, direction indicators, leather upholstery.	
Upholstery material	P.V.C. (leather extra)
Floor covering	Rubber
Exterior colours standardised: Any colour listed by International Paints, Ltd.	
Alternative body styles: 4-seat tourer, 2-seat drophead coupé	

Maintenance
Sump	11 pints, S.A.E. 20 (winter) 30 (summer)
Gearbox	2½ pints, S.A.E. 30
Rear axle	2½ pints, S.A.E. hypoid
Steering gear lubricant	Hypoid
Cooling system capacity	16 pints (2 drain taps)
Chassis lubrication: By grease gun every 3,000 miles to 6 points, every 5,000 miles to 7 further points (one-shot lubrication of front suspension by pedal every 100 miles).	
Ignition timing	4° b.t.d.c.
Contact-breaker gap	0.012 in.
Sparking plug gap	0.032 in.

Valve timing: Inlet opens 15° b.t.d.c., closes 55° a.b.d.c.; exhaust opens 55° b.b.d.c., closes 15° a.t.d.c.	
Tappet clearances (cold):	
Inlet	0.010 in.
Exhaust	0.012 in.
Front wheel toe-in	⅛ in.–1/16 in.
Camber angle	2°
Castor angle	4°
Steering swivel pin inclination	2°
Tyre pressures:	
Front	17 lb.
Rear	17 lb.
(For high speeds, 22 lb. and 20 lb.)	
Brake fluid	Girling
Battery type and capacity	Two 6-volt, total 54 amp. hr.

Perhaps the most delightful feature of the Morgan is the colossal "punch" which the engine delivers at low revs., for the car is so light that it responds beautifully to the accelerator pedal. Too many of the cars which I have tried lately have seemed over-geared and sluggish, giving no performance unless the gear lever were used energetically. The Morgan has a splendid gearchange, but it can also be driven all day on top gear. I drove the car on a cross-country journey which involved some winding country lanes. The rev-counter frequently fell back to 800 r.p.m. on the corners, but even uphill the machine accelerated briskly away on top gear. Yet, 50 and 75 m.p.h. may be exceeded on second and third speeds when one requires rocket-like acceleration. The test car had a rather prominent exhaust-note at peak revs.

Both at the front and at the rear, the suspension of the Morgan has a limited

JOHN BOLSTER TESTS

THE MORGAN PLUS FOUR

I ALWAYS look forward immensely to my road tests of Morgans. These high-performance cars have all the attractions of the Vintage sports models, and are ideal touring vehicles for typical English roads. I had tested the Ford-, Vanguard- and TR2-engined Morgans, but now the TR3-engined version has come along, with wire wheels as an extra, which has given me an excuse for another delightful week of "Morganatic Motoring".

I need not tell you that the chassis is the same as it has always been! Those straight Z-section members still pass beneath the back axle, from which they are suspended on short semi-elliptic springs, and in front (of course) one finds sliding stub axles on pillars, with helical springs. The gearbox nestles between the seats, with a short, central lever projecting from its lid, and it is attached to the engine by a duralumin bell housing with a central tubular extension. In other words, the Morgan is still a Morgan.

The open two-seater body is very well made, and has no rattles. The luggage space, normally hidden by the tonneau cover, is suitable for the carriage of a child sitting sideways, which the younger Bolsters much appreciated. The body owes little to aerodynamic research, but " . . . isn't it nice," said the lady on my left, "to be sitting behind a real bonnet again, with a hinge down the middle and lots of louvres." The amateur mechanic will bless that bonnet, for engine accessibility is really first class.

The Morgan has one of the best hoods I have used. The frame opens up out of the luggage boot in one quick movement, and the actual hood, of best quality heavy material, then buttons down with no difficulty at all. Why it should be so easy to fit I do not know, but even at 100 m.p.h. there is not the slightest sign of flapping—most hoods flap at 80 m.p.h. and tear or blow away before the hundred mark is reached! I understand that the sidescreens of my car were prototypes, but with their sliding panels they were truly excellent.

Naturally, the driving position is dead right, and as one moves off a touch of the accelerator pedal causes the seat to press one firmly in the back. The new engine certainly gives more power, and the acceleration figures are a useful improvement over those of the TR2-engined version. This car has really brilliant acceleration right up to 80 m.p.h., and it is only as 90 m.p.h. is approached that the wind resistance begins to slow the upwards rush of the speedometer needle.

Curiously enough, the new car is no faster than its predecessor. With the hood and sidescreens erect, it will register an honest, timed 100 m.p.h. in both directions, but I was unable to squeeze any more out of it. However, the wire wheels carry larger section tyres, and I ran them at the low pressure which the makers recommend. I feel that a few strokes on the tyre pump might have given me those extra m.p.h.

★

★

travel. On bumpy roads, the car is subject to some sharp up and down movement, and the ride is definitely hard. Yet, the handling is admirable, and corners may be taken with considerable enterprise. The steering is "quick", and the controllability on wet roads is particularly good. The machine runs straight and true at 100 m.p.h. and the springs do not "wind up" during a sprint getaway. Although the steering is not particularly light, the increase in tyre section has made no difference to its "feel".

The brakes look small, but the car weighs very little. At 100 m.p.h., the powerful braking effect of the wind, plus the retarding influence of four relatively large cylinders, slows the vehicle rapidly to 70 m.p.h. or so, when normal braking is required. I was able to heat the brakes up to the point where they were a little uneven, but only by very hard driving. I have no doubt that the wire

POWER HOUSE. Under the bonnet is housed the potent Triumph TR3 engine delivering 101 b.h.p. at 5,000 r.p.m.

Acceleration Graph

wheels are better than the discs for brake cooling.

A very pleasant feature of the Morgan is the way in which it will put up high average speeds without attempting to hurry. Other cars are overtaken with almost contemptuous ease, and the controllability and moderate size both assist in the rapid and safe negotiation of difficult or crowded roads. There is something very pleasant, too, about the excellent all-round visibility and the sense that one has of being a part of the car. On one journey, I had been enjoying these qualities, and the sensation of driving an open car on a summer evening. Then, as night fell, it began to grow cold. Instead of putting on my overcoat, I stopped for a few moments to raise the hood. So, in saloon-like comfort, I sat behind the powerful beams of the headlamps, and continued to put the miles astern. The Morgan is a sports car, but it is thoroughly practical and civilized, and the seats are really comfortable.

The Plus-Four, with TR3 engine, is a fast car of marked personality. For some, the ride may be too hard and the appearance may lack that suggestion of Detroit. For the man who has to live with his sports car all the week, as well as at week-ends, however, this machine is an excellent buy. Many a dreary duty journey will be rendered thoroughly enjoyable, and routine maintenance will be found to be particularly easy. Above all, the Morgan is a worthy partner for the art of driving fast safely.

FUNCTIONAL. The cockpit of the Morgan is devoid of frills and is in the true sports car tradition.

Specification and Performance Data

Car Tested: Morgan Plus-Four two-seater. Price £645 (£968 17s. including P.T.). Extra: wire wheels £32 10s. plus £16 5s. P.T.

Engine: Four cylinders 83 mm. x 92 mm. (1,991 c.c.). Pushrod-operated overhead valves; 8.5 to 1 compression ratio; 101 b.h.p. at 5,000 r.p.m. Twin SU carburetters. Lucas coil and distributor.

Transmission: Borg and Beck 9 ins. single dry-plate clutch. Four-speed Moss gearbox with short central lever on top of box, connected to clutch by extension shaft in duralumin housing. Ratios, 3.72, 5.1, 7.3 and 12.5 to 1. Short open Hardy Spicer propeller shaft. Salisbury hypoid rear axle.

Chassis: Z-section underslung at rear. Independent front suspension by stub axles sliding upon extended king pins against helical springs. Cam and sector steering. Semi-elliptic rear springs with sliding trunnion blocks at back and silent-bloc bushes in front. Girling hydraulic dampers, telescopic in front, piston-type at rear. Girling 2LS hydraulic brakes in 9 ins. drums. Extra: knock-on wire wheels fitted 5.60-15 ins. tyres.

Equipment: 12-volt lighting and starting. Speedometer, rev. counter, ammeter, clock, water temperature, oil pressure and fuel gauges. Extras on test car: heater, spotlamps, reversing light.

Dimensions: Wheelbase, 8 ft.; track, 3 ft. 11 ins.; overall length, 11 ft. 8 ins.; overall width, 4 ft. 8 ins.; turning circle, 30 ft.; weight, 16 cwt.

Performance: Maximum speed 100 m.p.h. Speeds in gears, 3rd 78 m.p.h., 2nd 52 m.p.h., 1st 30 m.p.h. Standing quarter-mile 17.6 secs. Acceleration, 0-30 m.p.h. 3 secs., 0-50 m.p.h. 7.4 secs., 0-60 m.p.h. 10.6 secs., 0-80 m.p.h., 18.4 secs., 0-90 m.p.h. 29.6 secs.

Fuel Consumption: Driven hard, 28 m.p.g.

*A fully illustrated catalogue
may be obtained on request from*

THE MORGAN MOTOR CO., LTD.

MALVERN LINK, WORCESTERSHIRE   Telephone: Malvern 106

MORGAN "plus four" COUPE

In Body And Chassis THE IMMUTABLE MORGAN
Hews To A Vanishing Status Quo, But Its Power And
Performance Put It In The Sports Car Avant Garde

"LO AND BEHOLD, up popped Lew Spencer in the Morgan again! Spencer, who enjoys the role of giant-killer with his green machine, presently *leads* MotoRacing's Pacific Coast sports car racing point standings in the Production Over 1500 cc category, pacing such marques as 300SL, Corvette and Porsche."

Commenting on this startling notice in a recent issue of our friendly contemporary, Morgan-importer Rene Pellandini said, "Sure, it's fantastic. Also, Barbara Windhorst has been mopping up consistently well for Morgan in ladies' events, beating Lotus, Corvettes and all comers. But let's face it, we've got a good combination working: the TR3 Morgan, good drivers, and, in Claude Brun, a mechanic in a million."

Since its introduction in 1951 the Morgan Plus Four has come up from behind inconspicuously but steadily to become an outstanding racing contender both outside of and within its class. The race-worthiness of the 1951 chassis with its 40 year old sliding-pillar front suspension was largely kept hidden by its reliable but mere 68 bhp Standard Vanguard engine. Then in 1954 the Plus Four was offered with either the Vanguard or the 90 bhp TR2 engine, the latter providing a 32 per cent increase in output with no increase in weight. Pounds per horsepower dropped from about 27 to 20 and the Plus Four suddenly seized power in the 2-liter production class . . . except in the presence of AC- and Arnolt-Bristols. Then, in '57, the Plus Four acquired the TR3 100 bhp engine and became even more of a bomb on the street or road course, resulting in its high position today — not just in its class, but in overall standings as well.

High-point man Lew Spencer has been a Morganatic since '53 and he has owned one each of the three versions

of the Plus Four just described. There were just over 3,000 miles on the odometer of his new, TR3-engined, red convertible coupe when we rendezvoused at the SCI's desert-mountain test area in the Southwest. Along for the ride and to put miles on a new machine was young Claude Brun. He is Pellandini's top go-fast mechanic, and first barked his knuckles as an apprentice in a racing garage in his native Cannes, on the French Riviera. His mount was Baby Doll Number 3, a shiny green Sebring-type Morgan competition roadster. With only 65 miles on its engine, test runs were out of the question.

With a full tank of fuel the convertible weighs nearly 2,100 pounds, making it the heaviest car Morgan has built. But even so it pulls only 20.7 pounds per horsepower, wringing wet, and is a torrid package even with our test car's numerically-low axle ratio of 3.73.

Taking first things first, entry is easy and is far from being a shoe-horn operation. Under the leather upholstery of the seats are pneumatic bladders which may be inflated to adjust both seat height and softness. The support and comfort that these seats provide cannot be improved upon. Foot room is good, the pedals are not crowded together and all controls are handy with the exception of the fly-off hand brake lever, which is situated far forward on the transmission tunnel. A large tachometer and gage cluster are located directly in front of the driver. The speedometer, which includes a trip odometer and a clock, is in front of the passenger . . . a location of dubious convenience.

The TR3 engine, with its high, oversize intake ports and big dual SU's, fires at the first spin even under temperature conditions that cause vapor lock in many engines. It idles at a busy 850 rpm, sounding content rather than nervous. For a racing start you put in the pleasantly light clutch

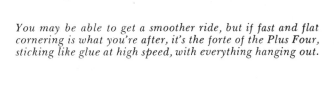

and poke the stubby shift lever into first, rev to 4,000 or so and let the clutch out as fast as possible without breaking the rear wheels loose. The clutch is ideal. It takes hold solidly, smoothly and without a trace of chatter or grabbing no matter how it's used. The car digs out instantaneously without any momentary hesitation due to rear-spring windup. In about 3.5 seconds you're at the 5,000 rpm red line and chop the shift lever downward into second. The gears crash painfully but they mesh. The synchronizers can't be beaten on third and fourth whether shifting up or down but, going either way, you must hesitate for an instant if you want to make it into second quietly. Double-declutching into first is easy, which can't be said for the gearbox that normally goes with the TR engine.

The TR Plus Four comes equipped with a Moss transmission whose internals are approximately identical to those in the Moss Jaguar box . . . which also tends to crunch when second is engaged. Coupling such a massive gearbox with the TR engine certainly should insure lifetime freedom from any sort of transmission failure. Spencer says, "We used to worry about the second-gear crunch until we tore a gearbox down after an hour's race in which we showed it no mercy. There wasn't a mark. Beyond that, I lost the clutch at San Diego and tried jamming the thing into gear with all my might. The sounds of protest were so horrendous that I gave that up and gloomily looked forward to the amount of damage we'd find when the box was opened. Again, not a mark. No abuse seems to make the slightest impression on it."

As the data table shows, this is one hot-accelerating machine. On the straight and level it will run off and hide, for example, from Triumph TR3's, AC Aces or Lancia Aurelia G.T.'s. Its nicely spaced transmission ratios keep the acceleration curve steep right out to the top limit of third, which is about 82 mph and 5,700 rpm. Beyond that, performance begins to get leisurely as direct drive to the 3.73 ratio takes over.

We were unable to achieve the 100-plus mph claimed for this car, as well as for the ten per cent less potent TR2 Plus Four. One reason is that in the interest of standardization we use a uniform one-mile approach to the timing trap for all top speed runs. At the end of the mile the test car still was unwinding, but very slowly, and our highest tach reading was 4950. These runs were made with top up and windows closed. With top down, windows and windshield removed the reduced frontal area would have made the century mark easy to break in this distance. But we were concerned with testing the convertible in normal road trim.

In the course of testing we did run the engine experimentally out to 5,700 rpm in second and third. Even at that point there was none of the machine-gun clatter often heard at peak in many pushrod engines. In competition Morgans the TR3 engine is balanced, red-lined at 6,000 and it can be taken to 6,500 although to no advantage. Only beyond six does the valve gear acquire that coming-unsoldered sound.

Even with the 3.73 axle gears (most competition models are fitted with 4.11) the TR3 Plus Four has surprisingly strong pulling power at low speeds. And it gives any sort of fuel economy that you care to drive for. During speed tests we recorded 19 mpg; by pussy-footing we were able to get 33 mpg.

Since Lew Spencer has raced several TR-engined Morgans and now owns his second, we asked him about the unit's reliability. On the street, he says, you just drive it and drive it and do a little tuning when you happen to be in the mood. Racing, of course, is different. Although the engine holds its tune extremely well you naturally sharpen it before every race to be sure of getting peak performance. But when they are raced, when they're being run constantly at very high revs, TR's are hard on lower-end bearings. The practice of the Pellandini equipe is to drop the pan after every racing outing and, as a matter of precaution, to replace the con-rod big-end bearings. After every third race the engine is pulled, thoroughly checked, valves are ground and all lower-end bearings are renewed.

If you attend the races you cannot have helped noting how exceptionally fine properly driven Morgans look in the turns. They go around very fast and with hardly a trace of body roll or tire noise; they just stay dead flat. To the man behind the wheel they feel as fine as they look. We have rarely taken our standard test curve so fast — above 65 mph — and with such confidence and ease. The car sticks and sticks until the rear end begins to move outward, very gradually and slightly. A little less throttle and it tucks in; a

The original number-one Morgan (Esquire) at the controls of the original number-one Morgan (automobile), vintage 1911.

shade more and it moves a shade farther out. You have to be going pretty unreasonably fast to hang it out far, and Spencer has learned that you must drive far over your head to put one of these entirely predictable, forgiving machines into a spin.

This is one of the reasons that he and many loyal Morganites like him can't be pried away from the marque. After his second Morgan, Spencer stepped up to a Corvette. This lasted just about long enough for him to order a new Morgan from the factory. He says, "I like the feel of the car. You get a complete sense of being part of it." Says Nanette, his wife, "And it's a little different. When we had the Corvette every time we turned around we were waving at ourselves."

The Morgan is the delight of iconoclasts and non-conformists. It pretends to resist progress with its ancient — but so effective — suspension and with its carefully preserved vintage look. At the same time it keeps sufficiently abreast of the times to be a top competition contender. The tiny factory with its annual output of perhaps 500 cars is indifferent to the millions of dollars to be made on the

MORGAN "PLUS FOUR" COUPE

Price at East Coast .... $2855 (incl. Fed. Tax)
U. S. Importer:

Worldwide Auto Import	Fergus Imported Cars
1968 So. Sepulveda Blvd.	1717 Broadway
West Los Angeles, Calif.	New York 19, N. Y.

PERFORMANCE

TOP SPEED:

Two-way average	98.0 mph
Fastest one-way run	99.6 mph

ACCELERATION:

From zero to	seconds
30 mph	3.4
40 mph	5.3
50 mph	7.8
60 mph	11.8
70 mph	16.5
80 mph	21.9
Standing ¼ mile	17.8
Speed at end of quarter	73 mph

SPEED RANGES IN GEARS:

I	0-33 mph
II	6-58
III	8-82
IV	11-top

SPEEDOMETER CORRECTION:

Indicated Speed	Timed Speed
30	29
40	38
50	46
60	56
70	66
80	75
90	84
100	94

FUEL CONSUMPTION:

Hard driving	19 mpg
Average driving (under 60 mph)	28 mpg

BRAKING EFFICIENCY (10 successive emergency stops from 60 mph, just short of locking wheels).

1st stop	.59	6th	.50
2nd	.59	7th	.45
3rd	.59	8th	.44
4th	.55	9th	.44
5th	.54	10th	.44

SPECIFICATIONS

POWER UNIT:

Triumph TR3	Water-cooled, in-line four
Valve Operation	Pushrod overhead valves, in-line
Bore & Stroke	3.27 x 3.62 in (83 x 92 mm)
Stroke/Bore Ratio	1.11/1
Displacement	121.5 cu in (1991 cc)
Compression Ratio	8.5/1
Carburetion by	Two SU side drafts
Max. Power	100 bhp @ 5000 rpm
Max. Torque	117½ lbs-ft @ 3000 rpm
Idle Speed	850 rpm

DRIVE TRAIN:

Transmission ratios	
I	3.45
II	1.98
III	1.40
IV	1.00
Final drive ratio	3.73 (4.11 optional)
Axle torque taken by	leaf springs

CHASSIS:

Frame	Open channel sections
Wheelbase	96 in
Tread, front and rear	47 in
Front Suspension	Sliding pillar, coil springs
Rear Suspension	Rigid axle, semi-elliptic leaf springs
Shock absorbers	Telescopic front, piston-lever rear
Steering type	Cam and sector
Steering wheel turns L to L	2
Turning diameter, curb to curb	33 ft
Brakes	Girling hydraulic, 2LS front
Brake lining area	121 sq in
Tire size	5.50 x 16

GENERAL:

Length	144 in
Width	56 in
Height	48 in
Weight, as tested	2370 lbs
Weight distribution, F/R as tested	47/53
Fuel capacity	13.2 U. S. Gallons

RATING FACTORS:

Specific Power Output	0.83 bhp/cu in
Power to Weight Ratio	23.7 lbs/hp
Piston speed @ 60 mph	1745 ft/min
Braking Area	102 sq in/ton
Speed @ 1000 rpm in top gear	20.7 mph

102

Morgan-owner pride of ownership is reflected in engine room of Spencer's car. TR3 is chromed and porcelainized.

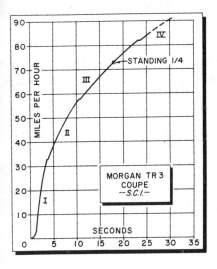

Plenty of leg room, air-inflated seats, polished wood are touches that make the Morgan a truly distinctive machine.

export market and seems to have no aspirations beyond that small and militant clientele that its somewhat offbeat products attract.

Typical Morgan owners delight in their cars' idiosyncracies. They beam and say, "Don't expect a Morgan to fit you. Either you fit it or you forget it." Actually, the range of seat-adjustability of the latest Plus Four is such that a six-foot-two owner of our acquaintance sits at the wheel of his car with legs comfortably extended. They say, "You can feel if a penny is facing heads or tails if you drive over it in a Morgan." That might be true if it weren't for the pneumatic seats that make insignificant any harshness that may be present in the ride. Except for a pronounced tendency to reflect the periodic blips of tar strips in concrete pavement, the Plus Four's ride is extremely free of vices.

The car does demand the sort of care that it will get only from the affectionately appreciative enthusiast. One of its mixed blessings is the instrument panel of mahogany — varnished smooth as glass — and, in the case of the convertible, door moldings of the same. The wood is beautiful . . . as long as it's properly maintained. In a closed car such maintenance is inconsequential but in an open car constant attention is required. A tonneau cover or top and windows should be used to protect the woodwork from exposure to the weather. And, depending upon the success of this care, the wood still should be refinished periodically. Most Morgan owners enjoy these attentions to their pets. Spencer, for example, has had many parts of his engine chromed and has had his intake manifold coated with black porcelain. It's a beautiful job that cost just $4 at Pacific Porcelain Products in Los Angeles.

The Morgan body contains a good deal of wooden framing and keeping the wood, the frame and the sheet metal as united as they were when delivered calls for strict discipline. Says one owner, "Just let the body go and in a year you have something that sounds like a tin can full of marbles. But if you go over the car with wrench and screwdriver once a month and keep all the joints tight, the structure stays like new. It's like the MG-TC in that respect. And better paint never has been put on a car. Morgans take a polish like nothing else."

The Plus Four has its negative aspects that even ardent devotees don't try to defend. Vision, for example, is excellent until the convertible's top goes up. After that, the rear quarters of the top are completely blind. The convertible's windows are not of the roll-up type. They are framed units that can be bolted to the upper edges of the doors or removed entirely. When in place they make arm signals impossible because only the forward portion of the glass can be slid open. Ventilation, however, is no problem, as it is with some two-seaters when the weather equipment is in place. The rear portion of the top is zippered and can be worn open.

This, plus the window openings, plus the ability of the top to be furled open over the occupants' heads in "coupe de ville" style, insures completely ample air circulation. A Smith's heater is standard on the Plus Four for the U. S. and it can drive you out of the car if both vents are opened and the rheostat twisted all the way. Demisting ducts are not standard but they can be ordered and, in damp weather, they most definitely are needed. The convertible is quite water tight.

Bystanders might object to the Plus Four's vigorous exhaust note but it certainly is inoffensive to the car's occupants. Our one objection to this machine deals with its brakes. The stock linings are soft and have an indifferent bite even when strong pedal pressure is used. After three hard stops from 60 mph the linings began to smell strongly, and by the eighth they were smoking more than a little. Such brakes are discordant with such a spirited sports car and they need improvement. For racing, Pellandini goes to Frendo competition linings and Spencer reports that these stand up to the most severe punishment. In a one-hour go on the tight Paramount Ranch course they show no signs of weakening, he states.

Other criticisms of the Morgan? Well, the top starts drumming loudly above 40 mph. Spencer says that all it takes to stop this is stuffing a pair of driving gloves between the forward top bow and the fabric. The factory might take note of this. A couple of cents' worth of padding could eliminate this annoyance.

Among the many detail improvements that Morgan continues to inject into this apparently little-changing product, the current Plus Four has gained four inches in internal width. Overall width remains unchanged, but the rear fenders are narrower and the passenger area is much more spacious. The car's steering has also been improved greatly and now is about three times lighter than before, while none of its quickness and accuracy has been sacrificed. Backlash adjustment is provided.

Optional accessories for the Plus Four include wire wheels of the strong triple-laced type. Their spokes are known to break under racing stress, but they are much stronger than the more common double-laced variety.

Another option is a deep-finned light alloy sump. It holds almost two quarts more oil than the stock pan and provides much better cooling of the lubricant. It also looks hairy. Also readily available are aluminum fenders . . . all four of them. These items are standard on the competition Sebring model, along with beefed-up frame and suspension. Some of the options are available from the large parts stock of Pellandini's Worldwide Automotive Imports Inc. in Los Angeles and from Fergus Motors in New York, distributor for the eastern U. S. Others must be ordered from the British factory.

In response to the question, "How come you bought a Morgan?" most Plus Four owners have an excellent pat reply: "For less than $3,000 how can you possibly beat it?"

Griff Borgeson

ROAD TEST MORGAN PLUS-4

There'll always be a Morgan, especially winning a race

THE long-prevailing philosophy in the small English factory where Morgan automobiles are made is one of lofty disdain toward the fluctuating fashions that less conservative companies call progress. Some time in 1936, when the concern introduced its first sporting 4-wheeler, it was decided that a peak had been reached and that further basic change was completely unnecessary. The passing years, bringing with them changes in every facet of the automobile, have made no discernible impression at the Morgan works. On the contrary, every alteration in standard practice has been met with a truly massive indifference (call it fidelity to tradition if you wish), and change, when there is change at all, has been so slow as to be

almost undetectable. The Morgan of today is the Morgan of the past, and, in all likelihood, the Morgan of the future.

Therefore, after testing the TR-2-engined version of the car back in 1955 (February), we assumed that there would be no more Morgan testing for some years to come. Until only a short while ago this assumption was quite valid, and aside from our test of the new (and somewhat ill-fated) model 4-4 (Road & Track, June 1957), our experiences with the Morgan were largely confined to watching it win races. Our chance to renew acquaintance came when we were advised of a semi-competition model with the following extras available: aluminum body and fenders $175, competition exhaust system $125, disc

Either left- or right-hand drive can be obtained on order.

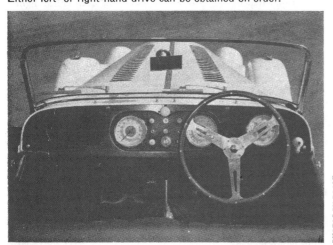

The twin SU carburetors meet a redesigned inlet manifold.

Twin 6-volt batteries are carried under the luggage space.

brakes (front) $158, triple-laced wire wheels $195, finned aluminum oil sump $75, and electric fuel pump $25.

There are other accessories available; the wooden-rim steering wheel and tonneau cover are examples. One extra item that we did not understand at all was offered for $40 and described as "strengthened front frame and gearbox mounts." To us, this seems perfectly ridiculous. We can understand many extras offered for competition work only, such as a higher-than-standard-compression ratio or stiffer dampers. But we cannot agree with a policy that obviously says, "Our cars are strong enough for the streets and if you intend to race you should expect to add bracing or they will break." In our opinion, when a manufacturer sells a sporting-type machine to a customer, he has an obligation to make that machine strong enough to take any normal use—and normal, applied to sports cars, includes racing.

In any case, our test car was fitted with all of the previously mentioned racing extras and, as a strong clue to the type of use that it will get, it had been ordered with right-hand drive. This last item won't make the car go any faster in a straight line but will help the driver through the predominantly right-hand turns on road circuits. The tires fitted to our test car were clinchers in deciding this particular car's fate: they were the latest in Dunlop racing rubber.

The Morgan has changed scarcely at all in appearance. The wire wheels lend a touch more in keeping with the character of the car than the old discs, but that is almost the only change. Several minutes of pensive studying did reveal that the car's tail ends a bit less abruptly than previously; otherwise, everything is as we remembered. Recalling the rather free use of lumber in the steel-bodied Morgan, we probed around under the aluminum skin of the new competition machine. We are happy to report to fanciers of the traditional half-timbered English coachwork that carpentry is still a required skill on the Morgan team. Perhaps it is just as well that Morgan Motor Company has never decided to institute mass production of its cars. If they were to do so, they might soon be committing such depredations on Sherwood Forest that Robin Hood and his Merrie Men would be left quite homeless. (For those of you who feel an impulse to leap to the de-

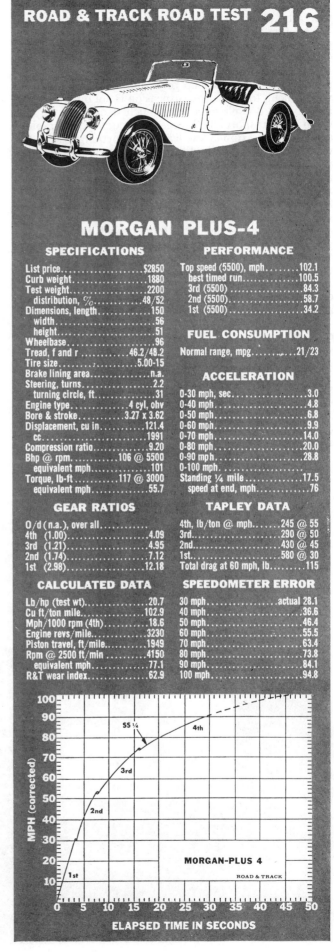

MORGAN PLUS-4

SPECIFICATIONS

List price	$2850
Curb weight	1880
Test weight	2200
distribution, %	48/52
Dimensions, length	150
width	56
height	51
Wheelbase	96
Tread, f and r	46.2/48.2
Tire size	5.00-15
Brake lining area	n.a.
Steering, turns	2.2
turning circle, ft	31
Engine type	4 cyl, ohv
Bore & stroke	3.27 x 3.62
Displacement, cu in	121.4
cc	1991
Compression ratio	9.20
Bhp @ rpm	106 @ 5500
equivalent mph	101
Torque, lb-ft	117 @ 3000
equivalent mph	55.7

GEAR RATIOS

O/d (n.a.), over all		
4th (1.00)		4.09
3rd (1.21)		4.95
2nd (1.74)		7.12
1st (2.98)		12.18

CALCULATED DATA

Lb/hp (test wt)	20.7
Cu ft/ton mile	102.9
Mph/1000 rpm (4th)	18.6
Engine revs/mile	3230
Piston travel, ft/mile	1949
Rpm @ 2500 ft/min	4150
equivalent mph	77.1
R&T wear index	62.9

PERFORMANCE

Top speed (5500), mph	102.1
best timed run	100.5
3rd (5500)	84.3
2nd (5500)	58.7
1st (5500)	34.2

FUEL CONSUMPTION

Normal range, mpg	21/23

ACCELERATION

0-30 mph, sec	3.0
0-40 mph	4.8
0-50 mph	6.8
0-60 mph	9.9
0-70 mph	14.0
0-80 mph	20.0
0-90 mph	28.8
0-100 mph	.
Standing ¼ mile	17.5
speed at end, mph	76

TAPLEY DATA

4th, lb/ton @ mph	245 @ 55
3rd	290 @ 50
2nd	430 @ 45
1st	580 @ 30
Total drag at 60 mph, lb	115

SPEEDOMETER ERROR

30 mph	actual 28.1
40 mph	36.6
50 mph	46.4
60 mph	55.5
70 mph	63.4
80 mph	73.8
90 mph	84.1
100 mph	94.8

MORGAN-PLUS 4

ROAD & TRACK

ELAPSED TIME IN SECONDS

fense of that legendary English outlaw, we must point out that, after all, the Morgan factory was there first.)

The first principle of modern chassis design dictates that a car should have a rigid frame and a supple suspension. This condition is the exact opposite of that in the Morgan. The frame of this car is so limp that, when it is parked with one wheel up on a hump, its doors can be very difficult to open. The suspension is not quite unyielding—but it doesn't miss it by much. However, the end result is great sport: the Morgan will corner quite rapidly and probably exhibits less lean than anything else in the world. The front wheels still slide on vertical posts (giving what is often called perfect geometry) and the live rear axle still fastens to the time-honored leaf spring. The arrangement may not be one that we would choose, but it has been used on the Morgan from the very first and it still gives acceptable results.

When we tested the 1955 Morgan with the TR-2 engine, our report stated that the car reminded us of the old MG-TC with muscle. It still does, but with even more muscle. The standard engine is now the TR-3, which has 100 bhp, and the optional competition engine, as fitted to our test car, has 106 bhp. Adding to the car's performance (in acceleration at least) were a 4.09 rear-axle ratio—replacing the standard 3.73—and a completely new set of transmission ratios. The Morgan has used the Jaguar gearbox for some time. However, it is not mounted directly behind the clutch, nor is an extension used to place the gearshift lever near the hand. Instead, the transmission is nearly 3 ft behind the engine. This necessitates a rather lengthy extension shaft between clutch and transmission, but the gearshift lever stirs things inside the box in a very direct fashion. The very latest close-ratio gears are used in the new cars.

The increased horsepower, lower total weight and new gearing have made the Morgan into an even better quar-

ter horse than it used to be. The standing quarter was covered in only 17.5 sec, with a speed of 76 mph at the end. The same figures for the old car were 18.3 sec and 74 mph, respectively.

Top speeds were almost identical; we could have bettered our figure under top-up conditions, but all runs were strictly of the open-air variety. The top bows were in place, but evidently someone had forgotten to put the fabric (which snaps on after the bows are up) in its proper stowing place.

All small improvements notwithstanding, the Morgan has not really changed its character since our first meeting. The big difference is in its competition. In 1955 there were others who, like Morgan, clung to the past and produced the high-wheeled, swoop-fendered classics that so completely met the definition of a sports car. With the disappearance of all other holdouts, like HRG, and the absorption of others into larger, better financed firms (MG into BMC, Singer into the Rootes Group), Morgan is left to stand alone. It would be grossly unfair to compare the Morgan directly with other sports cars being produced today. One must remember that the Morgan is now unique. In a field that is largely dominated by cold science, the Morgan is still produced on intuition and with an eye toward the sporting past more than the turbine-engined future.

By statistical standards, one can prove that the Morgan is out of date. Other cars of the same engine displacement sell for less money, are faster and more comfortable, yet handle just as well. However, these other cars do not, and probably never can, inspire the kind of loyalty and affection that devoted Morgan owners give to their truculent beasties. There are cars and there are cars, but the Morgan is well on its way to becoming a legend as the very last of the "hang the comfort, let's have sport" automobiles.

For a classic sports car, a less compromising radiator grille would be more suitable.

the driver's hand, it is separated from the engine by an extension shaft which is enclosed in a light alloy tube from the bell housing. A short, straight lever, pivoting in the lid of the box, avoids the need for any remote control. The front brakes are discs, but the less highly stressed rear brakes are of the drum type, which are better for the hand brake; the wheels are, of course, "knock-on".

The engine is the well-known Triumph TR3 unit. It is a straightforward design, with wet liners and pushrod-operated overhead valves. Developing 100 b.h.p. at 5,000 r.p.m. and plenty of torque in the lower ranges, it is a compact and comparatively light unit which is ideal for such a car. Unlike so many sports cars, the gearbox has well-spaced ratios without that fatal gap between second and third speeds.

JOHN BOLSTER TESTS

THE MORGAN PLUS FOUR

A Modern Sports Car with Charm and an Outstanding Personality

THE vintage car is all the rage, and more and more people like to read about them, tell lies about them in pubs and clubs, and even drive them. The reasons are not far to seek, for the modern sports car, with its all-enveloping body and soft suspension, is simply not so much "fun" to drive as were its forbears, nor does it look like a powerful piece of machinery, ready to be unleashed.

The Morgan has a very modern performance, as its competition successes prove. Yet, alone among current cars, it has that hard, glued-to-the-road suspension, that narrow cockpit, and that long, louvred bonnet with separate mudguards, all of which are dear to the heart of the vintagent. It is an entirely individual car, but it is an individuality that keeps the order books full, and which also causes the present writer to be numbered among its admirers.

However, the Morgan that I have recently been using had one big advantage over the vintage type of sports car. It had disc brakes, and these render the very considerable performance an even greater asset, because one can use "the lot" all the time without ever sparing a thought for the anchors. Let me say, straight away, that the knowledge of this immense braking power lying dormant adds immeasurably to the pleasure of hard driving. In the past, I have found that drum-braked Morgans tended to pull to one side or grab when the brakes were applied repeatedly at high speeds. With discs, one can rely on as many straight-line stops as one wants, and there is never a sign of distress. Truly, the disc brake is the biggest single step forward that has been made for many a year.

LYING DORMANT: Disc brakes provide immense braking power and in the Morgan you can use "the lot" without sparing a thought for the anchors. The brake pedal requires firm pressure, but the car does not snake or deviate from the straight line under braking.

For the rest, the Plus Four remains a sports two-seater of moderate overall dimensions, powered by a lusty 2-litre four-cylinder engine. The chassis is still the Z-section structure that we have known for so long, passing at full width beneath the back axle, and narrowing towards its attachment to the traditional Morgan front end. For more than 50 years, Morgans have had the pillar-type independent front suspension with helical springs. This year, the steering is much lighter if a little less "quick", and a pedal allows hot engine oil to be diverted occasionally to the suspension guides, which also form the king pins.

At the rear, underslung semi-elliptic springs locate the hypoid axle, and the short, open propeller shaft is attached to the centrally mounted gearbox. In order to bring the box back to a point beneath

The body of the Morgan is a two-seater, with a disappearing hood which covers the luggage space when erect. One sits well down but the forward view is good, and the walnut instrument panel is furnished with all the right dials. Morgans vary individually, I find, and I could have done with a bit more adjustment on the seat squab to get me further away from the steering wheel. This could certainly be arranged without difficulty. In passing, I must regret the deletion of the outside door handles, and remark on a few odd draughts and water leaks round the signalling flaps of the sidescreens and the front of the driver's door. The last few Morgans I have driven were completely snug, and the fault could soon be rectified in this new car.

"New", in fact, was the operative

SPECIFICATION AND PERFORMANCE DATA

Car Tested: Morgan Plus Four two-seater. Price £645 plus £269 17s. 6d. P.T. Extras: Wire wheels and knock-on hubs, £32 10s. plus £13 10s. 10d. P.T.; disc brakes, £10 plus £4 3s. 4d. P.T.; Duraband tyres, £4 15s.

Engine: Four-cylinders 83 mm. x 92 mm. (1,991 c.c.). Pushrod-operated overhead valves. 8.5 to 1 compression ratio. 100 b.h.p. at 5,000 r.p.m. Twin SU carburetters. Lucas coil distributor.

Transmission: Borg and Beck 9 ins. single dry-plate clutch. Four-speed Moss gearbox with short central lever on top of box, connected to clutch by extension shaft in duralumin housing. Ratios 3.72, 5.1, 7.3 and 12.5 to 1. Short open Hardy Spicer propeller shaft. Salisbury hypoid rear axle.

Chassis: Z-section underslung at rear. Independent front suspension by stub axles sliding upon extended king pins against helical springs. Cam and sector steering. Semi-elliptic rear springs. Girling hydraulic dampers, telescopic in front, piston-type at rear. Girling hydraulic disc brakes in front, 9 ins. drum-type at rear. Knock-on wire wheels fitted 5.60-15 ins. Dunlop Duraband tyres.

Equipment: Twelve-volt lighting and starting. Speedometer, rev-counter, ammeter, water temperature, oil pressure and fuel gauges, flashing indicators.

Dimensions: Wheelbase, 8 ft. Track, 3 ft. 11 ins. Overall length, 11 ft. 8 ins. Width, 4 ft. 8 ins. Turning circle, 30 ft. Weight, 16 cwt.

Performance: Maximum speed, 104.6 m.p.h. Speeds in gears, 3rd 82 m.p.h., 2nd 60 m.p.h., 1st 38 m.p.h. Standing quarter-mile, 17.4 secs. Acceleration, 0-30 m.p.h., 3 secs.; 0-50 m.p.h., 7.2 secs.; 0-60 m.p.h., 9.6 secs.; 0-80 m.p.h., 18.8 secs.

Fuel Consumption: Driven hard 25 m.p.g.

word, for the car was handed to me with barely 500 miles on the clock. I put on another 1,000 before taking the performance figures, and then found that I had the fastest Morgan ever tested by AUTOSPORT. Previous models had just about touched "the ton", but this one was timed at 104.6 m.p.h. under far from ideal weather conditions, nor did I increase the tyre pressures above the normal touring recommendation. Quite a bit more speed could be achieved on a really still day, but as this would entail taking the rev-counter well into the red, I did not subject the fairly new engine to such abuse.

The rear axle ratio suits the engine admirably, for although it allows 90 m.p.h. cruising on the motorways, it also renders the car extremely lively on top gear. One can accelerate so strongly without changing down that the employment of the gear lever may be almost forgotten if desired. Nevertheless, the ratios are especially well chosen, and

second speed is a splendid gear that may be used almost as much as third on the road.

The test car was fitted with the optional Dunlop Duraband tyres, which are reinforced with steel wire. These contributed to the very high cornering power of the car, and even during extremely fast driving there was no sign of tyre scream. The understeering tendency of earlier Morgans was not present in this instance, and one could fairly fling the car through corners in a most refreshing manner. The traction was also impressive, as the acceleration figures bear witness. On wet and greasy roads, the controllability was good unless actual wheelspin was induced by over-accelerating on the gears, when a fairly sudden breakaway had to be corrected.

The lighter steering is very pleasant, especially at town speeds. Skid correction calls for more wheel movement, but this is by no means excessive. The car is very steady at its maximum speed, de-

The graph shows MAX. 104.6 M.P.H. and ¼ MILE marked.

ACCELERATION GRAPH

MORGAN PLUS FOUR

manding no conscious direction from the driver. The brake pedal requires fairly firm pressure, but the sheer power of retardation can be used with confidence because the car never deviates or snakes.

The character of the ride is influenced by the fact that both the front and rear suspensions have limited travel. Small bumps are well absorbed, but the larger irregularities are certainly felt. Such a suspension system would not be suitable for a family saloon, but it is by no means out of place in a sports two-seater and there are many who will prefer it to the softer type of springing.

An important point is the excellent accessibility. Very frequently, the man who buys this type of car is an accomplished mechanic, and his maintenance chores or more elaborate adjustments can all be carried out more quickly and easily because he does not have to stand on his head or perform the other contortions that so many cars now demand. The body is thoroughly practical, but one regrets the absence of door pockets and the cubby hole could do with a lid. The horn button on the instrument panel may occasionally be pressed in place of some other switch, and the direction indicators are not self-cancelling.

The Morgan Plus Four has considerable charm and an outstanding personality. In the hands of the right kind of driver it is nearly unbeatable, and the roadholding and braking are more than adequate for the very real performance. There are many smoother, quieter, and more comfortable cars, but if the object of the exercise is really high average speeds in absolute safety, there is nothing to compare with the Morgan at less than twice its price. The fuel consumption is also quite moderate, especially if the top gear flexibility is exploited.

EXCELLENT ACCESSIBILITY: Maintenance chores or elaborate adjustments can be carried out quickly and easily because the mechanic does not have to "stand on his head" to perform such operations.

THE LAST OF THE CLASSICS?

A visit with Peter Morgan, who steadfastly maintains family tradition

STORY BY ALAN BECK

THE OLD, DIE-HARD, wind-in-the-face, frozen-eared, rugged motoring individuals used to find solace in the fact that two honest sports cars were still being produced —the HRG and the Morgan.

In their book all cars were effeminate hybrids unless they rode like a McCormick Reaper, had outboard fenders, with weather gear limited to vestigial or token tops, carried properly mounted wire-wheel spares, and were both light and tough.

Now that HRG has been gathered unto its forefathers, the Morgan, they feel, is left to carry on the tradition single-handed. To this breed of sports car purist, the Morgan is the whooping crane of the automotive world. It is a marque whose name is not to be bandied about by Johnny-come-latelys to the sports car fraternity.

The old school sports car drivers, given their way, would make it illegal for Morgans to be owned or driven by teenagers, elderly women, beatniks, or those who get store-bought grease jobs. Given their way, they would breed K-3 Magnettes with Morgans and sell their offspring only to such knowledgeables as owners of topless TC's and graduates of Watkins Glen, classes of '50, '51 and '52.

To these iconoclasts of motordom we would recount our visit to their Mecca, Malvern Link in Worcestershire, England, last fall.

The essence of all that is good and true for Morgan owners everywhere.

The low, red-brick factory bore no sign. They might be making doughnuts inside for all the outside world could tell, but the initials "M.M." set in the bricks hinted that it might be Morgan Motor Co., Ltd. It was. The elder Mr. Morgan, who made the first 3-wheeler in 1910, died last summer, and his son, Mr. Peter Morgan, is carrying on the business and the tradition.

This was the first time we had ever approached the private office of an automotive mogul. In a moist palm we clutched a business card and a letter of introduction. A vintage lady bore them into the *sanctum sanctorum*. What lay within? Wall to wall carpeting? Contemporary furniture? Wastebaskets with tassels?

"Come in," said Peter Morgan, a windblown sort of chap wearing a sport coat with leather patches on the elbows. "Won't you sit down?" There wasn't anywhere to sit; the two oak chairs were obviously being used to pinch-hit for tables, both holding papers of one sort or another. Mr. Morgan cleared them out. An old-fashioned desk, planked squarely in the middle of the office, was loaded with paper work and illuminated by a single drop light from the ceiling. On the walls were photographs of earlier Morgans, including the first 3-wheeler built some 50 years ago. On the wall was a plaque listing the many racing triumphs of Morgan down through the years, and it was interesting to me to see that the first record was dated 1912.

We told Peter Morgan of several Morgan legends in America:

(1) That Morgan was the world's smallest automotive manufacturer and produced six cars a week. Answer: "No. We're up to nine cars a week now, have a capacity for 12 a week, and would like to triple production."

We asked how he allotted his output. "America gets 80% of our cars and we split the shipments 50-50 between the East Coast and the West Coast."

(2) All Morgans since the first one have been painted by the same man and he is still using the same paint brush. This obviously distressed Mr. Morgan, but being a true English gentleman, he gave us a straight and courteous answer. "Several years ago one man *did* paint all the Morgans and he used a paint brush—several paint brushes, in fact. Today, however, TWO men paint the cars. One puts on the two undercoats and the other puts on the two color coats." He added thoughtfully, "They use a spray gun."

(3) The Morgan suspension is so stiff you have to hold a piece of inner tube between your teeth

"My father built a unique sports car in 1910. It is my aim to build the type of car he would be proud to offer for sale today"—Peter Morgan.

when driving down a cement highway. Peter Morgan's comment: "Father would have liked that."

This characteristic, incidentally, is closer to truth than to humor. Any Morgan owner, in showing off his machine, will suggest that you check the rather stiff front suspension by pushing down on the bumpers. You do so, and nothing gives, not even the split fraction of an inch! Is this good? Well, the Morgan drivers seem to like it. And the passengers can bring along their own pieces of inner tube.

Talk drifted to the Morgan design, and the front end in particular. Like Morgan owners in America, Peter Morgan is not too happy about the present grille and faired headlights, he too preferring the more classic treatment of the flat radiator and separately-mounted lamps typical of the older cars.

"If the general conception of styling in the future is to produce a more individual car with greater character, we hope to revert to something more like the original in future design," he said. "The big problem is the head-

lamps. Our supplier discontinued making individually mounted lamps, so we were forced to the present design. The old squared-off radiator was the very devil to keep clean, but you can tell American Morgan owners that the old design hasn't been forgotten."

We brought up a sore subject. "The sports car press in America commented unfavorably on your strengthening of the front section of the frame on your lightweight racing models, but not putting this beefed-up feature on the stock road cars."

"It was a misunderstanding," said Peter Morgan. "It was intended solely for trials and rally cars—not cars for racing. English trials and European-type rallies are far rougher on cars than smooth racing surfaces. However, because of the criticism, and not because of necessity, we have been equipping every car with this strengthened frame section for some time now."

We wondered what brought about the end of the famous Morgan 3-wheeler. They are still a familiar sight buzzing about the English hedgerows. "Originally it was a money proposition," said Mr. Morgan. "The purchaser had a tax advantage in buying a vehicle with fewer than 4 wheels and under 1800 pounds weight. That model was discontinued when we started mounting the heavier Vanguard engine in 1950."

Remembering the three months' waiting period for delivery of our roadster, we asked about deliveries of the superb two-passenger convertible, and that answer to a family man's prayer, the Morgan 4-seater.

"It takes a bit longer," he conceded. Our own observations in the factory would indicate that only a very patient man should place an order for one of these models. The big push is to try to keep pace with the demand for the popular roadsters.

Mr. Derek Day, shipping manager, graciously showed us every inch of the factory, where hand craftsmen and office workers number about 100. With difficulty we kept our hands in our pockets while walking by the bins of spare parts. Several dozen finished Morgan Plus-Four roadsters (tourers, as they are called in Britain) were lined up awaiting shipment and we asked to see one of the extra-light, aluminum bodied, competition models. "They

The winning Morgan team in the 1952 RAC Rally:
136—L.A.G. Goodall, 137—P.H.G. Morgan, 138—W.D. Steel.

GUY GRIFFITHS

Each Morgan grille is still hand made.

The Morgan has its faults, but so does a pinto pony. Most sports cars leak in a driving rain, but only in the Morgan does a snow storm come right on inside the car. It is one of the few cars in the world which could use windshield wipers on the *inside* of the windshield. We have never heard of another car on which the frame flexes one jump ahead of the shock dampers. On the other hand, who cares about a top on a Morgan? And the only thing that will go around a corner any faster than a Morgan is a greased monkey with Michelin pads on his rear feet. Of course, a bit of corrugated surface may find you doing a Waltzing Matilda, but after all, it was you who had the temerity to exceed the recommended tire pressures.

The Morgan is non-adjustable. Either you fit the Morgan or forget the whole deal. The average driver from 5 ft 9 in. to 6 ft 1 in. will have no difficulty. All others are on their own. The *top* of the seat adjusts back and forth, but the bottom stays put. Personally, we find it the most comfortable seating arrangement of all comparable sports cars.

The individuality of the Morgan extends right down to the very cushions you sit on. Inside the leather is an inner-tube sort of arrangement—you literally sit on air.

Ash framing is fabricated in the carpentry shop.

Door latches are installed before the metal is added.

all look alike," said Derek, as he went about lifting bonnets. "Here's one," he said. "See, the only difference to the eye is in the manifolding." The possibilities of a personally modified competition Morgan are really interesting.

Reducing the weight of this stock vehicle that hits the scales at 18 cwt by adding an aluminum body, PLUS the owner's notions of further heating up a 100-bhp TR-3 engine—well, it's a matter of which comes first, the point of no return or utter collapse of the pocketbook. But when it does occur, you have a rare sight indeed—the sight of a classic-bodied, old-time sports car showing a clean pair of Dunlops to such powerhouses as 300-SL's, Corvettes, and Porsches.

The photos tell their own story—veteran employees working alongside of young apprentices—careful, painstaking hand operations every inch of the way—an atmosphere of loyalty and pride in every department—the smell of ash shavings in the carpentry shop—the nostalgic sight of what has been called a "contemporary classic," taking shape under the hands of men who wouldn't know an assembly line from a tailfin.

We stopped for a moment and talked to some of the men at Morgan. Most of them have worked there all of their business lives. They are proud of their product, and anything less than their best work just isn't good enough. These men obviously are craftsmen first and employees second.

But back to our tour. One back room at the factory contained half-a-dozen dusty, road-begrimed tourers. "Those," said Mr. Derek, "belong to Americans who took delivery on their cars here at the factory, and then enjoyed a British vacation. Now we will ship the cars back for them . . . when we get time," he added. We trust this puts an intriguing bee in your bonnet, and we can definitely recommend a two weeks' tour of Cornwall, the north Devon coast, and Wales.

This rather screw-ball personal suspension works perfectly. The suspendee can adjust his seat to hard, medium or invalid cushion merely by blowing up the rubber innards or letting some air escape. Oddly enough, this air doesn't leak out. This is an unusual arrangement, but as the little Martian said about eating his girl friend's gloves, "Don't knock it till you've tried it."

The Morgan is not for the man who dislikes car-puttering. About one month after purchase it sounds as if every nut and bolt of the old-fashioned construction has started to loosen (a fact about which you were duly warned in the manual). However, one Sunday afternoon of tightening up several thousand nuts seems to do the job permanently. Road grime and Father Time seals them fast.

Then there is that irritating matter of the air cleaners. The trouble is that there aren't any! There are some things that you can't pack under a Morgan hood and one is a TR-3 engine with air cleaners. So the cleaners have to go. But, as Peter Morgan pointed out, "These are the new SU *dustproof* carburetors, so you really don't need cleaners." We settled for some copper window screening over the intake ports to exclude the larger bugs. Incidentally, this makes for an interesting whistle effect when stepping down on the gas at around 40 mph, a sound rather reminiscent of mother's old tea kettle or a 1925 Buick. (Dustproof SU pots are identifiable by not having any vent holes drilled through the brass caps of the oil reservoirs.)

Name almost any sporting marque you choose and you will find steady "progress" from original hairiness to smooth, svelte comfort. Not so, Morgan. It still goes jolting along like the Allards and the TC's of the past. But at a popular price you can still break 0 to 60 in under 10 sec and, with proper amateur tuning, crack the 100-mile-an-hour mark with ease and as smoothly as with a machine costing twice the price. The gas mileage (though it really doesn't matter) is creditably high. And among the plus factors is one which many rank high on the list in judging a sports car—it is happy and at home at 80 to 90 miles an hour, yet is tractable at 25 and 30. It has that settle-down-and-purr quality when moving along at top road speeds.

All in all, the rough-riding lightweight from Malvern Link holds a unique place in the sports car world today—it is the last of the classics. And it is heartening to know that Peter Morgan has every intention of keeping it exactly that way.

Shaping body panels. He's been with Morgan for years.

A Morgan getting a "rub down" after painting.

A row of Morgans awaiting export to America.

The late H.F.S. Morgan's personal car.

Slight modifications to the chassis in order to accommodate a wider gearbox are in no way discernible from an exterior view of the car which remains unaltered. Flashing indicators are now standard on both Morgan ranges.

NEW ENGINE FOR MORGAN 4/4

Series III Model has Ford 105E Engine and Four-speed Gearbox. Improved Steering on 4|4 and Plus 4 Ranges

PRINCIPAL item of interest in the range of Morgan models for 1961 is the fitting of the 997 c.c. o.h.v. Ford Anglia engine in place of the former 1172 c.c. side-valve type. The Ford 105E unit is used complete with clutch and gearbox, so that this latest Series III 4/4 model also has four speeds in place of the former three. In addition, improved steering and a new instrument panel incorporating toggle switches have been adopted. This new Series III model supercedes the Series II.

So far as the 2-litre, Plus Four range is concerned, the three models, two-seater, four-seater and coupé, are continued, but with steering improvements corresponding to those on the 4/4 and a similar toggle-switch type of instrument panel. A further point to note is that disc brakes, formerly an extra, have now been standardized at the front on the Plus Four models.

To revert to the Series III 4/4, the new 105E Anglia engine is used in standard form with 8.9 to 1 compression ratio, developing 39 b.h.p. net at 5,000 r.p.m., compared with the 36 b.h.p. net at 4,500 r.p.m of the 100E side-valve engine formerly used. For the present, at least, tuned versions of the engine are not being offered and there is accordingly no Competition version, but there are, of course, various conversions offered by tuning specialists, so that buyers with competition work in mind can readily have appropriate conversions carried out for themselves.

The 105E engine fits neatly into the existing underslung Morgan chassis with its unique Z-section side members and vertical-coil-spring independent front suspension. To accommodate the new gearbox, which is a little wider than the old, the frame has been modified very slightly in plan view and advantage has been taken of the change to increase foot room slightly at the same time. To this end, the scuttle structure has been extended laterally without, however, altering the actual bonnet width.

Engine Mounting

The unit is carried at three points. At the sides it is supported on the standard rubber mountings approximately midway along the cylinder block and, at the rear, there is a further rubber mounting below the gearbox. Stout bearers extending to the side members are used for the front mountings and the rear of the unit rests on a bridge piece bolted to the longitudinal connection between two chassis cross members.

In order to avoid a long and awkwardly shaped gear lever—which would be necessary if a direct-acting lever were retained—a simple but neat form of remote control is adopted. For this, a short vertical shaft terminating in a suitable knuckle end takes the place of the standard Ford gear lever and this is connected to a horizontal shaft sliding in a tube universally mounted in rubber in the scuttle structure at the front; this universal mounting acts as a fulcrum so that movements of the horizontal shaft are transmitted to the gearbox stub.

The action appears slightly unusual at first, in that changes between first and second and between third and top involve a horizontal push-pull movement of the gear lever knob, but once the fact has been grasped that the movement is, in effect, identical with that of a normal remote control except that the gear lever shaft is carried forwards from the knob instead of downwards, the entire action becomes clear, and a short run on one of the new models showed that the change is both easy and positive. The arrangement also caters for the lifting action required for reverse.

In conjunction with the existing 4.4 to 1 hypoid final drive, the new gearbox gives overall ratios of 4.4, 6.2, 10.5 and 18.0 to 1 (compared with the 4.4, 8.25 and 15.07 of the former three-speed gearbox), but reverse is somewhat lower at 23.0 to 1 compared with 19.71 to 1. The tyre size is unchanged so that engine/road speed relationship remains unaltered in top at 16.0 m.p.h. per 1,000 engine r.p.m., but the indirect ratios are now better spaced for overtaking purposes.

So far as the steering is concerned, a new variable-ratio steering box by Cam Gears has been adopted and this, in conjunction with a shorter drop arm, gives lighter steering with little extra wheel movement, the number of turns of the steering wheel from lock to lock now being 2¼ compared with the former 2. This applies to both the 4/4 and Plus Four models.

The Ford 105E engine, which fits neatly into the existing underslung chassis, develops 39 b.h.p. at 5,000 r.p.m. in untuned form. It may, of course, be extensively modified for competition work.

New Engine for Morgan 4/4

The new central switch panel on the facia is somewhat similar to the former type except that toggle switches are now used for the panel light and wipers. There is also a large central toggle-type switch for the flashing direction indicators which, incidentally, are now standardized on the 4/4 as well as the Plus Four. In the case of the latter, space is also provided for additional toggle switches for fog and road lamps when fitted.

So far as prices are concerned, the Series III 4/4 sells for a basic figure of £520 which, with purchase tax of £217 15s. 10d., gives a total of £737 15s. 10d., this representing an increase of £22 on the basic price compared with the previous Series II model.

For the Plus Four, prices remain as before with disc brakes, namely:—

Two-seater, basic £655, P.T. £274 0s. 10d., total £929 0s. 10d.

Four-seater, basic £670, P.T. £280 5s. 10d., total £950 5s. 10d.

Coupé, basic £710, P.T. £296 19s. 2d., total £1,006 19s. 2d.

All the Plus Four models are, of course, fitted with the Triumph TR engine.

MORGAN 4/4 SERIES III (WITH FORD 105E ENGINE)

ENGINE

Cylinders	4 in line, with hollow cast-iron 3-bearing crankshaft.
Bore and stroke	80.96 mm. x 48.41 mm. (3.187 in. x 1.906 in.)
Cubic capacity	997 c.c. (60.84 cu. in.).
Piston area	31.92 sq. in.
Compression ratio	8.9:1.
Valvegear	In-line vertical o.h.v. operated by pushrods and rockers from chain-driven camshaft.
Carburation	Solex 30ZIC2 downdraught carburetter, fed by mechanical pump from 8-gallon tank.
Ignition	12-volt Lucas or AC oil-filled coil, with centrifugal and vacuum timing control, and 14 mm. Champion N5 sparking plugs.
Lubrication	Rotor pump, full-flow filter, (½-pint capacity) and 4-pint sump.
Cooling	Water cooling with pump, fan, thermostat, and pressurized radiator. 12-pint water capacity.
Electrical system	12-volt 36 amp. hr. battery charged by 20-amp. dynamo.
Maximum power	39 b.h.p. net (41 b.h.p. gross) at 5,000 r.p.m. equivalent to 102 lb./sq.in. b.m.e.p. at 1,590 ft./min. piston speed and 1.22 b.h.p. per sq. in. of piston area.
Maximum torque	52.85 lb. ft. net (55 lb. ft. gross) at 2,700 r.p.m., equivalent to 131 lb./sq. in b.m.e.p. at 860 ft./min piston speed.

TRANSMISSION

Clutch	Ford 7¼ in. single dry plate with hydraulic actuation. 4-speed with direct top gear and synchromesh on upper 3 ratios.
Overall ratios	4.4, 6.2, 10.5 and 18.0. Reverse, 23.0.
Propeller shaft	Open Hardy Spicer.
Final drive	Hypoid bevel.

CHASSIS

Brakes	Girling hydraulic; two leading shoes at front.
Brake dimensions	Drum internal diameter, 9 in., friction lining area, 87.7 sq. in. working on 141 sq. in. rubbed area of drums.
Front suspension	Independent by coil springs and stub axles sliding on vertical guides. Vertical Armstrong telescopic hydraulic dampers.
Rear suspension	Semi-elliptic springs and rigid axle controlled by Armstrong lever type hydraulic dampers.
Wheels and tyres	Bolt-on, pressed-steel wheels with 5.20-15 tubeless tyres.
Steering	Cam Gears cam-and-peg variable-ratio steering gear.

DIMENSIONS

Length	Overall, 12 ft. 0 in.; wheelbase, 8.0 in.
Width	Overall, 4 ft. 8 in.; track, 3 ft. 11 in.
Height	Overall, 4 ft. 3 in.; ground clearance, 7 in.
Turning circle	31½ ft. diameter.
Kerb weight	13 cwt. unladen (without fuel but with oil, water, tools, spare wheel, etc.).

EFFECTIVE GEARING

Top gear ratio	16.0 m.p.h. at 1,000 r.p.m. and 50.6 m.p.h. at 1,000 ft./min. piston speed.
Maximum torque	2,700 r.p.m. corresponds to 43.44 m.p.h. in top gear.
Maximum power	5,000 r.p.m. corresponds to 80 m.p.h. in top gear.
Probable top gear pulling power	195 lb./ton approx. (Computed by The Motor from manufacturer's figures for torque, gear ratio, and kerb weight, with allowances for 3½ cwt. load; 10% losses and 60 lb./ton drag.)

ROAD IMPRESSIONS OF THE KIEFT-MODIFIED MORGAN PLUS-FOUR

HAVING acquired a taste for "rorty racers" when testing Ken Rudd's 185-b.h.p. Austin Healey 3000, we quickly accepted the opportunity to try a Kieft-modified Morgan Plus-Four. The Kieft Sports Car Co., Ltd., is now situated in Princip Street, Birmingham, and is in the process of rejuvenation. At the moment conversions are being manufactured for the Triumph Herald and TR3-engined cars, while a Formula Junior car is in the prototype stage and will be racing next season, and the eyes of Lionel Mayman, who is well known in the racing world, are firmly set upon the new 1½-litre Formula 1.

Meanwhile the Morgan conversion can be obtained in various stages according to the state of tune desired. Stage 1 is an exchange cylinder head which is machined for higher compression and gas flowed, while valves are ground in and fitted with stronger springs; the head is supplied complete with gaskets for £29 5s. The next stage (1A) consists of having the engine capacity increased to 2.2-litres and the fitting of larger pistons, which costs £51 2s. 6d. This results in a quite considerable increase in power. Alternatively, if one wishes to keep within the 2-litre limit for racing or rally purposes, an exchange cylinder block is available at £47 10s., together with a set of high-compression pistons costing £26 10s., which comprises Stage 2.

The test car, which is a veteran of many races and rallies, was fitted with Stage 1 head, Stage 2 block and pistons, an improved exhaust manifold and silencer with twin pipes emerging from under the driver's door, and an oil cooler which is fitted beneath the radiator. The S.U. carburetters are fitted with polished ram tubes, the inlet pipes are lagged with asbestos, and a heat shield is fitted between carburetters and exhaust pipes. The bodywork is modified at the rear so that the spare wheel (shod with a Dunlop R5 racing tyre) is fully enclosed, and a light alloy undertray is also fitted. There are bodywork modifications of another kind which were caused at Becketts Corner, Silverstone, during a race, the details of which are recorded in writing on the still unpainted wing.

The only other modification to the Morgan is the use of the optional low axle ratio, which is most suitable for circuit racing and hill-climbs, etc. Otherwise the car is a perfectly standard model having the 11-in. Girling disc brakes on the front wheels.

Collecting the "Moggie" from Birmingham, we soon discovered that everything said and written about Morgans was true : the ride is hard, the steering heavy and, added to this, the exhaust note is fruity, to say the least. With well over 100 b.h.p. to cope with 16½ cwt. of Morgan the performance is brisk, and if the throttle is depressed in the vicinity of other motorists or pedestrians they cannot fail to be aware of its presence. Fortunately the car is perfectly flexible and early engagement of top gear reduces the noise level to manageable proportions, so that policemen do not immediately reach for their notebooks.

As the October afternoon was sunny we ventured onto the A45 Coventry road with the hood down, and such is the design of the Morgan that one could easily imagine that the year was 1930. The long, tapering, heavily louvred bonnet, the high-set ungainly wings with lamps perched either side of the radiator grille, all combined to take one back to the days when cars were cars and sports-car drivers

were strong men. The stiff blast of cold air, somewhat alleviated by the heat from the engine, was refreshing at first but numbing after a few miles of 80-m.p.h. cruising, and when the Motorway was reached we stopped at a filling station to fill one of the two 7-gallon tanks and to shamefacedly erect the hood, while the attendant remarked that "They were grand old motors." We didn't have the heart to tell him that the car wasn't a year old.

On the open road the Kieft-Morgan is exhilarating to drive. The ride only becomes objectionable on really bad surfaces, when the car does its best to knock the breath from the occupants' bodies and the steering wheel has to be gripped hard if the driver wishes to avoid having it snatched from his hands. The axle ratio does not allow tremendous speeds to be reached, but 5,000 r.p.m. in top gear, which represents 96.5 m.p.h., is reached with ridiculous ease and 6,000 r.p.m. can be held if necessary. The TR engine, which seems sluggish and reluctant to rev. in its standard form, really howls like a 1100 Climax with the Kieft mods, and consequently becomes more pleasant to use. One peculiar factor which manifests itself with the low axle ratio is the inability of the engine to settle for a particular cruising speed as the revs. will go straight off the clock in top gear if allowed.

POWER HOUSE.—The TR3 engine is hidden by the aluminium plate which shields the carburetters from engine heat. The S.U. carburetters are fitted with ram tubes.

Road-holding with the Dunlop R5 tyres is good in the dry but they tend to accentuate the hard ride. In the wet, which predominated for almost the entire duration of our tests and which precluded the taking of acceleration figures, the Morgan was definitely "twitchy" and required careful handling. Having recently driven another Morgan in a similar state of tune at Goodwood we can vouch for the fantastic road-holding of this car, which would make an ideal beginner's racing car. There seems little likelihood of any major changes to the Morgan specification in the foreseeable future and, indeed, Lionel Mayman assures us that they sell well in the U.S. (where 90% of the production goes) *because* of the design and not in spite of it. With the expenditure of something over £1,000 the Morgan buyer will receive from Kieft a very accelerative sports car of distinctive lines which will be capable of winning its class in races, sprints and hill-climbs without the expenditure of a great deal more money—what more could the enthusiast ask ?—M. L. T.

[The Arden Racing and Sports Cars Ltd. point out that Kieft Sports Car Co. Ltd. is not the sole distributor for Arden conversions as mentioned in our November issue, but only the concessionaires for Formula Junior engines and five-speed gearboxes.]

◆◆

TRIUMPH ROADSTER CLUB

Following the announcement in our columns some months ago, this Club is now fully organised and membership forms are now available from Barry Cutter, 26, Ravensbourne Avenue, Bromley, Kent.

VINTAGE LINES characterise the Morgan Plus-Four. The test car was fitted with Dunlop racing tyres which emphasised the firm suspension but enhanced roadholding on dry roads.

THIS CAR will genuinely exceed 120 m.p.h. in full road trim. Chris Lawrence's well-known Morgan Plus Four outside John Bolster's home during its stay at Horsham.

JOHN BOLSTER TESTS A

Morgan with a Difference

The Remarkable Lawrence-tune Car

THE subject of this week's test is a Morgan with a difference and, as the French say, *vive la différence!* The actual car which I have been putting through its paces is the machine with which Chris Lawrence has been so successful in races. It is, in fact, the prototype from which the Morgan Motor Co. have developed their new Super Sports model, which I hope to test in the spring. In the meantime, however, it was thought that a preliminary canter with the Lawrence car would be of interest, as it is basically a well-worn 1956 model with a genuine *racing* mileage of some 7,000, in addition to at least six times that in fast road motoring.

This machine has the same body and chassis specification as the Super Sports. That is to say the body is panelled in aluminium instead of steel, and there are knock-on wire wheels, disc brakes and an oil cooler. Racing-type bucket seats are fitted, but it is likely that these too will be standardized on the Super Sports. The only "extra" on the test vehicle was an undershield.

The engines of the Super Sports Morgans are to receive the "Lawrence-tune" treatment at Westerham Motors, of which Chris Lawrence is managing director. Each engine will have its crankshaft, clutch, flywheel, connecting rods and pistons specially balanced by Jack Brabham (Motors), Ltd. The head will be polished and gas-flowed, and the ports will be modified to mate-up with special

induction and exhaust manifolds. Two dual-choke Weber 42 DCOE6 carburetters will be fitted plus a Lawrence-designed camshaft. The result of all this is a very useful power increase throughout the working range, with some extra revs. at the top end and an addition of 20 per cent. to the maximum b.h.p.

The car just tested had an old TR2 engine instead of the TR3 unit which is now standard. The compression ratio had been raised to 10:1 and the Weber carburetters were of 45 mm. size instead of 42 mm. It was, in fact, tuned a little further than the production cars will be, the winning of races being regarded as more important than the flexibility which is desirable for everyday driving.

It is difficult not to be amazed at the good handling qualities of the Morgan chassis. The traditional pillar-type suspension is still employed in front, and the short, flat underslung semi-elliptic springs locate the rear axle. The low wide frame has unusual Z-section members, and is stiffened by the body, particularly at the front end.

Yet, this ultra-simple vehicle is possessed of exceptional controllability even at three-figure speeds. Its behaviour is always entirely predictable, and corners may be taken just about as quickly as by machines of much more elaborate specification. If you are the kind of chap who wants to buy a Morgan, you are not worried about the absence of a boulevard ride. This almost vintage sports car is a tough, effective device, and it is of satisfactorily low weight.

The standard Morgan Plus Four is a lively and economical sports car which can achieve 100 m.p.h. The Super Sports has not yet been timed, but a full 115 m.p.h. is envisaged. Having put the stop-watch on the Chris Lawrence car I can state that this astonishing vehicle will genuinely exceed 120 m.p.h. At this speed on the standard axle ratio, the engine revolutions are approaching 6,000, but the carefully balanced unit seems quite safe at such velocities, at all events for short periods.

The acceleration figures which I recorded were marred by some dampness of the road surface, a condition which it is hard to avoid at this time of year. There was a good deal of wheelspin at the getaway, which is difficult to prevent

WEBERS as well as a fabricated exhaust system, a polished head with raised compression and several other modifications account for the car's fantastic acceleration.

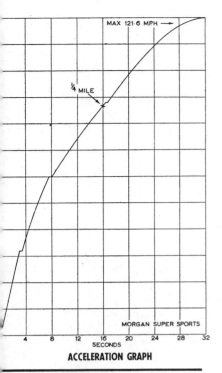

ACCELERATION GRAPH

MORGAN SUPER SPORTS

MAX 121·6 MPH →

¼ MILE

The Lawrence Morgan

on any fast car with a rigid axle. Nevertheless, the sheer performance is something which puts this Morgan in a class far beyond any normal sports car, and one can understand the almost monotonous series of victories which it has gained.

It would be true to say that the standard Morgan, although a fast car, could easily be controlled at higher speeds than those of which it is capable. This is proved by the current test car, which is still fully controllable when all its great power is exploited. The clutch shows no signs of distress, and did not appear to be getting unduly hot when the acceleration figures were taken. Some discretion must be exercised when starting off in first gear or excessive wheelspin may be induced even on a dry road.

The standard hood and sidescreens were used when the performance figures were taken. In this guise, the car was somewhat noisy, due to the short exhaust system which terminates approximately below the driver's seat. In fact, the noise is by no means excessive when heard outside the vehicle. Racing sparking plugs were employed during the performance testing, but it was necessary to keep up the revs. in order to maintain them in a clean condition. For all ordinary road work, relatively "soft" plugs were fitted. Some misfiring was apparent after crawling through a thick fog, but a short burst of hard driving soon cured the trouble.

As is usual with twin-choke Weber carburetters, cold starting was achieved by giving three or four preliminary pumps with the accelerator. This worked every time, and the engine showed no tendency to stall thereafter. Naturally, the fuel consumption was considerably heavier than that of a standard Morgan, but not unreasonable in view of the very high performance.

Complete new TR3 engines to Super Sports specification, including balancing, Weber carburetters, and manifolds, cost £220, and there is also an exchange plan, while the various components may be bought separately. For further informa-

tion, contact Westerham Motors, Ltd., 69A Avenue Road, Acton, W.3. The complete Super Sports Morgan is to be available as a new car for £1,250 including P.T. This must represent the greatest performance for the least money which is at present available.

SPECIFICATION AND PERFORMANCE DATA

Car Tested: Morgan Super Sports ("Lawrence-tuned").

Specification: As standard car previously tested with wire wheels and disc brakes, plus tuned engine with 10 to 1 compression ratio and two twin-choke Weber carburetters. Oil cooler, undershield, aluminium body panels.

Performance: Maximum speed 121.6 m.p.h. Speeds in gears: 3rd, 88 m.p.h.; 2nd, 60 m.p.h.; 1st, 32 m.p.h. Standing quarter-mile, 16 secs. Acceleration: 0-30 m.p.h., 2.8 secs.; 0-50 m.p.h., 5.8 secs.; 0-60 m.p.h., 7.6 secs.; 0-80 m.p.h., 13.8 secs.; 0-100 m.p.h., 20.4 secs.

Fuel Consumption: 15-18 m.p.g.

LOOKING very purposeful. Note the oil cooler at the front, the bonnet air scoop and the efficient-looking aluminium under-tray.

PLUS 4 TWO SEATER TOURER

An attractive Two-seater with ample power for either fast touring, or competition work. Each seat has its own pneumatic cushion with an adjustable single back squab. A large luggage compartment is provided into which the hood folds out of sight when not in use. The petrol tank holds 12 gallons, and is fitted with a quick action filler. Speedometer and Rev. Counter are fitted. A Fuel Gauge, Water Temperature Gauge, Ammeter and Oil Pressure Gauge are fitted to all Plus 4 models.

S.C.W. | FULL ROAD TEST

Twins, but they can be told apart. Left is the green Morgan Plus Four
tell-tale disc wheels. Right is Ron Coulston's red one with hood

CLYDE HODGINS DRIVES THE

LEGENDARY TR3 ENGINED

Racing type steering wheel and cockpit of Coulston's Morgan.

THREE young Sydney men are
responsible for the return to
major Australian car racing of a
famous English car. The car is
the Morgan, which has been setting world records for the past 50
years. The trio are Ryde brothers
Ken and Barry Ward and Rock-
dale watchmaker Ron Coulston.
The Wards have obtained the distribution rights for the Morgan
which had not been sold on our
shores for the past eight years.
Coulston, a committeeman of the
Australian Sporting Car Club
which organised the Redex and
Ampol Trials, is their first happy
owner.

Coulston persuaded the Wards
to hurry plans for setting up a
Morgan sales agency as he wanted one of these potent, but old-
fashioned looking vehicles for the
opening meeting at Warwick
Farm. He engaged top sports
and sedan driver, David Mackay,
to take the wheel for the race.
This race Morgan made history by
winning the production sports car
event — the first race held on the
the Farm layout. In taking the
checkered flag Mackay beat a line-
up of MGAs, Healeys and a TR3.

Morgan history dates back to
1899 when the teenage son of a
Hereford rector, H. F. S. Morgan,

demonstrator of the Ward Brothers, with hood erected and the
down and the racy wire wheels showing to advantage.

MORGAN PLUS FOUR

had a rather risky ride down a steep hill in a cyclecar. Just over 10 years later the first Morgan was born — in the form of a three-wheeler with a 8 hp twin cylinder JAP engine, a tiller and a single seat.

In 1912 H. F. S. Morgan set a Brooklands record, covering 59 miles 1120 yards in an hour. The car had two wheels up front, with independent suspension and a single wheel behind. One of these fantastic vehicles then could be bought for as little as 80 guineas. When the three-wheeler Morgan proved too outstanding a winner in RAC trials it was barred, after which the company brought out their first four-wheel car.

A Standard Motor Co. engine was fitted in 1938, together with a Moss gearbox mounted centrally in the chassis. During the war the Morgan factory, with the exception of the service and spares departments, was turned over to production of Army equipment.

Three-wheelers were discontinued in 1950, by which time the four-wheelers had become a big export earner for Britain. In 1954 the Triumph TR2 engine was fitted, followed by the TR3 two years later, raising bhp to 100, the same as today. Most recent introduc-

tion to keep Morgans up with the times has been the fitting of Girling disc brakes and knock-on wire wheels for racing.

Coulston has built up a name as one of the best trials navigators in NSW over recent years. He accompanied clubmate Bill Burns in the 1957 Ampol (in a Holden) and the 1958 Ampol (in the ex-Jack Middleton Jaguar XK120) hardtop. In the second trial they had a chance of winning the big car class but blew a head gasket on the last day. Last year Coulston found he suffered from car sickness when he was a passenger and not driving. As a result he looked round for a car which he could enter in trials and sports car races. He decided on the Morgan after much research.

He says the Morgan has harder springing and consequent superior roadholding than other sports cars in its price range. But he says it is not as good-looking as the Triumph TR3. Here I hastened to point out the Morgan is a car which will readily grow on the public, like the Volkswagen.

The Morgan Company is still a family concern and all cars are hand-built, so that on ordering clients can have many extras installed at little cost. Morgan have

always attempted and usually succeeded, in producing cars that owners can use with confidence in their daily vocation, or again awards in competition with other cars. They offer a car that in addition to sheer speed has the comfort and controllability so essential to a car for use under modern road conditions.

Morgan claim their bodywork is coach built of distinctive design from the best materials obtainable. An important point in these days of high costs is the ease with which the car can be maintained and repaired if necessary. As well as having exceptional performance the Morgan also is a comfortable long distance touring car which should give long life, plus economy and trouble-free motoring.

Basic Australian price of the Morgan is £1525 (inc. tax). Extras, if ordered with a new car are knock-on wire wheels £68; special induction and exhaust system £63 and Dunlop Duraband tyres £10. At these prices I can see the Wards receiving a lot of orders for the Morgans, which have a factory production of one car daily.

Four models of the Morgan are available. Three are plus fours

119

with TR3 motor — the two-seater tourer; two-seater coupe and a four-seater tourer. The tourer has cutaway doors and a large luggage compartment which is normally hidden by the back leather cover. It has a 12-gallon petrol tank with a quick action filler. The coupe has doors flush with the back of the car and sliding side windows. Windows do not have any inside mechanism to cut into elbow room. The four-seater has a petrol tank of nine gallons, fitted below the rear seats and the body is lengthened to accommodate passengers in comfort. Battery is moved from behind the front seat to under the bonnet.

Fourth model is the two-seater tourer 4/4 Series III, fitted with a Ford 10 hp engine of 996 cc capacity as on the Anglia, which meets the demand for a light but powerful sports car at a reasonable price. With a four-speed gearbox this Morgan is well known for its fuel economy and excellent power to weight ratio.

I have driven the first two Morgans imported by the Wards. They are a green standard one of the Wards which was not run in and the red racing one of Coulston. The standard version has a compression ratio of 8.5 and a rear axle ratio of 3.7. Coulston had compression raised to 10.2 and runs his Morgan on Shell 100 racing petrol. For increased acceleration, apparently with the Warwick Farm circuit in mind, he had a Jaguar rear axle fitted with low ratio of 4.28.

With the new rear axle, the Coulston Morgan had a most optimistic speedometer. On our top speed run on our test strip an indicated 114 worked out at an actual 96.9 mph. But over 60 mph the acceleration of the Coulston Morgan was amazing. From 60 to 80 mph took only 5 sec, compared with 9.2 sec for the standard version.

The standard Morgan plus four reaches 100 mph at 5000 rpm, while the racing one does 95 mph at 5500 revs, though it gets their far quicker. The four cylinders TR3 motor needs hardly any elaboration. It has a capacity of 121.5 cu in or 1991 cc. Bore and stroke are 3.268 × 3.622 in or 83 × 92 mm. With the bonnet opening from both sides, ease of getting to the engine is a big point in its favor. The twin SU carburettors go into a redesigned inlet mani-

In racing trim, Coulston's Morgan flies round the Warwick Farm circuit.

The easily accessible engine compartment showing the twin SU carburettors which go into a redesigned inlet manifold.

fold. Engine design is straight forward with wet liners and pushrod operated overhead valves. Lubrication is force feed by epicyclic geared pump, with an oil pressure gauge on the dashboard. Cooling is by water pump and fan, belt driven with an automatic thermostat.

The patented chassis is still of Z section structure, passing at full width beneath the rear axle and narrowing to attach to the famous Morgan front end. The front wheels have a pillar type independent suspension with helical springs which has been patented by Morgan for 40 years. The springs are longer than previously, giving more movement and softer travel. Double acting tubular type shock absorbers are fitted to the front springs.

The Moss gearbox setup is one of the unusual, but good, features of the Morgan. Clutch housing and transmission are separated by about 18 inches of cast tube and clutch shaft. The box thus rests handily at the forward edge of the seats, so that the lever goes right down into the doings without the aid of remote controls.

Since the gear layout and casing are substantially the same as in the Jaguar, the unit is more than strong enough and has excellent ratios. The direct lever provides easy control, though the green Morgan on our cover, still not run in, was naturally a little stiff. Travel between gears is so short that at times you doubt if you are really in the ratio you have chosen.

Synchromesh was unbeatable on our acceleration runs from a stop. Security from going into reverse by mistake also has been taken care of. The lever has to be lifted, which needs quite an art till you become accustomed to it.

Gear ratios are 3.73, 5.24, 7.38, 12.85 and reverse 12.85 to 1. Transmission is a Hardy Spicer propeller shaft with needle roller bearing universal joints. With the alternate axle ratio of 4.27 instead of the standard 3.73, the Coulston Morgan really took off, though top speed was naturally down slightly.

Incidentally the new axle was fitted by the Jaguar experts at Bryson Industries, who had the Morgan franchise till 1953, when it was allowed to lapse. This Mog has surprising pulling power at low speeds, going from 0 to 30 in 3.2 sec, to 50 in 7.2 sec and to 90 in 19 sec. Really pressed the Morgan just reaches 90 in third at peak revs, which time could be even bettered if you really wanted to thrash it.

The Dunlop Duraband tyres, which are similar to the famous Michelin X, produced an unusual cornering squeal at low speeds on hairpin bends, but once on the open road their roadholding was superb. The wire wheels, fitted as an extra, give extra lightness, though rule out the fitting of tubeless tires even for Mr Average Motorist,

Physical culture instructor Sheila Burgess of Bankstown adds color to the front view of the Morgan. The flutes along the bonnet top distinguish the plus four from the four/four, which has a Ford Anglia engine.

despite what the tyre company experts may say. It appears each spoke rivet gives extra outlets for tiny air bubbles to escape. Tyre size is 5.60 by 15 in.

Brakes are really outstanding, thanks to the discs on the front which give increased confidence for high cruising, knowing subconsciously that at least you can pull up in safety. Using our Bronder brake graph, the Morgan, with all anchors out, stopped from 20 mph in 16 ft 4 in, which rated as excellent.

The Duraband tyres, which are reinforced with steel wire, took away a lot of the understeering

which has been attributed to the Morgan. It could be flung through the corners in a most refreshing manner. The cam gear steering with two and a quarter turns from lock to lock is very direct and the turning circle is 32 ft. The Morgan is an ideal trials car as well as for racing. It will go wherever you have the strength to point it. The rear end just follows along and never tries to go off on a line of its own.

Instruments are neatly grouped on a steel panel with a polished walnut surround. The most important instrument, the rev counter, is sighted through the right side of the steering wheel. Through the left side are noticed the gauges for oil, amps, water and fuel. Speedo, with total and trip mileages are situated in front of the passenger, which could be alarming if you were taking your nervous grandmother on a fast country trip.

Also present are switches for wipers, panel lights, fog light and the popular manual choke, lights combined with ignition switch, warning lights for high beam and generator with a plug to take a trouble light. The trafficators are not self cancelling.

The Morgan windscreen comes off by unscrewing four studs. With the hood erected, a big window makes visibility clear in the back.

I picked Ron Coulston up at 5 am one Sunday morning to go out to the SCW test strip in his Morgan. The Plus Four is kept under covers as Ron already has a Peugeot for trials work and a small Renault for jogging round the suburbs.

The Mog had not been used for three weeks, but started up quickly after we had poured in a can of fuel. Seating was comfortable with the driver or passenger being able to adjust his own cushioning by adding or letting out air of the separate pneumatic style seats.

Handbrake is of the fly-off type, though I felt it was a little hard to reach in its position forward of the gearlever.

Our tests were carried out with the hood down and the windscreen up, in which style Ron felt the Mog went better.

Over the flying quarter mile the Morgan averaged 96.1 mph with a build up of only about half a mile each way.

The Morgan should soon become a popular sight at our races and

hill climbs. It has the real look of the vintage sports car, not being changed by the whim of a designer to follow the latest trend. It has the long louvred mudguards so dear to the heart of the vintage fan. It also proudly displays running boards and an engine compartment which can be lifted up from either side, depending at which section of the engine you wish to work on. Doors are cutaway at the top and are covered by the slip on side curtains when the clipped-on hood is in position.

Some people may find the Brooklands type steering wheel with aluminium spokes and wood rim a little close for comfort. Door handles have been eliminated, so that to enter the Mog you have to awkwardly put your hand under the side flaps. It appears also that a little water and odd draughts could penetrate round the windscreens in really dirty weather. But the real sports car boys claim that weather does not matter in such a fabulous machine.

Another trick with the Morgan is the horn button, which is situated on the dashboard. At first I had the idea it was for screen washers.

Top speed on our runs was a timed 96.9 miles per hour on the test strip, with the optimistic speedo showing over 110. Average of the runs worked out at 96.1.

With a test limit of 5500 revolutions per minute, which Ron considered high enough (and rightly so) the Morgan gave figures as good and better than Mogs used for racing in Europe and America.

Calculating on figures supplied by Ken Ward, who says the Coulston Morgan does 18.1 miles per hour at 1000 rpm, the car should have a top speed of 99.5 mph, with 77.5 in third, 58.9 in second and

34.5 in first.

We were unable to ascertain accurate torque figures so have for record purposes used those of the standard model — 118 lb/ft at 3000 rpm.

There was no brake fade during our tests, while the Mog stopped from 20 mph in 16 ft 4 in (rated excellent) using our brake gauge.

Best time for the standing quarter mile was 17.5 sec, with an average of 17.7 sec. Corrected speed at the end of this stretch was 90 mph.

Since this article was written the green standard Morgan was sold, unhappily for Barry Ward, who had taken out his provisional racing licence and had hoped to assist Coulston carry the Mog banner at Warwick Farm and Katoomba.

The Mog is a car ideally suited for the backyard mechanic due to ruggedness, ease of accessibility and the confidence that TR3 parts are readily available. Maintenance chores and other adjustments can be carried out without the use of a hoist or by having to inch your fingers into awkward corners. The body is most practical, but there is an unfortunate absence of those little gimmicks which make driving a little more comfortable, such as pockets in the doors and a lid to the cubby hole on the dashboard.

In the hands of the right owner, who respects its beauty and vices, the Morgan Plus Four can be almost unbeatable. It is a real performer, especially in Ron Coulston's version, and is matched with excellent roadholding and quick stopping brakes.

Perhaps there are some cars which are smoother, quieter or more comfortable, but not at the price. Just ask any Mog owner. #

A sleepy Ron Coulston after our 5 am run.

COULSTON MORGAN + 4

PERFORMANCE

TOP SPEED:

Two-way average	96.1
Fastest one way	96.9

ACCELERATION:

(test limit, 5500 rpm)
Through gears:

0-30 mph	3.2
0-40 mph	5.3
0-50 mph	7.2
0-60 mph	9.1
0-70 mph	11.4
0-80 mph	14.1
0-90 mph	19.0
Standing quarter-mile average	17.7
Standing quarter-mile, best run	17.5
Speed at end of quarter	90

MAXIMUM SPEED IN GEARS (calculated):

(at 5500 rpm)

I	34.5
II	58.9
III	77.5
IV	99.5

SPEEDOMETER ERROR:

30 mph actual equals	indicated 34 mph
40 mph actual equals	ind 46 mph
50 mph actual equals	ind 57 mph
60 mph actual equals	ind 69 mph
70 mph actual equals	ind 80 mph
80 mph actual equals	ind 92 mph
90 mph actual equals	ind 103 mph

TAPLEY DATA:

Maximum pull in gears:

I	580 at 30 mph
II	430 at 45 mph
III	290 at 50 mph
IV	245 at 55 mph

BRAKING:

Fade: Nil
Stopping from 20 mph .... 16 ft 4 in

CALCULATED DATA:

Weight as tested (two men)	19½ cwt
Max bhp	103 at 5500
Max torque	118 lb/ft at 3000
Lb/hp	21.8
Mph/1000 rpm top gear	18.1
Mph at 2500 ft/min piston speed top gear	81.5
Cub/cm/lb ft torque	15.3
Bhp/litre	43.2
Bhp/ton as tested	100.4

SPECIFICATIONS

PRICE:

£1666 (including tax, but without raised compression or lower rear axle ratio).

ENGINE:

Type	four cylinders
Valves	pushrod operated overhead
Cubic capacity	2380 cc
Bore and stroke	83mm x 92 mm
Compression ratio	10.2 to 1

Carburettors: Two SU (type H6)
Fuel pump: AC mechanical

CHASSIS:

Type: Deep Z shape side, 5 cross members of tubular section.
Track: 3 ft 11 in
Suspension: Independent vertical coil, rear, half-elliptic springs
Dampers: Armstrong hydraulic
Brakes: Girling disc, 11" front; 9" drum rear
Clutch: Borg and Beck 9" single dry plate
Steering: Cam and peg
Tyres .... Dunlop Duraband

GEAR RATIOS:

I	12.85
II	7.38
III	5.24
IV	3.73

GENERAL:

Length overall	12 ft
Width	4 ft 8 in
Test weather	fine, no wind

Tests made on dry, bitumen-bound gravel road with driver and one passenger. High-speed runs made with hood down and windows off. All times averaged from several runs in opposite directions, using where applicable a corrected speedometer.

A Faster Morgan

Distinguishing features of the latest Plus Four Morgan are a deeper windscreen and lower door sills.

Ford Classic Engine and Disc Brakes for the 4/4.

Improved Coupé and Tuned Lightweight in Plus 4 Range

NEARLY 40% more power and a like increase in torque have been given to the Morgan 4/4 for 1962 by the adoption of the 1,340 c.c. Ford Classic 315 engine in place of the 997 c.c. Anglia power unit used on the 1961 models. In addition, Girling disc brakes have been fitted at the front to cope with the increased performance. These new features increase the basic price by only £10, which brings the figure to £530 (with British purchase tax, £774 3s. 1d.)—the lowest sum for an over-1,000 c.c. sports car in this country.

The Triumph TR-engined Plus Four models are continued largely unchanged, but improved vision is provided on the coupé, and the Lawrence-tuned engine and lightweight body announced as special extras at the Show last year are now combined in a catalogued version at £900 basic (£1,313 14s. 9d. with P.T.). The remaining Plus Four models (2-seater, 4-seater and D.H. Coupé) continue at unchanged prices. Plus Four models, incidentally, are now fitted as standard with the latest 2,131 c.c. TR4 engine but the 1,911 c.c. unit can still be supplied as an optional extra.

* * *

The new Series IV, 4/4 model is identical in external appearance to the Series III and, indeed, the only differences are the fitting of the longer-stroke Ford engine (complete with gearbox), a modification of the gear change and ratios, and the adoption of front disc brakes. Judging by a brief run in the new model, however, the new engine has revolutionized performance, not merely by reason of the extra power available (the output has gone up from 39 to 54 b.h.p. net), but because it is developed lower in the range and is accompanied by a big increase in torque (from 53 lb. ft. to 74 lb. ft.), which is also produced lower in the r.p.m. range. The result is an outstanding top-gear performance as well as much snappier acceleration when full use is made of the gears.

Used in standard form, the Classic unit drops neatly into the existing chassis frame and is stated to involve no change in weight. It has been possible to arrange a very neat form of remote control which retains conventional gear positions: a short vertical lever from the box is attached by a rubber-bushed joint to a straight horizontal lever which terminates in the usual knob at its rear end and enters a close-fitting tube at its forward extremity; this tube is flexibly mounted in rubber in the bulkhead and acts as a fulcrum, the rubber mounting permitting the necessary angular changes; movement of the lever within the tube allows fore-and-aft motion. Thus changes between first and second gears, or between third and top, are effected by a simple push-pull motion of the knob, whilst movements across the gate merely involve a side-to-side action; similarly, reverse can be obtained by lifting the knob and moving it outwards—all of which may sound slightly complicated but is simple and effective in practice.

Somewhat unexpectedly in view of the increased power, the rear axle ratio has been lowered fractionally (from 4.4/1 to 4.56/1), but the car is still fairly high geared and is notably free from fuss. Actual performance figures must await a full road test, but the prototype tried appeared to have a maximum in the region of 90 m.p.h. The new front disc brakes are the familiar Girling type, but a notable point is the large (11-in.) discs used, giving an exceptionally large rubbed area for a car weighing only 13 cwt.

CONTINUED ON PAGE 151

A push/pull remote control gear lever (*left*) is fitted to the Classic-engined 4/4. (*below*). It has conventional gear positions.

A maximum speed of 115 m.p.h. is claimed from the supersports Plus 4 model fitted with the Lawrence-tuned TR engine shown here.

Road Research Report: Morgan 4/4 Series III

● The Morgan Motor Company observed its 50th anniversary in 1960 and celebrated the event by introducing the 4/4 Series III. The least expensive Mog, it uses English Ford's 105E overhead-valve engine and four-speed transmission.

Viewed dispassionately, the Series III is notable for its decidedly dated styling, its uncompromisingly harsh ride and passenger accommodations that are practically medieval. However even a ride around the block should be enough to convince you that the neo-classic Morgan cannot be viewed solely as an object on four wheels. Its styling has a fierce practicality, reflecting the basic soundness of its engineering, and possesses no small amount of flair. The ride must be analyzed in terms of what it does for the driver, giving illusion-free information about what the car is doing in relation to the road at all times. As 'for the passenger accommodations, well, who ever decided sports cars should ride like baby buggies and be equipped with power tops and wind-up windows anyhow?

Our Road Research Report extended more than 1100 miles, including driving at both Thompson Raceway and Lime Rock Park. The car broke in without fuss (other than some boiling over which we will discuss later), used no oil and proved to have good fuel economy.

The performance of the Series III is better than the Series II which it replaces, although the latter in its hopped-up form (see SCI, November, 1957) will outdrag the new car. The Series II was powered by the old flat-head Ford engine and used a three-speed transmission. While the Series III will provide good all-around performance, one consideration in our deciding to test it was to find out what kind of basis it might be for using some of the speed equipment available for the 105E mill. After discussing the features and faults of the standard 4/4 we'll give you a run-down on the bolt-on, bore-out, boost-up bit. The other reason for our wanting to test the Series III was to get reacquainted with the classic sports car.

There are only a few external differences between the Series II and the Series III. The new car uses different taillights (like those on the MGA 1500) and the side curtain fasteners are on the outside of the door. This latter change eliminates the annoyance of snagging a sleeve on the hardware during violent cockpit maneuvers.

VIRTUALLY HAND-BUILT

The overall appearance is enhanced by a smooth blending of straight and curved lines. The hand-made radiator grille (Morgan employs 68 persons directly concerned with turning out the virtually hand-built cars) flows into a long hood that probably fools some bystanders into thinking it's covering a straight-eight. The car gives the impression of being quite long although its actual exterior dimensions are tidy. The rake of the front fenders and the sweep of the flattened tail section add to the illusion. The single Lucas driving light mounted low-down for best illumination in fog helps too and supplements the no-nonsense air of the car. There are no frills. The standard Dunlop disc wheels are perforated to help brake cooling and the hub caps are smooth chrome-plated discs. There's no need for bold script to tell the world it's a Morgan (that fact is noted only by the Morgan emblem on the grille surround); anyone who knows anything about sports cars recognizes the *marque* at a glance. The externally mounted spare and the louvers on the side of the hood are in keeping with the functionalism of the whole car. To some it may look "old fashioned" but to sports car buffs, the people who buy them as fast as they're built, Morgans are as up to date as tomorrow's headlines.

After picking up the Mog at Fergus (pausing momentarily to admire some of the TR-3-engined Plus Fours) we put a few miles on it before heading for Thompson Raceway. We made the trip in a steady downpour and, to put it mildly, driving over 200 miles under such conditions put the car in a very unfavorable light. Despite the snug appearance of the top, rain poured in over the windshield, around the edges of the side curtains and dripped steadily on the drivers right ankle from under the cowl. Being a true enthusiast's car, it had no heater or defroster. If you want ventilation you're supposed to leave the top at home since there are no vents and the flaps in the side curtains won't stay up by themselves. Under such conditions we weren't disposed to witty banter so we occupied ourselves with bailing out the cockpit and keeping the windshield reasonably unfogged.

If the Mog had a top arrangement like that on the Sprite, leaks at the leading edge would probably be minimized. Since it doesn't an owner could cement some rubber weatherstripping to reduce the waterfall effect.

HANDLES LIKE A WINNER

Once at the track we abandoned the top altogether to take some laps. Despite the persistent rain and the squishing every time we moved in the seats the 4/4 proved a real ball to drive. The handling of the car is one of its strongest virtues and skids could be provoked only with deliberate wheel movements. The billiard-table-flatness and the light, quick steering kept things in hand at all times. The Dunlop Gold Seal tires gave a good bite with predictable breakaway and good recovery characteristics. The car had a sure-footed feel in spite of track conditions although on the open road when the surface got very rough it tended to skate, with control diminishing in direct proportion to the frequency and intensity of the bumps. The effect of tire pressures on road behavior may be clearly demonstrated in the Mog. If they are too high the ride will rattle the fillings from your teeth while those that are too low will make the car behave like a greased snake on a hockey rink. For best results (a reasonable compromise of ride comfort and control) use the recommended figures or 2 or 3 psi more.

The car seemed badly geared for the Thompson circuit with second gear the key offender. Over-revving in second or lugging in third were the only alternatives in some corners and lap times suffered as a result. It was impossible, furthermore, to peak out in fourth and third was too low for the length of the straights.

At Lime Rock things were better. For one thing the sun was shining. In addition the corners didn't require using second gear, third providing enough dig through the tighter sections. However it still wasn't possible to wind it out all the way in fourth. Comparing the two sessions, Lime Rock brought home the need for more power while gearing played the dominant role in the Thompson turnings.

The Ford four-banger with its single-throat Solex carburetor had excellent responsiveness, with no slack or binding spots noticeable in the cable linkage. Tromping on the loud pedal (and it was just that with the straight-through "silencer" mounted on the car) caused a pleasant "wonk" sound as air rushed into the carb. The air cleaner, if you care to call it that, resembles a small sheetmetal roof. Stuck on top of the carb, with no filter element, it's enough to prevent a mechanic's false teeth from falling in but that's about all.

The engine started with a twist of the key even after standing in heavy rain. It idled smoothly with a pleasant mechanical whirr and seemed free from vibration in all ranges. In its standard form, it develops 39 bhp at 5000 rpm, compared to 36 bhp at 4500 rpm in the former model.

Our only real complaint concerning the engine was its tendency to overheat in traffic. With only a two-bladed fan, air flow at low speeds is restricted and the car lacks the louvers on top of the hood that other Morgans had. However, by the time you read this a four-bladed fan will be standard equipment. The lack of a water temperature gauge complicates the overheating question; not even a warning light is fitted. A gauge could be installed without much work and we'd recommend it.

Even with the hardest running, the lowest gas mileage figure we recorded was 25.8 mpg. This was when the engine had only about 350 miles on it and had been driven mostly in traffic. We reached a high of 29.7 mpg cruising at 60 to 65 mph. There was every reason to believe the figure would improve as the engine continued to limber up. Regular fuel was all that was needed; there was no trace of pinging or running-on and (seemingly) any old-volatile substance would work fine, although Morgan recommends using premium.

The new engine slips neatly into the underslung Morgan chassis with its unique Z-section side members and vertical coil spring independent front suspension. Consequently Series II owners shouldn't have much trouble installing one of the new units together with the four-speed box if they should want to. The transmission is a little wider than the three-cog box and the frame has been modified slightly to accommodate it. At the same time interior foot room has been increased by widening the internal cowl/firewall section, but without widening the actual hood width. The engine is mounted at three points. Two of them are on the sides of the block with the third under the transmission. The clutch and bell housing are wholly within the engine compartment.

UNUSUAL SHIFTING ARRANGEMENT

To avoid the awkwardly long shift lever which would be necessary if a direct-acting prong were used, a simple remote control is adopted. The shift pattern, consequently, is a little weird as the lever projects almost horizontally from the firewall. A short vertical shaft projecting from the transmission is rigged to a suitable joint on the horizontal lever. The latter, in turn, is mounted at its forward end in a tube which is mounted in rubber to permit fore-and-aft and side-to-side movement. The shifting motion is like thrusting with a fencing foil. To shift from neutral to first, the shift knob is lifted slightly and jabbed forward in one motion. From first to second the action is like pulling a broom stick downstairs. It's not as screwy as it sounds. Shifting can be done rapidly and accurately; the required motions are quite small and there is a crisp feel to the gate. While we wouldn't give the arrangement an unqualified endorsement, it's effective, easy to learn and it adds to the "far out" quality of the whole car. The car accelerates in a businesslike manner, a sharp brrap issuing from the tailpipe, up to about 65 mph. Over that speed additional notches on *Continued on page* 130

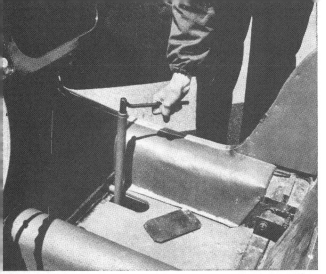

The 4/4's jacking system requires that the occupant get out, remove the seat and support, then slip the unit into the frame.

Morgan fans mourned the passing of the flat radiator grille and short front fenders, but the modernized front end is attractive.

Representative of the hot 105E engines is this by Lawrencetune with twin-throat Webers, increased compression and new cam.

There's only one word for the Mog: rakish. Its sweeping fenders and long flat hood go well with its classic handling and ride.

Rich leather hides the wood floorboards and gives the Morgan a quality feel. The suction rear view mirror is a Mog institution.

As mentioned in the text, the Shorrock supercharger is an easy step for increased power. Here's one on a stock Anglia engine.

Road Research Report:
MORGAN 4/4 SERIES III

Importer: Fergus Imported Cars, Inc.
1717 Broadway
New York 19, New York

Worldwide Automotive Imports, Inc.
South Sepulveda Boulevard
West Los Angeles, California

Number of U.S. Dealers: 50
Planned annual production: 250
Dollar value of spare parts in U.S.: $40,000 + EnFo dealers

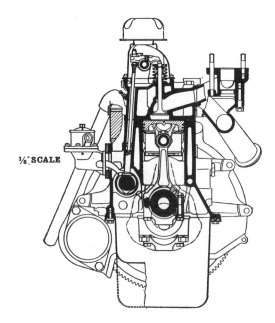

⅛ SCALE

PRICES

Basic Price	$2340
Options fitted on test car	None
Total price of car as tested	$2340
Options available:	
Heater & Defroster	65
Special color paint	50
Tonneau cover	45
Second driving or fog light	20
Luggage rack	57
Disc brakes on front wheels	80
Competition kit, including aluminum cylinder head, intake and exhaust manifolds, two SU carburetors, heavy duty valve springs and tachometer	200
Hood strap	12
Heavy duty front suspension	35

OPERATING SCHEDULE:

Fuel recommended	Regular
Mileage	25-31 mpg
Range on 9.5 gallon tank	235-295 miles
Oil recommended	SAE 10W/30
Crankcase capacity	3 quarts (4 with oil change)
Change at intervals of	2000 miles
Number of grease fittings	11
Lubrication interval	2000 miles (see text)
Most frequent maintenance:	Oil sliding axles (200 miles)

ENGINE: (Ford 105E)

Displacement	60.8 cu in, 997 cc
Dimensions	Four cyl, 3.19 in x 1.91 in
Valve gear	Pushrods, vertical overhead valves in line
Compression ratio	8.9 to one
Power (SAE)	41 @ 6000 rpm
Torque	53 lb-ft @ 2700 rpm
Usable range of engine speeds	1000-5300 rpm
Correct piston speed at 5000 rpm	2055 fpm

CHASSIS:

Wheelbase	96.0 in
Tread	47.0 in
Length	145.0 in
Ground clearance	7.0 in
Suspension: F, ind., coil spring, sliding pillar; R, rigid axle, semi-elliptic springs.	
Turns, lock to lock	2.7
Turning circle diameter between curbs	L 38 ft, R 34 ft
Tire and rim size	5.20 x 15, 4J x 15
Pressures recommended	16 F, 18R
Brakes: type, swept area	7 in drum; 141 sq in
Curb weight (full tank)	1570 lbs
Percentage on driving wheels	55

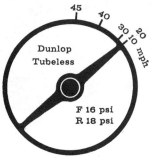

Dunlop Tubeless

F 16 psi
R 18 psi

45 40 30 20 10 mph

Steering Behavior

Wheel position to maintain 400-foot circle at speeds indicated.

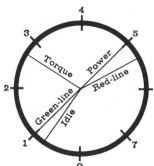

Torque   Power
Green-line   Red-line
Idle

Engine Flexibility
RPM in thousands

DRIVE TRAIN:

Gear	Synchro?	Ratio	Step	Overall	Mph per 1000 rpm
Rev	No	5.40		23.70	—3.2
1st	No	4.11	—	18.10	4.1
2nd	Yes	2.40	72%	10.54	7.1
3rd	Yes	1.41	70%	6.21	12.1
4th	Yes	1.00	41%	4.40	17.1

Final drive ratio: 4.40 to one; no options at present.

ACCELERATION:

Zero to	Seconds
30 mph	5.9
40 mph	10.7
50 mph	16.6
60 mph	25.8
Standing ¼ mile	23.0

1 Horn button
2 Speedometer
3 Odometer reset
4 Ammeter
5 Fuel gauge
6 Oil pressure
7 Windshield wiper switch
8 Trouble light socket
9 Driving light switch
10 Panel light switch
11 Turn signal light
12 High beam light
13 Turn signal lever
14 Ignition warning light
15 Choke
16 Ignition switch
17 Headlight switch

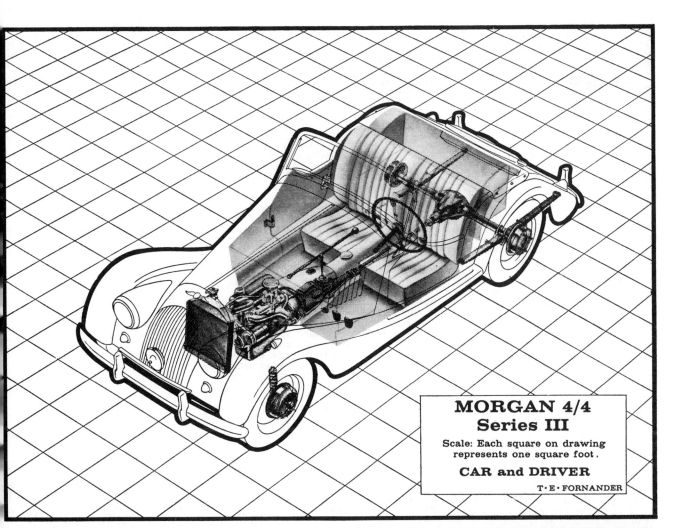

MORGAN 4/4
Series III

Scale: Each square on drawing
represents one square foot.

CAR and DRIVER

T·E·FORNANDER

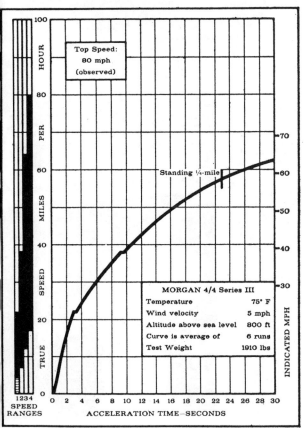

Top Speed:
80 mph
(observed)

Standing ¼-mile

MORGAN 4/4 Series III

Temperature	75° F
Wind velocity	5 mph
Altitude above sea level	800 ft
Curve is average of	6 runs
Test Weight	1910 lbs

HOUR PER MILES SPEED TRUE

INDICATED MPH

SPEED
RANGES

ACCELERATION TIME—SECONDS

ROAD
RESEARCH
REPORT: MORGAN
4/4 SERIES III

*Continued from
page* 126

the speedometer become harder to carve and a long flat stretch of road is a prerequisite. Once accelerated, virtually any speed up to the maximum can be held for as long as road conditions permit in view of the light loading on the oversquare engine.

The 4/4 has one of the nicest interiors we've seen in a car regardless of its price. The doors, transmission tunnel and frame side members are covered with leather. Our car was a gloss black and had cherry red upholstery, a good combination and a wise choice for the exterior if you are prone to collecting chipped paint since there's no matching problem for touching up. The floor and the forward section of the frame rails are sensibly covered with ribbed rubber. The workmanship of the interior trimmings and exterior of the car were outstanding.

The leather seats are unique though they've been a Morgan fixture for years. They have a one-piece back which has adjustment for a small amount of rake. The seating position is nearly perpendicular and the big Bluemels Brooklands wheel sticks out at right angles to the walnut dashboard so the appearance of the driver behind the wheel is like a Grand Prix Kilroy. The seat cushions are merely leather containing air bags which can be inflated for the desired amount of softness. All of the pedals are of the pendant variety with heel-and-toeing the brake and accelerator a matter of shoe size.

The dashboard, as can be seen from the diagram, lacks a tachometer and a water temperature gauge but has both an ammeter and ignition warning light. The horn button is convenient to the steering wheel. Toggle switches on the central "console" replace pull-types used on the Series II. The factory informed us a tachometer will be available soon. Even the arch-conservative Morgan now starts on the key (hear that, BMC?).

Some amount of body shake, particularly the doors, is visible as the frame racks over rough surfaces. The doors open fairly wide but getting in and out gracefully is hampered by the step-down seating and the steering wheel. The low-cut profile gives a convenient arm rest although on chilly days with the side curtains off the wind gives a kidney punch. The driving position is quite low so the low windshield does a good job of wind protection. The wipers have only one speed and it's not fast enough for a heavy rain.

The car looks best with its top down, although the 4/4 does not have the top-up ungainliness that Morgan Plus 4 4-seaters have. The top itself is plasticized cloth, completely removable from the ribs. The fabric snaps onto the upper edge of the windshield and has no gasketing. Snaps are also used for the rear attachment. The framework is hinged at each side and collapses out of sight. Putting the top up is best done with two people. Rear quarter vision is restricted by the lack of windows such as those on the MG TD. Luggage space is in the classic sports car manner. the sole compartment being the well behind the seats and that is quite narrow and not very deep. A luggage rack is a Morgan accessory.

In testing the Series II we called Morgan the "staunchest guardian of the vintage look, ride and feel." This is true too of the Series III and a further vintage virtue it maintains is construction. Of the car's total weight, for example, some 45 pounds are wood. This oldest (and very vintage) body-making material is used for framing the doors and constructing the rear wheel wells as well as the floorboards and platforms for the seat cushions. Another contribution to the vintage aspect is its front suspension. Nominally independent, it was first used by H.F.S. Morgan, founder of the firm, as early as 1909 (in prototype form). It consists of a coil spring wrapped around a vertical bar on which the stub axle can slide up and down. A tubular shock absorber mounted vertically forward of the sliding unit is used on each wheel. The sliding axle is lubricated by pressing a toe button on the middle of the firewall, just over the transmission tunnel. The factory recommends this "one-shot" lube at least every 200 miles. Holding the plunger down for a few seconds permits some engine oil to flow to the suspension's working parts and a slight drop in oil pressure is noticeable while the button is down. In addition, however, the axles have grease nipples to be lubricated every 3000 miles, the grease is said to be helpful in retaining the oil supplied by the one-shot system.

Morgan is a great believer in the tenet that lubrication is cheaper than overhaul and is very specific in its instructions stressing the importance of preventive maintenance. It encourages drivers to do their own maintenance, giving a very complete owner's manual but for those who are not so inclined the neighborhood Morgan or English Ford dealer should have a full supply of parts and factory-trained mechanics. Morgan stresses three points in ownership. The first two are regular lubrication and keeping brakes adjusted properly. The third is "the necessity of keeping nuts, bolts and screws tight." An honest car, the Morgan's components are easy to reach and aren't mysterious.

Some 4/4 owners may find they want more power. The stamina of the 105E engine has been amply demonstrated in its rapid acceptance by Formula Junior builders. From its initial modest 39 bhp it can be transformed into a fire-breathing 85 bhp tiger.

The simplest step is to order your Morgan with the factory Competition Kit (probably Aquaplane components) which includes an aluminum cylinder head, new intake and exhaust manifolds, two S.U. carburetors, heavy duty valve springs and a tachometer. The price, installed on new cars, is $200.

This could be in conjunction with the $80 kit for front wheel disc brakes which boost the swept area from 141 to 325 square inches, although we should note that the stock brakes seemed well-suited to their job. A third performance option for serious drivers would be the heavy-duty front suspension kit at $35.

Another option on new cars that is not available at this time in the United States, is to order your car with a supercharger. This can presently be done in England. The supercharger is a Shorrock eccentric-rotor, vane-type blower which mounts on the left side of the engine just above the generator. Available from the Allard Motor Co., Ltd., 24-28 Clapham High Street, London S.W.4, England (there is no U.S. agent at this writing), it's priced at about $210 not including shipping, taxes, etc.

Driven by a single vee-belt, the blower uses a single 1½-inch S.U. carb which comes in the kit. It is lubricated with engine oil and is driven at engine speed. It develops a maximum boost of 6.5 psi according to Allard. They say bench testing of the blown engine shows power is increased 56.4 percent to 61 bhp at 5000 rpm. At 5500 rpm, 63 bhp is produced while at 3200 rpm, no less than 37 bhp is developed. Figures in an AUTOCAR test on a blown Anglia said pulling power in lower gears was improved and the top speed went from 79 to 91 mph. It's logical to conclude the benefits of super-

charging would be multiplied in the lighter Morgan.

Another way to more go is to install a rebuilt engine. The advantages of this over the supercharger route are that you can end up with exactly the degree of power you want and, by buying components, you can do as much as you can afford at a given time. A photo representing the possible results shows the Lawrencetune engine available from Westerham Motors Ltd., 69a Avenue Road, Acton, London, W.3., England, whose engines are from $490 up.

Cosworth Engineering Ltd., Florence Road, London N.18 is one source of rebuilt engines and equipment. According to W. Brown, the general manager, their main concern is producing engines for F. Jr. cars but they do sell them for other uses too. Two variants are available, the "75" and the "85" bhp units,

priced at about $785 and $925, respectively, f.o.b. the factory. Mr. Brown said the "75" units are currently producing "more than 80 bhp at 7000 rpm and are more tractable than the more powerful engine." The compression ratio is about 10 to one in both engines.

Both the "75" and the "85" engines are fully balanced and the maximum power is guaranteed to at least equal the nominal listing through dynamometer testing before the engines are shipped. Both used special pistons, lead-indium main and rod bearings, oversize intake valves, heavy-duty exhaust valves, heavy-duty springs, and two Weber carbs.

Another source for engines and equipment is G.S.M. Cars Ltd., makers of the G.S.M. Delta. Fine Cars, Inc., 152-154 West 56th Street, New York 19, N.Y., is the distributor. Among their offerings are these engine assemblies which include transmission, carburetors, exhaust header, starter and generator: 60 bhp with standard gear box, $755; 60 bhp with close-ratio box, $930; 75 bhp with close-ratio box, $1315 and 86 bhp with close-ratio box, $1835. Among the individual items available from Fine Cars are: intake manifold for Weber dual-throat carb, $45; Weber carb, $84; exhaust header set, $60; T3 camshaft, $50; air cleaner for Weber carburetor, $17. The firm also sells a laminated steering wheel for $55.

G.S.M. offers three stages of tune on the 105E engine. The first consists of mounting the special intake and exhaust manifolds, and the related items. Stage II features the addition of heavy-duty valve springs and the camshaft. Stage III includes all of the above plus a high-compression head and bigger intake valves.

A further source of supply for some speed equipment for the 105E is Tec Auto, 198 Glen Street, Natick, Massachusetts. Among the items currently available are the Speedwell "full-flow" four-branch exhaust manifold and Servais mufflers. The prices, including shipping, are $49.95 and $22.95.

The Aquaplane Company, Ltd., Oulton Broad, Suffolk, England supplies many hop-up items that can be bought in kits or as separate units. As we mentioned, we believe this firm supplies the equipment for the factory-installed competition kit although up to our deadline for this Road Research Report we had not seen one. Aquaplane was the supplier of equipment for the hopped-up Series II we tested.

Among their equipment, with approximate prices f.o.b. the factory, are an intake manifold with two S.U. carburetors, pipes and linkage (NA/900/2SUK) $63 and air cleaners for the above (NA/AF250/SU), $2.80 each. A less expensive dual manifold is their NA/900/-SOL/K which comes with one Solex carburetor, to match the stock unit and includes pipes and linkage, priced at $45.64. Air cleaners (NA/AF/250/SOL) are $2.80 each.

A racing alloy flywheel (NA/1000/R) is priced at $32 and weighs about one-half as much as the stock iron unit. One with a steel face (NA/1000/R/SF) for greater durability costs $35.

The NA/1400 exhaust manifold is recommended for use with either of the dual intake manifolds. Of a free-flow design, it's priced at about $25. Contributing nothing in the way of power but useful for prolonging engine life and reliability, the oil cooler kit may be

considered. Priced at about $33, its part number is NA/3000/OC/FF.

Heavy duty exhaust valves (NA/-KE965) are priced at $14 per set. Similar intake valves (NA/INLET) go for about $5.80 per set. Oversize exhaust valves (NA/KE965/OV) are about $15 per set while heavy duty valve springs (NA/825/R) are about $6.30 per set.

Aquaplane's finned alloy valve cover (NA/SPEC/5) is priced at $11.50 and the electronic tachometer (NA/1500/-ELEC) lists at $37.80. According to our most recent price list, the Aquaplane Alloy Superhead (NA/6000/S) was to be available shortly. We believe this is the head that is available on the 4/4 but we have no price on it.

In lieu of Morgan taking the initiative (and we wouldn't be at all surprised if they will), we offer this suggestion. Swap the existing 105E engine for one of the new 109E engines used in the just-announced Ford Consul Classic 315. It's essentially a stroked Anglia mill.

Displacing 1340 cc, it has an 8.5 to one compression ratio and develops 56.5 bhp at 4900 rpm in stock form, equal to the output of many 1500 cc sedans. The 109E uses the same block as the 105E. Its bore is identical but the stroke is increased from 1.90 to 2.562 inches. A different cylinder head is used, having deeper combustion chambers for the larger displacement. Valves and springs are the same, but the pushrods are longer. The pistons in each are identical and the extra length of the crankshaft throws has been accomplished by shortening the con rod centers. Slight changes were made in the intake and exhaust manifolds, but not in the port sizes.

The gearbox used with the 109E is the same as the Anglia's (and, of course, the Morgan's). To take the added power of the bigger engine, you'd do well to install the Classic's heavier-duty clutch which is the same diameter as the Anglia's but has stronger springs. Alternate rear-end ratios, according to Morgan, will be available for the Anglia-engined 4/4 and one or more of these should be useful if you go to the 109E engine.

Rather than buying a complete 109E (and that could be quite difficult since, at present, there are none available in the U.S.) you could possibly "modify" your 105E engine to its specifications. Reportedly development of the two engines was carried on simultaneously by EnFo with the beef needed for the larger being built in from scratch. Consequently if you could get the bigger engine it should be a sound basis for further power probes with something over 100 bhp within the reach of a skilled mechanic.

The 4/4 should be a wise choice for a sports car. Its price is not cheap, but neither is its finish and you are buying a certain degree of exclusiveness, much more than you buy with one of the mass-produced *bolides*. The simplicity of its mechanical components should encourage home maintenance yet the car isn't fussy so that it doesn't have to be a "full-time hobby." Its operating expenses should be low and world-wide Ford service should set an owner's mind at ease once that fateful day comes when it does need major work. Its desirability among enthusiasts should keep its resale value relatively high.

The 4/4 Series III restates the basic definition of the term sports car: transportation for driver and passenger with a high degree of performance, safety, convenience—and fun! —C/D

THE DAY THE MORGANS ARRIVED

Interest in this classic British sports car has been revived with the arrival in Australia of the firm's range of 4/4, Plus Four and Supersports models.

THREE brand spanking new Morgans, their gleaming paintwork and chrome-plate hidden under a grimy film of protective grease, stood in formation one day recently on the concrete slab at Sydney's Darling Harbor wharf. They had just been slung from the hold of the Shaw Savill vessel the *Iberic*, after completing the long sea voyage from Worcestershire, in the West country of England near Wales, to Sydney, New South Wales.

Two — a Lawrence-tuned Super Sports and a Plus Four — were bound for prospective owners while the third car, a Ford Classic-engined 4/4, was to go on show until a buyer turned up. The consignment represented the second batch of this classic British-as-the-British sports car to reach our shores in just over a year after a period of several years when the prospect of obtaining a new Morgan seemed a remote chance for Australian enthusiasts of the marque.

Morgan's re-introduction to this country has come as a direct result of one man's devotion to the car. He is a young Sydney engineer, Ken Ward, who in 1960 obtained the sole Australian franchise for Morgan cars after an exchange of correspondence with Mr Peter Morgan, general manager of the firm and son of the founder, the famous H. F. S. Morgan.

Not so long ago, H.F.S., as he was affectionately known to Morganeers the world over, died just short of seeing the 50th year of production of the cars bearing his name. Morgan bolted together his first three-wheeler in 1909 and saw many thousands of the "trikes" built in the next 30 years. Offering a startling performance at a very low cost, they became one of the most popular light sports cars in England.

Over the side of the Iberic comes a mouth-watering new Morgan Supersports. This is one of the famous Lawrence-tuned cars and the first to reach Australia.

Ken Ward's interest in Morgans began when he bought his first 4/4 — a well-worn 1949 drophead coupe — back in 1955. He admits to being merely interested in them at the time. Now, he's a "fanatic". It wasn't long before he sought out other Morgan owners and the end result was that the Morgan Car Club of Australia came into being. This revived enthusiasm which had begun to wane because of the difficulty of obtaining information or spares.

Membership in NSW has grown to around the 30 mark and includes two three-wheelers, one of which was featured in SPORTS CAR WORLD'S Classics Salon for November, 1960. Both these reside in the same Sydney suburb and one is undergoing complete restoration at present. They are the only known survivors of several which reached the State in the 1930s.

Gently, now! Wharfies steady the sling as £1800 worth of car descends the last few feet on terra firma. All body panels and guards are in aluminium.

Morgans officially ceased to come to Australia in 1952, although several 1954 models found their way to Western Australia around the middle 1950s. One day in 1960 Ken and his brother Barrie were asked why no new Mogs were coming into the country. "It was a good question," says Ken. "It prompted me to dash off a letter straight away and begin going around the customs offices finding out how one went about importing cars." By the end of the year the first two Morgans, both Plus Fours, had arrived, one for Ron Coulston in NSW and the other for a South Australian customer.

Coulston's car is well known on the racing scene. Just after it reached his hands the engine was removed, rebored and fitted with Ferguson tractor sleeves to bring the capacity out to 2.3 litres. Other modifications took the developed horsepower to well over the 100 mark, and in this tune it vanquished all opposition in the production sports car race and impressed everyone with its acceleration and surefootedness on the rain soaked track.

Last season, Barrie Ward raced his green Morgan Plus Four with consistent success in NSW and Queensland. This is a standard car with a stock engine developing about 100 bhp, but it gave him regular class wins and a temporary production sports car outright lap record at Brisbane's Lakeside.

Ken has set up a workshop in which he tends Morgans of all vintages and in general keeps them on the road. When spares are either unobtainable or have to be brought from England, Ken sets to and makes them himself. Plans are under way to develop the distributorship and these include the building of a showroom and service centre.

Morgan production has reached 500 a year. They are still handmade to a certain degree, but to keep down costs, a number of component parts are used. Recently, an owner queried the factory why they didn't step up their output. Back came this answer: "We don't produce more than we can sell and we don't sell more than we can produce!" It was a forthright statement typical of the company's attitude and showed that they didn't care a stamp about what other manufacturers were doing. They intend to go on making their highly individualistic sports cars as long as

David McKay drove this Plus Four to an easy win at Warwick Farm's first meeting. It has hot, 2.3-litre engine similar to new Triumph TR4.

people still want to buy them. The day they don't seems further away than ever.

Morgan will meet any individual requirement, even to small things like extending the seat adjustment and the range of optional extras includes wire wheels, badge bars, genuine leather upholstery and full tonneau covers.

The car has undergone little styling change throughout the years, but its performance is quite out of keeping with its vintage appearance. The Plus Four is a genuine 100 mph machine, whilst the aluminium-bodied Super Sports has been road tested at better than 120 mph in England and has scored many resounding victories over such opposition as the RS60 Porsche.

Newest car of the range—and the cheapest—is the 4/4, which was reintroduced at the London

Iberic shipment included this beautiful ivory Plus Four. Wharfies in the hold literally handled it with kid gloves. Note how car is placed in the sling.

THE DAY THE MORGANS ARRIVED

Motor Show last October. This has only a moderate performance as it is equipped with a standard 54 bhp Ford Consul Classic 1340 cc engine. However, its price of £1200 in Australia will appeal to many as a range of conversion kits are readily available for this versatile engine, which can be made to give over 100 bhp in its most highly-tuned form. The high-geared 4/4 is extremely suitable for touring and the company may ultimately offer an optional "super" version for the competition-minded.

Mainstay of the company for the past several years, the Plus Four has earned itself a worldwide reputation since it was introduced in the early 1950s. Selling for £1416 in Australia, it is probably still the best buy performance-wise on the market, although one has to pay extra for such niceties as wire wheels and special tyres.

Possibly the biggest single improvement to the Plus Four has been the fitting of disc brakes, which are much more suited to the car's high cruising speeds than the old drum brakes. The TR3 power unit is very lightly stressed and on the 8.5 compression supplied in standard trim it pushes out 100 bhp at only 5000 rpm. Flexibility and good gear ratios are two of the Plus Four's biggest assets and given a good road it can maintain 80 to 90 mph very comfortably.

In view of this, it is not surprising that the Super Sports gets up to the speeds that it does. We are all looking forward to the first competition appearance of the first one brought to Australia and the lucky owner, Alby Sedaitis, has promised SPORTS CAR WORLD a run in this remarkable car.

Bodywise the Super Sports is identical to the Plus Four. However, the use of aluminium panelling has cut the weight down considerably. Actually the Super Sports came about as a result of developmental work carried out on a 1956 Plus Four by British specialist Chris Lawrence. His racing successes encouraged the works to produce a really fast car *genuinely* ideal for road or circuit use.

Each Super Sports engine has had its crankshaft, clutch, flywheel, con-rods and pistons balanced by Jack Brabham Motors while Lawrence has worked over the head. The car comes supplied with twin double choke 42DCOE Weber carburettors feeding the bigger inlet valves through a pair of beautifully designed induction manifolds. The exhaust manifold is a bunch-of-bananas system and a special camshaft is fitted. These

Morgan trio on parade after initial clean-up. Car on left is Plus Four, one on right the newly announced 4/4 and car behind is the Supersports.

modifications result in a 20 percent horsepower increase and an extra 1000 revs.

For £1885 the Super Sports gives a performance bettered by very few sports cars and probably only one other in this price bracket. Figures quoted by the factory give it a standing quarter-mile time of well under 17 seconds and a 0-60 time under eight seconds, in addition to an 85 mph third gear and 60 mph second gear.

Morgan also intend making the Super Sports engine available to owners of Plus Fours or supplying just the manifolds and Webers. #

At 70 years of age, the world's richest man, Mr J. Paul Getty, recently drove the latest Lotus Formula Junior around a British circuit — and thoroughly enjoyed it! In next month's issue of SPORTS CAR WORLD, Gordon Wilkins brings you an interview with Mr Getty, plus his scheme to present a British driver with the car.

The instrument and control layout is neat and very convenient. The centre panel contains an inspection lamp socket which can also take the leads from a trickle charger.

The Morgan 4/4

IT would be a mistake to judge the Morgan 4/4 on the strength of an ordinary trial run. Drivers who are thoroughly conditioned to modern cars find it difficult initially to accept a vehicle that departs so far in so many ways from the current trend. But a real acclimatization, such as we obtained by driving our Morgan nearly 2,000 miles in the first week of its test, reveals some fascinating traits and strongly recalls the almost forgotten virtues of the traditional type of sports car of which this is almost the only surviving representative.

Morgan fame nowadays rests mainly on the high-performance Plus Four with its 2-litre Triumph TR3 engine. The Series IV 4/4 is a less ambitious and considerably cheaper model powered by the 1,340 c.c. Ford Classic engine and gearbox in standard form. In other mechanical respects the two cars are almost identical; the same massive brakes are used in both, wheelbase, track and overall dimensions are also much the same but the 4/4 is considerably lower. By virtue of smaller tyres and an engine which permits a big reduction in the bonnet and scuttle height, it has been possible to design a body which is 3 in. lower. For the same reasons it scales some 2½ cwt. less than its larger brother.

Good Acceleration

EVEN for a 1,340 c.c. car weighing only 14½ cwt. the Morgan has an unexpectedly good top gear performance, and its acceleration from rest through the gears is impressive, 50 m.p.h. being reached in 11.9 sec. and the quarter mile completed in 20.9 sec. For road use, however, some of this acceleration might with advantage be sacrificed in favour of higher gearing which would give easier high-speed cruising, better fuel consumption, a more useful second gear and probably a higher top speed. The timed two-way 80.3 m.p.h. which we recorded was slightly less than we had expected; bad weather conditions may have had something to do with this but power seemed to fall off very rapidly above 4,900 r.p.m., at which speed the engine is supposed to peak. Our highest one-

In Brief

Price (as tested) £530 plus purchase tax £199 15s. 3d. equals £729 15s. 3d.

Capacity	1,340 c.c.
Unladen kerb weight	14½ cwt.
Acceleration:	
20-40 m.p.h. in top gear	9.6 sec.
0-50 m.p.h. through gears	11.9 sec.
Maximum top-gear gradient ..	1 in 9.3
Maximum speed ..	80.3 m.p.h.
"Maximile" speed ..	78.0 m.p.h.
Touring fuel consumption	32.0 m.p.g.
Gearing: 15.5 m.p.h. in top gear at 1,000 r.p.m.	

The Morgan 4/4

way speed (82.6 m.p.h.) corresponded to nearly 5,400 r.p.m.

The Ford engine proved both smooth and mechanically quiet but a fairly prominent exhaust note and an unsilenced air intake produced a high internal noise level with the hood and side screens in place. Thus, on good main roads any cruising speeds over 65-70 m.p.h. felt rather too fussy to use for long periods. In third gear 55 m.p.h. is usefully available and constantly used but in second peak revs correspond to about 32 m.p.h. and although this speed can be exceeded quite easily, second remains essentially a town gear; only the sharpest bends justify its use in country motoring.

The remote gearchange is ingenious and unusual. The gearlever knob appears in a conventional and convenient position but it is coupled to a horizontal lever instead of a vertical one, which is constrained at its forward end to slide to and fro inside a tube and linked at a point along its length to a vertical rod projecting from the gearbox. Thus changes between first and second or between top and third have a short push-pull action which is a little stiff but delightfully rapid; the other changes, which involve crossing the gate, need rather more practice as there is a tendency to overshoot the neutral position when coming out of the existing gear. On the whole, the system works extremely well and powerful synchromesh copes easily with fast changes between ratios which are rather widely spaced for sporting use.

The engine can be a little temperamental in the warming-up stage; full choke brings almost immediate over-richness whilst part choke gives stable fast idling with a tendency for the engine to cut dead if the throttle is opened quickly. When the car is warm this bottom-end flat spot disappears in mild weather but remains prominent when temperatures are around freezing point.

The Cockpit View

THE Morgan feels different as soon as one sits inside it. It is tailored for a driver about 5 ft. 10 in. tall and although there is no seat adjustment of the usual sort it is possible for a shorter legged driver to replace the bottom edge of the single-piece softly sprung squab in an alternative position some 2 in. further forward than normal; this gives a rather more reclining angle which is, in fact, more comfortable than the normal very upright position. Separate air cushions fit on sloping wooden bases between the deep propeller shaft tunnel and the high door sills which conceal the Z-section side members. After sitting for a long period in this car one wonders why pneumatic seats have gone out of favour since very few if any other forms of upholstery combine such comfort with light weight and freedom from bounce.

A comfortable feeling of being housed well inside the Morgan is accentuated by the closeness of the windscreen and the facia, an arrangement which certainly has advantages in bad weather when rain and dirt on the glass impair vision less than with most cars. It is noticeable too that there is relatively little back draught when the car is driven in open form whether the sidescreens are fitted or not.

The steering wheel, which necessarily comes unfashionably close to the driver's chest, is also close to the facia on which the controls are grouped in such a way that many of them can be used by extending a finger without removing the hands from the rim. The horn button appears just to the right of the wheel, the light switch, wipers, screenwashers and direction indicators just to the left. The last are non-cancelling and the green warning light adjacent to the switch is too far from the line of sight to be conspicuous in daylight.

It is very difficult to avoid resting the left foot on the clutch, to the detriment of the carbon thrust pad, because there is nowhere else to put it except flat on the floor. At night this involves rather a long

movement to the foot dipswitch which is attached to the bulkhead immediately above the clutch pedal. Further to the left, above the transmission housing, is a small and very inaccessible pedal which should be pressed every 200 miles or so in order to lubricate the vertical guides of the front suspension with engine oil under pressure.

The same brakes which arrest the 100 m.p.h. Plus Four Morgan have a very easy time stopping the lighter 4/4. On the road the required pedal-forces felt high but not as high as our measured tests revealed them to be; it may well be that the effectiveness of the 11 in. front discs increases with temperature rise in hard road driving. After some 1,500 miles it was necessary to bleed the hydraulic lines to remove air which was allowing excessive pedal travel and after a similar mileage the travel had again increased appreciably. This air leak was presumably due to some minor defect in our particular car. Heel and toe operation of brake and accelerator proved easy and convenient.

Excellent Handling

THE driver surveys the road ahead over a long low sloping bonnet which is flanked by separate-square section wings surmounted by small traditional side-lamps; all these "aiming marks" make the Morgan particularly easy to place accurately and it can be driven very close to kerbs and verges with confidence. We have already mentioned the close-up driving position but the steering characteristics and ratio (2⅔ turns from lock to lock) make large movements of the wheel unnecessary except on sharp corners. When large angles of lock are needed the steering becomes rather heavy but normally it is light and almost free from reaction. A small amount of play does not appreciably affect its straight-line stability and the driver has little work to do even on bumpy cambered roads.

More than any other factor it is the

It is fairly easy to get in and out of the Morgan because of doors which extend well forward. A surprising amount of luggage can be packed into the well behind the seats, particularly as the detachable hood occupies little space when folded up.

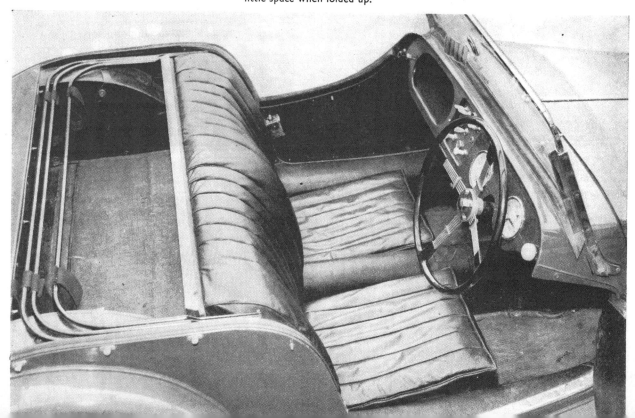

THE Motor

MAKE: Morgan. TYPE: 4/4 Series IV.
MAKERS: Morgan Motor Co., Ltd., Malvern Link, Worcs.

ROAD TEST • No. 16/62

DATA

CONDITIONS: *Weather: Wet and cold with strong wind. (Temperature 40° F., Barometer 28.9-29.0 in. Hg.) Surface: Wet tarmacadam. Fuel: Premium grade pump petrol (approx. 97 Octane Rating by Research Method)*

INSTRUMENTS

Speedometer at 30 m.p.h.	8% fast
Speedometer at 60 m.p.h.	7% fast
Speedometer at 80 m.p.h.	5% fast
Distance Recorder	1% fast

WEIGHT

Kerb weight (unladen, but with oil, coolant and fuel for approximately 50 miles) .. 14¼ cwt.
Front/rear distribution of kerb weight 48/52
Weight laden as tested .. .. .. 18¼ cwt.

MAXIMUM SPEEDS

Mean lap speed around banked circuit 80.3 m.p.h.
Best one-way ¼-mile time equals 82.6 m.p.h.

"Maximile" Speed (Timed quarter mile after one mile accelerating from rest.)
Mean of opposite runs .. .. 78.0 m.p.h.
Best one-way time equals.. .. 81.0 m.p.h.

Speed in gears

Max. speed in 3rd gear	64 m.p.h.
Max. speed in 2nd gear	42 m.p.h.
Max. speed in 1st gear	25 m.p.h.

FUEL CONSUMPTION

48 m.p.g.	at constant 30 m.p.h. on level
41½ m.p.g.	at constant 40 m.p.h. on level
35½ m.p.g.	at constant 50 m.p.h. on level
31 m.p.g.	at constant 60 m.p.h. on level
25½ m.p.g.	at constant 70 m.p.h. on level
21 m.p.g.	at constant 80 m.p.h. on level

Overall Fuel Consumption for 2,786 miles, 95.5 gallons, equals 29.2 m.p.g. (9.67 litres/100 km.)

Touring Fuel Consumption (m.p.g. at steady speed midway between 30 m.p.h. and maximum, less 5% allowance for acceleration) 32.0 m.p.g.
Fuel tank capacity (makers' figure) 8½ gallons

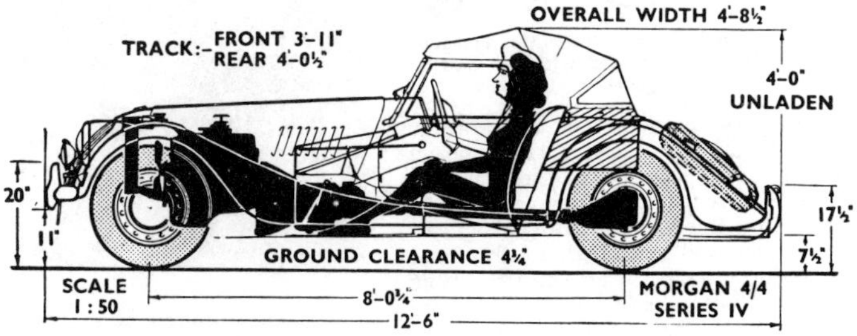
OVERALL WIDTH 4'-8½"
TRACK:- FRONT 3'-11" REAR 4'-0½"
4'-0" UNLADEN
20"
11"
17½"
7½"
GROUND CLEARANCE 4¾"
SCALE 1:50
8'-0¾"
12'-6"
MORGAN 4/4 SERIES IV

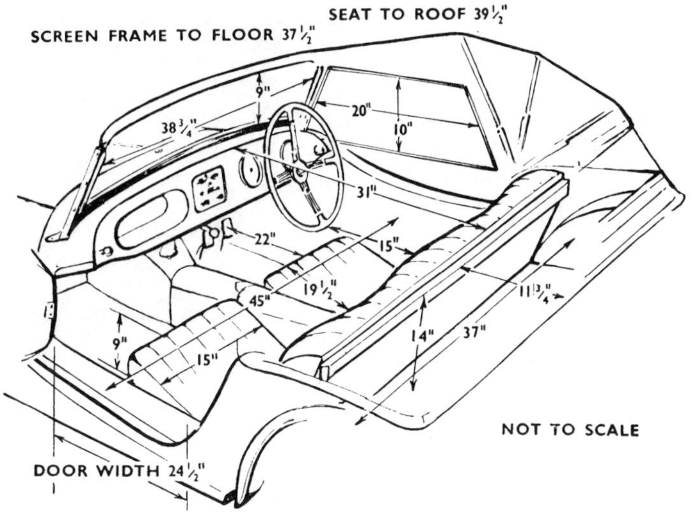
SEAT TO ROOF 39½"
SCREEN FRAME TO FLOOR 37½"
9"
20"
10"
38¾"
31"
22"
15"
19½"
45"
11¾"
14"
37"
9"
15"
NOT TO SCALE
DOOR WIDTH 24½"

BRAKES from 30 m.p.h.

0.99 g retardation (equivalent to 30½ ft. stopping distance) with 150 lb. pedal pressure.
0.91 g retardation (equivalent to 33 ft. stopping distance) with 125 lb. pedal pressure.
0.78 g retardation (equivalent to 38½ ft. stopping distance) with 100 lb. pedal pressure.
0.64 g retardation (equivalent to 47 ft. stopping distance) with 75 lb. pedal pressure.
0.43 g retardation (equivalent to 70 ft. stopping distance) with 50 lb. pedal pressure.
0.23 g retardation (equivalent to 130 ft. stopping distance) with 25 lb. pedal pressure.

HILL CLIMBING at sustained steady speeds

Max. gradient on top gear	1 in 9.3 (Tapley 240 lb./ton)
Max. gradient on 3rd gear	1 in 6.4 (Tapley 345 lb./ton)
Max. gradient on 2nd gear	1 in 4.1 (Tapley 525 lb./ton)

ACCELERATION TIMES from standstill

0-30 m.p.h.	4.4 sec.
0-40 m.p.h.	7.9 sec.
0-50 m.p.h.	11.9 sec.
0-60 m.p.h.	18.6 sec.
0-70 m.p.h.	27.1 sec.
Standing quarter mile	20.9 sec.

ACCELERATION TIMES on upper ratios

	Top gear	3rd gear
10-30 m.p.h.	9.8 sec.	6.3 sec.
20-40 m.p.h.	9.6 sec.	6.2 sec.
30-50 m.p.h.	10.6 sec.	7.4 sec.
40-60 m.p.h.	12.4 sec.	10.2 sec.
50-70 m.p.h.	15.5 sec.	— sec.

STEERING

Turning circle between kerbs:

Left	33 ft.
Right	33¾ ft.
Turns of steering wheel from lock to lock	2⅔

Specification

Engine

Cylinders	4
Bore	80.96 *mm.*
Stroke	65.07 *mm.*
Cubic capacity	1,340 *c.c.*
Piston area	31.9 *sq. in.*
Valves	*Overhead (pushrod)*
Compression ratio	8.5/1
Carburetter	*Zenith downdraught, VN 2*
Fuel pump	*AC mechanical*
Ignition timing control	*Centrifugal and vacuum*
Oil filter	*Full flow*
Maximum power (net)	54 *b.h.p.*
at	4,900 *r.p.m.*
Piston speed at maximum b.h.p.	2,090 *ft./min.*

Transmission

Clutch	7¼ *in. Ford/Borg and Beck s.d.p.*
Top gear (s/m)	4.56
3rd gear (s/m)	6.44
2nd gear (s/m)	10.93
1st gear	18.80
Reverse	24.65
Propeller shaft	*Hardy Spicer open*
Final drive	*Hypoid bevel*
Top gear m.p.h. at 1,000 *r.p.m.*	15.5
Top gear m.p.h. at 1,000 *ft./min. piston speed*	36.2

Chassis

Brakes .. .. .. *Girling hydraulic, disc front and drum rear*
Brake dimensions:
Front .. .. .. 11 *in. dia. discs*
Rear .. 9 *in. dia. drums,* 1¾ *in. wide*
Friction areas: 77 *sq. in. of friction lining* (17 *front,* 60 *rear) operating on* 324 *sq. in. of rubbed area.*
Suspension:
Front: Independent by coil springs and vertical guides.
Rear: Live axle on semi-elliptic springs.
Shock absorbers:
Front .. .. *Armstrong telescopic*
Rear: .. .. *Armstrong lever type*
Steering gear .. *Cam Gears, cam and peg*
Tyres .. .. .. 5.20—15 *tubeless*

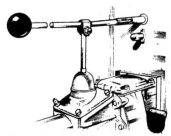

This drawing shows how the Morgan remote control is used with the Classic gearbox.

A centre-hinged bonnet provides first-class accessibility for the Ford Classic engine. A minor irritation is the necessity to open one side to inspect the dipstick and the other side to add oil.

Although the whole car is only 4 ft. high, there is plenty of headroom for a tall man with the hood up.

behaviour on corners that endears the 4/4 to its driver. Hard springs, heavy damping and a slightly flexible chassis is not the current recipe for good roadholding but it keeps the Morgan wheels surprisingly well attached to the road and reduces roll to an imperceptible amount. Most remarkable, however, are the ease and safety of handling in the breakaway region when tyre adhesion is at or near its limit. The rear wheels start to slide first but there is no sharp and sudden movement, merely a gentle transition which needs no particular skill to correct and control. Thus a driver of very ordinary ability can throw the car into corners, wet or dry, and hang the tail out in a way which feels and probably looks extremely professional with little or no fear of the car's taking charge.

Quite low tyre pressures of 16 to 18 lb./sq. in. are recommended. For fast cornering we found that 16 lb. front and 18 lb. rear gave good results although even more can be used at the back with advantage. Such pressures are low enough to avoid rattles, shakes and harshness on bad roads but the overall impression given by the suspension is one of considerable firmness. Rear springing which is softer than that at the front allows considerable pitching on certain surfaces and on bad secondary roads the cruising speed must be limited to stop the short travel suspension crashing against its stops. Ground clearance is also small and the back of the body may sometimes touch the road after a bad depression.

Weather Protection

A SEPARATE button-on plastic hood which fits over a simple folding frame is easy to put up single-handed in a reasonably short time. The sidescreens have fixed windows of flexible plastic and button-down signalling flaps. When the car is left standing, rain tends to creep in between the hood and the tops of these screens and fall on to the seat cushions; at high speeds it infiltrates in small quantities along the top and bottom edges of the windscreen and, especially in cross winds, in rather larger quantities at the sides.

It is inadvisable to splash through deep puddles too fast as quite large quantities of water can be forced in through the removable jacking covers under the seats. In these circumstances the recirculating heater has enough power to keep the inhabitants warm but it does little to avoid internal misting; there are no demisting ducts to the windscreen and the sidescreens need continual wiping. Although the plastic rear window is a reasonable size, the hood leaves blind spots in the rear quarters which are particularly noticeable in town traffic.

However, potential Morgan owners are unlikely to be deterred by these shortcomings; our not very hardy testers survived all these conditions and worse, including snow and ice, without apprec-

iable discomfort. The only possible reason for buying such a car is the sheer fun of driving it fast on suitable roads and for £730 the 4/4 provides a remark-

able amount of pleasure with low running costs.

Coachwork and Equipment

Starting handle .. .. None	Locks: with ignition key .. Ignition only
Battery mounting Under luggage compartment at rear	Glove lockers .. One in passenger's side of facia
Jack .. .. Screw pillar type	Map pockets .. .. None
Jacking points .. Sockets in cross member under each seat	Parcel shelves .. .. None
Standard tool kit .. Jack and wheel nut spanner	Ashtrays .. .. None
Exterior lights: 2 head, 2 side, 2 stop/tail, rear number plate lamp.	Cigar lighters .. .. None
Number of electrical fuses .. .. Two	Interior lights .. .. Instruments only
Direction indicators .. Non-cancelling flashers	Interior heater .. .. Optional extra, Smith's re-circulating type
Windscreen wipers .. Twin blade electric, not self parking	Car radio .. .. Not available
Windscreen washers Optional extra, Lucas electric	Extras available: Leather upholstery, heater, screen washer, fog lamps, badge bar, special steering wheels, knock-on hubs and wire wheels, luggage carrier, wheel trim.
Sun visors .. .. None	
Instruments: Speedometer with trip and total mileage recorder, oil pressure gauge, fuel gauge, ammeter.	Upholstery material .. .. Leathercloth
Warning lights: Ignition, main beam, direction indicators.	Floor covering .. .. Rubber
	Exterior colour standardized .. 6. Others at extra cost
	Alternative body styles .. .. None

Maintenance

Sump .. .. 4 pints S.A.E. 30 in summer, S.A.E. 20 in winter	Tappet clearances (cold):
Gearbox .. .. .. 1¼ pints S.A.E. 80	Inlet .. .. .008 in.
Rear axle.. .. 2 pints S.A.E. 90 hypoid	Exhaust .. .. .018 in.
Steering gear lubricant .. .. S.A.E. 140 oil	Front wheel toe-in .. .. ⅛ to 3/16 in.
Cooling system capacity 12 pints (2 drain taps)	Camber angle .. .. 2°
Chassis lubrication: By grease gun every 3,000 miles to 4 points and every 5,000 miles to 9 points.	Castor angle .. .. 4°
Ignition timing .. .. .. 6° b.t.d.c.	Steering swivel pin inclination .. .. 2°
Contact breaker gap .. .014 to .016 in.	Tyre pressures:
Sparking plug type .. .. Champion N5	Front .. .. 16-18 lb.
Sparking plug gap .. .. .. .025 in.	Rear .. .. 16-18 lb.
Valve timing:	Brake fluid .. .. Girling
Inlet opens 17° before t.d.c. and closes 51° a.b.d.c.	Battery type and capacity .. 12 v., 43 amp hr.
Exhaust opens 51° before b.d.c. and closes 17° a.t.d.c.	Miscellaneous: Sliding front suspension guides lubricated with engine oil by pressing a pedal for few seconds every 200 miles.

THE
MORGAN
4/4 SERIES IV

PATRICK McNALLY
TESTS

THE last of the genuine sports cars: that is a phrase so often attached to the marque Morgan, and one it richly deserves. I have just finished testing one of the small Morgans, the 4/4 series IV, which is fitted with 1,340 c.c. Ford engine and gearbox, and have come to the conclusion that this car, like all other Morgans, is a true sports car if ever there was one.

However, it is better to explain, here and now, that really to appreciate a Morgan it is necessary to cover many miles of various roads before making judgment; a merely casual flirtation tends to leave one doubting the car's virtues, but the full-blooded affair makes one realize just how good a car it is. This is certainly not the car for a man who believes in creature comforts, for there are few of these. The hard ride would also, no doubt, be criticized by such a man, as would the weather protection. But for the true enthusiast a Morgan must be the answer, for few cars are as exhilarating to drive.

The series IV employs the same chassis as its predecessors, with the very attractive, if antiquated, body shape. Ash is used for such parts as flooring and bulkheads, and the rear wings and doors, too, all have wood sub-frames. The overall effect is a light-weight, extremely rigid construction, the dry weight of which is 12 cwts. 2 qtrs.

The front suspension is unchanged, with sliding pillars and coil springs. These sliding axles are fitted with a lubrication system which is operated from inside the car. The shock absorbers are mounted behind the coil springs, and the suspension is set up with 4 deg. of castor and 2 deg. of camber, with approximately $\frac{1}{8}$ in. toe in. The rear is by slim elliptic springs with Armstrong dampers. The spring blades are actually enclosed in the chassis section, which has the effect of restricting their travel by acting as bump stops.

Girling brakes are fitted to all four wheels, 11 ins. discs on the front with leading calipers, and leading and trailing shoes in the drums on the rear. The hand brake operates on the rear wheels by means

of cable and rods, while 15 ins. bolt-on wheels, with cooling slots, are fitted all round.

The engine is the 1,340 Ford unit—the engine of the test car being fitted with a special camshaft and a single 1½ in. H 450 carburetter and a four branch exhaust. All these items are optional equipment.

A Ford four-speed box, with standard ratios, is mated to the engine by a single dry-plate hydraulically operated Ford clutch. Gear ratios are: 1st 4.1, 2nd 2.4, 3rd 1.42, with direct on top. The 4.56 to 1 hypoid rear axle is three-quarter-floating. Worm steering is employed.

The windscreen is flat and low, but forward vision, even with the hood up, is good. The seats consist of one large double back-rest, which straddles the prop-shaft tunnel, with individual seats. These are adjustable for rake by moving the back-rest, but, on full adjustment, the driving position is far from "straight-armed". Instrumentation consists of a speedometer, fuel and oil pressure gauges. Neither rev-counter nor temperature gauge is standard.

On the road, the car is remarkably light and easy to manoeuvre, whilst the 1,340 engine is well up to the job of propelling the car in a suitable manner. Maximum speeds through the gears proved to be 25 m.p.h., 43 m.p.h. and 68 m.p.h., although the effective maxima were 20 m.p.h., 40 m.p.h., and 62 m.p.h. Close-ratio gears would no doubt be a great improvement.

The performance figures were excellent,

the little bomb reaching 60 m.p.h. in 10.5 seconds, whilst the 30 and 50 figures proved to be 3.25 seconds and 7.25 seconds respectively. However, 80 m.p.h. took longer to reach, and 19 seconds was the best figure recorded.

The Plus Four, its elder and very desirable

SPECIFICATION AND PERFORMANCE DATA

Car Tested: Morgan 4/4 series IV two-seater tourer, price £600, plus P.T. £125 11s. 3d., total £725 11s. 3d.

Engine: Four-cylinder 80.96 mm. × 65.07 mm. (1,340 c.c.). Push-rod-operated overhead valves; compression ratio 8.5 to 1, 62 b.h.p. at 5,000 r.p.m. Single SU carburetter; coil and distributor ignition.

Transmission: Single dry-plate clutch with hydraulic operation; four-speed gearbox, synchromesh on 2nd, 3rd and top. Ratios: 4.56, 6.4, 10.9 and 18.6 to 1. Open propeller shaft; hypoid axle.

Chassis: Steel body and chassis. Independent front suspension, vertical coil spring. Cam gear steering. Semi-elliptic rear springs; telescopic dampers on front, lever type hydraulic rear. Girling disc brakes on front, drums rear, bolt-on disc wheels fitted with 5.60 × 15 ins. tyres.

Equipment: 12-volt lighting and starting. Speedometer; fuel, oil pressure and ammeter gauges. Flashing indicators.

Dimensions: Wheelbase 8 ft. Track 3 ft. 11 ins. Overall length 12 ft. 1 in. Width 4 ft. 8 ins. Weight 12¾ cwt.

Performance: Maximum speed 92 m.p.h. Speeds in gears: 1st, 20 m.p.h., 2nd, 40 m.p.h., 3rd, 62 m.p.h. Standing quarter-mile 18.1 s. Acceleration: 0-30 m.p.h., 3.25 s.; 0-50 m.p.h., 7.25 s.; 0-60 m.p.h., 10.5 s.; 0-80 m.p.h., 19.0 s.

Fuel Consumption: 27-30 m.p.g., driven hard.

Extras on Car Tested: Pass light, screen washer, quarter lights in hood, wheel trims, map reading light and hand throttle.

sister, had better watch out, for little sister is catching up!

The road holding must be described as interesting. To begin with, tail happiness tended to make one cautious, but after a time, when it was found that the tail could be hung out as much as one required with no fear of it running away, liberties were taken and the tail was slid freely. The ride is hard, and thus tends to belie the speed at which corners are negotiated, for there is little roll. A certain amount of hop was detected over rough surfaces, but the word tramp can't be mentioned—even with a heavy-footed take-off.

The steering was so low-geared that over-correction was difficult—a useful feature on a potential "tail-chaser".

The slight over-steering tendency was naturally more apparent in the wet but certainly could never be a criticism of the car—in fact quite the contrary.

The brakes deserve the highest praise. As with every other disc-braked Morgan I have driven, they inspired the utmost confidence. There were no signs of fade or judder, and they always pulled the car up in a straight line.

From personal experience I know one failing on front disc-braked Morgans. If one is not very careful, oil from the one-shot lubrication system gets on the disc pads, and the brakes start to pull. But to be quite fair, this never occurred during the testing period.

The weather protection is much better than on previous models, but rain still finds its way up under the side screens. A rubber strip now stops water seeping under the hood where it is attached to the windscreen —a great improvement.

With the hood down and side screens in place, motoring is a real pleasure: plenty of fresh air without too many draughts.

Petrol consumption is quite reasonable, working out at between 25-30 miles per gallon. Oil consumption, with the 109 E engine, is negligible.

Great fun can be had with this delightful little car, which even in novice hands should be extremely safe.

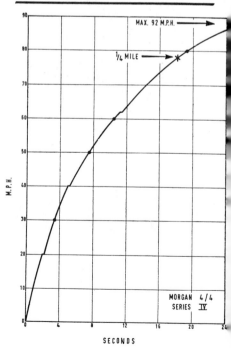

ACCELERATION GRAPH

SPORTS CARS UNDER £700

THE £659 MORGAN 4/4

The last sports car in the vintage style

UGH!—The Morgan does not take too kindly to water as a good deal of it seems to find its way into the car.

All the other cars dealt with in this series of road tests of under £700 sports cars are in the 1,100-c.c. category but the Morgan 4/4 is available with the 1,340-c.c. or 1,500-c.c. Ford Classic engines, giving the Morgan the best performance of the cars tested in this series and the worst fuel consumption, a fact of motoring life which seems inescapable.

With the 1,340-c.c. engine the Morgan 4/4 is known as the Mk. IV and costs a total of £659 2s. 1d. with the engine in standard form. With the 1½-litre engine and all-synchromesh gearbox it is known as the Mk. V and costs a total of £683 5s. 5d., once again with the engine in standard form. The car submitted to us for test was in actual fact the Competition version of the Mk. IV which uses a single S.U. carburetter on a new inlet manifold in conjunction with a 4-branch exhaust manifold. Production cars of this type also have a rev.-counter but the test car was not so fitted. With these modifications the price of the test car came over our £700 limit, working out at £731 12s. 1d. The standard models will of course be slower and have better fuel consumption.

There is not a lot which can be said about the Morgan which has not already been said many, many times, as, apart from engine

UNCHANGING.—The Morgan changes little over the years, only the curved grille and headlights distinguishing this one from pre-war versions.

and gearbox variations, the design changes very little over the years, only slight body changes serving to distinguish the present model from its pre-war counterparts. The chassis has two deep Z-shaped side-members with five bracing cross-members, the front suspension is the same sliding pillar type patented by Morgan 40 years ago except that longer coil-springs are used, the rigid rear axle runs above the chassis side-members and is sprung on semi-elliptic leaf-springs, but a concession to modern trends is shown in the braking system, which uses 11-in. Girling discs on the front wheels and 9-in. drums at the rear.

There is little comparison between the Morgan and the other cars in this series as the others have been developed to the extent where they can be considered as completely weatherproof, comfortable touring cars with most of the amenities of comparable saloon cars, but the Morgan stays determinedly rugged and spartan, with few of the refinements which most modern sports-car drivers demand. Getting in and out is a problem as the cut-away doors are narrow, the door sill is high, and the end of the scuttle provides a pointed edge to impale kneecaps with great accuracy. There are no external door handles so it is necessary to lift the flaps on the detachable sidescreens to reach inside and open the doors. However, as the flaps button down to keep out the rain it is sometimes necessary to bend the metal framework of the sidescreen to gain access unless you detach the sidescreen in its entirety, which is simple enough as the knurled knobs are on the outside. Once inside driver and passenger sit on upholstered cushions loosely placed on wedge-shaped wooden boxes which have no method of adjustment, and they lean against a one-piece back-rest which is also not adjustable. The driver is confronted by a huge 17-in. Bluemels 4-spoke steering wheel which is too large for the cramped conditions of the cockpit, as well as rubbing the driver's trousers. The brake and throttle pedals are well placed in relation to each other for heel-and-toe changes but due to the wide gearbox tunnel there is no room to rest the left foot, which makes things difficult, especially as the Morgan handbook implores the owner (in large capital letters) not to rest his foot on the pedal. The dipswitch is placed above the clutch pedal on the bulkhead and the plunger for front suspension oiling is above the gearbox tunnel. This plunger diverts engine oil to the sliding axles and should be pressed every 200 miles or so, although there is a childish tendency to do it more often, just to see the drop in oil pressure on the gauge. However, this can soon empty the sump, so is not really recommended.

The wooden dashboard follows normal Morgan practice with two cream-coloured instruments placed either side of the steering column, that on the right being a rather erratic Smiths 90-m.p.h. speedometer with trip and total odometer, and the other one containing fuel contents, ammeter and oil-pressure gauges. A horn button is placed on the outer edge of the dashboard to the driver's right and in the centre is a batch of toggle switches in a separate panel which cover the operation of the panel lights, fog and spot-lamps (although the test car only had a spot fitted), direction indicators, and windscreen wipers. Pull-out knobs operate the choke and headlamps, a tiny press-button works the electric wind-screen washers, and starting is by the ignition key. Warning lights in this panel show when the headlamp main beam is in operation, when the dynamo is not charging and when the flashing indicators are working. A 2-pin socket for an inspection lamp is also fitted in the centre panel.

In front of the passenger is an unlidded cubby-hole, which, with the space behind the seats, forms the only luggage accommodation in the car. To the left of the locker is the knob for the Smiths recirculatory heater which is fitted to the bulkhead. Of the items mentioned, the heater, spot-lamp and windscreen washer are all extras, costing £15 4s. 6d., £8 12s. 2d. and £4 16s. 1d., respectively, the price for the spot-lamp including the badge bar on which it is mounted. There is also a vast range of other extras (some of which many people might consider as essentials), such as wire wheels, leather upholstery, rear bumper, tonneau cover, wooden steering wheel, seat belts, luggage carriers, etc.

Having accustomed oneself to the cramped driving quarters of the Morgan it is quite refreshing to peer along a proper bonnet once more, with separate wings showing just where to point the car. Visibility is good through the flat screen but side and rear vision is rather restricted and the tiny rear-view mirror is inadequate.

Morgan have not adopted a proper remote-control arrangement for the gear-lever but have fitted a push-pull lever like that used on the older 4/4 model and such cars as the 2 c.v. Citroën and Renault 4. This takes some getting used to and although satisfactory changes can be made, the box is nowhere near as pleasant as that on the Ford from which the gearbox is taken. It is difficult to judge distances across the gate and we confess to hitting 1st occasionally when going from 2nd to 3rd, while we found reverse difficult to locate. However, we soon became accustomed to the peculiarities of this lever without coming to like it much. Clutch pedal pressure is light so that reasonably fast shifts can be made with determination.

The Morgan weighs in at around 13 cwt. dry so the Ford engine endowed it with fairly brisk acceleration, which places it ahead of the other cars tested in this series as far as performance goes. It is relatively noisy in the Morgan, setting up a sympathetic vibration somewhere in the car when approaching peak revs, but it will pass through this period and smooth out until valve bounce is reached. The gearbox is not unduly noisy and the main source of noise at speed comes from colossal wind roar around the wind-screen pillars, which is also the source of numerous draughts inside the car which become a little too uncomfortable in really cold weather. Fortunately with the heater fan switched on at full blast the heat just about counterbalances the incoming draughts. Another fault found on the test car was its lack of weather protection, the screen becoming almost as wet on the inside as on the outside in heavy rain, and as there are no such refinements as demisting slots on the scuttle a plentiful supply of

MORGAN 4/4 SERIES IV

Engine : Four cylinders, 80.96 × 65.07 mm. (1,340 c.c.). Push-rod-operated overhead valves. 8.5 : 1 compression-ratio. 56.5 b.h.p. at 5,000 r.p.m.

Gear ratios : 1st, 18.8 to 1; 2nd, 11 : 1; 3rd, 6 : 1; top, 4.56 : 1.

Tyres : 5.60 × 15-in. Dunlop C41 on bolt-on disc wheels.

Weight : 13 cwt. (dry).

Steering ratio : 2¼ turns lock-to-lock.

Fuel capacity : 8½ gallons. (Range approximately 230 miles.)

Wheelbase : 8 ft.

Track : Front, 3 ft. 11 in.; rear, 3 ft. 11 in.

Dimensions : 12 ft. × 4 ft. 8 in. × 4 ft. 4 in. (high).

Price : £545 (£659 2s. 1d. with purchase tax). Competition model as tested : £760 4s. 10d.

Makers : Morgan Motors Ltd., Pickersleigh Road, Malvern Link, Worcestershire.

clean rag is necessary to keep the screen clear on the inside.

The ride of the Morgan is softer than previous Morgans we have tried due to the longer coil-springs, but it still has about the harshest ride of any current production sports car. On smooth main roads the ride is quite acceptable, small bumps not being particularly noticeable, but as soon as any serious undulations are crossed the suspension bottoms viciously, lifting the occupants out of their seats and dropping them back with a spine-jarring crash. There is also some scuttle shake under these conditions, a problem which is nearly always present in cars of this type of construction. The harshness of the suspension spoils high-speed driving for most people as it is necessary to reduce speed drastically when running on bad roads. On smooth roads the 4/4 will cruise quite happily at an indicated 80 m.p.h., although with its 4.56 : 1 axle ratio the engine sounds quite busy. It should be possible to fit the 4.1 : 1 ratio of the Classic for quieter cruising in the higher speed ranges. On the present ratio the car will reach speeds of 27, 45, 65 and 90 m.p.h. in the gears, but engine

OLD ENGLISH PERPENDICULAR.—Just about the last of the traditional sports cars which remained popular until the '50s, the Morgan 4/4 still looks handsome.

MODIFIED.—The 1,340-c.c. Ford Classic engine of the Mk. IV 4/4 is shown in competition trim with single S.U. carburetter and 4-branch exhaust.

r.p.m. is near 6,000 r.p.m. at maximum speed. Acceleration from rest to 60 m.p.h. in 13.7 sec. is some 2 sec. better than the Spitfire and 2.7 sec. better than the Midget, while it shows an even greater improvement to 70 m.p.h. with a time of 17.4 sec., which is 4.3 sec. faster than the Spitfire and 5.6 sec. quicker than the Midget. It must be remembered, however, that the Morgan is the more expensive Competition model.

The actual performance figures, with the best run in brackets, are shown below.

0–30 m.p.h.	..	..	3.5 sec.	(3.1 sec.)
0–40 „	..	..	6.2 sec.	(6.0 sec.)
0–50 „	..	..	10.2 sec.	(10.0 sec.)
0–60 „	..	..	13.7 sec.	(13.4 sec.)
0–70 „	..	..	17.4 sec.	(17.0 sec.)
s.s. ¼-mile	..	..	19.0 sec.	(18.9 sec.)

On smooth bends the Morgan handles particularly well as the taut suspension allows little roll, and it is possible to make the C41 Dunlops squeal heavily without inducing breakaway on dry roads. On bumpy corners axle hop is experienced and the driver is given the feeling that the front and rear suspensions are out of phase, the front end dancing about noticeably while the tail sits down fairly happily. The steering is reasonably light and with only 2¼ turns lock-to-lock corrections are easily made, but a smaller steering wheel and more elbow room in the cockpit would give the driver more confidence as he sits in a rather hunched-up position.

The brakes are smooth, powerful and progressive, and stop the car well under all circumstances with no sign of fade or grab. However, the umbrella-type handbrake fitted under the dashboard is completely out of character with this type of car although working reasonably well.

It seems incredible that a car which has changed only in small details, apart from various different engines, since well before the war is still selling at all, but the small factory is still quite busy sending cars all over the world. Much of the credit for this must go to Chris Lawrence and Richard Shepherd-Barron, whose exploits with the Lawrencetune Morgan Super Sports have brought the car to the notice of a much larger public due to their numerous competition victories. The fact remains that the present-day sports-car buyer demands a far higher degree of comfort and habitability than the Morgan offers. Compared with its competitors in the under-£700 class the 4/4 has less interior room, less luggage space, a much firmer ride and a general lack of refinement and detail finish, while many buyers in this price class may feel that a petrol thirst of 28.5 m.p.g.. which is what we obtained, is too much compared with the 33.7 m.p.g. of the Spitfire and 39.2 m.p.g. of the M.G. Midget.—M.L.T.

Morgan 4/4 (1958)

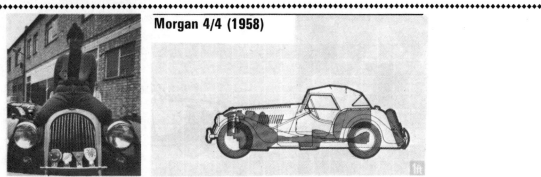

Griff Griffiths, 34, runs a car-tuning business in Willesden, North West London. He races a Volkswagen at weekend autocross meetings.

Other than the Volkswagen, the only cars I've ever owned have been Morgans. I started with a three-wheeler and as far as I'm concerned the Morgan is the only car on the market.

It has character and personality. When you get behind the wheel you feel you are teaming up with an old and trusted friend.

I've heard people say that the driving position is cramped. But when I'm driving I want to feel that the car is a part of me, reacting to my moods. Another thing about Morgans is that they are all just a bit different—you have to treat them like individuals.

I have driven other cars but there was nothing exciting or stimulating about them.

Some people think Morgans are a menace on the road. They don't understand. Once bitten by the Morgan bug you've got the disease for the rest of your life.

PRICE
now £200
new (1958) £748
COST
per week £3 6s
running £3 2s
depreciation 4s

AA Driving the Morgan 4/4 for the first time can be disenchanting thanks to its three-speed gearbox. You change into top gear when the needle has passed the 40 mph mark and as you do so performance drops off dramatically. Then an enthusiast says: 'Keep it in second until you reach the 50s.' You take his advice and discover a brisk little sports car without any flat spots at all.

Fitting the 1,172 cc Ford Anglia engine and gearbox helped to make the 4/4 the cheapest open two-seater on the British market ten years ago. It catered for people with more enthusiasm than means, but tuning kits were available. The test car had a special manifold and twin carburettors.

With practice the horizontal gear shift permits fast, smooth and silent gear changes. The clutch, though heavy, has plenty of bite.

Above 60 mph, at which the 4/4 cruises comfortably, fuel consumption drops from the normal 32-35 mpg to below 30 mpg.

Neither steering wheel nor seat can be adjusted and the driver hasn't much elbow room. The pedals are well placed but the only convenient place to rest the left foot is on the clutch.

Morgan roadholding has always been good. The springs are firm and on good surfaces the ride is reasonably comfortable. The light steering is high enough geared to make the car respond to quite small movements of the wheel and tight corners can be taken without fuss. Both foot and hand brakes are powerful.

Points to watch : Morgan front suspension sliding pillars (king-pins) need replacing about every 20,000 miles : if the front wheels can be rocked to and fro at top and bottom, call in an expert. There's quite a lot of wood which should be tested for rot by poking it with a penknife. Slack door hinges are cheap and easy to replace.

SPECIFICATION
Engine—1,172 cc, 4 cylinders, producing 36 bhp at 4,500 rpm
Transmission—3 forward gears, no synchromesh on first
Suspension—independent front, leaf rear
Brakes—drums all round
Tyres—5.20 x 15
SPARE PARTS Engine £45
Clutch £3 10s
Gearbox £25 10s
Silencer £7 15s
Tyre (cross-ply) £6 12s 6d

MORGAN 4/4 and SUPER SPORT

A Return to Paradise

ONCE UPON A TIME (1910) there was a gentleman who lived and worked in the little town of Malvern, which is situated among the verdant hills of Worcestershire, in England. Being engaged in the motor trade, the gentleman in question, H. F. S. Morgan, not unnaturally became

quite a motoring enthusiast, and built for his own use a 3-wheeled motorcar. This creation was noteworthy for many things, not the least of which was a novel front suspension, with stub-axles sliding on vertical posts; propulsive power being supplied by an air-cooled V-twin Peugeot engine. So pleased was the gentleman that he bestowed his own name upon the car and promptly formed a, manufacturing company for the purpose of producing additional examples. It is a measure of Morgan's satisfaction with what he had wrought that the 3-wheeler, in various close derivations, remained the company's stock-in-trade for the following 26 years. At various times during that period, to indulge the whims of the spoiled masses, such frills as electric lighting, front-wheel brakes and a reversing-gear were added, but the basic vehicle was unchanged.

Then, in 1935, it was noticed that the 4-wheel chassis was

coming into vogue, and the following year a new model was brought out as a companion-piece to the faithful Edwardian tricycle. With typical restraint, the new car was designated "4/4," which was an oblique way of indicating that it had that many wheels and cylinders, respectively. A wheel may have been added; nothing of the original's character was lost. The Morgan 4/4 was, like the earlier tricycle, quite light and a most effective instrument for sporting events, and this again pleased H. F. S. Morgan mightily, with the predictable result that the pattern established would endure. And, as a matter of record, the pattern has not been changed appreciably to this day, some 27 years later.

A description of that first 4-wheeler will do nicely for both it and today's 4/4, the series-V. The front stub-axles still slide on posts, with a long coil-spring above the axle and a short one below to take jounce and rebound. Telescopic dampers provide the necessary bounce control. Actually, the present car is slightly different: the suspension posts have been angled-in to permit a somewhat larger and softer spring, with more travel. The rear suspension, which is a conventional live axle, is clamped to a pair of leaf springs, after the established fashion, and the only change worth mentioning here is that the rear shackles, which had consisted of slotted trunnions through which the spring-ends extended, have been changed to the almost universally used H-shackle. Lever-type dampers were then, as now, used for the rear axle.

The frame configuration of the 1936 4-wheeler has also been continued. In this, a pair of Z-section longitudinal frame members follow the outer body contour, being bolted to the front suspension's supporting structure at the front and terminating at the rear spring shackles with precious few (and mostly ineffectual) cross-members between. The lower legs of each frame Z are turned in, to support the wooden flooring, and it must be admitted that whatever other faults the arrangement may have, it has the advantage of allowing the car's occupants to be seated very low, inside the frame-rails.

Bodywork, hand-fitted steel paneling, was and is tacked and wood-screwed to a timber framing, and it does little to stiffen the extremely supple chassis. As a concession to what Morgan considers to be the popular fancy, there has been a re-styling: the early flat-slab radiator has been shrouded behind a rounded shell, with curved vertical grille bars, and the cutaway sections around the forward ends of the front fenders have been closed. At the rear of the car, the traditional twin spare-wheels are gone and the stern is slightly flattened. Again, the changes have not been substantial and, frankly, most of the Morgan fanciers we have questioned would prefer a return to Pure-Perpendicular styling. Be that as it may, the present car is a far, and welcome, cry from the contemporary pontoon-fendered fashion, and the 4/4 series-V rates very high with those who like Early-British styling—as a surprising number of people do.

Throughout its 53-year history, Morgan has made a prac-

tice of purchasing major mechanical elements, such as the engine, from outside suppliers—heavy manufacturing equipment being entirely absent at the Malvern works. At present, engines are supplied by Standard-Triumph (whose TR-4 engine powers the plus-4) and by Ford of England, makers of the 116-E engine and all-synchro 4-speed transmission used in the 4/4. No modifications are made for this particular application; the engine is taken out of its crate and installed in the car. The one change is that Ford employs an air-cleaner, and Morgan replaces this useful item with a small shield, the sole purpose of which is, apparently, to prevent mechanics from dropping their tools down inside the carburetor throat and to protect the underhood paint from backfire flames. Needless to say, this device does nothing to soften intake-air noise, and one's progress through traffic, at light throttle openings, is heralded by a thin, subdued, teakettle whistle. At greater throttle openings, any of the more subdued sounds, up to and including shouts between driver and passenger, are drowned by the decidedly boisterous exhaust.

One curious problem we encountered with the 4/4 was a carburetion defect that persisted even after the entire carburetor jet-block had been changed. Our test car was one of the very first of the series-V cars to be built, and we think that the combination of a straight-through muffler and removing the air-cleaner upset the Ford engine's carburetion. Fiddling with the car revealed that it would run fairly cleanly if the choke were pulled a trifle, and that is the way it was driven most of the time. Obviously, this made it impossible to get a true picture of the car's fuel consumption characteristics. We did manage about 28 mpg, overall, with the choke in continuous operation, so the 4/4 should be quite a gasmiser when perking properly.

Strangely enough, the engine would run quite well on full throttle, and our acceleration runs were made with the choke off. This made the engine a bit ragged at part throttle, but we were able to make our runs. However, considering that the times obtained were only fractionally better than those listed by one of our English contemporaries for the previous series-IV model, with the 1340-cc engine, we would guess that the car is capable of better performance.

One happy result of the use of this stock Ford engine is that it has made the Morgan extremely docile and pleasant as a day-in, day-out transportation car. The engine's torque curve is very flat, holding over 90% of maximum from 1500 rpm all the way up to 4000 rpm, which covers a 4th-gear speed range from 25- to 65-mph. Reduced to practical terms, this means that the Morgan can be driven briskly without a lot of rowing at the gear lever. We would also like to toss in an admiring word about the engine's smoothness; the usual 4-cylinder shake is entirely absent, and this gives one the impression, probably quite accurate, that the mechanical elements are all working in harmony and that reliability will be one of the car's strong points. Certainly, the engine's basic layout

MORGAN 4/4 and SUPER SPORT

would seem to support this impression. It is blessed with a short stroke, an enormously strong 5-mainbearing crankshaft with generous bearing area, and plenty of water-jacketing down the full length of the cylinder bores and around the valve seats and guides in the cylinder head. Those who are more interested in performance than reliability will be pleased to learn that they can have both in large measure. Complementing the engine's inherent sturdiness is a very real potential for high power output. There is, for example, the all-separate port layout and the lightweight valve gear, and the success of those smaller, but basically identical, Ford engines used in Formula Junior racing tells us that considerably more than the stock 64 bhp can be extracted.

Much of that which is good may also be seen in the transmission to which this engine is coupled. Its most outstanding feature is that it has synchromesh on all 4 ratios, and the synchro is so powerful that even fast, slam-through shifting produces no crunch. It is a development of the transmission introduced with the first "80-bore" Ford engine, the 109-E, and for use with the 116-E the case has been lengthened slightly to accommodate the synchro. Also, the low-gear reduction was changed; with the larger engine, which has much more torque, the necessary stump-pulling force could be obtained with less gearing-down. Consequently, 1st gear was brought up nearer 2nd. Unfortunately, 2nd had been staged to be a sort of substitute for a synchro-low for making rolling starts in traffic, and it is too low. There is, as a result, a long jump from 2nd to 3rd, and this uneven ratio-staging has rather a bad effect on acceleration—although the effects of this are minimized by the engine's broad torque range. Happily, 3rd and 4th are staged close together, and 3rd is a very useful ratio for highway passing: the engine will pull strongly up to about 5000 rpm, and that is equivalent to 57 mph.

Climbing into the 4/4's cockpit (and that word describes the passenger compartment better than any other), one finds

that here, too, Morgan has been faithful to tradition. The first thing to smite the eye is the instrument panel planking, which we usually loathe, but which is entirely in keeping with the overall character of the Morgan. Instrumentation, on the 4/4, is scanty. There is a speedometer, which proved to be much more accurate than is generally the case these days, and beside it is a matching round face into which are grafted oil-pressure and fuel-level gauges, and an ammeter. There is no water-temperature indicator, but we understand that any serious overheating will be signaled by plumes of steam from the hood louvers.

Most of the main controls are well positioned, and there is a surprising amount of room around the pedals—although not so much that there is any place to rest one's clutch-foot except on the clutch pedal. The hand-brake is operated through an umbrella-grip handle, hidden up under the dash, and the steering wheel itself is set close to the instrument panel—so close, in fact, that one's knuckles constantly find their way across the horn button, located on the panel. The really strange control is the gear-change lever: this device extends back horizontally, and is manipulated with a push/pull motion. The arrangement is odd, but it is the most direct approach to providing an extension from the lever on the transmission, which is hooked (through a clevis) to the push/pull rod. The rod's forward end slides in a tube that is, in turn, fixed to the firewall by a swivel. After one becomes accustomed to this oddity, it works fine, but it is seriously lacking in esthetic and sales appeal, and is to be replaced by a more conventional remote-change mechanism.

Creature comforts are present in varied quantities. There is no heater or demisting equipment, but there is enough engine-heat and even with the top erected, enough drafts, to make this lack a relatively minor annoyance. The wipers clear only a small portion of a very small windshield, but the cockpit is so short that one's nose is quite near the windshield and even through a tank-driver's window the view of the road would be reasonably good. The close-coupled cockpit layout does bring one somewhat too close to the wheel for comfort. But for these exceptions, the cockpit is comfortable. The inflated-bladder seat cushions do a lot to insulate one's rump from random road-shocks and vibration; the seat-back, although too upright, is well padded and comfortably contoured; and there is, surprisingly, plenty of width.

For the actual performance and handling evaluation of the Morgan, the 4/4 was taken to the Willow Springs (California) road-circuit. Lew Spencer, the western-U.S. distributor

The Super Sports has these leather-covered bucket seats . . . . . .   *Which will soon be available to replace the 4/4's semi-bench.*

for Morgan motorcars, accompanied us and brought along his own competition Plus-4 Super Sports. This car has the same lowered body lines as the 4/4 (the standard Plus-4 having a somewhat higher hood and cowl) but all of the paneling is in aluminum. Its engine is basically Triumph TR-4, but in the Super Sports the basic engine is further developed for power by equipping it with a special camshaft, a pair of double-throat Weber carburetors, an "extractor-type" exhaust manifold and the compression is increased. Fully "prodified," the TR-4 engine thus equipped will deliver close to 150 bhp, and that will propel the lightweight Morgan along very rapidly indeed.

Pulling a 4.1:1 final-drive ratio, Spencer's Super Sports was a most impressive performer. We used a 6000-rpm limit, which held the top speed to 106 mph, but gave us a standing-start ¼-mile in 16.2-sec, with a terminal speed of 88 mph. No special technique was required; the TR-4 engine has plenty of wide-range torque and we simply blipped the engine up to about 3500 rpm and banged in the clutch, going away feathering the throttle for a few feet to limit wheel-spin and then applying all vigor.

After circulating for a few laps to familiarize ourselves with the rather tricky Willow Springs course, we began to press the cars a bit, both the 4/4 and Super Sports, and

discovered something very interesting: that limp-chassis, antique-suspensioned Morgan is one of the best-handling, most forgiving automobiles in the world. It does not have exceptionally good adhesion, especially on a bumpy surface, but it behaves in exactly the same manner every time, and with little experience on the part of the driver, it can be drifted, slid, skidded and just generally flung about in a fashion that would be suicidal in many a more modern sports car. Most remarkable was the fact that it handled very much the same at all speeds. There are 2 turns at the course in question that tighten as they end and one is taken at about 40 mph; the other at just short of 100 mph. Both of these could be taken in exactly the same way, easing on the throttle half-way around to skid away some speed, then exiting at full-blast in a great, long drift. Virtually all other cars require that the driver take into accounting his absolute speed.

Actually, we must confess that only the Super Sports was driven this way; the 4/4 would not go fast enough to require any technique at all on the faster bends. On lower-speed turns, however, it behaved just like its more powerful brother.

Apart from the power advantage, the Super Sports had the benefit of good, contour-fitting bucket seats and a full complement of instruments. These things are, we understand, to be made available in the 4/4 and we would certainly recommend

MORGAN 4/4 and SUPER SPORT

that the prospective Morgan buyer willingly hand over the money for these extras. The bucket seats have thin backs, and provide more room in the cockpit, enabling the driver to use the arms-out driving stance, and the additional instruments might just tell him something important.

All of the current crop of Morgans have exceptional brakes. Drum-type brakes are used at the rear wheels, but those in front are equipped with 11-in. discs, and they do provide impressive stopping power.

Of all the things we noticed about the Morgan, the only ones that truly gave us pause were the many areas where the car was poorly finished. There is some myopic fiend at the factory who wields a large coarse brush dripping with a dull, tarry black paint, and this person feels obliged to coat the engine compartment and the area behind the seats, where the top is stowed, with this mess. With a little more consistency, this would not be too bad, but he slathers it on the engine, etc., where it is not needed and leaves the ragged ends of brush strokes showing where coverage *is* required.

Regardless of the finish, and the primitive suspension (the front-end bottoms on every bump of any consequence), and the lack of protection against the elements, we were greatly taken with the Morgan. Super Sports or 4/4, they were more fun than anything else we have tried lately and we would be disappointed if Peter Morgan (H. F. S.'s son, who now heads the company) were to suddenly introduce a new, modern Morgan. Of course, after 27 years that is unlikely. Barring that sort of catastrophe, the Morgan will continue as man's last link with that great and glorious time when people were more interested in sporting qualities than in keeping dry and warm.

The Super Sports' elaborate and impressive carburetion . . . . .

Contrasts oddly with the 4/4's single, puny Zenith "pot."

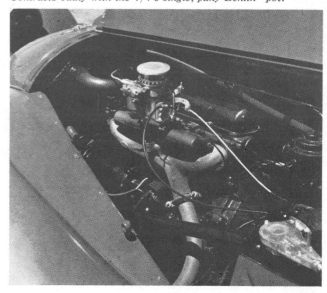

SCALE: 10" DIVISIONS

DIMENSIONS

Wheelbase, in	96.0
Tread, f and r	47.0
Over-all length, in	150.0
width	56.0
height	51.0
equivalent vol, cu ft	248
Frontal area, sq ft	15.9
Ground clearance, in	5.7
Steering ratio, o/a	n.a.
turns, lock to lock	2.6
turning circle, ft	33.5
Hip room, front	2 x 16.0
Hip room, rear	n.a.
Pedal to seat back, max	40.0
Floor to ground	6.5

CALCULATED DATA

Lb/hp (test wt)	30.1
Cu ft/ton mile	102.8
Mph/1000 rpm (4th)	16.1
Engine revs/mile	3740
Piston travel, ft/mile	1785
Rpm @ 2500 ft/min	5250
equivalent mph	84
R&T wear index	66.7

SPECIFICATIONS

List price	$2545
Curb weight, lb	1542
Test weight	1925
distribution, %	47/53
Tire size	5.60-15
Brake swept area	324
Engine type	4-cyl, ohv
Bore & stroke	3.19 x 2.86
Displacement, cc	1499
cu in	91.5
Compression ratio	8.3
Bhp @ rpm	64 @ 4600
equivalent mph	74
Torque, lb-ft	81.5 @ 2300
equivalent mph	37

GEAR RATIOS

4th (1.00)	4.56
3rd (1.41)	6.43
2nd (2.40)	10.9
1st (3.54)	16.1

SPEEDOMETER ERROR

30 mph	actual, 31.6
60 mph	60.0

PERFORMANCE

Top speed (4th), mph	80
Shifts, rpm-mph	
3rd (5000)	57
2nd (5200)	35
1st (5300)	24

FUEL CONSUMPTION

Normal range, mpg. (see text)

ACCELERATION

0-30 mph, sec	3.9
0-40	7.0
0-50	10.7
0-60	16.5
0-70	26.6
0-80	
0-100	
Standing ¼ mile	20.6
speed at end	65

TAPLEY DATA

4th, maximum gradient, %	9.5
3rd	14.6
2nd	23.1
Total drag at 60 mph, lb	115

ENGINE SPEED IN GEARS

ENGINE SPEED IN RPM
2000 3000 4000 5000

ACCELERATION & COASTING

SS¼

SS¼

4th

3rd

2nd

1st

4/4
SUPER SPORT

MPH

ELAPSED TIME IN SECONDS
5 10 15 20 25 30 35 40 45

The Morgan radiator grille lifts as one piece with the alligator bonnet. Combined sidelamps and winking indicators are built-in under the headlamps

Morgan Plus Four Plus

CLOSED GLASS FIBRE BODY

PRICE

	Basic £	Total (inc. P.T.) £ s d
Morgan Plus Four Plus	1,055	1,275 7 1

AS an addition to the Morgan Plus 4 model range (with Triumph TR4 engines), a new version with smooth, closed bodywork is introduced today, called the Morgan Plus Four Plus. In practically all mechanical details it is identical with the traditional open version (which continues in production), but its moulded glass fibre body is entirely new.

An enquiry from Greece, about the idea of mounting a special body with streamlined styling on the Morgan chassis, finally sparked off this new design, and the prototype was completed in March this year. Although some may see a resemblance to the Jaguar XK150 at the front end, and to a Lotus Elite at the rear, the overall appearance of the car is quite distinctive, and the head and sidelamps are built into the front of the wings. Slightly reduced in size, the familiar Morgan radiator grille is retained, and the Plus Four Plus has the same bumper bar and overriders at the front as the open Plus 4; but

at the rear there are wrapround extensions to the bumper, made of chromed glass fibre—an unusual feature.

This is one of the first Morgans to feature a curved windscreen and winding side windows. The windows themselves are of almost semi-circular shape, and slide up or down in contact with the straight leading edge of the frame, giving a ventilation space at the rear, but they do not drop completely out of sight into the doors. The car has the usual Morgan arrangement of individual pneumatic seat cushions for two, with a shaped one-piece backrest. Behind this is a deep trench for luggage,

Specification

ENGINE
No. of cylinders... 4, in-line (water-cooled, front mounted)
Bore ... 86mm (3·38in.)
Stroke ... 92mm (3·62in.)
Displacement ... 2,138 c.c. (131 cu. in.)
Valve position and operation ... Overhead, pushrods and rockers
Compression ratio 9 to 1
Max b.h.p. (net)... 105 (net) at 4,750 r.p.m.
Max. b.m.e.p. (net) 148 p.s.i. at 3,350 r.p.m.
Max torque (net) 128 lb./ft. at 3,350 r.p.m.
Carburettor ... 2 Stromberg C.D.
Fuel pump ... AC mechanical
Tank capacity ... 10 Imp. gallons (45·5 litres)
Sump capacity ... 11 pints (6·25 litres)
Oil filter ... Full flow, renewable element
Cooling system ... Water pump and engine-driven fan
Battery ... 12 volt, 54 amp. hr.

TRANSMISSION
Clutch ... Borg and Beck 9in. dia. single dry plate

TRANSMISSION (cont.)
Gearbox ... 4-speed centre floor change, synchromesh on 2nd, 3rd, top.
Overall gear ratios Top 3·73, 3rd 4·49, 2nd 6·51, 1st and reverse 11.08.
Final drive ... Hypoid, 3·73 to 1.

CHASSIS
Frame ... Underslung platform chassis
Brakes ... Girling disc front, drum rear, no servo
Disc size ... 11in. dia.
Drum size ... 9in. dia., 1·75in. wide shoes
Suspension: front Independent, sliding pillars, coil springs
rear ... Half elliptic leaf springs
Dampers ... Armstrong telescopic front, lever arm rear
Wheels ... 72-spoke wire wheels standard
Tyre size ... 5·60—15in.
Steering ... Cam gear
Steering wheel ... Brookland 17in. four-spoke
Turns, lock to lock 2·25

DIMENSIONS
Wheelbase ... 8ft 0in. (244cm)
Track: front ... 3ft 11·5in. (121cm)
Track: rear ... 4ft 1in. (124cm)
Overall length ... 12ft 8in. (389cm)
Overall width ... 5ft 1in. (155cm)
Overall height (unladen) ... 4ft 3in. (129cm)
Ground clearance (laden) ... 7in. (17·8cm)
Turning circle ... 32ft 0in. (976cm)
Kerb weight ... 16·25 cwt (dry)

PERFORMANCE DATA
Top gear m.p.h. per 1,000 r.p.m. 21
Torque lb./ft. per cu. in. engine capacity ... 0·98
Brake surface swept by linings 325 sq. in.
Weight distribution ... F. 53 per cent R. 47 per cent

Morgan
Plus Four Plus..

The side window is seen here lowered as far as it will go—the door curvature prevents it from disappearing completely from view. The chromium-plated bumper wraprounds are of thick glass fibre, and shine more brilliantly than the chrome-on-steel centre section and overriders

supplementing a fair amount of stowage space around the spare wheel in the boot, which is lockable.

Both doors can also be locked, and have deep pockets for oddments. They are hinged well forward and are unusually broad, allowing easy access. The same four-spoke steering wheel is fitted, but there is a different facia panel, with rev counter and a matching compound instrument including fuel, temperature and oil pressure gauges, and an ammeter, in front of the driver. Switches for lights, single-speed wipers, and the winking indicators—which are not self-cancelling but have an audible flasher unit as well as a warning light—are in the centre of the panel; to the left is the speedometer. A facia cubbyhole and grab handle occupy the passenger's side of the panel.

Twin exterior catches concealed in the inlets on either side of the radiator grille, and one central safety catch, secure the bonnet, which is hinged at the rear and opens wide enough for good access to the engine. A 10-gallon fuel tank fed from a large snap filler cap

is housed beneath the boot floor.

It is claimed that the improved airflow with this more streamlined body has raised the maximum speed to about 107-110 m.p.h. Dunlop RS5 tyres and 72-spoke wire wheels are standard equipment. The Four Plus Four is being sold only as a fixed-head coupé, without any open bodywork alternative, so as not to cut across the existing production of Morgan Plus 4s; it is essentially an alternative model, aimed primarily at the European market. It is, of course, a hand-built car in small-scale production, but present output is in the order of two per week.

Road Impressions

Seated in the Plus Four Plus there is an impression of considerably more space than the exterior view would suggest, probably as a result of the generous glass area and the room behind the seat backrest. Visibility is good, although one tends to sit rather low in the car. Screen pillars are narrow, and the width of the curved rear window adds to the

impression of being almost entirely surrounded by glass.

For ride comfort, this is essentially a car for good roads, since the suspension has limited travel and is ultra-firm. Heavy steering on sharp corners gives an impression of exaggerated understeer. The engine drives through a Moss four-speed gearbox, and really invigorating performance is available. In a quick run around the Malvern hills the forceful hill climbing and ability to rush up to 75 or 80 m.p.h. on short stretches of straight, using the excellently high third gear, underlined the low weight of the new body—only 16½cwt in running trim.

With the prototype there was rather more engine and transmission noise than there should be with production models, but the level of wind noise was low and there was an absence of squeaks or rattles. Morgan state that they aimed to steer clear of glass fibre body construction until they could be sure of the rigidity and high standard of exterior finish with good door and body fits, which has been obtained in this new model.

CONTINUED FROM PAGE 124

In the Plus Four range of Triumph TR-engined cars, the only change, apart from the engine and the tuned, lightweight version, lies in a reshaping and enlarging of the windscreen of the drop-head coupé, together with a lowering of the door sills to give better vision at the sides as well as at the front. The new screen has been deepened by 1¾ in. and both the top and bottom frames curved to blend with the scuttle line. The glass is flat as before.

The Lawrence-tuned supersports Plus Four has a claimed maximum speed of 115 m.p.h. The crankshaft, connecting rods, pistons and flywheel are fully balanced and other features include a special camshaft, two dual-choke Weber carburetters, modified manifolding including a four-branch exhaust system, a polished and gas-flowed cylinder head, a 9/1 compression ratio and an oil cooler. Maximum output is 115 b.h.p. at 5,500 r.p.m.

In the body of this model, the panelling and wings are of aluminium alloy, but steel is retained for the scuttle structure in the interests of rigidity. With wire wheels, which are also standard on this version, the dry weight is 15¾ cwt. A lower (4.1/1) rear axle ratio and Dunlop RS5 tyres are available as extras.

All models in both the 4/4 and Plus Four ranges have the classic vertical-coil Morgan front suspension, a Z-section chassis frame underslung at the rear, and Girling disc-front/drum-rear brakes.

MORGAN 4/4 SERIES IV SPECIFICATION

Engine.—Cylinders, 4 in line with hollow cast-iron 3-bearing crankshaft. Bore and stroke, 80.96 mm. × 65.07 mm. (3.19 in. × 2.56 in.); 1,340 c.c. (81.77 cu. in.). Piston area, 31.92 sq. in. Compression ratio, 8.5/1. Valvegear, in line overhead valves operated by push rods and rockers from single chain-driven camshaft. Carburation, Zenith 32VN pump-type downdraught carburetter, fed by AC mechanical pump, from 9-gallon tank. Ignition, 12-volt coil, centrifugal and vacuum timing control 14 mm. Champion N5 sparking plugs. Lubrication, rotor pump, full-flow filter and 4-pint sump. Cooling, water cooling with pump, fan and thermostat, 12-pint water capacity. Electrical system, 12-volt 36 amp. hr. battery. Maximum power, 54 b.h.p. net (56.5 gross) at 4,900 r.p.m. Maximum torque, 74 lb. ft. (net) at 2,500 r.p.m.

Transmission.—Clutch, Ford/Borg-and-Beck 7¼-in. single dry plate with hydraulic actuation. Gearbox, four-speed with direct drive on top gear; synchromesh on upper three ratios. Overall ratios, 4.56, 6.44, 10.9 and 18.7; rev. 24.0; open propeller shaft; hypoid bevel final drive.

Chassis.—Brakes, Girling hydraulic, disc at front and drum at rear; front discs, 11 in. dia., rear drums 9 in. dia. × 1¾ in. wide. Brake areas, 77.4 sq. in. of lining (17 sq. in. front plus 60.4 sq. in. rear) working on 325 sq. in. rubbed area of discs and drums. Front suspension, independent, by vertical coil springs and sliding axles; Armstrong telescopic dampers. Rear suspension, semi-elliptic leaf springs, rigid axle and Armstrong lever-type dampers. Wheels and tyres, Dunlop 4-stud disc wheels (wire type with knock-on hubs extra) and 5.20—15 tubed or tubeless tyres. Steering, Bishop cam.

Dimensions.—Overall length, 12 ft. 1 in.; wheelbase, 8 ft.; overall width, 4 ft. 8 in.; track, 3 ft. 11 in. Height, 4 ft. 2 in.; ground clearance, 7 in. Turning circle, 31 ft. Kerb weight, 13 cwt. (without fuel but with oil, water, tools, spare wheel, etc.).

Effective Gearing.—Top gear ratio, 15.4 m.p.h. at 1,000 r.p.m. and 36.2 m.p.h. at 1,000 ft./min. piston speed. Maximum torque at 2,500 r.p.m. corresponds to approx. 38.6 m.p.h. in top gear. Maximum power at 4,900 r.p.m. corresponds to approx. 75.5 m.p.h. in top gear.

MORGAN:

the last horseless carriage

THE MORGAN'S SECRET, OF course, is that it's antique only in looks and feel. In every important basic respect it offers startling value for money. The Four-Four we tested had the optional competition engine—really Ford's twinchoke GT 1500—which adds another £73 to the bread and butter model's £683. It offers really tremendous performance, roadability and finish for *less* cash than any open rival.

Really you can say that with this 1500cc version the Four-Four has finally arrived. Up to now it has always carried (and deserved) a slight taint as the hearty, Triumph-powered Plus Four's poor relation—a slow slogger for die-

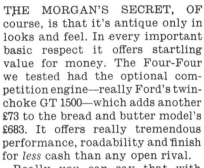

hards whose nostalgia turned out to be stronger than their sense of proportion. The original 105E Ford Anglia engine gave it less performance than many small saloons, and even the 1340cc Classic-powered version which followed left owners wondering what they could do to get over the feeling they were overbraked and underprivileged. Then last year Morgan decided to settle for the then-new five bearing variation on Ford's original theme, and at one blow the factory found it had made a killing with far more performance than rival Spridgets and Spitfires for very little more money (just £42 more to be exact).

The competition model, of which this is the first-ever road test, carries the attack still further into enemy territory. Even for dedicated moderns, who may feel that they're having to put up with all those old-fashioned outward survivals just for the sake of a bit of toe, its appeal is undeniable. And for the unashamed traditionalists who make up much of Morgan's market it represents a step forward in an era when they've become all but resigned to marking-time.

How does Morgan do it? Briefly, by keeping weight down and refusing to let unessential extras push prices up. Even in GT form the Ford 116E is a cheap engine—yet Morgan thinks, and so do we, that it's an ideal one for any small sports car application. It's also a reasonably light engine, and since

FACTS — MORGAN 4/4 COMPETITION

How much?	£756 tax paid
How fast?	94 mph
	Acceleration 0–30 3.1 sec, 0–40 5.5 sec, 0–50 7.6 sec, 0–60 11.9 sec, 0–70 18.8 sec
How thirsty?	26.7 mpg
How big?	150 in long, 56 in wide, 51 in high
How heavy?	1544 lb
How hairy?	Four-cylinder water-cooled in-line cast iron pushrod five-bearing engine at front driving rear wheels; 1498 cc developing 78 bhp on 9 to 1 compression; disc front, drum rear brakes; suspension by coils and sliding pillars (front) and leaf springs and rigid axle
How often?	Greasing at 4 and 9 points every 3000 and 5000 miles, oil change every 5000 miles
How roomy?	two-seat, two-door steel and ash roadster, open rear boot

the Four-Four's Z-section chassis and simple wood-frame body are also essentially modest in basic poundage the only remaining task is to make sure the resultant package has enough eye-appeal to get its message across. Those now-unique traditional lines and obvious tailor-made looks see to that, and carefully controlled factory economics (see production story on pages 24-25) do the rest.

Reactions to the Morgan's prewar styling vary with the individual. We got one or two laughs, and we did find one fellow who congratulated us on a fine restoration job, but by and large we were staggered at the instant, unalloyed affection the little car's rugged outline inspired in the most unlikely quarters. Girls in particular fell for it in a big way.

Before we let in the clutch let's take an analytical look round. Structurally, the Morgan begins and ends with its chassis—a simple, flexible combination of almost-straight steel side members and tubular crosspieces, with the unique sliding-pillar independent front suspension which the company has specified without a break since 1911 rigidly attached up front. Rear suspension is by very flat leaf springs with a rigid axle. The engine sits well back in the chassis, yet the bonnet is so long that the gearbox still comes no further rearward than the toeboard. Accordingly Morgan has had to develop a unique remote-control change mechanism with a long horizontal lever working in a fulcrum on the scuttle and meeting an extension from the gearbox itself one-third along between fulcrum and knob.

Steering is by cam and peg in the time-honoured Morgan way, and the brakes are the same as for the heavier and more powerful Plus-Four—mighty 11in discs on the front, nine-inch drums behind.

The scanty, rakish bodywork offers some unusual advantages. Engine accessibility is first class because the bonnet sides reach all the way down to crankcase level, although it's a bit of a nuisance having to open one side of the centre-hinged cover to check the oil and the other to top-up. Separate wings are a help from the driver's point of view, in that they make accurate placement in narrow lanes an easy thing—and it's a special advantage having a car which stays the same width all the way back, so that if the front goes through the tail will too.

Luggage room is the only area (aerodynamics apart) in which a modern silhouette would help materially. The Morgan's flush tail holds nothing apart from a generous fuel tank and the part-recessed spare wheel, and the area behind the seats provides no more room than the equivalent space in a Sprite: in other words there's no counterpart to the lock-up boot, however small, on mass production rivals. The rather roughly finished abaft-seat area will in fact hold two good-sized soft bags. Anything bigger tends to interfere either with visibility (hood up) or stowage for the weather equipment (hood down). For holidays we reckon the optional luggage rack is essential.

The hood itself is simple yet adequate. The actual car we tested —not the one in the pictures—was the personal property of Morgan sales manager Jim Goodall and its chassis and body had seen several years of service. Accordingly it was excusable that the hood

fasteners should have been so stiff as to be almost unusable; new cars we tried were no worse in that respect than most. Rigid, non-flap sidescreens struck us as showing more forethought than usual and the hood fabric fitted so well that it neither vibrated nor leaked. We can't say as much for the windscreen, although some adjustment of the rubber flap between frame and scuttle checked the flow.

You clamber into the Morgan through hatches rather than doors, flopping backside first into your seat and hauling in any spare limbs afterwards. (Hint for batchelors: she'll love you better if you open her door and *don't* stay to watch.) The cockpit is hardly spacious. Tall men have just enough legroom. The individual pump-up rubber seat cushions give reasonable support, but the one-piece sprung backrest is uncomfortably upright even at the rearmost of its several alternative positions. Driving attitude is the real old Brooklands type. You sit hunched over the wheel, elbows tucked-in and forearms and shoulders doing all the work. This is the exact opposite of the currently fashionable straight-arm, Jim Clark position—and yet it has its uses. The Morgan's steering is heavy and direct, with only 2½ turns from lock to surprisingly generous lock, so that it's a help to be able to get some beef into it. And having such a short distance between yourself and the flat, low windscreen helps when it comes to seeing past rain and spattered insects as well as keeping out the direct back-blast of the wind.

Cockpit equipment is all there. Instruments clustered in three dials right before your eyes include speedo, tachometer, engine thermometer and oil pressure and fuel gauges. The wheel in our car was the optional Brooklands four-spoke

fully sprung type, vast and nostalgia-laden. An enormous chrome-plated nut at its centre gave rise to one or two hoary wisecracks and probably wouldn't do your chest much good in a crash. The horn, for the record, is in its traditional sports-car location on the dash—as if you hadn't guessed. Other minor controls include crisp switches for road and instrument lights and wipers and a sideways toggle control in the middle of the dash for the direction indicators; there's also a socket.

Ford's GT engine was always an easy starter, and the one in our test car showed the usual perfect decorum. It needed little choke and always pulled strongly from cold. Sound insulation in the Four-Four is minimal, so that you get plenty of long-forgotten vintage mechanical noises such as a loud sucking sound from the filterless carburettor intake and a healthy thrum from the valvegear.

The gears all have synchromesh, and first slips in easily every time. The odd change mechanism takes time to master—but only because you tend to expect more difficulties than you actually find. Even reverse goes in without contortion; the general feel reminded us of the smaller Citroens, Ami-6 and 2CV. Upward changes are instantaneous and so in theory are the downward ones, though our car had had its second-gear synchro fiended at some time in the past.

Ratios are the same as for the Ford GT saloons; ie, second is too low. Otherwise the box is there to be used, and third in particular gives a splendid rush of acceleration right up into the late 70s. The engine feels powerful and yet always seems to work well within its capabilities. Taking 6000 rpm as a sensible ceiling, we got gear speeds of roughly 35, 50 and 75 mph and with the hood up (when streamlining is better) we managed a two-way maximum close enough to 95 which is just over 6000 on the dial. The Morgan is lower-geared than any of the Ford-built cars which use this engine, and it interested us to see how it felt at high cruising revs. The answer is: fine. The unit seems to revel in more or less constant activity, and at a steady 85 (5400) or so on the motorway it just couldn't have been happier. And as for noise, the sound of the wind ripping round all those vertical posts and louvres effectively killed any of that.

We feel tempted to say the Four-Four handles like a tap. Anyway,

it's either on or off. With the tyres at the recommended 18lb all round you can make it understeer or oversteer to order simply by backing-off or applying more power in a corner. In fact, there's even a built-in safety valve. Accelerating in, say, second through a sharpish turn you can hang the tail out a full 45 degrees just for the hell of it and then if something goes wrong catch it again at once by taking your foot off the accelerator. It really would be hard to find a safer car to play boy-racers in, and as well as bags of fun you have the certain knowledge that your cornering speeds are at least as good as an MGB's or a TR's—and probably a good deal better.

Brakes too are top-class. High pedal pressures (you have to work hard at everything in a Morgan) yield spectacular, four-square results with neither nose-dive nor wheel locking drama.

Steering is heavy and direct and not really the most precise in the world. Our car had a trace of lost motion around the dead-ahead position, but it could have been wear. Road shocks are not unduly noticeable—probably because you're already feeling them through the chassis, which takes some fearful shocks on occasion because of the inflexibility of the suspension. This is really the biggest limitation for habitual fast drivers. It's absolutely essential to slow down for bad bumps and, even when you do, quite a lot of the road irregularities which most postwar cars absorb completely get through in no uncertain fashion. Rough corners set the back axle dancing madly, too. Since it's much worse if you try pumping the tyres up any higher to avoid scrub in slow corners (which can be a hazard otherwise) the only real answer is to go easy except on the smoothest main roads.

Is this a good reason to stay away from the Four-Four? We think not. Nowhere else can you get such spectacular straight-line performance for so little money. Almost no other cars can have such a big braking reserve. None are safer and few faster in smoothly surfaced bends. And you get the thrill of owning a car so obviously and honestly different it's guaranteed to set every atom of pride aflame in any enthusiast breast. ✵

IT'S LIKE WANDERING casually into 1920. You push open a little blue door and step out of sunlit, sleepy but unmistakably present-day Malvern Link into a low, pine-panelled room bursting with memories—a room lined from floor to ceiling with posters bearing lurid pictures of gay flappers draped over fiery red three-wheelers and boasting of the hillclimbing exploits of The Perfect Runabout. There's even a glass case full of showpiece samples of turnery and cutting. 'That's where they put it when they make anything that fits' someone unkindly remarked.

They? As if there could be any doubt. This trim anteroom is your introduction to the Morgan Motor Company Limited, Britain's oldest privately owned automobile manufacturer, purveyor of sports cars to the nobility and gentry since 1911—last stronghold of the wood frame and hand-beaten steel construction method in which all others had their foundation, final bastion of the square-rigger style of passenger-car architecture, successful upholder of a proud and unbroken tradition in times which have seen the demise of most of its traditional opposition.

Behind a faded inner door managing director Peter Morgan—tall, 45, soft-spoken, gently mannered—struggles daily with the manifold problems involved in keeping what he freely admits is a virtual museum-piece of a car in competitive production. Oddly enough, his biggest worry is not maintaining production but increasing it to the point where American dealers, who manage to swallow 85percent of the tiny factory's total production 'without even trying,' feel it's worthwhile hanging on to their franchises and persuading customers to be patient while their cars are screwed together rather than stomp off and buy off-the-peg elsewhere. Present output level is 10 cars a week, three up on the late-'50s figure, and already Morgan is talking about pruning certain models out of the range because they take up man-hours which could be better spent putting the ceiling up to 11 or even 12. Even now the activity is tremendous for such a small plant. Since each car takes roughly six weeks of fairly continous work to put together, there are always at least 60 chassis in various stages of completion scattered about.

Production starts in the carpentery shop, where seasoned ash planks from the timber-yard outside arrive to be sawn first into convenient lengths and then into patterned shapes for assembly into the screwed and glued body frame which forms the basis of every Morgan car. Meanwhile chassis workers are bolting crossmembers to the forged steel side rails, bought outside, and installing the engines which lie ranged in long rows just as they come from Ford and Standard-Triumph.

Then the skilled work starts in earnest. The carpenters have already taken pains to make individual doors fit properly in their frames, wedging and clamping the wooden components *in situ* and then screwing and glueing them down. Now panelbeaters take each section in turn and clothe it with steel, shaping the graceful tail and bonnet panels, tapping the intricate scuttle assembly into line, wheeling-in the strengthening ribs and turning over all the edges with traditional hammer and steel.

Painters with hand spray-guns take over at intervals, applying black preservative to the wooden frames and building up layers of undercoat, sealer, primer and cellulose finish between hand-rubbings to individual panels and finally to the completed body as a whole. Multi-curve pressings (wings, air-intake cowl) arrive from the stores where they wait after delivery from the big contractors in Birmingham to be painted, dried in a special dustproof enclosure and finally bolted on last of all. The carpenters arrive again, this time with their varnished planks of solid African walnut for the dash. Then it's off to the trimming shop in a corner by the door.

There the atmosphere is positively domestic. Middle-aged women sit along one wall at their sewing machines, pleating and tucking just like mum. Upholsterers with tack-hammers tap away at their folded strips of leather (for the door tops), vinyl plastic (for door panels and seats) and neatly tucked and bordered lengths of carpet. Other workers wrestle with the studied intricacies of hood-sticks and webbing straps, coaxing the pliable weatherproof plastic to guarantee a draught-free fit. No-one speaks.

Then there's the wiring loom – fed into prefabricated channels like technicolour spaghetti, red, blue, green, yellow, black; connected to instruments and lights which have at last begun to fill vacant sockets in panelling and dash. The cars come alive. Men arrive to start the engines, stick on the export labels, apply a final coat of polish, disappear for a quick burst round the block: it's the end of the line.

Are Morgans better-made than other cars? Probably not. The difference is just that they're made by people, all the way, with human minds and human hands watching how they go. For some owners there's comfort in the thought that the same simple, nut-and-bolt mistakes which can lead to trouble on the road will respond to equally simple investigation and repair. If something falls off a Morgan you screw it on again. No need to take a tin opener and lever the spot-welds apart . . .

The Morgan unmoving — static delight.

ROB LUCK DRIVES... THE MAGNIFICENT

The enthusiast's fundamental or a boulevardier's disillusionment, t h e Morgan is a permanent fixture amid the confusing fluxes of modern motoring.

"I͟T'S a Road Test car," I said. He didn't hear. The tacho said two grand and the engine was noisy.

"How much did you get it for — 'bout thirteen hundred quid? Oh, jeez it's beautiful."

He lifted up the side curtain flap again: "Did you get it out near the Nepean Highway — about 900 miles on the clock — almost new?" He was

Where it all started — wood frame chassis on Morgan England assembly line.

Smooth straight classicism. Quarter windows are useful local addition.

Unclad for open action. Wire wheels are optional.

MOG

SPORTS CAR WORLD · ROAD TEST

half gasping, gesticulating wildly.

I nodded.

"I was going to buy it. I didn't have the dough—it's bloody mighty. How much did you get it for?"

"It's not mine — I didn't buy it, — it's a road test car," I repeated.

"Beauty, beauty. Good luck to you." I still wasn't sure if he had heard. The light was

English excellence — a driver's cockpit.

changing to amber.

"I won't stop you," he said. I protested I would stop, but he didn't hear me.

"Beautiful!" He said finally, patting the soft top reverently. "Absolutely beautiful," — and disappeared into the night.

I never saw him again, but even this far from the incident, I swear there were tears streaming down his cheeks.

MELBOURNE is rarely moved by anything — anything at all. Our road test Moggy was an exception. Melbourne — en masse — goggled, gaped, stepped half under moving traffic in awe and even waved at the immaculate British racing green Morgan 4/4 Competition model that we romanced with for a whole weekend in Melbourne.

Why, I am still not sure. I am half suspicious that most thought it was an immaculately restored vintage racing sports car of God-knows-how-

An invitation to pleasure — instrumentation is adequate, equipment spartan, finish good.

far-back. Many would just have been curious at seeing such an unusual car, for there are few on Victorian roads. Some, I suppose, were fascinated by its old, odd lines, or perhaps half guessed it was some sort of modern link with the past. One thing for sure — only a handful recognised it.

But moody Melbourne — it yielded us weather all the way from torrential downpour to warm sunshine — was clearly impressed and the many, many incidents will long be remembered.

Firmly implanted in our minds are little glimpses of Morgan lovers, pessimists and even the uninformed. After all, in what other car would you be forced into the kerb by a Jeep at a drizzly 40 degree 2 am to meet the straight-talk demand of a bod and bird as to what the hood was doing up. And what of the surly clot who coolly requested from the driver's seat of his new Galaxie at a certain set of traffic lights as to what vintage that "neat little heap" might be— only to be firmly shut down when the green light flashed? What indeed? A profuse apology and some sensible queries at the next set of lights where he was quietly squeezed out again — all without exceeding the arbitrary 35 mph limit. There again there was the Holden driver who didn't believe that every gear in the box could be swapped effortlessly without the clutch (yes, including first) until he was sat in the passenger's seat and appointed chief observer for a successful (and graunchless) experiment. By far the worst in a long line of me-toos and know-alls was the chap who observed with quiet professional air that it was undoubtedly the better car of its time — the TC being the other (Oh, my God!)

If we assume that people who still regard Morgans as ancient, backward or outdated didn't get further than the heading on this script we need not offend them. If we assume they are still reading — well, here come both barrels. Such people have very little concept of true sporting motoring, almost no sense of values and absolutely no ability at all to evaluate a product for its market, intended purpose, or price range. Strangely, although very few people criticise the Morgan, even fewer have any thought at all about

DETAILS OF THE
MORGAN 4/4 SERIES V
COMPETITION MODEL

SPECIFICATIONS

DIMENSIONS:

Wheelbase	8 ft 0 in.
Track, front	3 ft 11 in.
Track, rear	4 ft 1 in.
Ground clearance	7 in.
Turning circle	32 ft 0 in.
Turns, lock to lock	2¼
Overall length	12 ft 0 in.
Overall width	4 ft 8 in.
Overall height	4 ft 3 in.

CHASSIS:

Steering type	cam gear
Brake type	11 in. discs front, 9 in. drums rear
Swept area	NA
Suspension, front	independent by Morgan patent (sliding pillar)

it. This could be attributed to any of a hundred different reasons: the product is not readily available, it is not marketed actively in competition against other makes and it does not cater to the whimsical, impatient, intolerant un-sporting or, for that matter, weak kidneyed. This latter could just be the most important reason for the Morgan's general — as opposed to isolated — lack of acceptance in the modern sports car picture. We know of a top go-kart man who was banned from racing because of its jarring effect on his kidneys — it is the only reason we can think of for staying away from the Morgan.

Let it be clear by way of introduction to the car itself that it is the only car designed 20 years ago that is still 10 years ahead of its time in most respects. A rash statement, surely? I think not. Almost every criticism which is levelled at the Morgan involves the inability of human beings to adapt to its minor diversions from the (modern) conventional. The accent, of course, is on the words *minor* and *modern* and these diversions can be summed up basically as three things — appearance, ride, and weather equipment. All are directly attributable to human weaknesses.

Actually the car excels with its weather equipment — it has fewer leaks from the hood than any production soft top sports car we have driven — and that includes some way over the Morgan's modest price. We refuse to go deep into the question of looks because it is an intensely personal matter — but it should be noted that the attention the car drew (whether because it looked like a vintagent or not) from the average people on the street was not equalled by the Pontiac Parisienne we also happened to drive on the same visit.

Bases for establishing ride qualities can be determined by a variety of conflicting motives. Do you want the ultimate in ride or the ultimate in handling? Most modern cars try to approach the problem by aiming for the maximum ride comfort and then balance this with the best handling possible to satisfy the needs of a softened generation of customers. Morgan way back in the 1910s decided roadholding should be the prime aim as the road conditions were then poor

Speaking of horses — well worked Cortina has 78.

enough to ensure a car designed for good ride on the bad conditions came out well down on the handling side.

The company's policy hasn't changed over the years and Morgan could well argue that there should be no need to change, either — because the road conditions are obviously far better. If you think Morgan is being presumptuous to assume that the modern human being should appreciate the car's unmodified qualities I suggest you don't bother to tell the company — ever since its inception it has been over-subscribed with customers and under-equipped for production. You therefore arrive at the unique situation of a company which could quite easily select its customers. Morgan, of course, isn't so silly; but there again it doesn't suffer the problems of other manufacturers with regard to customer satisfaction, so why worry?

Suspension, rear	semi elliptic leaves
Shock absorbers	double acting telescopic front Armstrong hydraulic rear
Tyre size	5.60 x 15
Weight	13 cwt
Fuel tank capacity	8½ gals
Approx cruising range	230 miles

ENGINE:

Cylinders	four in line
Bore and stroke	80.97 mm by 72.82 mm
Cubic capacity	1499 cc
Compression ratio	9 to 1
Fuel requirement	97 octane
Valves	pushrod operated, overhead
Maximum power	78 bhp at 5200 rpm
Maximum torque	NA

TRANSMISSION:

Overall ratios —	
First (synchro)	14.76
Second (synchro)	9.8
Third (synchro)	5.7
Fourth (synchro)	4.1
Final drive	4.1 to 1
Mph per 1000 rpm in top	18.1 mph

PERFORMANCE

Top speed average			108.6 mph
Fastest run	(6200 rpm)		112.4 mph
Estimated safe maximum	(6500 rpm limit)		117.6 mph
Maximum, first	(6500 rpm limit)	37	mph
Maximum, second	(6500 rpm limit)	53	mph
Maximum, third	(6500 rpm limit)	88	mph
Maximum, fourth	(6200 rpm limit)	112.4	mph
Standing quarter mile average			17.6 secs
Fastest run			17.0 secs
0-30 mph			2.7 secs
0-40 mph			4.6 secs
0-50 mph			7.1 secs
0-60 mph			10.4 secs
0-70 mph			14.2 secs
0-80 mph			18.4 secs
0-90 mph			24.9 secs
0-100 mph			NA
0-60-0 mph			14.2 secs

	Top	Third
40-60 mph	9.2 secs	5.5 secs
50-70 mph	10.5 secs	6.5 secs
60-80 mph	14.7 secs	10.6 secs
70-90 mph	9.8 secs	NA

Fuel consumption, cruising	28 mpg
Fuel consumption, overall	24 mpg

This all adds up to the much referred-to dray cart ride (or worse) but handling so phenomenal that the car becomes almost unshakeable in its intention of staying to a committed line. This is just as we found the 4/4 Competition Morgan we tested in Melbourne.

The car was handed over to us by Morgan Sports Car Distributors (Vic) of St Kilda — a small emergent firm born out of a close association of three ardent Morgan followers. All three have owned Morgans at some time or other and have campaigned successfully a Plus 4 competition model and 4/4 Competition in hill climbs. Jeff Hall and Digby Thackeray are two of them — but the third shall be nameless for reasons of his own choice.

In just a couple of years they have developed full workshop facilities that enable them to handle the strictest demands of customers (from routine servicing to a complete re-build, and a spare parts stock that is somewhat more than comprehensive for a small-turnover company. The road test car was immaculately prepared. Time hadn't allowed the standard rubber to be swapped for high-speed equipment, but our speed tests were conducted well away from public contact, on Riverside Dragway. In all other respects the presentation was faultless and indicative of the absolute thoroughness with which each car is treated. After taking delivery from England the cars receive special modifications for local conditions. Each is carpeted throughout (replacing rubber mats on the floor) and the heavy duty vinyl hood is inserted with additional clear plastic quarter windows to give better rearward vision.

An exterior mirror is also added, together with an ashtray and gearshift modifications (more of that later). Subsequent to our road test other modifications will also be made to all future cars imported: the jacking point slots in the floor (you just lift up the carpets and drop the jack through from the inside) will be better sealed against water and dust admission. The problem was only a small one which developed from an improper factory seal. The sidescreens occasionally popped outwards with air pressure inside the cockpit during high speed runs, leaving small slots through which draughts could be admitted. Future cars will be fitted with sealing tabs to prevent this.

The finish of the Morgan was immediately noticeable to even an untrained eye. The British racing green paintwork was deep and flawless, the vinyl hood and upholstery of thick and lasting quality and all metal joints finely matched. The dashboard was solid polished walnut and the all-black trim fitted beautifully.

The Morgan is still built of a wood skeleton frame on the strong, light chassis, but additional support comes from proper sheet metal pleating and re-inforcing tube in the stress spots. There is never a trace of scuttle shake or panel movement and if the suspension thumps hard into a bump the whole car moves as one. This probably leaves the occupants as the only shock-absorbent factors present and they yield in proportion to their own insulation: slim people inevitably suffer worst.

In the steer seat the driver is confronted with a large diameter thin-rimmed plastic wheel and a slightly impressive trio of dials. The chromed steering wheel fastening nut would give the safety wallahs a fit of the screaming heeby jeebies and it doesn't particularly help the cockpit aesthetics, either. However, the horn is easily found (sometimes accidentally) just under the lip of the wheel on the upper dashboard. Right above the chrome steering nut and well placed to be subconsciously visible to the driver even when his eyes are on the road is the Smiths-origin 8000 rpm tachometer. We rarely exceeded 6500 on our acceleration runs apart from an occasional close-to-seven-grand, but even 6500 rpm was enough to yield a 17.2 second quarter and 6000 rpm in top was 108.6 mph with plenty of wind-out left (6500 rpm is 117.6 mph, so there). We would venture to state that using a full seven thou before each shift-up the car would comfortably devour the quarter in the high 16-second bracket. As well-worked Cortina motors such as this are regularly taken to 7500 rpm by track exponents with rare expense, the safety margins seem well conceived. The engine is of course fully balanced. What else would you expect of Morgan?

The speedometer to the right of centre reads to an unassuming 110 mph and though it was almost dead accurate we couldn't find a stretch of road long enough to wind the car out past the 112 we once timed. The speedometer is matched by an identical size combination dial housing fuel gauge, oil pressure and amp meter. When running, the Morgan usually registers 45-50 lb/sq in. and if you see much below 30 on the dial — even at idle — you can switch off and get out the spanners. To the left of the instruments a recessed switch-panel caters for headlights, panel lights, wipers (very feeble) power point take-off (radio, razor, Halda Speed Pilot etc), choke, ignition, turning indicator, spare (fog or spot) and generator and turn-indicator tell-tales. To the left a felt-lined glovebox has no lid, and under the dash edge a passenger's ashtray is attached. A rear vision mirror is suction-cup applied to the windscreen centre. The handbrake is pivoted on the passenger's side of the transmission tunnel and is of the fly-off type (yes, for gymkhanas, if you like). The Morgan gearshift is normally an atrocious pudding stirrer which wanders out from somewhere under the dash (a la Renault R4) and is operated like a fencer parrying an opponent. However, showing resourceful engineering genius the company devised a hook-up linkage utilising a normal short stick shift operating through the conventional H-pattern. It works perfectly and as explained earlier the Cortina box can still be shifted without the clutch with no effort. About half an inch is the maximum gate travel between slots.

The car's performance potential could be summed up best by saying that there isn't a production car within $1000 of the Morgan 4/4's modest price that could hope to even look competitive on the racetrack. In stock form the Morgan is a potent little racer and demure street hack in one. It prefers to be kept always above 2000 rpm, but is so tractable that it can be pottered away from a dead stop in third without touching the throttle, and if you don't mind cleaning the plugs every 1000 miles or so you can forget the over-2000 rpm rule. There again you needn't worry about the thoughtless location of the fuel filler — the car demands only normal super grade petrol.

The controls are so straightforward they wouldn't frighten mother, and yet the pedals are carefully aligned for heel-and-toe (of course) and the steering is set for sensitive hands. There is barely more than a twitch of the fingers necessary to swap gear ratios and the gate is so positive it wouldn't confuse a learner-driver. In fact all the controls are designed to leave the' driver with the maximum amount of concentration devoted towards keeping the thing on the road. This the car does almost by instinct under normal conditions, but a good driver soon finds that the Morgan is utterly forgiving at its limits as well and rarely leaves itself without an escape route. The power is astounding for medium-pace corners and for high speed bends the sheer stickability is the car's most salient feature.

For those who are still unconvinced and prefer the easier life — the hood doesn't flap at high speed, the cockpit is almost breeze free with the hood down, a half-tonneau is standard, and the car is basically comfortable for its occupants (we would prefer a little more squab padding). For those who are partly convinced you could fit

Koni adjustable shockers and fiddle the ride for a little more softness without hurting the handling.

Surprisingly the car will go almost anywhere (superior traction). During our tests it never suffered axle tramp (although wheelspin was noticeable with high rpm) and it found its way without protest through near-bog conditions, which almost stopped a Viva.

Braking is faultless and full-effort stops could not induce either the big front discs or the rear drums to lock or hook. The car always pulled up faithfully and total lack of fade was a further reassurance.

Despite a thorough search we failed to locate one basic or significant failing except perhaps that the lights are not much good over 100 mph. We rather feel anyone who wants to achieve that speed regularly at night would also be interested in fitting a spotlight for his own sake. In fact, we have only one minor criticism — we would like to see the tiny red tell-tales installed in the top of the parking lights. It would fit the overall image rather well.

But just to let the Morgan owner know he is fortunate to be among the ranks of the distinguished, a neat little device affixed to the bulkhead gives him a constant reminder. It is just a small pressure button which the driver must depress every 50-100 miles or so just to keep the Morgan patent front suspension constantly lubricated. It rather reminded us of an external gear-lever or handbrake or a Klaxon horn and was undeniably a faint glimpse of tradition — so typical of the little intimate touches Morgan builds into its cars.

It is all part of the Morgan picture — tradition with performance. The 4/4 could never disappoint a discriminating buyer.

The price, by the way is just $2860 including the recent rise in import tax. Anyone for poor man's racing?   #

CAR and DRIVER ROAD TEST

Morgan Plus 4

You either accept a Morgan as you accept the Himalayas, or you go on to more splendid things, say, butterfly collecting. A Morgan merely *is*. That should be enough.

In this mock Edwardian decade, in which we have taken to reproducing the cut-glass bowls and high-button shoes of our grandfathers, we are committing the curious paradox of banishing, at the same time, the authentic relic of their motoring hours.

We are consigning the Morgan to history. The last of the great coal carts, a car almost unchanged since 1910—except for the addition of a fourth wheel, a few minor suspension changes to go with, and a slightly updated engine—a pure antique, and our federal government has decreed it is no longer to be brought to our shores.

It is not to be expected that a firm which has survived with the same basic design for almost 60 years will give up easily. No, Morgan swears it will be back in 1969 with an all-new car. But "all-new" is an anathema to Morgan, always has been, and though surely the company will try to meet our federal standards, their own traditions might subvert that accomplishment.

But the classic Morgan as we have known it, perfectly safe, even exciting, for generations of enthusiasts, has suddenly been put beyond the pale for our colorless, antiseptic, spoon-fed citizens. It is almost like a retroactive Coast Guard examination of the Titanic.

If the all-new '69 Morgan is stillborn—through the device of Dr. William Haddon's midwifery—it will be a near-fatal blow to the Morgan Car Company, which sells almost two-thirds of its production in this country. The Morgan Car Company, like its product, is not quite prepared to survive in our contemporary world.

Peter Morgan (contemplating the '69 with some annoyance, you may be sure) continues to build a four-wheeler his founder/father would admire: a simple, wood-braced, hand-formed artifact that is so much a tribute to Henry Frederick Stanley Morgan it is barely distinguishable from the car he built in the late Thirties when he reluctantly made a square of a triangle and bowed to the fad of the four-wheeler. It still takes weeks to build a single car, the glue pot still bubbles at

Malvern, and although production is up to 12 cars a week, the Morgan is basically a hand-built, hand-formed motorcar.

It is hard to imagine that the 90 or more artisans who create the Morgan will survive when Morgan sales are cut back 65%. They must be the last of the great blacksmith/coachbuilder car families—scorning the National Health Service, voting Conservative, setting off to work with great dignity and purpose. Nor can they be young men anymore. What must they think of our government's edict, which scorns a quality of workmanship we barely see any longer and celebrates instead the ideal of a machine-spewed plastic cocoon for anyone who ventures on the highway?

Their regret will surely be philosophical compared to that of the Morgan Owners Club in this country.

Representing a hard-core band of unreconstructed car nuts, the MOC considers anything built since 1936 a flash in the pan. They see nothing inconsistent in owning a 1967 Morgan—it is, after all, a brand new, perfectly restored car of the Thirties—even the Twenties. And there are no Invictas, no HRGs, no Squires left to own. There is only the Morgan.

They're not alone. The Chairman of the Board of Governors of the Sports Car Club of America will watch the Morgan go with great regret. So will a feisty young man from Southern California. So will a pretty graduate student in Washington, D.C.

Lew Spencer was one of the great Morgan drivers in the late '50s when he ran "Baby Doll," at the head of the pack in almost every Class C-production event on the West Coast. He humbled the previously all-conquering Bristols in his dark blue, Weber-carbureted lightweight, and made an enviable reputation that led him to a factory ride with Shelby American.

Carl Swanson was the 1966 National Champion in E-production, winning the Riverside race for the title in the only Morgan in a pack of Porsches. And although Pat Mernone has given up driving, she was a familiar figure in a G-production

Morgan in the Northeast Division.

When word got out that the classic Morgan would very likely be off the market, there was a run on the cars, and all that was available to us was a tacky 4-seater which was duly delivered to our garage. With a photographer assigned, the test strip reserved, and a proper mood carefully cultivated, we set off. The 4-seater wouldn't start. Nothing could persuade it to. Nothing in the world. Typical. We went back to the office to call the distributor and found a call waiting for *us*. A salesman had been out to our garage with a customer, the car had been sold, and would we mind taking another? Of course not, but didn't the man know the car wouldn't start? Of course he did, and so did the customer, and it didn't make a bit of difference in the world. The customer was a *Morgan* buyer, he said, as if that would explain it all. In fact, it explained it perfectly well. Antiques are not meant to run on time. Antiques are meant to be looked after, tended, coaxed. It is a reaffirmation and a joy when an antique won't start. How else can you be sure it's an antique?

We discovered the answer to that when we got our 2-seater the next day. Our Technical Editor had approached the Morgan steeped in his era's belief that everything on a good car works. This product of the bright new generation was appalled by the Morgan. The door opened from the inside—and, at that, it opened reluctantly and sagged a little on the hinges. The seat was adjustable—as it has always been—only by inflation of the seat cushion. And the flat windshield was only inches away from the Bluemels steering wheel, which was, in turn, only inches away from the driver's chest. Our Technical Editor drove the car in its drag strip trials, got out, and took the train back to the office. "It's a stone," he said in disgust. He was born 20 years too late for the Morgan—poor soul. It's all a matter of approach.

Park a Morgan in a country lane in the autumn sun near a tree so that the dappled sunlight can reflect from its long, louvered hood, hinged at the top. Park it so its wire wheels glisten, so its leather seats invite you to tour winding back roads. Park a Morgan in the city on a Sunday morning and watch a father, trailing a troop of daughters, look at the car with wistfulness and envy. Park a Morgan in the rainy night with the tonneau zipped and see the drops bead on its taut surface. And when you come to drive it, stand back a moment and look at its stance: long in the engine, short-coupled rear. Only one spare tire these days (there used to be two, and not so long ago at that), sitting vertically at the back; high wheels, forthright fenders—genuine fenders, fenders as they were meant to be. And as you get in the

thing you notice about a Morgan. Everything's so damn direct. You feel every pebble on the road through the steering wheel, and your foot (time and marshmallow cars have made it clumsy) seems to operate directly on the engine. You can't get the Morgan operating smoothly for miles. Ah, but when you do—and when you find a relatively smooth surface—you understand what was exciting about sports carring in the Thirties. You understand how Lew Spencer humbled the Bristols, and Carl Swanson the Porsches. You understand *laissez faire* motoring at its best. Twitch the wheel, and out goes the tail of the Morgan. Just as far as you want, for just as long as you want, for just the result you want. Fangio used to set up a slide

imprudent enough to set forth upon a bad road, you will live to regret it. A tar divider strip will launch the Morgan on a flight that would put a Hell Driver to shame—a genuine bump will qualify you for flight pay. Still, it's not the take-off that gets you; it's the landing. About three landings a week should be tops. Anatomically. If you're contemplating a Morgan, see your doctor first.

With all this, however, there's a generous portion of performance. The Morgan—lighter than the TR-4—performs smartly in the quarter-mile, turning 81.2 mph in 16.9 seconds. Add the smooth-track handling, and things begin to make sense. Top speed is about 110 mph; our test car was taken up to 95 mph and was still pulling when our Technical Editor backed off.

The problem with our Technical Editor was that he actually tried to *understand* the Morgan, what it was, what it did, where it managed to fit into the community of nations. What the Morgan meant in the greater scheme of things. Futility. You either accept a Morgan as you accept the Himalayas, or you go on to more splendid things. Butterfly classification, phrenology, alchemy. A Morgan merely *is*. That should be enough.

If Peter Morgan's all-new '69 dies a-borning, and it might, it would be more proper to say a Morgan merely *was*, our federal safety standards have seen to the past tense. And that is a sad, sad thing for many. Oddly, one of those many was a 9-year-old boy who came with us when we went out to photograph this almost-last-of-the-Morgans. It was four in the morning and it was raining, and the boy was up for the first time in his life of his own choice at that evil hour. The city streets were empty, as the Morgan, top down, bucked and snorted by darkened buildings and through a long tunnel to the parkway. He had never been in a roadster in the rain, that 9-year-old. Most especially not a Morgan, and he was perfectly delighted to find that, at 50 mph, he wasn't getting wet. He loved the bouncing, darting behavior of the car in the rain on the bumpy expressway—he had never really been in a car anything like this one, he said. In fact, he said, it was almost as though he had never been in a car at all before. Of course he hadn't. This 9-year-old, almost the last 9-year-old ever to experience it, was bounding around in the passenger seat of a car of another era. He was taken back in time by that Morgan, in the rain and the darkness. And he couldn't help but respond to it.

It's no use saying the Morgan is a put-on in 1967, it's no use saying it's the last of the new antiques. There was virtue to the Thirties, a simplicity, and a demand on the human to participate that we've long since given up. And that's what the Morgan means, and that's what we're shipping off, perhaps forever. The Thirties are gone—for the best—and goodbye. Now, it seems, Farewell to the Morgan. ●

Should you be imprudent enough to set forth upon a bad road in a Morgan, you will live to regret it. A tar divider strip will launch the car on a flight that would put a Hell Driver to shame—a genuine bump will qualify you for flight pay.

Morgan—opening the door from the inside —listen to the pneumatic cushion sigh as you settle down in the cockpit and stretch to reach the pedals; your right leg, knee and thigh pressed tight against the transmission tunnel. Of course everything is close: the wheel and the wooden dashboard with its big, round simple instruments; shouldn't they be? Where did this arms-out stuff come from, anyway? Surely not Morgan, not MG, not Bugatti. Why did the great Tazio Nuvolari forever have his elbows crooked out when he was sawing away at the wheel of his Alfa?

The Morgan starts—when it starts—on a familiar key. The 2.2-liter TR-4 engine fires with a well-known sound (somehow changed by its surroundings). Depress the clutch (God, it's hard), crunch the old Jaguar gearbox non-synchro low gear, and you're off. Directly. That's the very first

for each corner. Be Fangio; the Morgan makes it easy. And you can *see* what you're doing. *Everything* you're doing. You can see the front fenders pounding from the sliding pillar front suspension (welds will break in exactly the same places on those fenders in time; they always have, they always will). You can look out over the side and see the bump that put the Morgan five feet in the air; a bump a Porsche would have brushed aside. And later—straining to turn around in front of the full-length mirror at home—you will see the beginnings of the bruises on your backside. The steering, like the rest of the car, is direct, almost too direct. You have to give a great wrench on the wheel to go anywhere, and any subtlety is absolutely lost on the Morgan. The result is a dramatic change in direction, with a suddenness that is startling. And should you be

MORGAN PLUS 4

Importer/Manufacturer: Booth & Cowley Inc.
444 West 55th Street
New York, New York

Number of dealers in U.S.: 35

Vehicle type: Front-engine, rear-wheel-drive, 2-passenger sports car, steel chassis, steel/wood/aluminum body

Price as tested: $3,850.00
(Manufacturer's suggested retail price, including all options listed below, Federal excise tax, dealer preparation and delivery charges; does not include state and local taxes. license or freight charges)

Options on test car: Heater and defroster ($65.00), wire wheels ($140.00), wooden steering wheel ($38.00), tonneau cover ($38.00), map pockets ($15.00)

ENGINE

Type: Water-cooled, 4-in-line, cast iron block and head, 3 main bearings
Bore x stroke . . 3.39 x 3.62 in, 86.0 x 92.0 mm
Displacement . . . . 130.5 cu in, 2138 cc
Compression ratio . . . . 9.0 to one
Carburetion . . . . 2 x 1-bbl Stromberg
Valve gear . . . . pushrod-operated overhead valves, mechanical lifters
Power (SAE) . . . . 104 bhp @ 4700 rpm
Torque (SAE) . . . . 132.5 lbs/ft @ 3000 rpm
Specific power output . . . . 0.80 bhp/cu in, 48.7 bhp/liter
Max. recommended engine speed . . . 5500 rpm

DRIVE TRAIN

Transmission . . 4-speed manual, synchromesh top three gears
Clutch diameter . . . . 9.0 in
Final drive ratio . . . . 3.73 to one

Gear	Ratio	Mph/1000 rpm	Max. test speed
I	2.97	6.9	38 mph (5500 rpm)
II	1.75	11.8	65 mph (5500 rpm)
III	1.20	17.2	86 mph (5000 rpm)
IV	1.00	20.6	103 mph (5000 rpm)

DIMENSIONS AND CAPACITIES

Wheelbase . . . . 96.0 in
Track . . . . F: 47.0 in, R: 47.0 in
Length . . . . 144.0 in
Width . . . . 56.0 in
Height . . . . 52.0 in
Ground clearance . . . . 7.0 in
Curb weight . . . . 1846 lbs
Test weight . . . . 1982 lbs
Weight distribution, F/R 50/50%
Lbs/bhp (test weight) 19.0
Battery capacity . . . . 12 volts, 57 amp/hr
Generator capacity . . . . 480 watts
Fuel capacity . . . . 14.4 gal
Oil capacity . . . . 6.0 qts
Water capacity . . . . 8.5 qts

SUSPENSION

F: Ind., Morgan-type sliding pillars, coil springs, telescopic shock absorbers
R: Rigid axle, semi-elliptic leaf springs, lever-type shock absorbers

STEERING

Type . . . . cam and peg
Turns lock-to-lock 2.5
Turning circle . . . . 37.5 ft

BRAKES

F: 11-in. Girling solid discs
R: 9 x 1.75-in. cast iron drums
Swept area . . . . 324 sq in

WHEELS AND TIRES

Wheel size and type . 4.5J x 15-in wire wheels, knock-off hubs
Tire make, size and type . . . . . 5.60 x 15 Dunlop RS, 4-ply nylon, tube type
Test inflation pressures . . . F: 28 psi, R: 30 psi
Tire load rating . . . . . . 740 lbs per tire @ 24 psi

PERFORMANCE

Zero to	Seconds
30 mph	2.6
40 mph	4.6
50 mph	6.7
60 mph	9.2
70 mph	12.8
80 mph	16.5
90 mph	21.6
100 mph	27.0

Standing ¼-mile . . . . . . 16.9 sec @ 81 mph
80–0 mph panic stop . . . . 262 ft (0.81 G)
Fuel mileage . . . . 22–25 mpg on premium fuel
Cruising range . . . . 317–360 mi

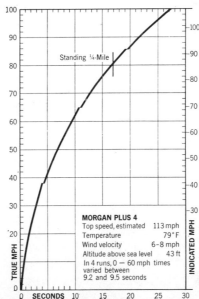

MORGAN PLUS 4
Top speed, estimated 113 mph
Temperature 79°F
Wind velocity 6-8 mph
Altitude above sea level 43 ft
In 4 runs, 0 — 60 mph times varied between 9.2 and 9.5 seconds

A

BRACE

OF

MOGGIES

ROAD TESTS OF THE
ELUSIVE
MORGAN PLUS 4 PLUS
AND THE
MORGAN 4/4

Confusing ain't it?

(Photo Michael Ware)

THE MORGAN PLUS 4 PLUS

WHEN this car was announced at the Motor Show of 1963 by the small Malvern firm, most Morgan enthusiasts, and there are many, dismissed it as a gimmick, and some were heard to remark that it was not a "real" Morgan. With only 47 of these G.T. cars behind them in 2½ years many will think the critics were right—but were they? Peter Morgan claims that he never wanted to make more than 50 cars, and in fact he budgeted to cover his design costs on this number. As to whether the car is a gimmick we say an emphatic "no", and it certainly is a *real Morgan ;* everything is Morgan except for the shape.

The chassis is the same as for the ordinary Plus 4 model, onto which the first class fibreglass body made by E. B.

(Staffs) Ltd. of Stoke on Trent has been fitted. The engine and running gear are as per the Plus 4, namely the TR4 engine, Moss gearbox and Salisbury back axle. The suspension at the front is the well-tried independent unit which Morgans have been using for years (and years), sliding pillars with coil springs, whilst at the rear there are semi-eliptic leaf springs. The lubrication of the front suspension is a daily task accomplished by depressing a button on the cockpit floor for five seconds first thing in the morning. This allows a certain amount of engine oil to flow through and replenish the supply. The car weighs just over 16 cwt. which is the same as the open Plus 4; the G.T. car however is a better aerodynamic shape and is therefore just that little bit faster. The TR unit gives the car effortless cruising in the upper 80's (when the law allows) with a top speed well over the 100 mark. Though the motor is completely tractable at low speeds, it does not become really smooth until 3,000 r.p.m. shows on the clock and above this speed it really comes into its own, propelling the car along with effortless ease and commendable silence. The cars are handbuilt to order, like all Morgans, and at the moment there is a waiting time of over 14 weeks.

The car which Morgans lent us was in fact the original prototype 869 KAB first seen at the 1963 Show and it has now covered well over 50,000 miles. Much of the pre-production testing was on the Continent over rough pavée in France and Belgium. Now that all the bugs are ironed out the car is used as Peter Morgan's personal transport and he alternates between this and a Ferrari! The car is of course well known to trials enthusiasts as Peter uses it in most M.C.C. long distance events to very good effect. In a car that has had such a chequered background one might expect many faults, but apart from some clutch and gearbox

General Specification Plus 4 & Plus 4 Plus

Cubic Capacity.—130·5 cu. ins. (2138 c.c.).

Bore and Stroke:—3·386 in. × 3·622 in. (86 mm. × 92 mm.).

No. of Cylinders.—Four.

Compression Ratio:—9 : 1.

Firing Order.—1, 3, 4, 2.

B.H.P.—105 at 4,750 r.p.m.

Oil Capacity.—11 pints. Refill 10 pints.

Valve Timing.—(With valve rocker—clearance set at 0·040 in.—when Ex. and Int. Valves of No. 4 Cyl. are rocking). Inlet opens 17° B.T.D.C. Inlet closes 57° A.B.D.C. Exhaust opens 57° B.B.D.C. Exhaust closes 17° A.T.D.C.

Valve Rocker Clearance.—With engine cold: Inlet 0·010 in. (0·250 mm.). Exhaust 0·010 in. (0·250 mm.).

Ignition Timing.—With distributor points just opening, set to fire at 4° B.T.D.C. Contact breaker gap 0·015 in. (0·350 mm.).

General Specification

Cooling.—By water pump and fan, belt driven with automatic thermostat. Radiator grille chromium plated on brass.

Chassis Frame.—A special feature of the car and is a patented design. The side members are deep Z-shape, arranged to give ample steering lock, together with maximum width. This arrangements also permits a low floor at the same time saving weight. There are five cross members of boxed or tubular section. The front end is easily detachable and follows usual Morgan practice.

Gearbox.—All Plus 4 models. Four speed and reverse. Synchromesh on 2nd, 3rd and top. The gears are changed by a short lever fitted direct to the top of the box, which is connected to the engine by a large electron casting forming the clutch housing. The position allows a low and forwarding placing of clutch and brake pedals, a short propeller shaft and good weight distribution.
     Overall Ratios: Top 3·73, 3rd 4·49, 2nd 6·51, 1st, 11·08, reverse 11·08 to 1. All 4/4 Series V. Four speed and reverse. Synchromesh on all forward gears. The gearbox is mounted directly behind the engine and the gears are changed by means of a simple and effective remote control through a pull and push mechanism.
     Overall Ratios: Top 4·56, 3rd 6·4, 2nd 11, 1st 16, reverse 17·8 to 1.

Transmission and Rear Axle.—A propeller shaft with needle roller bearing universal joints transmits power from the gearbox to the Salisbury rear axle, which is of the built-up tubular type, fitted with Hypoid gears having a ratio of 3·73 to 1 on the Plus 4 and 4·56 on the 4/4. An alternative ratio of 4·1 to 1 is available to special order.

Wheels and Tyres.—Pressed steel with wide base rims fixed with four studs and covered with a chromium plated disc. Tyres fitted are Dunlop 5·60 in. x 15 in. Centre lock wire wheels are available as optional extra, Standard fitment on the Plus 4 Super Sports and Plus 4 Plus, along with high speed tyres.

Brakes.—Girling hydraulic type, operating on four wheels. Eleven-inch diameter disc brakes on front wheels, 9 in. x 1¾ in. drum brakes on rear wheels. The hand-brake is operated by cable with compensated linkage.

Steering Gear.—Cam Gear with 17 in. spring wheel, two and a quarter turns lock to lock. Turning Circle 32 ft. Track Rod and drag-link are fitted with Thompson Ball Ends.

Suspension.—The front wheels are independently sprung by a system patented by the Morgan Motor Co. and used by them with every satisfaction. The springs are longer than they have used in the past, giving more movement and softer travel. Double-acting tubular type shock absorbers are fitted to the front springs. The rear springs are semi-elliptical with Silentbloc bushes fitted at both ends, the springing being controlled by Armstrong hydraulic dampers.

Electrical Equipment.—Lucas 12-volt equipment with full set of lamps, flashing indicators, instrument panel lighting and dual windscreen wipers.

Ignition.—Coil and distributor with induction-operated advance and retard mechanism.

Instrument Panel.—The instruments are neatly grouped on a steel panel with a polished walnut surround. They include Speed Indicator with trip mileage; Revolution counter; oil, water, fuel gauges and ammeter. There are also sockets for Inspection Lamp and the usual switches to control lighting and turn signals. The 4/4 has above equipment, except Revolution Counter and Water Temperature Gauge. A revolution counter is standard equipment on the 4/4 Competition Model.

Bodywork.—Is constructed of sheet steel panels on a robust ash wood frame. It is individually produced and has the advantage of being easily repaired if accidents should occur. Upholstery is carried out by hand in good quality vynide material, or leather if specified at extra cost mentioned below.
     Detachable tops are fitted to the open cars which can be stowed when open in the luggage compartment or behind the rear seats in a four-seater. The Drophead Coupe has a hinged top which folds neatly into the back of the body when open, but can be erected in the half open position if desired.

Standard Finish.—Westminster Green, Crimson, Kingfisher Blue, Smoke Grey (Light Blue), or Broken White. Upholstery Black. Any deviation from the above will entail an extra charge of £10 for paintwork and £10 for upholstery carried out in leather and/or special colour.

Dimensions, (approx.).—Wheelbase 8 ft.   Track, front 3 ft. 11 in., Rear 4 ft. 1 in.
        Overall Length 12 ft.   Plus 4 Plus 12 ft.
        Overall Width 4 ft. 8 in.   Plus 4 Plus 5 ft. 3 in.
        Ground Clearance 7 in.

Height:	Plus 4 two-seater & Coupe	4 ft. 4 in.	
	Plus 4 four-seater	4 ft. 5 in.	
	4/4 and Plus 4 Plus	4 ft. 3 in.	
Weight:	Plus 4 two-seater	16½ cwts.	1850 lb.
	Plus 4 four-seater	17 ,,	1900 ,,
	Plus 4 D/H Coupe	17½ ,,	1960 ,,
	Plus 4 Plus	16¾ ,,	1875 ,,
	4/4 & Competition Model	13 ,,	1460 ,,

MORGAN PLUS 4 PLUS

ENGINE		STEERING		Front Seat Comfort:	Good
Starting:	Fair	Ratio:	Good	Legroom:	Excellent
Idling:	Good	Kick Back:	Good	Driving Position:	Good
Flexibility:	Good	Caster:	Good	Headroom:	Good
Vibration:	Good	Direction:	Good	Boot:	Fair
		Lock:	Excellent	Other:	Fair
TRANSMISSION				Ventilation:	Good
Clutch:	Average	BRAKES		Visibility:	Excellent
Gear Ratios:	Good	Fade:	Good	Heating:	Excellent
Synchromesh:	Fair	Pedal Pressure:	High	Instruments:	Good
Gear Change:	Fair	Response:	Good	Minor Controls:	Good
Gearbox Noise:	Fair	Balance:	Good	Headlights:	Good
Final Drive Ratio:	Good	Handbrake—position:	Poor	Wipers:	Good
Rear Axle Noise:	Nil	—action:	Good		
				SERVICE	
SUSPENSION		BODY		Frequency:	Average
Roadholding:	Excellent	Finish—exterior:	Good	Accessibility:—plugs:	Average
Roll Stiffness:	Good	—interior:	Good	—spare wheel:	Good
Ride:	Morgan!	Sound Level:	Good	—battery:	Good
Traction:	Good	Weatherproof:	Good	—radiator:	Good
Ground Clearance:	Good	Entrance:	Good	—dipstick:	Average

	m.p.h.		m.p.h.
MAXIMUM SPEED (estimated)	110	SPEEDS IN GEARS	
SPEED	secs.		First—35
	0–30— 4·4		
	0–40— 6·6		Second—57
	0–50— 9·6		
	0–60—13·2		Third—83
	0–70—15·1	Price: £1,276	
Fuel consumption 28.5 m.p.g.			

these days that the factory are unable to supply cars for press use—every car that is made is bespoke, long before the chassis arrives from Rubery Owen Ltd. The car tested was fitted with the standard disc wheels (most people prefer wire wheels) as these are more satisfactory for the hard use the car gets in production car trials and autocross. The suspension too had been slightly modified with stronger rear springs and competition dampers on the front. The chassis of the car is basically the same as the Plus 4, only certain cross-bracing changes being made to accept the Ford engine and gearbox. Onto this intentionally flexible chassis is fitted a simple but most attractive looking body mounted on an ash frame. All the body panels are made by Morgans, only the front wings coming from an

MORGAN 4/4

ENGINE		STEERING		Front Seats:	Good
Starting:	Excellent	Ratio:	Good	Legroom:	Good
Idling:	Excellent	Kick Back:	Good	Driving Position:	Unusual
Flexibility:	Excellent	Caster:	Good	Headroom:	Good
Vibration:	Fair	Direction:	Good	Boot:	Nil
		Lock:	Fair	Other:	Fair
TRANSMISSION				Ventilation:	Good
Clutch:	Good	BRAKES		Visibility—forward:	Good
Gear Ratios:	Fair	Fade:	Good	—rearward:	Poor with hood up
Synchromesh:	Excellent	Pedal Pressure:	Fair	Heating:	Good
Gear Changes:	Good	Response:	Excellent	Instruments:	Good
Gearbox Noise:	Good	Balance:	Good	Minor Controls:	Good
Final Drive Ratio:	Good	Handbrake Position:	Good	Headlights:	Excellent
Rear Axle Noise:	Nil	—action:	Fair	Wipers:	Good
SUSPENSION		BODY		SERVICE	
Roadholding:	Superb	Finish:	Good	Frequency:	Average
Roll Stiffness:	Good	Interior:	Good	Accessibility:—plugs:	Good
Ride:	Morgan	Sound Level:	Fair	—battery:	Fair
Traction:	Excellent	Weatherproof:	Good	—radiator:	Good
Ground Clearance:	Good	Entrance:	Fair	—dipstick:	Good

	m.p.h.		m.p.h.
MAXIMUM SPEED (estimated)	102	SPEEDS IN GEARS	
SPEED	secs.		First—30
	0–30— 3·1		
	0–40— 5·2		Second—46
	0–50— 8·0		
	0–60—10·8		Third—76
	0–70—13·7	Price: Series V £714	
Fuel consumption 32.5 m.p.g.		Series comp £787	

noise it would appear to have stood the test of time very well indeed. The engine was in first class order, though it tended to use a little oil. On this car the side windows are of perspex (glass is used on the production models) which tends to bend a little at high speed creating some wind roar, which we know from an earlier experience of a production car is eliminated with the glass windows.

The car took a little starting in the mornings, but needs little choke and the temperature gauge soon shows "N" after only a couple of miles of motoring. When hot the engine always started easily. In traffic the car would trickle along very happily in third, and a quick dab on the throttle would quickly bring in brisk acceleration; that in the middle range was particularly good. The 70 m.p.h. limit was in force all the time we had the car, but we felt that it really needed an overdrive unit, especially on top gear. The gearbox has a very chunky feel to it and is a little slow to use, but very precise. It is possible to beat the synchromesh if one is a little over-exuberant. The petrol consumption over 1,500 miles worked out at exactly 28½ m.p.g.

It looks a big car when one is sitting in it looking out, and there is much more room inside than in one of the open models; in fact 7½ inches more elbow room. This has been achieved by making use of every inch of the very deep doors, in which there is a very useful sized map pocket. Water did tend to seep down into this, however, resulting in sodden maps! On the prototype there are two individual seats with a common bench back, but later models are all fitted with most comfortable bucket seats. The transmission tunnel is deep and while it divides the seating without cramping the feet-room, a little more room for the clutch foot would be appreciated. Behind the seats there is a very useful space for stowing soft baggage or one suitcase. Though there are two foot wells here, I cannot see anyone trying to use it as a 2 plus 2! There is a very good glove pocket, much deeper than usual in fact, so much so one can lose things in it. The instrumentation is good, though the speedometer is a little far to the left. In front of the driver is the tachometer (with a needle which tends to swing erratically) and a circular dial containing the oil, water, ammeter and fuel gauges. The pedals are well placed and it is possible to heel and toe comfortably. The handbrake is badly positioned on the passenger side of the tunnel, well forward.

The side windows are nearly circular and wind down almost completely into the doors. It was found that a good level of ventilation could be obtained by a permutation of window opening and heater setting. The heater is a Smith's re-circulatory type and was very efficient indeed. The windscreen seems huge with very slender pillars and the rear window is pleasantly wide, giving first-rate all-round visibility. The doors too are very wide making for easy entrance and exit.

Some of the initial critics were sure that the fibreglass body mounted on the well-known Morgan whippy chassis would result in the body breaking up very quickly. There was not a sign of a crack on the body (except on the boot, which had taken the brunt of a fall off a ramp!) and it is a credit to the builders of this body that there has been no fault in this direction. Perhaps it is the fact that a coupe body makes it exceptionally strong. We were told of one car which had rolled, without much apparant damage! If the body has strengthened the chassis it certainly has not effected the superb roadholding. From some angles the body can be said to be ugly, but taken overall the effect is very pleasing and different. The Autocar described it as a cross between an Elite and an XK150. The wide bonnet is hinged at the scuttle and lifts well clear of the engine, giving good accessibility for servicing. The grille is the only give-away of the car's ancestry, being a slightly modified form of the grille

that has been in use since 1936. A 10-gallon fuel tank lives under the floor of a reasonably-sized lockable boot, though the spare wheel does take up some of the space. Again one suitcase or a number of soft bags can be carried with ease. The wheels are 72-spoke knock-on's, shod with standard Dunlop Road Speed tyres. There are Girling discs on the front with drum at the rear, which stop the car well from high speed, though they require quite a high pressure. The clutch requires firm pressure whilst the steering, particularly at low speeds, is very heavy—not a woman's car this! The lights are good and are dipped by the usual Morgan switch above the clutch pedal which takes some getting used to.

We have deliberately left the road-holding till last, because this is where the car really shines, and it is this department which really makes the car a Morgan. The road holding of Morgans is well-known and this model is as good as any of them. It is difficult to break the rear away, but when it goes it is completely controllable. The car tested was fitted with Armstrong Selectaride suspension which worked well, but to get the best from the car it should be left on one of the harder settings, which although giving a firmer ride allows the car to show off its road holding to the best advantage with minimum body roll. The ride on any setting is distinctly vintage and sporting, but most people would expect and demand this from a Morgan. On really rough roads taken at speed it was pretty uncomfortable as the car tended to kick its heels in the air, resulting in the occupants leaving their seats.

In all a first class slightly vintage G.T. car which is perhaps a little highly priced at £1,276. Anyone who has a hankering after a Morgan but who wants something a little more cushy than the more spartan open models need look no further than the Plus 4 Plus. Sign an order form and we are sure Peter Morgan's arm will be twisted into making you one.

THE MORGAN 4/4

THE Morgan 4/4 first appeared in 1936 and at that time it cost 185 guineas and was fitted with an i.o.e. Coventry Climax 1122 c.c. engine. The 4/4 has now reached the series V and costs £714 in basic form and uses the Ford 1498 c.c. engine. The 4/4 part incidentally stands for 4 wheels and 4 cylinders, because prior to the announcement of the new model in 1936 all Morgan products had been three-wheelers with motor-cycle engines. Over the years the model has been fitted in turn with the Standard o.h.v. engine, the Ford 100E and 105E and the later 1340 c.c. motor. Apart from the engine changes the car hasn't changed a great deal, and it still retains a delightfully vintage look, which causes a lot of fun with friends who congratulate you on a very good rebuilding job!

The 4/4 is made in two basic forms, the cheaper version known simply as the Series V fitted with a standard Ford Cortina engine but for an extra £73 you can buy the competition model which has the G.T. engine. The car tested was the latter version and belonged to Mike Ware, Curator of the Montagu Motor Museum. Morgans are in such demand

Well, well, back to Vintage Viewpoint.

outside firm. Both the exterior and interior finish is of a very high standard. At the front, the usual Morgan sliding pillar suspension is fitted, and at the rear semi-elliptic 5-leaf springs. The long bonnet hides the Ford engine mounted well back in the chassis, and all items under the bonnet are very easily accessible. The bonnet is hinged down the middle, which means you have to check the oil level on one side, and replenish on the other. The car is strictly a two-seater, with space behind the seats to stow a small amount of luggage or one medium-sized suitcase, though with the hood down, space is further-restricted. There is an optional luggage grid which fits over the exterior-mounted spare wheel and this would be essential for owners in the habit of carrying anything but the minimum of luggage. Mounted in the tail under the spare wheel is an 8-gallon fuel tank. The battery is situated under the floor of the luggage compartment, which keeps it well away from any heat. Though this is an awkward place to get at, it only needs checking when the car is serviced, so is in fact a good idea. The tools are kept in an open topped box mounted across the scuttle under the bonnet. The hood when erected tends to spoil the lines of the car, but it is functional keeping out most of the rain, though water sometimes comes up through the floor if deep puddles are taken at speed. The standard sidescreens are not stiff enough and tend to blow away from the windscreen pillar at over 40 m.p.h., causing draughts and wind roar. The car tested had the optional extra sliding screens which when fitted correctly make the car very snug—there is also a very good heater. The snag to these sidescreens is that they have no means of being opened from the outside—so the Morgan driver is shut out of his car, as no door handles are fitted on the exterior! Most owners fit door handles from a Ford Popular to cure this oversight.

The small doors restrict entrance to the car a little, but once one is inside the seats, fitted with "blow up" squabs, are comfortable. There are two squabs with a common bench back, which is adjustable. Some owners would prefer a greater range of adjustment, but the Morgan is a car you have to adjust yourself to—not the car to you! The large Brooklands steering wheel seems to take up all the driver's cockpit, and the driving position is distinctly old-fashioned —none of the straight arm stuff here.

The engine starts immediatly the key is turned and needs little choke; once it is warmed up one is conscious of how smooth the Ford engine really is. Morgans suggest that 6,200 is about the top useful revs as valve bounce sets in after this, though they do not mark the rev counter with any red section at all. For normal motoring one need not bother to go over 5,500 to get a most useful performance. The only criticism to be levelled at the engine and gearbox department is the usual Cortina gap between second and third gear which drops you nearly 1,500 revs on the change. It's an all-synchro box which cannot be beaten however quickly the change is made. Because of the low bulkhead a normal remote control gear system cannot be employed and Morgans have worked out a most ingenious system which results in having virtually a push/pull gear change. In practice it works well, once you have got used to it, though it may slow the changes down a bit. Morgans claim a top speed of 95 m.p.h., but like most things Morgan this is conservative, top speed being just over 100 m.p.h. When the law allows, cruising in the 80's would be normal with bursts of 90 m.p.h. coming up easily. There is definitely a double pressure on the accelerator, the second pressure bringing in the second choke of the Weber carburettor and noticeably more power. The power-to-weight ratio is of course fantastic for a fully-equipped road car, as the car only weighs 13 cwt. (lighter than a Sprite or Midget) with an engine pushing out over 78 b.h.p. Up to 70 m.p.h. we found that the performance was better than the Plus 4 Plus. The suspension gives a hard ride, and the test car's modifications made it even harder. Cornering is out of this world, helped no doubt by the Cinturato tyres all round. It is possible to bottom the front suspension on some corners and on bumpy roads, but it appears to do no harm. On roads with an undulating top surface the ride is most uncomfortable and it is advisable to wear a lap strap to stay with the car. This is the worst fault in this department, but frankly one can put up with it as the car has so many virtues to offset it.

Some say the steering is heavy, but certainly it is not as heavy as the Plus 4 Plus; it has not got as generous an amount of lock however. The brakes are first class but need firm pedal pressure. The clutch is stiffish without being hard to depress. The dipswitch is mounted above the clutch pedal and is awkward to use at first. There is nowhere to rest the left foot whilst driving. The oiling button for the front suspension is above the gearbox, but as you only need to use it once a day, this position is of no consequence.

The Morgan Car

A message from Peter Morgan, Chairman and Managing Director of the Morgan Motor Co Ltd.

IT gives me a great deal of pleasure to realise that so very many people are still interested in Morgans old and new. In fact, considering the size of the company, and the output of Morgan cars over the years, we must be the most fortunate firm of motor manufacturers in existence, to have so much interest shown by our enthusiastic owners.

The 70th Anniversary of the introduction of the Morgan three-wheeler has now passed, and perhaps the question could be raised as to why the Morgan Motor Company did not mark the occasion themselves. Two reasons arise in my mind, firstly when discussing the future of the company with my father, HFS, before he died in 1959, neither of us felt we could stay the course and survive until the 80s, mainly due to the thoughts that the mass produced car would become so much cheaper compared with the hand constructed type of vehicle. Fortunately this state of affairs has not arisen up to the present time.

The second reason was a somewhat more personal one of my own, in so far that after the 50th year event at Malvern I remember thinking that we will work towards reaching

the 75th Anniversary and mark that occasion if and when it occurs.

To try and explain the survival of the Morgan would be a difficult and lengthy task, as so many factors undoubtedly arise. But possibly one answer could be due to trying to retain the general image of the Morgan, as a sporting car which is fun to drive, and which can give a good account of itself when running in suitable competition events.

The information provided in this supplement should provide everyone with a working knowledge of the history, performance, and specification of all four-wheeler Morgans built from 1936 to date, which may be something of a relief to my future working life — at the moment I seem to spend a fair proportion of my time acting as the company's unpaid historian! This does not mean, however, that I discourage customer contact, for without them we would most assuredly have no future to contemplate.

I hope your reading of this supplement gives you as much pleasure as I still derive from running the company which makes the cars. ●

Above, Peter Morgan, Chairman and Managing Director, (right) seen at the opening of a pub in Malvern dedicated to the marque.

Introduction

ALTHOUGH there are cynics who say that Morgan is alive, and well, and living in the 1930s, it doesn't seem to have deterred the paying customer. At the time of writing, Morgan are building cars to satisfy orders originally place *in 1974,* when the waiting period had cautiously been forecast as "about three years". They are now calmly accepting orders for 4/4 1600s and Plus 8s, while warning that there might even be a *ten year* wait for delivery to take place.

For at least the last 15 years, the demand for Morgans has far outstripped supply. Production at Malvern Link is never better than ten cars a week, or — in a good problem-free year — about 450 cars a year. It explains why any current-model Morgan is worth far more as a trade-in (especially more if it is a private sale) than it cost when new, and why certain unscrupulous customers have been known to take delivery of a new Morgan merely to sell it at a huge premium a week or so later. This is just an indication of the way that the Morgan cult continues to flourish.

It also explains why, when we talked to Peter Morgan before starting work on this special survey, that he expressed the hope that it would not stimulate demand any further, as "we have quite enough difficulty in keeping our present customers happy . . ."

You need to be a motorist with a hard heart if you cannot see the possible fun of owning a Morgan. In fairness, having bought one you would also be advised to develop a very hard bottom, for the suspension of all Morgans might charitably be described as "very firm". This, of course, is as it should be, for even a 1980-model Morgan is built according to the methods, and the standards, of the 1930s.

For the lover of thoroughbred cars, of

course, this situation is ideal. Here is a car which he can acquire, having much more performance than any actual 1930s car, but with modern and very effective brakes, and — hopefully — a traditionally coachbuilt body shell which has neither been butchered by several previous owners, nor suffered too much rot along the way. He is, in short, faced with the honourable pleasure of experiencing yesterday's motoring, today.

If the four-wheeler Morgan has one thing, above all other, it is character — which explains why it, quite literally, has no rivals. Other firms (and we won't name them here . . .) have tried to muscle in on the market in recent years, but have all failed, either because they had no sporting traditions, or could not develop any, and inevitably suffered the description of being "vulgar". No Morgan, not even the strange Plus Four Plus, ever set out to be other than it was — a simple, strong, and almost alarmingly

attractive sports car, and there are thousands of "Moggie" devotees who love it for that.

It also stands, virtually alone, in the ranks of a genuinely thoroughbred car, in being built by the same management, in the same factory, as it always has been. The present chairman and managing director, Peter Morgan, was already in the business when the first four-wheeler car became established at the end of the 1930s, and the company has been family-owned ever since it was established more than 70 years ago. That, of course, ensures the continuity of design, of thought, and of liaison with the customers which has always made Morgan such a friendly concern to do business with.

In the following pages we might not be able to satisfy every query about the Morgan motor car, its joys and its heartbreaks, or even of its little ways, but we hope we can make clear the necessary and practical facts about the various models built in the last 44 years.

Below, a Morgan worshipper pays his respects

Development of th

In this review of the four wheel Morgans, **Graham Robson,** chronicles the development of the marque, its competition activities, performance and fuel consumption facts, and the Morgan Sports Car Club.

Above, by 1938 (three years after its introduction) slight changes occurred to the bodywork and "easy-clean" wheels replaced disc type. Right, sturdy chassis and Coventry Climax engine.

TO make things crystal clear, and to encapsulate the entire development of four-wheeler Morgans in two sentences, I would say this: In general layout, today's Morgan is exactly like those built in 1936. In detail it is almost entirely different. Confused? Of course you are — but it nevertheless sums up the evolution of the Morgan motor car in the last 44 years.

The very first Morgan, a three-wheeler cycle car, was displayed in 1910, and descendants of that original layout were built until 1952. The original prototype four-wheeler Morgan sports car was built in 1935, and production cars went on sale early in 1936. Since then, about 12,500 Morgans of one type or another have been built, rarely at the rate of more than ten cars a week, rarely without the customers having to wait patiently in a queue for his car to be completed, and — in every case but for one model — they have incorporated traditional constructional methods and classic styling.

The fact that the same basic chassis layout has been retained from 1936 to this day, and that the same type and range of body shells and styles have usually been available, makes my task in describing the evolution of the cars much easier. In those 44 years, the only really big advance has been in the performance provided. There is also the rather sad fact that, because of the inflationary times in which we live, the price has continued to rocket upwards.

I must start, therefore, by describing the chassis and suspension layout. Each and every four-wheeler Morgan has been built on the basis of a simple but sturdy ladder-style steel chassis frame, in which the main side members are shaped in what is lovingly known by all Morgan enthusiasts as "Z Section", which is to say that the top flange of the side member is turned outboard, while the

bottom flange turns inboard. Box and tubular cross members provide cross-bracing, and at the front there is a built up cross-member to provide support for the coil spring and vertical pillar independent front suspension (the layout was adopted for the first three-wheelers, and has never basically been changed). The frame passes under the line of the back axle, and suspension is by half-elliptic leaf springs with no additional location.

In 44 years there have been two changes of wheelbase, which is rather fundamental, and several changes of track, which is not. The original 4/4s had a 92in wheelbase, while all the Plus 4s, and the 4/4s reintroduced in 1955 used a 96in wheelbase. The big Plus 8 needed a stretch to 98in (the extra two inches all being accommodated forward of the toeboard) to accommodate the massive Rover vee-8 engine.

4/4s fitted with Meadows gearboxes (those built up until 1939) will present real difficulties if gearboxes need work, as Meadows stopped making the boxes before the war, and have not been in the transmission business since then. Moss gearboxes of both types are easier to restore, as Morgan themselves took over manufacture of some components when Moss closed down a few years ago. There should be no impossible delay in obtaining parts for the Ford gearboxes fitted behind their appropriate Ford engines in 1955-1980 4/4s, though I should warn any D-I-Y man that there seem to be a myriad variations in parts used by Ford behind the "Kent" engines of 1959 to 1980.

In any and every case, a call to the factory (Malvern — STD 06845 3104/3105), and a discussion with Mr W. J. Walwyn, who is the Director in charge of the parts and purchasing departments, will usually result in the correct item being identified. To look into the stores at Morgan is to enter an Aladdin's cave as far as

a Morgan enthusiast is concerned.

If you ever saw a Morgan body being constructed when new, you would realise why a big stock of wood-framed body items, or doors, is not kept in stock, for every car is individually fitted out, with a great deal of attention, by craftsmen with a great deal of experience. It is probably as well to suggest that you treat the rebuilding of a Morgan as a restoration project (as of an out-of-production thoroughbred car) rather than one of simple repair, and replacement of standardised parts. Be careful, too, of assuming that one part might still be the same when fitted to a Morgan built, say, ten years later. Over the years, a great deal of detail change has persistently been carried out. Even a 1980 Plus 8 is rather different from a 1968 model, and the difference between a Plus 8 and, say, an early Plus 4, is considerable.

We seem to give this advice when commenting on *any* rebuilding or restoration project but: It is essential that you should be armed with as many motor car numbers — chassis, body, engine and even gearbox —

Below, interior of 1936 Morgan 4/4 — note large instruments and sprung steering wheel.

Below, Morgan 4/4 Drophead Coupe of 1938 had chunkier appearance with full doors, and built-in petrol tank.

morgan breed

when searching for spare parts. There is never any harm in contacting the factory regarding the originality of your car. Mark Aston, Morgan's sales manager, showed us the production ledger when we recently visited Malvern, and pointed out that a considerable number of details about any car are entered in the ledger when the car is being built.

Although a Morgan is by no means an easy car to keep in top-class condition (the main problem being to stop the body rot which inevitably attacks the woodwork), it is mechanically very simple and straightforward to lay bare. Unlike the truly complex enthusiasts' cars like the vee-12 E-Types, and the real pressed-steel rot boxes like Austin-Healey 3000s or MGBs, a Morgan is a simple, basic, strong, structure which can readily be restored to its original condition. Having seen, and heard, about the way in which spare parts, advice, and specifications can be dispensed, we are convinced that a Morgan is a perfect subject for restoration. At the end of the day, too, its behaviour makes it all worthwhile. ●

4/4 Model — 1936 to 1950

After prototype trials in 1935, when the original car was powered by a side-valve Ford 933cc engine, the 4/4 went on sale in 1936 with an overhead inlet/side exhaust Coventry-Climax four-cylinder engine of 1122cc. This was a familiar proprietary unit used by several concerns in the 1930s, including Triumph. For competition purposes, however, the engine capacity was awkward, and in 1939, after a satisfactory showing at Le Mans, an alternative "Le Mans Replica" model was offered, in which the engine size was reduced to 1098cc with a reduced cylinder bore. A feature of the layout, retained by Morgan for many years, was that a separate, central gearbox was mounted well back from the engines, and connected to them by a cast light alloy tube. Original gearboxes were supplied by Meadows, but from 1939 a Moss box was specified in its place. Even by 1939, when the company had produced less than a thousand cars of this type, they had become available in three different styles — the original two-seater sports car, a four-seater

"tourer" in which the rear seats were over the back axle, and in which luggage accommodation was non-existent, and a two-seater drop-head coupé in which a folding hood was allied to straight-top doors and slightly different rear styling.

By 1939, however, Coventry-Climax engine supplies were beginning to dwindle, and Morgan took up an offer from Standard to use a special overhead valve derivative of their Flying Ten unit. This was a 1267cc engine whose head was designed using experience gained in manufacturing overhead valve engines for the larger-engined SS-Jaguars, and was rather more powerful than the Coventry-Climax unit. Only 29 engines were actually used before the war intervened, but as there were no new Coventry-Climax engines available from 1945 onwards, it became the standard post-war offering. Strangely enough, Standard never used the engine for any of their own models — not even for the Triumph Mayflower, which would surely have benefited from using it. Indeed, the fact that the engine was especially built for

6 ☞

Above, four seater arrived one year after two seater.

Above, Morgan Plus 4 powered by Triumph TR2 engine by this time.

Above, 1954 Morgan Plus 4 shows transition to cowled headlamps but retaining twin spare wheels.

Development of the Morgan breed

Morgan was a major factor in the big change which followed in 1950, for 1267cc supplies, quite simply, became impossible to guarantee.

The original Morgan four-wheeler car, therefore, was phased out in 1950, and replaced directly by the Standard Vanguard engined Plus 4.

Plus 4 (and derivatives) — 1950 to 1968

The Plus 4, which took over from the original 4/4, needed a four inch wheelbase stretch to accommodate the much bulkier 2088cc Standard Vanguard engine and to allow a little extra space in the cockpit. At the same time the wheel tracks and the overall width were increased by two inches, a slight but worthwhile improvement. Like the later 4/4s, the Plus 4 had the separate Moss gearbox, which was connected to the engine by a lengthy cast tube.

The Plus 4 was substantially faster than any previous Morgan, but its TR2-engined development of 1954 was even more exciting, and now, perhaps for the first time, Morgan had a car which was potentially an outright winner in rallies and some types of racing. Once the TR engines became optional, most customers specified them, although Vanguard engined cars continued to be built until 1958.

Right from the start, in 1950, the "usual" three body options were available, and from the autumn of 1953 there came an important styling change, when the original up-standing radiator and separate headlamps gave way to a sloping grille and semi-fared in lamps. This, however, was only a temporary solution, for one year later the sloping radiator was replaced by the curved style used to this day.

An important and rather special body option, officially available from the autumn of 1954, was the *four*-seater drop-head coupé style, really an amalgam of four-seater tourer and coupé hood layout (but it was by no means as simple as that). According to factory records, a mere 51 of these cars were built, the last being delivered in January 1957, and the majority being built with Vanguard and some with Triumph TR engines.

From the mid-1950s until 1968, when the Plus 4 was finally discontinued, it received steady but essentially detailed improvement, which included extra body width, the availability of front wheel disc brakes (from spring 1959), and the uprating of the TR engines to accord with Triumph's own usage. Thus, the last of the Plus Fours had a 2138cc TR4A engine and 104bhp (DIN), compared with 1991cc and 90bhp (gross) in 1954.

There were two important sub-derivatives of the Plus 4:

Plus 4 Super Sports — 1961 to 1968

Between 1961 and 1968, 101 of these cars were built, with 1991cc or 2138cc Triumph TR engines tuned and greatly modified by the Chris Lawrence organisation. Depending on the final tune chosen, they could have up to 125bhp, and because they had mainly light-alloy bodies they were much more accelerative than the standard product.

There were no obvious styling changes, but the changes were immediately obvious when the bonnet was raised, and the twin-choke Weber carburettors and special manifolding was revealed. An engine oil cooler was standard, as were wider 72 spoke wire wheels, and some cars had individual bucket seats instead of the normal bench seats. Nearly all had two-seater sports bodies, but a handful were built with 4-seater and with 2-seater coupé styles.

Plus 4 Plus — 1963 to 1967

This was the only Morgan built which didn't look like a traditional Morgan. Peter Morgan was led to believe that a more modern style was needed to keep his company going in the late 1960s, and developed a full-width bubble-top coupé style, in conjunction with John Edwards of EB Plastics (who supplied the shells complete), using glassfibre. The inspiration was the Debonair GT body (also made by EB Plastics), and the Plus 4 Plus has often been accused of having an XK150 nose and a Lotus Elite rear.

The chassis was absolutely unmodified Plus

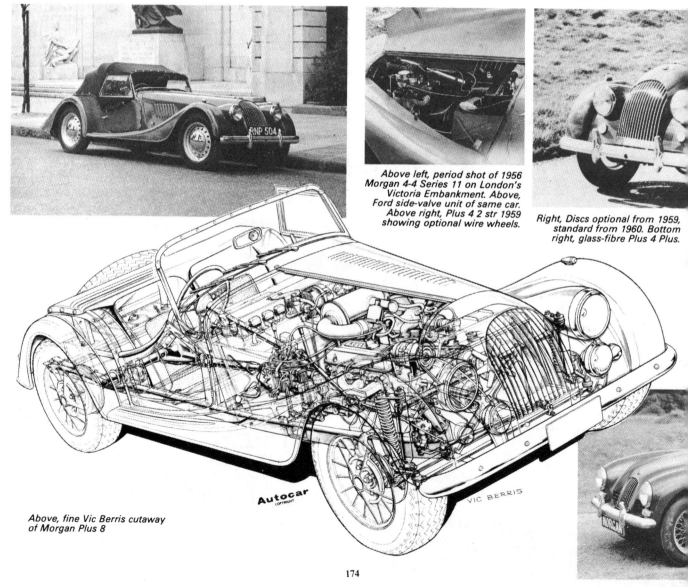

Above left, period shot of 1956 Morgan 4-4 Series 11 on London's Victoria Embankment. Above, Ford side-valve unit of same car. Above right, Plus 4 2 str 1959 showing optional wire wheels.

Right, Discs optional from 1959, standard from 1960. Bottom right, glass-fibre Plus 4 Plus

Above, fine Vic Berris cutaway of Morgan Plus 8

4, and the 2138cc TR4 engine was standard. However, although Peter Morgan campaigned the works prototype with great success in British events, the model was not a success. Peter always says that he was misled by the original advice tendered — that the people who said that Morgan should modernise its image were not potential customers anyway, and therefore did not know what they were talking about — and never committed the same mistake again.

Over the years the fiction has grown up that 50 cars of this type were built, but a study of factory records shows that precisely 26 cars were delivered, the last of all leaving Malvern Link in 1967.

4/4 models built from 1955 to date

These cars, which are now much the most numerous of all Morgans, should not be confused with the original 4/4s of 1936-1950, from which they are very different. The 4/4 was re-introduced in 1955 to fill in a marketing gap at a cheaper price than the Standard-Triumph engined Plus 4s then in production. With suitable detail re-engineering, they used the Plus 4's 96in wheelbase frame as their base but have only ever been offered with two-seater and four-seater tourer bodywork.

They were the first-ever Morgans to have gearboxes in unit with their engines, and the first officially (but not in one-off form) to be equipped with Ford engines. They come in five different basic varieties:

The SII had a side-valve 1172cc Ford engine and three-speed box, and was built from 1955 to 1960

The SIII, complete with overhead-valve 997cc engine and four-speed box, was only built in 1960-1961

The SIV had a 1340cc engine, and was built from 1961 to 1963

The SV had a 1498cc engine, and was built from 1963 to 1968

The 4/4 1600 (not the SVI, please . . .) has a 1599cc bowl-in-piston engine, and has been on sale continuously from 1967 to date.

Just to confuse everyone, it should be noted that there was a tuned SII "Competition" from 1957 to 1960, an SV "Competition" from 1963 to 1968, and that the current 4/4 1600 was originally a "Competition" derivative of the basic 4/4 1600, which had the less highly-tuned Ford engine of that size.

It is interesting to note that the current 4/4 1600, which is being built at a slightly higher rate than the Plus 8, is at least as powerful as the TR2-engined Plus 4 of the mid-1950s, though it is lighter and has a 400cc smaller engine.

Not all 4/4s had disc brakes, which became optional in 1960 for the SIII, but were standarised for the SIV from the end of 1961.

The 4/4 is still, of course, in full production, with steel-panelled or alloy-panelled body, and as I have already stated, the waiting list for new deliveries is presently quoted at ten years!

Plus 8 — built 1968 to date

By the mid-1960s, Standard-Triumph were only building wet-liner four-cylinder 2138cc engines for their own TR4A sports cars, and for Morgan, so when the new TR5 was revealed in the autumn of 1967, powered by a dry-liner six cylinder engine, it was clear that the Plus 4's days were numbered.

Peter Morgan chose to use a Rover vee-8 engine of 3528cc in place of the old TR4A engine after politely refusing a takeover bid for his company from Rover, and after considering alternative engines like the six-cylinder TR5 unit (too long), and the vee-8 Triumph Stag engine (still only a prototype). The first ever Plus 8 prototype was built in 1967, and used a Plus 4 frame, but it was a real shoe-horn job, and the 1968 production car had a lengthened and widened frame so that the vee-8 engine could drop in more easily, and require no external body panel changes. Compared with the 4/4 1600, which has a 48in wheel track, the track of the original Plus 8 was 49in at the front and 51in at the rear; from October 1973, and current models have a 52in front track and a 53in rear track.

Apart from minor though significant development changes, the main alterations to the Plus 8s have been to the transmission arrangements. The first cars, built up until May 1972, had a Plus 4-type of centrally-mounted Moss gearbox. From May 1972 until the end of 1976, the vee-8 engine was directly mated to the Rover 4-speed all-synchromesh box used in the P6B 3500 saloon model. From the beginning of 1977, not only was the engine uprated to the new SD1 saloon car standards (155bhp (DIN) instead of 143bhp (DIN)), but it was mated to the new five-speed all-synchromesh gearbox also found in that car, and in the TR7 and TR8 models.

The Plus 8 has only ever been sold with the two-seater sports style, like that of the 4/4 1600 but significantly wider. From October 1975 to January 1977 there was a light-alloy bodied "Sports Lightweight", but this has now been replaced by a normal option of light-alloy panelling to the normal bodywork. All Plus 8s have cast-alloy road wheels, which have never been available on the 4/4s; conversely, there has never been a wire wheel option on the Plus 8.

No automatic transmission Plus 8 has ever been marketed, though one prototype was built. ●

Morgans since 1936 — the march of horsepower

Model	Years Built*	Engine size, and power
4/4	1936-1939	Climax 4-cyl, 1122cc, 34bhp (gross) at 4500rpm
44 Le Mans Rep	1939	Climax 4-cyl, 1098cc
4/4	1939-1950	Standard 4-cyl, 1267cc, 40bhp (gross) at 4300rpm
Plus 4	1950-1958	Standard 4-cyl, 2088cc, 68bhp (gross) at 4300rpm
Plus 4	1954-1962	Triumph 4-cyl, 1991cc 90bhp (gross) at 4800rpm — from 1957, 100bhp (gross) at 5000rpm**
Plus 4 Super Sports	1961-1968	Lawrencetune Triumph 4-cyl, 1991cc, 116bhp (gross) at 5500rpm
Plus 4	1962-1968	Triumph 4-cyl, 2138cc, 100bhp (net) at 4600rpm
Plus 4 Plus	1963-1967	Triumph 4-cyl, 2138cc, 100bhp (net) at 4600rpm
4/4 SII	1955-1960	Ford s.v. 4-cyl, 1172cc, 36bhp (gross) at 4400rpm
4/4 SII Competition	1957-1960	Ford s.v. 4-cyl, 1172cc, 42bhp (gross) at 4800 rpm
4/4 SIII	1960-1961	Ford ohv 4-cyl, 997cc, 39bhp (gross) at 5000rpm
4/4 SIV	1961-1963	Ford, 4-cyl, 1340cc, 54bhp (net) at 4900 rpm
4/4 SV	1963-1968	Ford, 4-cyl, 1498cc, 60bhp (net) at 4600rpm
4/4 SV Competition	1963-1968	Ford, 4-cyl, 1498cc, 78bhp (net) at 5200rpm
4/4 1600	1967-1970	Ford, 4-cyl, 1599cc, 74bhp (net) at 4750rpm
4/4 1600 Competition	1967 to date	Ford, 4-cyl, 1599cc, 88bhp (net) at 5400rpm — later re-stated as 86bhp (DIN) at 5500rpm
Plus 8	1968 to date	Rover, V8-cyl, 3528cc, 151bhp (net) at 5200 rpm — later re-stated as 143bhp (DIN) at 5200rpm — from autumn 1976, 155bhp (DIN) at 5250rpm

* Calendar Year
** Between 1955 and 1957, TR2/TR3 engine power changed progressively from one extreme to the other; there were several subdivisions, some quoted as 95bhp (gross) at 4800rpm.

Morgans Since 1936

T HE chart in this section has been assembled with the help of Morgan, and takes account of several discrepancies thrown up by other well-documented sources. Because of these discrepancies, and without an exhaustive and time-consuming study of Morgan's own chassis records, it is likely that the figures quoted will differ very slightly from others published elsewhere.

It does seem, however, that about 12,500 four-wheeler Morgans have been built since production began at the beginning of 1936 — and that total continues to increase at the rate of nine or ten cars every week, which is the practical capacity of the works at Malvern Link.

It has not been possible to separate detail statistics of the popularity of the various two-seater, coupé, or four-seater body styles and — because the chassis were built as normal Plus 4s until the bodies were added — the 26 Plus 4 Plus cars have been included in the total for the Plus 4 production achievement.

To stem all criticism, and to answer arguments, Morgan themselves state that there were:

26 Plus 4 Plus models, built from 1963 to 1967

101 Lawrencetune Supersports Plus 4 models, some with 1991cc and some with 2138cc engines, built from 1961 to 1968

51 Four-seater coupé Plus 4s, built between 1954 and 1957.

Incidentally, of the 12,500 four-wheeler Morgans, 883 cars were built between 1936 and 1939. Morgan historians also like to emphasise the difference between "flat radiator" and "cowled radiator" models, so in this context I should state that a total of 2094 "flat radiator cars" appear to have been built.

Family Tree

Year	Model			
1936	4/4			
1950		+4 (V)		
1954			+4 (TR)	
1955		4/4 SII		
1958				
1960		4/4 SIII		
1961		4/4 SIV		
1963		4/4 SV		+4+
1967				
1968		4/4 1600		Plus 8
1980				

Note: V = Vanguard engine, TR = Triumph TR engine.
A few cars of each superseded model were probably delivered in the year after which they were officially discontinued.
All Morgans except the Plus 8 had four-cylinder engines; that of the Plus 8 is a vee-8. Production of 4/4 1600s and Plus 8s continues unabated.

Above: the 1938 4/4 which cost £190. Below, left, the small production glass fibre Plus Four Plus and right, the current Plus Eight.

Morgan Models: When built? In what numbers?

Model	Engine	When Built	Chassis Number Sequence	Number built	
4/4 Series I	Coventry-Climax 1122cc	1936-1939	1 to 2081	789	
	Coventry-Climax 1098cc	1939-1946		65	Grand Total
	Standard 1267cc	1939-1951		578	1436
	Ford various	1936-1939		4	
Plus 4	Vanguard 2088cc	1950-1958	P2100 to 6853	893	
(includes 26 Plus 4	TR2 1991cc	1954-1956	(early Triumph-engined cars carried suffix "T", while	366	Grand Total
Plus coupés)	TR3/TR3A 1991cc	1956-1962	Vanguard engined cars carried suffix "P")	1871	4754
	TR4/TR4A 2138cc	1962-1968		1523	
	Supersports 1991/2138cc	1961-1968		101	
4/4 Series II	Ford svl 1172cc	1955-1960	A200 to A586	387	
4/4 Series III	Ford ohv 997cc	1960-1961	A589 to A648	59	
4/4 Series IV	Ford ohv 1340cc	1961-1963	B650 to B855	206	Grand Total
4/4 Series V	Ford ohv 1498cc	1963-1968	B856 to B1495	639	4451
4/4 1600	Ford ohv 1599cc	1968 to date	B1600 to B4760 at October 1980*	3160	
Plus 8	Rover 3528cc	1968 to date	R7000 to R8830 at October 1980*	1830	Total 1830

*Production continues unabated.

Morgans in Competition

The Lawrence/Shepherd-Barron Plus 4 at Le Mans in 1962 behind the 3 litre Ferrari of Noblet and Guichet and, insert, the same car, which was placed 13th and won the 2 litre class.

ALTHOUGH every Morgan car ever made was sturdy, relatively light, and had very responsive handling, that didn't automatically make it a good competition car. I think it's fair to suggest that the original 4/4s were somewhat under-powered, and that the opportunities for a Plus 8 to shine are rather too limited. In terms of "works" or "works-assisted" efforts, the hey day of the competition Morgan has been connected with the Plus 4.

On the assumption that it is properly protected underneath, a Morgan has always been well-suited to production car trials, and there is a history of success starting with the 1936 4/4s and coming up to date. In marque racing, or in formulae to which it is especially suited, a Plus 8 is ideal, and a fast Plus 4 (or Super Sports) has also been successful. Morgans were most prominent in rallies in the 1950s and early 1960s, when driving skill in tests, sprints and short hill-climbs had to be matched to the map-reading skill of the navigator on the road sections. Now that almost all worthwhile rallies are settled by the use of special stages, where strength allied to a good ground clearance is essential, a Morgan is quite unsuitable.

Many truly private owners, of course, have had their successes, but unless they were connected with the factory I have not found the space to include their efforts.

Trials

These were always close to the hearts of Morgan management, as the contestants were the types likely to buy new Morgans if they were impressed. H. F. S. Morgan entered the

very first 4/4 in the 1936 Exeter Trial, where he gained a Premier Award. Later that year three factory cars entered the "Edinburgh" and one gained a Premier award. Peter Morgan took a Silver medal in the 1937 Edinburgh, but undoubtedly their finest pre-war effort was in 1938, when HFS and Peter Morgan both gained Gold Medal "Triple" awards for being unpenalised in that season's Exeter, Land's End and Edinburgh Trials.

Peter Morgan and W. A. G. Goodall continued to compete successfully in this type of event until the 1960s, with Peter in particular notching up Golds in cars as diverse as a two-seater coupé, and in the prototype Plus 4 Plus coupé. However, by now such trials had become social affairs, and it was in rallying that most of the prestige was to be gained.

Rallies

Between 1937 (when they first competed) and 1939, Morgan factory entries had a fine record in the RAC Rally, with George Goodall winning his class on three consecutive occasions each time in a Coventry-Climax engined car. Also in 1939, Jim Goodall (George's son) won the Scottish Rally outright, defeating among other cars a further six Morgans.

It took time for rallying to re-establish itself in Britain after the Second World War, but the new breed of RAC Internationals, the famous London, and the MCC Nationals, were all ideal for Morgans because of their combination of navigation and driving tests. Peter Morgan might well have won the 1951 RAC outright in a Plus 4, if he had not been outdone on the last test by the redoubtable Ian Appleyard and his Jaguar XK120, but Morgan won the Team

The Prodsport Plus Eight, now raced by Charles Morgan. This is the original road test car.

Morgans in Competition

Prize. A year later Messrs Morgan, Goodall and Steel won the RAC team prize again, and in that year Jimmy Ray's privately entered Plus 4 won the London Rally outright, a feat which he repeated in 1953. There were TR-engined Plus 4s in many major National events thereafter, which included "Doc" Spare taking third overall in the 1956 RAC Rally, and in Pauline Mayman becoming prominent in her famous car, registered EPM 324 (the letters were her initials).

Class wins were common place, but the Plus 4 was never a contender for outright victory in European events. In Britain, from the end of the 1950s, Brian Harper became *the* man to beat in his red Plus 4 — one of his finest drives being to win the 1959 London Rally. In the same year, incidentally, Peter Morgan was foiled from making a good show in the RAC Rally when he became embroiled in snow drifts in Scotland and had to make a huge detour to stay in the event; nevertheless, he finished sixth overall and won his class. Harper continued to win events outright — Welsh in 1960 and *Express and Star* in 1961 — before switching to a Sebring Sprite.

By this time, however, rallying was becoming very specialised, and the "homologation special" was becoming common, so further Morgan success was out of the question, especially when rough special stage events began to predominate.

Above, Morgans in historic racing. Plus Four SSs at Nurburgring, 1980 with Lucassen leading Hofmans. Below, Morgan representation at the 1954 Alpine Rally.

Races

The 4/4s racing career got off to a very creditable start in 1937 when Robert Campbell won the Ulster Trophy race on handicap, and when in the following month D. C. McCracken won the Leinster Trophy race. The big event of 1938, however, and one on which much Morgan folk-lore is based, was when Prudence Fawcett and her co-driver G. White entered a 1098cc 4/4 (with preparation help from Malvern) in the world-famous Le Mans 24 Hour Race. The little car had a very reliable and successful race, finishing 13th overall at an average speed of 57·2mph.

A year later, with Dick Anthony driving the car in place of Ms Fawcett (who never appears to have raced again), along with White, the re-engined (1122cc) 4/4 was taken to Le Mans once again. On this occasion there was all manner of trouble with petrol supplies, and sticking needles, which led to a breakdown out on the circuit, to Anthony *running* back to the pits for fuel supplies, but a very fine and fighting finish at an average speed of 64·53mph, in 15th position overall.

In 1952, however, the specially prepared Vanguard-engined Plus 4 of Lawrie and Isherwood broke down with engine failure, and there would be no further Morgan presence at the French circuit until 1962. By this time Chris Lawrence had begun to make a name for himself in highly tuned TR-engined Plus 4s, and it was he, with Richard Shepherd-Barron, who drove the well-known TOK 258 into a fine 13th place at Le Mans in 1962, winning the 2·0-litre class, and averaging no less than 93·97mph, all with no more trouble than a broken exhaust manifold pipe which did not take too much edge from the car's performance. It was the company's finest ever Le Mans performance.

Three years later, at Brands Hatch, Chris Lawrence (with John Spender) figured in a rather epic battle for the two-day 1000 mile Guards Trophy, in what was meant to be a production sports car race. The "Morgan" in question was actually a Super Sports Plus 4 chassis clothed in one of Lawrence's own super-streamlined SLR (Sprinzel-Lawrence-Racing) coupé light alloy bodies, and it was obviously quite fast enough to win such an endurance event.

On the first day, however, the unfortunate Lawrence suffered a big delay when a cracked front suspension pillar was found, and this delayed him by no fewer than 21 laps, and lost him the lead. On the second day, rather too late to do more than pull himself up a few places, the combination of SLR-Morgan, Lawrence and Spender led almost throughout, and averaged more than 75mph for a 500 mile "day".

By this time, however, Plus 4s were no longer really competitive in anything other than "marque" racing, though a young man called John Stapleton was beginning to make quite a name for himself in some club events. By the early 1970s, too, Chris Lawrence had been drawn back into a Morgan for racing, and enlivened several club events — his car was borrowed by Robin Gray to win the Spreckley Thoroughbred cars race at Silverstone late in 1973, a feat which he repeated on occasion in 1974. Within a couple of years a "works" connection, though rather tenuous, was re-established with racing when Charles Morgan (Peter's son) began to use MMC II, one of the very first Plus 8s, and a magazine test car, with some success.

To bring the story right up to date, however, I should mention that two Plus 8s performed with great distinction in Britain's first-ever 24 Hour race — at Snetterton, in June this year. Although it was Stirling Moss and Desiré Wilson who took the publicity, and it was an Opel which won the event outright, two Plus 8s (one prepared and entered by the Morgan Sports Car Club and one by the Morris Stapleton organisation) finished in third and fifth places. Clearly, in the right places, and in the right hands, the Plus 8 is still a highly competitive car. ●

The marque was usually well represented in the MCC's Land End Trial. This is the 1954 event.

Performance
& fuel consumption

IN a survey like this, we think it is important that full and impartially obtained performance details should be assembled, in tabular form. Normally we have no difficulty in being able to choose, and to provide the facts about almost every derivative of a design, or family of cars, which qualify for inclusion. With Morgan, however, we have a problem. The company was usually so confident of selling all its cars that it sometimes did not bother to provide a test car of one particular type. This certainly explains why our weekly contemporary, *Autocar*, only managed to lay its hands on seven Morgan test cars in 44 years!

Even that very limited opportunity to test the product would have been acceptable if the seven cars had been a representative selection. However, although there are two different pre-war 4/4 tests of Climax-engined cars, two different Plus 4s and two Plus 8s, there are no figures available for a Standard-engined 4/4, nor has any late-model 4/4 with the overhead valve Ford engine ever been tested.

So, what can we say? Firstly, with regard to the Standard-engined 4/4, the claimed engine power was 40bhp instead of 34bhp, on identical gearing, from which it might be assumed that the maximum speed was at least a true 80mph, and that acceleration would be significantly, but not dramatically, improved.

4/4s which have been built since 1968 have all had 1599cc engines, for which 86bhp (DIN)

is claimed, and for which the unladen weight is about 1650lb. This probably means that the car should be slightly more lively than a TR2-engined Plus 4 (for which the 90bhp was by no means a "nett" figure), and that it should have a maximum speed of at least 100mph. Let's guess (and it can be no more than that) at a 0-60mph time of around 11 seconds, a standing ¼-mile in about 17.5 seconds, and typical fuel consumption of better than 30mpg.

Finally, a word about the difference between the two Plus 8s. The first test car of 1968 still had the centrally-mounted Moss gearbox, in which top gear was direct drive. The 1978 car had the Rover "SD1" type of five speed gearbox, in which top gear was effectively an overdrive. In fourth gear, in fact, the new car was almost equally as outstanding as the original. No Morgan, incidentally, has ever been sold with an electrically-controlled overdrive, or with automatic transmission. ●

Going faster! a competition Plus Four with experimental hardtop which competed in 1961, often with Pip Arnold at the wheel.

	4/4 2-seater Climax i.o.e.v. engine 1122cc	4/4 4-seater Climax i.o.e.v. engine 1122cc	4/4 Series II 2-seater Ford s.v. engine 1172cc	+4 2-seater Vanguard ohv engine 2088cc	+4 2-seater DHC TR2 ohv engine 1991cc	+8 2-seater Rover ohv engine 3528cc	+8 2-seater Rover ohv engine 3528cc
Cost When New	£194	£225	£714	£880	£830	£1478	£5961
Road Tested in *Autocar*:	11 Dec 1936	12 Aug 1938	14 Sept 1956	27 April 1951	7 May 1954	12 Sept 1968	15 July 1978
Maximum speed (mph)	78	76	70	86	96	124	123
Acceleration (sec):							
0-30mph	6.1	7.0	6.9	4.6	3.5	2.3	2.2
0-40mph	–	–	–	–	–	3.5	3.5
0-50mph	15.9	17.3	18.0	11.3	9.0	5.2	4.6
0-60mph	28.4	28.3	29.4	17.9	13.3	6.7	6.5
0-70mph	–	–	–	28.0	17.5	8.6	9.0
0-80mph	–	–	–	–	24.5	11.8	11.4
0-90mph	–	–	–	–	35.9	14.5	15.4
0-100mph	–	–	–	–	–	18.4	20.2
0-110mph	–	–	–	–	–	25.7	31.0
0-120mph	–	–	–	–	–	42.9	–
Standing ¼-mile (sec):	Not recorded	–	23.5	n.r.	18.5	15.1	15.1
Top gear (sec):							
10-30mph	10.9	12.9	–	9.9	–	5.8	8.8
20-40mph	11.6	13.8	15.1	9.0	8.4	5.0	7.7
30-50mph	12.0	15.7	15.5	9.5	8.4	4.8	6.8
40-60mph	–	–	19.2	–	8.6	4.6	6.7
50-70mph	–	–	–	–	9.6	4.5	7.2
60-80mph	–	–	–	–	–	5.2	7.9
70-90mph	–	–	–	–	–	6.0	9.2
80-100mph	–	–	–	–	–	7.4	11.8
90-110mph	–	–	–	–	–	10.9	20.3
100-120mph	–	–	–	–	–	13.8	–
Overall mpg	35	35	36	24	30	18	20
Axle ratio	5.00	5.00	4.44	4.1	3.72	3.58	3.31
Unladen weight (lb)	1582	1642	1568	1904	1876	1979	2128

MORE INFORMATION FOR THE MORGAN ENTHUSIAST

Brooklands Books have been collecting motoring journals for nearly 40 years and have over 180,000 items listed in their files. Less than 10% of this material has found its way into books. As a company, our main objective has always been to make available to enthusiasts as much motoring literature as possible and therefore, we have decided to offer an added service for our readers - **Classic Car Files.**

Classic Car Files will be made up with articles etc. that could not be fitted into our regular books because of space limitations. They will in the main include road tests, new model announcements, and stories on tuning, racing, history and period advertising. They will be individually photocopied to order and will be presented in a laminated folder for safe keeping.

In 1989 we started a three volume Gold Portfolio programme to cover three and four wheeler Morgans which, with the publication of this book, is now complete. To supplement these books we are making available the following **Classic Car Files.**

Morgan 4 /Wheeler Classic Car File No. 1
Covering Plus/4, 4/4, and Plus/4 /Plus Models up to 1967.   **60 Pages - £10.00** plus P&P.

Morgan 4 /Wheeler Classic Car File No.2
Deals mostly with Plus/8 models between 1968 and 1992.   **60 Pages - £10.00** plus P&P.

Morgan 3/Wheeler Classic Car File No. 1
Approx. half of this file is made up of graphically beautiful advertising material from the 1930's, supplemented by stories and technical material drawn from more recent publications.   **60 Pages - £10.00** plus P&P.

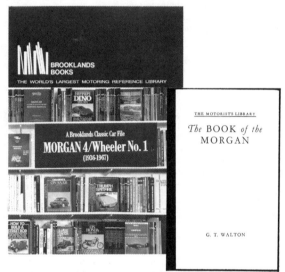

Two other out-of-print publications on Morgan can now be offered in photocopy form.

The Book of the Morgan
Published in 1930 by Pitmans. Approx. 108 small pages. 'A complete guide for owners and prospective purchasers of all Morgan three-wheeler models.   **£10.00 Plus P&P.**

The Morgan Three-Wheeler Handbook
Published privately about 1958. Approx. 62 duplicated quarto pages containing information for owners of JAP, Matchless, Anzani, Blackburne and Ford engined 3/wheelers.   **£10.00 Plus P&P.**

Postage & Packing : UK customers - £1.50. Overseas customers (surface) - £2.50: (air) - £4.00.
Payment: Sterling cheque or quote us your Visa, Access/Mastercard number. When ordering please quote credit card number, date of expiry, full name & address plus contact 'phone or fax number. Orders may be 'phoned, faxed or sent by post to:

Brooklands Books Ltd., PO Box 146, Cobham, Surrey KT11 1LG, UK.
Tel: 0932 865051   Fax: 0932 868803

All orders will be despatched within 14 days. Every effort will be made to make these photocopies as clear as possible, however, it must be remembered that some of the original material that we will be working from is over 70 years old!